At the Origins of German Liberalism:
the State in the Thought of Robert von Mohl

STUDIES IN POLITICS, SECURITY AND SOCIETY

Edited by Stanisław Sulowski
Faculty of Political Science and International Studies
University of Warsaw

VOLUME 35

PETER LANG

Paweł Lesiński

At the Origins of German Liberalism: the State in the Thought of Robert von Mohl

PETER LANG

Bibliographic Information published by the Deutsche Nationalbibliothek
The Deutsche Nationalbibliothek lists this publication in the Deutsche Nationalbibliografie; detailed bibliographic data is available in the internet at http://dnb.d-nb.de.

Library of Congress Cataloging-in-Publication Data
A CIP catalog record for this book has been applied for at the Library of Congress.

The publication was financed with use of funds forming part of the Preludium 15 competition of the National Science Center (Poland). Research project no.: 2018/29/N/HS5/01501, research project title: At the origins of German liberalism: the state in the thought of Robert von Mohl

Cover illustration: 1848 revolution in Berlin. Author unknown.
This illustration is in the public domain according to the information in https://commons.wikimedia.org/wiki/File:Maerz1848_berlin.jpg, (25.09.2020)

This work has been reviewed by: Lech Dubel
(Maria Curie-Skłodowska University)

ISSN 2199-028X
ISBN 978-3-631-81305-8 (Print)
E-ISBN 978-3-631-84580-6 (E-PDF)
E-ISBN 978-3-631-84607-0 (EPUB)
E-ISBN 978-3-631-84608-7 (MOBI)
DOI 10.3726/b17984

Peter Lang – Berlin · Bern · Bruxelles · New York · Oxford · Warszawa · Wien

This publication has been peer reviewed.

www.peterlang.com

"(. . .) therefore not a man exists for a state, but a state exists for a man."

Robert von Mohl

Table of Contents

List of abbreviations

1. Federal Constitutional Court - **FCC**
2. author's note - **author's footnote**
3. R. v. Mohl, *Das Staatsrecht des Königreiches Württemberg*, Erster Theil, Tübingen 1829. –**Staatsr.Württem.1.1829**
4. R. v. Mohl, *Das Staatsrecht des Königreiches Württemberg*, Zweite Auflage, Erster Band *das Verfassungsrecht*, Tübingen 1840. – **Staatsr. Württem.1.1840**
5. R. v. Mohl, *Das Staatsrecht des Königreichs Württemberg*, Zweiter Band, Tübingen 1831. – **Staatsr.Württem.2.1831**
6. R. v. Mohl, *Die Geschichte und Literatur der Staatswissenschaften in Monographieen dargestellt*, Erster Band, Erlangen 1855. – **Geschicht.und. Lit.1**
7. R. v. Mohl, *Die Geschichte und Literatur der Staatswissenschaften in Monographieen dargestellt*, Zweiter Band, Erlangen 1856. – **Geschicht.und. Lit.2**
8. R. v. Mohl, *Die Geschichte und Literatur der Staatswissenschaften in Monographien dargestellt*, Dritter Band, Erlangen 1858. – **Geschicht.und. Lit.3**
9. R. v. Mohl, *Die Polizeiwissenschaft nach den Grundsätzen des Rechtsstaates*, Erster Band, Tübingen 1832. – **Polizeiwiss.1.1832**
10. R. v. Mohl, *Die Polizeiwissenschaft nach den Grundsätzen des Rechtsstaates*, Erster Band, Tübingen 1844. – **Polizeiwiss.1.1844**
11. R. v. Mohl, *Die Polizeiwissenschaft nach den Grundsätzen des Rechtsstaates*, Erster Band, Tübingen 1866. – **Polizeiwiss.1.1866**
12. R. v. Mohl, *Staatsrecht, Völkerrecht und Politik*, Bd. 1. *Staatsrecht und Völkerrecht,* Tübingen 1860. – **SVuP.1**
13. R. v. Mohl, *Staatsrecht, Völkerrecht und Politik,* Bd. 3, *Politik,* Bd. 2, Tübingen 1869. – **SVuP.3.2**
14. R. v. Mohl, *Staatsrecht, Völkerrecht, Politik*, Bd.2, *Politik,* Bd.1, Tübingen 1862. –**SVuP.2.1**
15. Constitutional Tribunal - **CT**

Introduction

Is it possible for a law to exist and function in isolation from ideas? Is it possible to create a specific legal institution, without looking not only at what factual state it is supposed to achieve, but also whether this actual state can be regarded as justified, equitable, and rational? Undoubtedly, law is an instrument for influencing the behaviours of people. A legal norm is a specific manual on how to operate in specific factual conditions that function in real people's lives, that actually answers the question: "how?." Hence it says a particular individual how it should behave in a specific situation. However, can the examination of the law be reduced to the simple answer stating how to behave, or what sanction will be imposed on whoever fails to comply with the order or legal prohibition? Surely not. The second question that should be asked when analyzing specific legal institutions should be: "why?." The answer also requires the reason that motivated the legislator to introduce legal regulations towards specific entities, in specific conditions.

It is undeniably correct to say that a full-fledged understanding of law must also include an examination of the ideological, doctrinal reflection that accompanies the respective institution of law. Knowledge of the doctrine understood as "a systematic set of ideas, theories and political programs or their fragments, aiming to exert a real impact on reality"[1] allows the lawyer to go deeper into the area of knowledge it deals with.[2] The scientific discovery of the branch of political and legal doctrines is not limited to just theoretical broadening of the body of knowledge. Quite the contrary. We can put forward the thesis that it also has an extremely practical dimension. It allows a lawyer to avoid becoming just a "technician" in the service of power, a tool in the hands of other people, often pursuing very particular interests.[3] A lawyer operates one of the most effective and widespread tools to influence reality. Cutting such person off sources that

---

1 L. Dubel, *Historia doktryn politycznych i prawnych do schyłku XX wieku*, Warszawa 2009, p. 17. More about the post-war understanding of the history of political and legal doctrines: M. Jaskólski, *Szkice o Historii Doktryn Politycznych i Prawnych*, "Zeszyty Naukowe Uniwersytetu Jagiellońskiego DCCXII," "Prace z nauk politycznych," z. 23, pp. 13–16.

2 L. Dubel, *Historia doktryn politycznych i prawnych*. . ., p. 13. A. Bryl, *Między historią a teorią – kilka uwag na temat statusu doktryn politycznych i prawnych jako specjalizacji naukowej* [in:] *Myślenie o Polityce i Prawie, przedmiot, metoda, praktyka*, I. Barwicka-Tylek, A. Czarnecka, M. Jaskólski, J. Malczewski (eds.), Warszawa 2015, p. 46.

3 *Editors' note*, [in:] *Myślenie o Polityce i Prawie, przedmiot, metoda, praktyka*. . ., p. 11. A. Czarnota, *Czym była, czym jest a czym może być historia idei?* [in:] *Myślenie o Polityce i Prawie, przedmiot, metoda, praktyka*. . ., p. 65.

were developed over centuries of progress of civilization may deprive it of the ability to formulate judgments assessing whether a particular aspiration deserves legal sanction, or not. It is also correct to state that lawyers of every era are made responsible for the functioning of the political order.[4] So it is on their shoulders that the state, the whole political dimension of the common existence of people, function on solid, healthy and just grounds. *Ius est ars boni et aequi*, this maxim should guide every lawyer, and what enables a lawyer to judge what is good and just is the very study of political and legal thought, both in their historical, but also contemporary dimension. In addition, guided by the Roman maxim, we should also note that law is an art. It is not technical knowledge, it often fails to deliver simple answers, by mere substituting data into a formula. The above reflection underlies this monograph, which goes back to the thought, the doctrine to which many institutions of the state and law refer today.

Another assumption underlying the present monograph is the conviction that the state and the law are, *sui generis*, inseparable. These two concepts can be considered as conditioning each other. What would a lawless state be? Could it function without the set of norms telling its residents, how to behave in certain situations of their lives? What is more, could the law operate without the state, its organization and the executive apparatus providing instruments for implementing legal norms? The answer to the above questions must be negative.

Based on the above assumptions, the subject of the present work is the idea of the state in the thought of Robert von Mohl. This German lawyer and politician is considered one of the creators and popularizers of the *Rechtsstaat* concept. The rule of law[5] is undoubtedly one of the constitutional foundations of most civilized states today. However, Mohl's vision of the state is not limited to idea of the rule of law. The scholar presented a comprehensive vision of the state, and its role in human life. Therefore, the analysis of his views in this respect is part of the paradigm presented above, which is not only a kind of indissolubility of the state and law, but also postulates that at their foundations there should lay a definite and complete vision (doctrine, thought).

---

4 *Editors' note*, [in:] *Myślenie o Polityce i Prawie, przedmiot, metoda, praktyka...*, p. 11.

5 For the purposes of this publication the phrases "rule of law" and "legal state" are used equivalently. However it should be noted that the meaning of specific term "Rule of law" from English legal tradition does not perfectly cover with the meaning of the Rechtsstaat concept. The term "legal state" is used as a translation for Rechtsstaat, for example, by Dietmar von der Pfordten. More: D. v. d. Pfordten, *On the Foundations of the Rule of Law and the Principle of Legal State/Rechtsstaat*, [in:] J. R. Silkenat, J. E. Hickey Jr., P. D. Barenboim (eds.), *The Legal Doctrines of the Rule of Law and the Legal State (Rechtsstaat)*, Heidelberg, New York, Dordrecht, London 2014, p. 15

Another reason that we decided to take up this subject is the current condition of research on the state thought of Robert von Mohl. It will not be a mistake to assume that von Mohl and his achievements are far from popular a subject for research in Polish science. There is also no monogaphic study dealing with any aspect of the von Mohl idea (including the state). The merit of introducing the figure of the German scholar in Poland should be attributed to Adam Bosiacki. He modernized the sole work of a German scholar translated into Polish, namely the *Encyclopedia of Sciences of State*,[6] also writing the Polish introduction thereto. The ideas of von Mohl, primarily those related to his vision of *Rechtsstaat*, function as topics for several scientific articles and are present in collective studies and academic textbooks on the history of political and legal doctrines. It should not be surprising, however, that in German science, von Mohl's oeuvre was subjected to more frequent analyses, albeit it is difficult to compare it, even in terms of quantity, with publications devoted to such masters as Immanuel Kant or Wilhelm von Humboldt. The Mohl's idea of state was thus the subject of analysis by representatives of German science. However, publications on this issue are either relatively old (created e.g. in the 1960s) or have the form of scientific articles or single chapters in monographs, which are necessarily shorter forms.[7]

The above-mentioned reasons all justify taking up the subject of the monograph. Its purpose is a comprehensive synthesis and discussion of the vision of the state that was presented by Robert von Mohl. We will also prove the rationality and comprehensiveness of Mohl's understanding of the state. Furthermore, on the background of historical events, we will also prove that von Mohl was rooted in the achievements of two different eras, in his understanding of the role of state. Thus, on the one hand he will be still inspired by the absolutism era and its *Polizeistaat*,[8] on the other by the liberal reflection in the form of the *Rechtsstaat*

---

6 The explanation of the translation of phrase *Staatswissenschaften* into "sciences of state" is made in Chapter II.

7 A more detailed description of publications related to the scholar's ideas is made later in the introduction.

8 *Polizeistaat* - literally translated "police state" for the purpose of this work is understood as the idea of a state that is the counterbalance to the concept of *Rechtsstaat* (the rule of law, legal state) developed in the 19th century. It is a state that is seeking, through its extensive administrative apparatus, to provide its residents with maximum prosperity. However, such a state lacked civil liberties and equality before the law. Clerks of the administration apparatus serving the absolutist monarchy occupied the crucial position. German pharses "*Polizei*" and "*Polizeiwissenschaft*" were translated into "police" and "police science" respectively. It should be underlined that for the purpose of this

idea. It is the spread of the scholar's ideas between the two great epochs in the history of comprehending the state, and his attempt to synthesize them, that make his achievements a fascinating, and inspiring object of research.

The timeframe of our work is limited by the perspective of the scientist's life and work. It is, above all, the period from the beginning of the nineteenth century until the creation and the first years of the Second Reich. Due to the fact that von Mohl drew on the achievements of the enlightened absolutism, references will also be made to the second half of the 18th century. There is no doubt that the subject of the work defines von Mohl's ideas concerning the state as the main axis of the analysis. However, it will also present the concepts of other politicians, scientists and thinkers. They will not only provide specific benchmarks for the achievements of the Württemberger,[9] but will also give the present argument a cognitive depth. They will set the understanding of the state by von Mohl in a specific ideological context.

This work consists of five chapters, each of which has a specific role and research task.

The first chapter is primarily an introduction to the main topics of our analysis. Its task is to outline the general political and social picture of the German states in the nineteenth century. This objective is met with a brief overview of the most important events and ideological trends taking place in nineteenth-century Germany.[10] The main focus is pointing out and underlining the social and political unrest that took place in German areas throughout virtually the entire 19th century (until unification under the rule of Prussia). Economic and social issues were also raised, including the economic backwardness of Germany in relation to France and England, the industrial revolution and the related rise of the proletariat, and the urban bourgeoisie. We also stressed the issue of German reunification, the Spring of Nations in its territory, and the events of the Frankfurt Parliament. All this was superimposed on the formation of the German national

---

work the term "police" is not equivalent with todays meaning of "police" or "*Polizei*." DF Lindenfeld, *The Practical Imagination The German Sciences of State in the Nineteenth Century*, Chicago 1997, p. 6.

9 For the sake of the aesthetics of expression, in the present work will also call von Mohl the Württemberger, which will also emphasize his origin from one of the most liberal German countries.

10 Whenever the words "German area," "German states," "German lands" or "Germany" are used in the work, these will refer to all the states that in the nineteenth century could be included in the German cultural area, which were also part of the German Confederation, and later also of the Second Reich.

community, a sense of separateness and the specific German ethos. Attention was paid to the sentiment of many Germans to the times of enlightened absolutism, to life under the protection of the caring monarch in the *Polizeistaat*. However, conservative ideas were increasingly tested by the stratum of liberal (as for German conditions) middle class that was growing in strength, demanding civil liberties and the liberalization of political life. The period of the nineteenth century in Germany, until the proclamation of the Second Reich in 1871, was marked by a more or less intense battle between what was past (conservative) and what was new (liberal). Liberals (including von Mohl) were in favor of freedom of property, freedom of thought, basing the state on a written constitution and introducing parliamentary representation. At the other extreme there were the conservatives, who saw a chance to return to feudal relations, estate organization of society and the omnipotent power of the monarch through the restoration process. In this melting pot, the specific German version of liberalism was forged, which abandoned the aspirations of revolutionary change in favor of reform-oriented cooperation between the people and the authorities (the ruler).

The first chapter also presents the views of several thinkers, whose perception of the state can be considered emblematic for the ideological portrait of Germany at that time. The underlying intention of this research activity was to present the widest range of views represented at the time in Germany. The conservatives discussed are: Karl Ludwig von Haller and Friedrich Julius Stahl. The first of them referred to pre-revolutionary feudalism and was the creator of the idea of restoration. The second, who lived later than Haller, was also a bit more progressive than the latter. He was in favour of the *Rechtsstaat* concept (but only in its formal dimension). However, he criticized the understanding of the state characteristic of contemporary liberals. We also referred to the so called romantic vision of the state, as presented by Adam Müller. He treated it as a metaphysical being, but also a necessity for the individual that was aiding it. The eclecticism and uniqueness, as well as the specific turbidity of his conception, perfectly illustrate what ideological melting pot was the then Germany. The task of sketching the ideological picture of Germany at that time will be completed with presentation of views on the state of one of the most prominent German liberals at that time. We are talking about Karl von Rotteck. His views will demonstrate the other opposite, towards which the progressive part of Germany was heading. In addition, due to the nuances and differences in, for example, the perception of the issue of electoral law or the idea of separation of powers, an analysis of his views in comparison with the visions of von Mohl will demonstate that German liberalism was far from being an unambiguous current.

Every individual, and certainly an individual, who is politically aware and, moreover, actively participates in the life of the state, during its existence often even involuntarily, soaks up the trends of the reality in, which it finds itself. It was no different with Robert von Mohl. Therefore, the threads of the scientist's biography cannot be omitted. Our analysis of this aspect will prove that von Mohl was a child of his era. Coming from a respected, noble, bourgeois family, he received a thorough education and used it in both scientific and practical activities. His scientific activity was complementary to his political activities. In his works, he often used conclusions derived, for example, from activities in the Frankfurt Parliament.

The second chapter is also there to construct a background for von Mohl's state doctrine. Here comes the statement that for von Mohl the state was just one of many so-called "spheres of life" in which individuals function during their existence. From our analysis of the idea of "spheres of life," it also appears that, for von Mohl, the state was not something total, overwhelming the entire human existence. Therefore, other "spheres of life" and their relation to the state were also briefly discussed. Furthermore we also discussed the concept of goals of human life. It was also this concept that formed one of the cornerstones for the assumptions of von Mohl, used to construct the concept of state and the justification for its very existence.

One of the "spheres of life" listed by von Mohl was the society. Due to the fact that he was one of the first nineteenth-century German thinkers, who saw the existence of this phenomenon, we decided to devote a separate editorial unit to it. The idea of the sphere of society is very extensive in von Mohl and it also forms the background for his idea of the state. We started with presenting the Württemberger's assessment of the earlier scientific achievements in the field of society. It proved the scholar's great knowledge of the literature on the subject (although sometimes misinterpreted), forming an introduction to his original concepts. The answer to the so-called "*Soziale Frage*" (social issue) was one of the scholar's distinguishing features against the ideological background of contemporary Germany. We will prove that he was one of the first German writers, who noticed the formation of society and the proletariat. He also attempted to find a solution to the problems arising from this phenomenon. We will also present his perception of relations between the state and society, which is important also from the point of view of parliamentary representation (as discussed in chapter five). The analysis of the system of "sciences of society" in von Mohl's thought will function as a link to the issues raised in the next subsection.[11] The purpose of

11 The use of the term "sciences of society" and not "social sciences" was dictated by the

this research task is to demonstrate that von Mohl gave a similar rank to society, the state and the individual (and he created a separate pattern of sciences for all these entities).

The entire scope of knowledge relating to "sciences of state" proves the comprehensive approach of von Mohl to the phenomenon of state. An analysis of the Mohl's understanding of the state would be incomplete without discussing the scope of sciences related to the state derived by the scholar. The very concept of *Staatswissenschaften* (sciences of state), as well as their role and popularity in contemporary German science will be analyzed. Similarities and differences between the perception of sciences of state by von Mohl and other contemporary German thinkers (primarily Karl von Rotteck, Karl Theodor Welcker, Friedrich Bülau) will also be pointed out. We will prove that von Mohl's ambition was to create a system of sciences allowing the analysis of the state from all possible points of view. In addition to the law so he saw the state through the prism of politics and ethics. He was also not forgetting about the role of history and statistics in the state. This confirms that the state became the center of his scientific reflection. Another issue raised will be the ways for presentation of knowledge about the state. We will examine the encyclopedia of sciences of state, as a popular method of spreading the knowledge of state. It will be proved that von Mohl was in favor of popularizing it, formulating scientific statements in an easily accessible, and politically conscious manner.

Chapter three begins the discussion of the crucial content from the viewpoint of objectives of the present publication. It focuses on the analysis of the genesis and the concept of the state and its evolution during the entire career of Robert von Mohl. It corresponds to the spheres of life listed in chapter two, by indicating the differences between them and the state. What is discussed are also the ways for establishing a state, as distinguished by the scholar, and the goals it should be guided by. The research task undertaken in the thrid chapter is also to examine the constituent parts of the state, which von Mohl distinguished in its definition. Therefore, his concept was analyzed in relation to the concept of population and nation, "collective power," "collective will" and territory.

Von Mohl claimed that the state is a creation that is functioning for the people. That is why the significance of the population for the state, thoroughly analyzed by the scholar, was separated into an editorial unit devoted to it. In this aspect,

---

desire to avoid giving the von Mohl concept the same meaning that today refers solely to the concept of "social sciences." Similar translation of the verb *Sozialwissenschaften* was made by David F. Lindenfeld. Ibidem, p. 181.

among other things due to the nationalist tensions of that time, it seems important to present the Württemberger's views on the issue of the nation in the state. Therefore, the concept of individual rights in relation to the state resulting from belonging to such, and not another nationality, and their influence on the state was discussed. Our analysis of the Mohl's concept of "species and types of states" forms both a substantive link, and a brief introduction to chapter four. On the basis of opposites, it will bring out the features of one of the scholar's main considerations, i.e. the idea of *Rechtsstaat*.

As already noted, the idea of the rule of law (legal state, *Rechtsstaat*) was one of von Mohl's most extensive research fields. In order to achieve the goal of analyzing his concept of *Rechtsstaat*, we will start by presenting the perception of the origin of the rule of law and the assessment, by von Mohl, of the views of other scientists in this aspect. Then we will go on to investigate the very understanding of rule of law by von Mohl, and attempt to define it. It will be emphasized that von Mohl links the idea of *Rechtsstaat* with a sufficiently high development of the rationality of a given people.

One of the material aspects of the Mohl 's idea of the *Rechtsstaat* were the relationships between the individual (citizen) and the legal state. To discuss these relationships we will first demonstrate the understanding by the understanding of the term of citizen by von Mohl. Secondly, both the rights and obligations of citizens in the rule of law will be analyzed. We will also analyze the formal aspect of the legal state, examine the sources of law in von Mohl's and their mutual relations. Despite their universal nature, they also correspond to the *Rechtsstaat* concept, because von Mohl based his theory on a three-stage division of sources of written law. We also make a reference to the principles of the legislative process expressed by the scholar.

As part of chapter four, an analysis of the relationship between the absolutist police state and the rule of law in the doctrine of von Mohl is also provided. To this end, the concept of state activities through its administration will be discussed. We will present the principles of operation of the administration and "police" (*Polizei*) and their compliance with the principles of the idea of the rule of law. Mohl's vision of the issue of bureaucracy and the functioning of officials in the state was also raised. A separate issue will be the admissibility of the use of coercion by the state, demonstrated on the background of administrative activity. The issue of use of coercion by the state (in this case by its police) is worth quoting because it shows the duality of von Mohl's views, drawing from both the era of absolutism and liberalism.

The considerations undertaken as the main part of the publication will be closed by a chapter relating to the broadly understood issues of power in the state and its holders. This research task will begin with the analysis of the concept of power in the thought of Robert von Mohl and determination of the significance of his requirement of its indivisibility and irresponsibility. Next, the views of the scholar and their evolution in the field of parliamentary representation will be discussed. It was another topic that was subject to vivid discussion in the troubled nineteenth-century Germany. To deepen our argument on this subject, we added the description of the internal situation in relation to the development of the idea of parliamentarism. An attempt will be made to answer the question what shape of the parliamentary system did the scholar considered the most optimal one. In addition, the issue of the party system and the relationship between the vision of society and the parliamentary system will be analyzed. Evidence of moderation in liberal aspirations will be provided, by means of our analysis of von Mohl's understanding of democracy and his opposition to universal suffrage.

The work on the preparation of this publication involved a number of trips to research centers in Germany. They enabled us to collect the necessary scientific materials and literature on the subject, which were usually not available in Poland. Two visits were made to the Berlin State Library (*Staatsbibliothek zu Berlin*), and a monthly stay was conducted at the Faculty of Law of the Ruprecht Karl University of Heidelberg (as part of the scholarship of the DAAD, German Academic Exchange Centre). In addition, using funds obtained under the PRELUDIUM 15 competition of the National Science Center Poland (research project No. 2018/29/N/HS5/01501 entitled *At the origins of German liberalism: the state in the thought of Robert von Mohl*) a study was conducted in the Library of the Institute for European Legal History of the Max Planck Institute in Frankfurt am Main.[12] A number of scientific consultations took place, among others with dr hab. Małgorzata Łuszczyńska (Maria Curie-Skłodowska University in Lublin) professor UMCS, dr hab. Jarosław Kostrubiec (Maria Curie-Skłodowska University in Lublin), prof. dr hab. Adam Bosiacki (University of Warsaw), dr hab. Artur Łuszczyński (University of Rzeszów) professor UR, prof. dr. Martin Borowski (University of Heidelberg).

During the preparation of the work, we used mainly German-language sources and materials. However, the sole work of the German thinker published in Polish was a good reference standard. Works by other authors of that era were also used, and their detailed list is included in the References section.[13]

12 The PRELUDIUM competition is addressed to young researchers, who did not yet obtain the doctoral degree..

13 It should be noted that for the sake of clarity (including footnotes) a number of abbreviations have been used in the work, the scope of which has been included in the List of Abbreviations.

As for the German-language literature on the subject, it was naturally a richer resource than its Polish counterpart. During the preparation of the monograph we analyzed German monographs, articles and studies on all aspects of von Mohl's activity. Particularly noteworthy is the very extensive and comprehensive work by Erich Angerman (published in 1962). It provides a complete overview of the life and work of Robert von Mohl. The author focused on issues concerning the legal state, social problems, workers' issues and economic views, as well as the theory of administration and parliamentarism. However, he did not pay too much attention to the systematics of sciences of the state and the general understanding of the state by von Mohl.

Mention should also be made of several doctoral dissertations published in print by Johanna Hähnle and Eduard Schupp (both published in the interwar period). The first concerned the scholar's political ideas, and the second related to his economic views. Dissertations by Brigite Granzow (on the subject of Mohl's idea of parliamentarism) and Helmut Schmitz (on the general idea of the state) appeared after World War II. There is no doubt that the aforesaid publications refer to the concept of the state in Robert von Mohl's thought with varying intensity. However, we should note that all these are relatively short works (none of them exceeds 150 pages), written rather long ago, and often not using all the available sources.

It is worth noting the dissertation by Rolf-Jürgen Grahe from the 1980s, referring to civil rights, and the valuable work of Brigit Stöcker, dealing with the relationship between the concept of von Mohl and the principles of the "social legal state" (*Sozialer Rechtsstaat*) in Germany. The renowned German political scientist Klaus von Beyme published a collection of writings by Robert von Mohl, writing a valuable introduction to it. In addition to these publications, von Mohl's concepts are present in a large number of articles or chapters of monographs. All those used for the purpose of the present work are listed in the References section.

As already noted, concepts relating to the state in the thought of Robert von Mohl as the subject of scientific research, were undertaken quite rarely in Polish science. The scholar's views are present in textbook studies (among others by Lech Dubel). They also function as references, paragraphs or chapters in monographs (e.g. by Zbigniew Maciąg or Maria Gromadzka-Grzegorzewska). We should highlight, once again, also the merits of the aforementioned Adam Bosiacki. In addition to the activities already mentioned above, he is the author of publications relating to the world of German ideas and the rule of law in the thought of Robert von Mohl. Józef Nowacki also undertook an analysis of Mohl's idea of the state in his article.

The methodological assumptions adopted in the present work correspond to the methods assigned to the history of political and legal doctrines. The main idea was to determine what von Mohl thought about the state, and why he thought so. To this end, the views expressed by the German thinker were subjected to reconstruction, sythematization and evaluation. This action was also accomplished by placing von Mohl's views against the background of the era in which he lived.[14] To implement the methodological *modus vivendi* presented above, we applied research methods resulting from the interdisciplinary nature of political and legal doctrines.[15]

Therefore, during our work on the publication, we did not limit ourselves to the research methods proper for legal sciences. On the one hand, we functioned within them, as we attempted to study the doctrine that was the basis of normative regulations. On the other hand, in referring to the role of the state in the lives of citizens, their rights, and the very functioning of state institutions, was also entered the realm of political sciences.[16] We also applied auxiliary methods stemming from linguistics and history. The most important methods were the analytical-deductive method and the inductive reasoning. We analyzed the works of Robert von Mohl and other scientists using these methods. Theses contained in the publications were used and evaluated. The above method was also combined with the comparative (comparatistic) method, which was applied to indicate common features and differences between the views of von Mohl and other scholars. The biographical method, sourced from historical sciences, was applied to analyze the life of the German liberal. The institutional and legal method were also used, first of all for the analysis of legal issues arising in the *strict sense*. To present the research results, we aided ourselves with both the descriptive (doxographic) method, and the explanatory method. In the process

---

14 M. Maciejewski, T. Scheffler, *O doktrynologii: Rozważania dotyczące przedmiotu oraz metody doktryn politycznych i prawnych* [in:] *Myślenie o Polityce i Prawie, przedmiot, metoda, praktyka…*, p. 266.

15 Michał Jaskólski also writes about the interdisciplinarity of history of political and legal doctrines, more: M. Jaskólski, *13 różnych esejów o historii myśli politycznej i nie tylko*, Warszawa 2013, pp. 47–75.

16 On the admissibility of using political science methods in the study of political and legal doctrines: O. A. Górecki, *Metodologia głównych orientacji badawczych teorii polityki w analizie doktryn polityczno-prawnych* [in:] *Myślenie o Polityce i Prawie, przedmiot, metoda, praktyka…*, p. 233. More about methods used in political science: A. Łuszczyński, *Podstawy Metodologiczne Badań Politologicznych*, Rzeszów 2005, pp. 34–75.

of interpretation, paraphrase and translation of German sentences and phrases, methods known from linguistics, i.e. linguistic and sociolinguistic analysis, linguistic analysis, and written translation were all applied.

At the end of this publication, in addition to summarizing the arguments contained therein, the last research task was carried out, which assumed giving the modern dimension to Mohl's understanding of the state. For its implementation, the most important aspects of the idea of the rule of law in the thought of Robert von Mohl were compared with contemporary principles of the "social state" and "democratic legal state" in the systems of Germany and Poland. A concise analysis of the relationship between von Mohl's views and the understanding of these constitutional principles will allow us to demonstrate that there are many similarities between them. On the other hand, we will also stress the differences, primarily in terms of issues related to power in the state, sovereignty of the nation and the functioning of democracy.

Acknowledgments

Ending the introductory remarks the author would like to thank the person without whom this work would never be created, dr hab. Małgorzata Łuszczyńska UMCS professor. Her above-average patience and forbearance, respect and care demonstrated to the author while preparing this book must undoubtedly be regarded as far exceeding the generally applicable academic customs and practices.

The author would also thank, for his valuable advice and help, dr hab. Jaroslaw Kostrubiec. The author would also stress his gratitude for the substantive support provided to Professor dr hab. Adam Bosiacki and dr hab. Artur Łuszczyński, UR professor.

We also owe thanks for the warm welcome, advice and help provided during the research stay at the Heidelberg University to Prof. dr Martin Borowski, Head of the Chair of Public Law, Constitutional Theory and Legal Philosophy at the Faculty of Law of the Heidelberg University. Thanks to Mrs. Ingrid Baumbusch for all her help and kindness.

The author would also like to thank, for their support in the process of creating this publication, the management of the Institute of Legal Sciences of the Faculty of Law and Administration at UMCS, Professor dr hab. Leszek Leszczyński and dr hab. Marek Kulik UMCS professor. I also owe thanks to dr Barbara Warda, dr. Mariusz Banach Deputy Mayor City of Lublin and Mrs. Anna Kochalska-Wasak for their valuable advice and all the help provided.

There is no doubt that this work would not have been possible without the support of my loved ones, my family and friends. The author would like to thank his wife Diana, and parents Renata and Jan for their understanding, patience and unlimited support. Thanks are also due to the author's sister, Dr. Magdalena Lesińska-Staszczuk, who was always ready to provide valuable advice and help.

I would also thank, for help in collecting materials and inspiring conversations, my sincere colleague from school years Paweł Łapiński and also Maciej Szmygin. The author would like to express gratitude to Agata and Stefan Siegmann for the help and kindness demonstrated during his stay in Heidelberg.

Finally, the author would like to thank his departed Grandfather Jerzy Skrzypek, who was the first to introduce him to the world of history and politics, and initiated his passion that continues to this day.

Chapter I Robert von Mohl and his era

1.1. The sociopolitical situation of German lands from the beginning of the 19th century until the unification of Germany

The French Revolution marked one of the most important landmarks in the history of Europe and the whole world, but also for the history of Germany. This event triggered a process in the German lands that Michael Stolleis later called the "turn of the ages."[17] Liberal ideas carried by the French Revolution began to penetrate relatively quickly into the territory of the still existing First German Reich.[18] Initially, the revolutionary slogans of equality, freedom and political empowerment did not find a fertile ground in German states. This was mainly because in this area (in contrast to the then France and England), a strong urban bourgeoisie (which could take over the role of popularizing liberal and revolutionary ideas) had not yet developed. The nobility and the peasantry were conservative, and the social system was still based on the estate organization.[19] The fear of the negative effects of revolutionary changes, social unrest and terror that were all seen in case of France was also strong.[20] Therefore, many German thinkers, headed by Immanuel Kant, despite their praise for the ideas of freedom and respect for slogans of the French Revolution, rejected the violence and anxiety brought by it.[21]

In addition, the ideas of the French Revolution, proclaiming the sovereignty of the people and the need to break with the old order of the era of absolutism aroused particular fear and opposition among German monarchs, particularly in Austria and Prussia. The fears of the rulers of these two great countries resulted in the establishment of an alliance against revolutionary France between Austria

---

17 M. Stolleis, *Geschichte des öffentlichen Rechts in Deutschland*, München 1992, p. 42.

18 T. Paluszyński, *Historia Niemiec i państw niemieckich zarys dziejów politycznych*, Poznań 2006, p. 173.

19 It is noteworthy that the German lands of the late eighteenth and early nineteenth century were economically backward compared to France or England. More on the economic and social relations of the early nineteenth century in the German area in: W. Czapliński, A. Galos, W. Korta, *Historia Niemiec*, Wrocław, Warszawa, Kraków 1990, pp. 401–404.

20 M. Stolleis, op. cit. p. 42.

21 Z. Zieliński, *Niemcy Zarys Dziejów*, Katowice 2003, p. 113.

and Prussia. Tensions between these countries led to the 1792 Franco-Austrian War, which resulted in France capturing the western part of German Reich.[22] As a result of Peace of Basel, Republican troops entered German territories located on the left bank of the Rhine. In general, they were enthusiastically welcomed by the local population, counting on liberal changes in the social structure. The effects of France taking over control of the left-bank Rhineland included, inter alia, the proclamation of the first democratic state in German history, i.e. the Republic of Mainz.[23] The war events of the following years, the struggles of both the first and second anti-French coalition, and the French victories sealed by provisions of peace treaties concluded in Campoformio and Luneville and the conference in Rastatt, led to the consolidation of French domination and enabled Napoleon Bonaparte to control the situation in most of the German areas, according to French interests.[24]

At the same time, German nationalism and disagreement with the hegemony of their western neighbour began to slowly grow in the dominated countries. The sense of German national and cultural unity appeared, coupled with the belief in the need to establish one German state based on a national society.[25] The additional side effect of French domination of German lands was that the majority of Germans came to believe that the republican order of France does not fit the conditions of contemporary Germany.[26] The republic was not seen as the only proper *remedy* for the absolute monarchy. The fear of instability, as observed in France, therefore, caused the consent of most Germans to reform the monarchy, and not to abolish it.

Therefore, the population of most German states began to seek support in a monarchical system, where the ruler appeared as a caring guardian, attempting to secure the good of his subjects with aid of his officials.[27] The effect of this attitude was the deepening of the so-called the police state (*Polizeistaat*), i.e. a state where, as we already mentioned before, the most important goal was to ensure maximum happiness and care for the subjects. The one to pursue that

---

22 T. Paluszyński, op. cit. pp. 173–174.

23 Z. A. Maciąg, *Kształtowanie zasad państwa demokratycznego, prawnego i socjalnego w Niemczech (do 1949 r.)*, Białystok 1998, p. 65.

24 T. Paluszyński, op. cit., p. 175.

25 Ibidem, p. 181. Such postulates were included, among others, in the *Speeches to the German Nation* published in 1807 by Johann Gottlieb Fichte: J. G. Fichte, *Reden an die deutsche Nation*, Hamburg 1978.

26 Z. A. Maciąg, op. cit., p. 66.

27 F. Berber, *Das Staatsideal im Wandel der Weltgeschichte*, München 1973, p. 336.

objective was the monarch, and the subordinate, vast official apparatus. It should be emphasized that 19th century witnessed the crowning of the construction process of enlightened absolutism in Germany.[28] Another important event confirming the hegemony of France in western Germany was the formation of the Confederation of Rhine under its leadership.[29] It were the large southern German states: Bavaria and the homeland of Robert von Mohl, Württemberg that played the main role in that confederation. The rulers of these countries were elevated to royal dignities by Napoleon, and became his loyal, albeit puppet allies.[30]

The Confederation of the Rhine was completely subordinated to Napoleonic France. Domestic reforms in its member states were also an expression of dominance. They were patterned on the model of the ruling system in France. The introduction of the Napoleon Civil Code in the Rhine states played a significant role in this process.[31] It abolished privileges of estates and introduced equality of access to public offices. One should also remember that constitutions modelled on the French one were also introduced in many countries of the Confederation of Rhine.[32] They liberalized, to a large extent, political life, especially in countries such as Württemberg and Bavaria. For example, they included into the legal order of these countries the principles of equality of all citizens before the law or abolished serfdom of the peasants.[33] However, it would be unjustified to say that the states of the Confederation of Rhine were liberal constitutional monarchies. These countries sought to strike a balance between royal absolutism and the influence of the increasing bourgeoisie, demanding participation in government.[34]

---

28 Z. A. Maciąg, op. cit., p. 66. W. Conze, *Staat und Gesellschaft in der frührevolutionären Epoche Deutschlands*, [in:] *Entstehung des modernen souveränen Staates*, H.-H. Hofmann (eds.), Köln, Berlin 1967, p. 301.

29 T. Paluszyński, op. cit., p. 176. More: Z. Zieliński, op. cit., pp. 116, 118.

30 T. Paluszyński, op. cit., p. 176.

31 Z. Zieliński, op. cit., p. 118.

32 More on these reforms: D. Willoweit, *Deutsche Verfassungsgeschichte Vom Frankreich bis zur Wiedervereinigung Deutschlands*, München 2005, pp. 266–279.

33 Z. Zieliński, op. cit., p. 118. T. Paluszyński, op. cit., p. 180. It is worth noting that in Prussia, in the result of the defeat suffered in the war with France in 1806, also wanting to strengthen the state institutions it was decided to make changes called the "reforms of Stein and Hardenberg." They reformed the organization of the state, leading, among others to abolition of feudal relations, elimination of serfdom and servitudes. More about the reforms of Stein and Hardenberg in Prussia: Ibid, pp. 181–183, A. Dziadzio, *Koncepcja państwa prawa w XIX wieku – idea i rzeczywistość*, "Czasopismo Prawno-Historyczne," t. LVII, 2005, Zeszyt 1, p. 182.

34 M. Stolleis, op. cit., pp. 62–63.

Therefore, the system that prevailed in the so-called Rhine Germany, can also be referred to as the enlightened absolutism state system. It referred to the aforementioned forms of the "police state," as well as the *Wohlfahrtsstaat* or welfare state.[35] This resulted in the expansion of various types of administration and the introduction of a centralist bureaucratic system.

It is worth noting that the expansion of public administration, ordered with the task to care for the broadly understood well-being of citizens, was associated in Germany with the further development of the so-called *Ancien Regime* of "police science" (*Polizeiwissenschaft*). This also spurred the development the German area-specific administrative law (*Verwaltungsrecht*) and the very notion of "police" (*Policey*) denoted all branches of administrative sciences at that time.[36] However, despite the introduction of the principles of enlightened absolutism, the entire area of political and administrative power remained in the hands of the ruler. It is true that his task was to protect the safety of the subjects and to care for their well-being, but they were to be values provided under the individual's limited freedom, as limited by the bureaucratic apparatus of the state.[37]

The end of the French domination, as well as the Confederation of Rhine itself, were brought about by the events of the end of the Napoleonic era.[38] After the battle of Leipzig, other states of the Confederation of Rhine, mainly Baden and Württemberg, switched sides, joining the anti-Napoleonic coalition.[39] Question of future of Germany, including its organization and functioning of this complicated conglomerate of states and countries were not resolved until the Congress of Vienna.

One of the most important issues raised during the Congress of Vienna was of course the future of Germany and the so-called "constitutional question" *(Verfassungsfrage)*. In the result of decisions taken at Congress, the territorial

35 O. Kimminich, *Deutsche Verfassungsgeschichte*, Frankfurt am Main 1970, pp. 307–312. Such a system was also adopted by Friedrich, the King of Württemberg. The objective of this ruler was to build an efficient state, internally united, according to the French but also Prussian models. For example, as early as 1806, Württemberg had an organization of ministries (*Ministerialverfassung*), consisting of six main branches of administration: foreign affairs, internal affairs, justice, war, finance and education, as well as the so called "spiritual matters." More on this subject: K. Weller, A. Weller, *Württembergische Geschichte im südwestdeutschen Raum*, Stuttgart und Aalen 1972, pp. 212–214.

36 M. Stolleis, op. cit., p. 229.

37 A. Dziadzio, op. cit., p. 179.

38 W. Czapliński, A. Galos, W. Korta, op. cit., p. 441.

39 T. Paluszyński, op. cit., p. 185.

division of the German area was maintained.[40] The Confederation of Rhine was abolished and the German Confederation established in its place, with the dominant position of Austria. The political system of the German Confederation was based on the constitution called the "Constitution of the German Confederation" (*Deutsche Bundesakte*), and its supplement in the form of the Vienna Final Agreement (*Wiener Schlussakte*) of 1820.[41] From the very beginning, the existence of the German Confederation was marked by competition for domination between Prussia and Austria. On the one hand, Austria was becoming weaker and unable to reform its political and economic system, while on the other hand Prussia was strengthened by the reforms of Stein and Hardenberg, and subject to active and dynamic economic change.[42] The economic development, not only of Prussia, but also of other states of the German Confederation accelerated the lifting of internal fiscal barriers and customs. The effect of the growing dominance of Prussia was the inclusion of southern and central German states (which is also significant - excluding Austria) in the Prussian Customs Union (*Zollverein*).[43]

The process of the post-Napoleonic restoration brought specific political and social changes to German states. First of all, the return to the pre-Napoleonic social organization hit the middle class, who lost the main political gains of Napoleonic times. The German middle class, strengthened during the time of French domination, was, starting with the Congress of Vienna, the main animator of liberal aspirations and the struggle for social change.[44]

Despite the fact that the doctrinal basis of police states of the early nineteenth century in Germany was to ensure the broadly understood prosperity and happiness of their subjects, in the first half of the nineteenth century the division between the state - the royal administrative-police apparatus and society - was becoming more apparent. It should be emphasized that the police state was still the ruler's arbitrary state. The monarch was not limited by the will of national representation, officials were primarily subject to his orders, and not the provisions of generally applicable law. The deepening dichotomy between the monarch and society initiated the search for different paths of systemic reform. Neither revolution nor democracy was at stake. Both of them arose fear, of terror

40 E. Forsthoff, *Deutsche Verfassungsgeschichte der Neuzeit*, Stuttgart, Berlin, Köln, Mainz 1972, p. 85.
41 Z. Zieliński, op. cit., p. 126.
42 T. Paluszyński, op. cit., pp. 190–191.
43 Ibid, pp. 191–192.
44 Ibid, p. 188.

known from France, or the demagogy that was likely to develop in a democratic system. Therefore, the conviction came that the proper way of reforms would be to maintain a monarchy, in which the ruler's political position should be limited by law.[45]

The middle class began to play an increasingly prominent role in the societies of German states, gaining a strong position as a result of economic changes and the industrial revolution that began in Germany in the first half of the nineteenth century.[46] The gap between the poor and the rich, the bourgeoisie and the pauperized masses also grew further.[47] The nobility's advantage was beginning to weaken in the face of the stronger economic influences of the middle class. The aspirations of this social stratum in this period focused on the demands of introducing parliamentary government, a clear statutory definition of authority competence and its control by independent courts.[48] In order to implement the aforesaid ideas, the German bourgeoisie demanded the introduction of a state functioning on the basis of a social contract and constitution, freedom to dispose of property and participation in law-making.[49] It was at that time that the concept of the rule of law, or the legal state (*Rechtsstaat*) was ever more frequently referred to. During the first half of the nineteenth century, this idea had primarily political significance, personifying the opposition against the functioning absolutist state.[50] The state was then first understood as the result of social contract, which people are forced to conclude being unable to face challenges of their life alone.[51]

We find the sources of the *Rechtsstaat* concept in the works of Immanuel Kant and Wilhelm von Humboldt.[52] In their concept of *Rechtsstaat*, which was

---

45 Z. A. Maciąg, op. cit., p. 66–67.

46 J. Burska- Cieślak, *Geneza pojęcia socjalnego państwa prawnego w doktrynie niemieckiej*, [in:] *Państwo ustrój konstytucja studia*, L. Antonowicz et al. (ed.), Lublin 1991, p. 27.

47 Z. Zieliński, op. cit., p. 129.

48 J. Burska- Cieślak, op. cit., p. 27.

49 M. Zmierczak, *Kształtowanie się koncepcji państwa prawnego (na przykładzie niemieckiej myśli polityczno-prawnej)*, [in:] *Demokratyczne państwo prawne*, H. Rot (ed.), "Acta Universitatis Wratislaviensis," No 1457, p. 43.

50 The first use of the term *Rechtsstaat* appears in the work entitled *Literatur der Staatslehre* by Johann Wilhelm Placidius. According to this German scholar, *Rechtsstaat* was a state, whose goal should be to safeguard human rights, that is to say, the greatest freedom of individuals. Ibid., pp. 42–43.

51 M. Stolleis, op. cit., p. 123.

52 More on the concept of the rule of law in Kant's thought: K. Jońca, *Ewolucja pojęcia "Państwa Prawnego" w Niemieckiej Doktrynie Prawnej*, "Acta Universitatis Wratislaviensis" No 307, Przegląd Prawa i Administracji VII, Wrocław 1976, p. 215.

to be the opposite of the *Polizeistaat* "police state," Kant and Humboldt referred to the protection of individual as the main task for the legal state. For Kant, ensuring security and protecting legal order was therefore the main goal of the rulers of the state.[53] Wilhelm von Humboldt presented a similar belief. Referring to the state, he claimed that it shall not limit the freedom of its citizens.[54] For Humboldt, the task of the state was thus merely to create a framework, in which free individuals could operate. The state should limit their freedom as little as possible, avoiding actions aimed at caring for the well-being of its citizens.[55] Both Kant and Humboldt created the concept of the legal state as a state limiting itself solely to the protection of a legal order based on equal rights. Its tasks did not include caring for the well-being of society, which corresponds to the concept of the so-called night watchman, in line with the ideas of *laissez-faire*.[56] However, we should not forget about the then strong views postulating maintaining order restored during the post-Napoleonic restoration. The German science also refers to all reactions to the progressive-libertarian aspirations of the liberal movement as restoration processes. This reaction also resulted in the creation of concepts justifying the legitimacy of the royal power (which will be seen, for example, in works by Karl Ludwig von Haller).[57]

However, many German rulers were aware that return to the absolutist form of government, as known from the 18th century, was impossible, as it could threaten with a revolution.[58] The German monarchs, being also aware of the fiscal and tax needs of their countries, were also sensible to the need to create

---

A. Bosiacki, *Z zagadnień koncepcji państwa prawnego w myśli niemieckiej XIX w.*, [in:] *Pro bono Reipublicae, Księga jubileuszowa Profesora Michała Pietrzaka*, P. Borecki, A. Czohara, T. J. Zieliński, (eds.), Warszawa 2009, p. 44.

53 W. Buchner, *Kant - Państwo i Prawo*, Kraków 1996, p. 42.

54 More about Humboldt: M. Sobolewski, *Koncepcja państwa prawnego (Rechtsstaat) w doktrynie niemieckiego liberalizmu epoki klasycznej*, PIP 1980, z.2, p. 132. M. Chmieliński, *Wilhelma Humboldta idee ograniczenia państwa,* "Czasopismo prawno-historyczne," t. LIV 2002, z.1, p. 346.

55 M. Chmieliński, *Dwa niemieckie indywidualizmy: Liberalny Humboldta i anarchistyczny Stirnera*, "Studia Prawno-Ekonomiczne," t. LX, 1991, p. 60. Idem, *Atomizm a indywidualizm. Rozważania nad myślą polityczną i prawną Wilhelma von Humboldta*, Łódź 2004, p. 79.

56 A. Dziadzio, op. cit., pp. 180–181.

57 R.-J. Grahe, *Meinungsfreicheit und Freizügigkeit. Eine Untersuchung zum Grundrechtsdenken bei Robert von Mohl*, Münster 1981, p. 12.

58 R. Zippelius, *Kleine deutsche Verfassungsgeschichte. Vom frühen Mittelalter bis zur Gegenwart...*, p. 103.

representative bodies that would be binding the state (monarch) on the one hand, and the society on the other. In this way, in the individual German states, there appeared legal systems that combined the principle of monarchical governance and elements of the representation system.[59] The pattern for constitution, which was imposed on as many as thirteen states of the German Confederation, was the French Charter of 1814, which was an attempt to include the bourgeoisie in the country's decision-making processes.[60]

As a result of reforming the absolute monarchies, the first constitutions appeared in Germany, securing fundamental rights (e.g. personal freedom) or the responsibility of ministers before parliamentary assemblies. Full power, however, still remained in the hands of the rulers, whose constitutional prerogatives were, for example, legislative initiative or foreign policy.[61] The establishment of these constitutions was rather the result of cold, political calculations of monarchs, wishing to remain in power, with the smallest possible concessions made to that end. These acts were usually largely limited by them, and passive electoral rights to parliaments depended on criteria of nobility or wealth.[62]

The process of granting the first modern constitutions in German lands was also connected with the process of "positivisation" of fundamental rights, which is also important from the viewpoint on the position of an individual in Mohl's Rechtsstaat. The ideas of so-called "fundamental rights" (*Grundrechten*), "human rights" (*Menschenrechten*) and "civil rights" (*Staatsbürgerlichen Rechten*),[63] emerged in German states in the course of the French Revolution, but also the

---

59 A. Dziadzio, op. cit., p. 182. R.-J. Grahe, op. cit., pp. 17–18. These are primarily the states of southern Germany. More about the so-called 'Constitutional movement' (*Verfassungsbewegung*): T. Nipperdey, *Deutsche Geschichte 1800–1866 Bürgerwelt und starker Staat*, München 1991, pp. 273–274.

60 E. Forsthoff, *Deutsche Verfassungsgeschichte der Neuzeit. Ein Abriß*, Stuttgart 1961, p. 107.

61 R.-J. Grahe, op. cit., p. 20.

62 A. Dziadzio, op. cit ., p. 182. For example, in the 1818 Bavarian Constitution we find a statement saying: "The king is the head of state, holds all the powers of state authority and exercises it on the basis of the provisions contained in the constitutional act he granted." Full text of the constitution: http://www.verfassungen.de/de/by/bayern18–index.htm [access date: 13/02/2018].

63 More on the development of so-called "fundamental rights" in Germany in the nineteenth century and their relationship with the idea of *Rechtsstaat*: R. Wahl, *Rechtliche Wirkungen und Funktionen der Grundrechte im Deutschen Konstitutionalismus des 19. Jahrhunderts*, "Der Staat" Vol. 18, No. 3 (1979), pp. 321–348, K. Doehring, *Allgemeine Staatslehre, Eine systematische Darstellung*, Heidelberg 2004, pp. 214–224.

Enlightenment concepts of Immanuel Kant and German idealism.[64] German liberalism did not strive to openly break with the absolutist tradition and the outdated social order as in the case of France. Great codifications of the late 18th century, such as Prussian *Landrecht*, completely ignored the issues of broadly understood fundamental rights of an individual. At the beginning of the nineteenth century, all civil liberties, both economic and personal, were not introduced in a revolutionary (bottom-up) manner, but in a slow reform process of absolutist countries, following concessions of rulers for the benefit of citizens.[65]

Broadly understood fundamental rights were not derived from natural law ideas, or defined in abstract and general declarations, but introduced and guaranteed by rulers in precise normative acts, as the so called civil rights. They were associated with belonging to the state, and not, for example, with being a human being as such. In the first half of the 19th century, these rights were clearly distinguished from the general ideas of human rights. The fundamental rights positivisation process was the first approach of German states to protect citizens against abuses, primarily from the authorities. As Andreas Haratsch states, this proved to be insufficient security. Due to the fact that these rights were granted under laws by the head of the state (the monarch), there was still risk that they could be withdrawn or limited by him.[66]

We find the expression of mixing of the old, absolutist order with the new, liberal currents in Germany in the functioning of parliamentary systems combining state elements with elements of the idea of representation.[67] The parliaments of the constitutional German states of that time were based on the principle of bicameralism, where the upper chamber was reserved for aristocrats, and the lower for representatives of universities or nobility, according to the property qualifications. Therefore, it should be stated that the conflict was not resolved and society was not identifying itself with the state (monarch). On the one hand, these constitutions contained catalogues of civil rights, such as equality before the law or personal freedom. On the other hand, they rejected the principle of separation of powers, according to Montesquieu.[68] The monarch was still understood as head of state (*Oberhaupt des Staates*), to whom all power belonged.[69]

---

64 A. Haratsch, *Die Geschichte der Menschenrechte*, Potsdam 2010, p. 46.

65 Ibidem, p. 50.

66 R.-J. Grahe, op. cit., p. 95.

67 A. Dziadzio, op. cit., p. 183. More on the first constitutions in the German area: R. Zippelius, *Kleine deutsche Verfassungsgeschichte. Vom frühen Mittelalter bis zur Gegenwart...*, pp. 105–107.

68 A. Dziadzio, op. cit., p. 183.

69 E. Forsthoff, *Deutsche Verfassungsgeschichte der Neuzeit. Ein Abriß...*, p. 108.

The increasingly strong demands for liberalization of the Confederation's member countries met with the reaction of its authorities. Already in 1819, Austrian Chancellor Klemens von Metternich, at a conference in Karlsbad, pushed through preventive censorship of newspapers, a ban on student corporations and supervision of universities.[70] The aforementioned 1820 Final Act of the Viennese Conference also strengthened the royal power.[71] To sum up, the situation in German states before the Spring of Nations (*Vormärz*) should be described as the time of growing unrest. These resulted from changes in the social and economic structure (industrialization, pauperization, strengthening of the bourgeoisie), and the emergence of society and nation as concepts and political subjects. Romantic, liberal, democratic and socialist tendencies also increased. Romantic slogans proclaiming the need for a break-up, a protest whose goal would be to achieve freedom and equality of people were combined with liberal ideas, which were gaining more and more popularity in Germany.[72]

The development of liberal ideas in Germany went hand in hand with the development of market economy.[73] There was also an increasing conflict between liberal bourgeoisie, seeking to expand its political freedoms, and the conservative nobility.[74] Early German liberalism sought political empowerment of the middle class, which was then gaining importance. In its concepts it also referred to the idea of the so-called *Juste milieu*, i.e. the golden mean between royal rule and the rule of the crowd, fearing the negative effects of demagogy in politics.[75] Speaking of liberal aspirations in Germany, one cannot forget the democratic movement, which formed the most radical wing of liberalism. Representatives of this faction postulated, in addition to the abolition of the monarchy, political equality and the introduction of representative power from elections.[76] We should also bear in mind the beginnings of the socialist and workers' movement in Germany.[77] Potato blight, which affected large areas of the German Confederation in the mid-1840s, caused famine and general impoverishment. Rising unemployment

70 More about the so-called Carlsbad Decrees (*Karlsbader Beschlüsse*): M. Görtemaker, *Deutschland im 19. Jahrhundert Entwicklungslinien*, Bonn 1989, pp. 84–88.

71 Z. Zieliński, op. cit., p. 130.

72 E. Forsthoff, *Deutsche Verfassungsgeschichte der Neuzeit. Ein Abriß*..., p. 117. T. Nipperdey, op. cit., p. 286. T. Paluszyński, op. cit., p. 193.

73 More on this topic: M. Stolleis, op. cit., pp. 156–159.

74 T. Paluszyński, op. cit., p. 193.

75 W. Czapliński, A. Galos, W. Korta, op. cit., p. 460.

76 T. Paluszyński, op. cit., p. 195.

77 Z. Zieliński, op. cit., p. 132.

and strikes of the emerging working class began to appear in cities. The class conflict between the urban elite, getting ever richer and holding the means of production, and the emerging proletariat was growing. Thus, in the cities and industrial districts there emerged not only the groups demanding political freedoms, but above all those raising social claims. This created a fertile ground for the emerging principles of socialist and communist doctrine.[78] Conservatism, dating back to the 18th century, also played a significant role. Representatives of the conservative trend, such as August Wilhelm Rehberg and Karl Ludwig von Haller, opposed rationalism and contractualism, opposing them with their idea of the historical origin of the state. Conservatism referred to the system of estates of the realm, referring to the rule of aristocracy and the patrimonial power of the monarch in the state.[79]

Speaking of the political picture of the German area of the first half of the 19th century, one cannot ignore the question of the unification of Germany, which was perceived differently by the respective ideological currents. German liberals postulated so-called bottom-up union, stemming from the social movement, which was also to involve systemic reforms. Whereas the so-called top-down union found support among Prussian or Austrian monarchs and, contrary to the first concept, proclaimed the preservation of the current constitutional principles.[80]

The Spring of Nations, initiated by the 1848 French Revolution in Paris, was in fact the opposition of the population (primarily the bourgeoisie), expressed in relation to the ruling European monarchs. The main postulate raised by the revolting societies was, therefore, the restoration or introduction of liberty and freedoms in a liberal spirit, which were abolished as a result of the restoration process. In addition, the richer middle class sought political empowerment,

78 T. Paluszyński, op. cit., pp. 195–196. On the beginnings of social democracy, communism and the workers' movement in Germany: M. Görtemaker, op. cit., pp. 189–206. More on the social democratic movement in Germany: A. Czubiński, *Węzłowe problemy rozwoju socjaldemokracji niemieckiej (1847–1993)*, Poznań 1994.

79 W. Czapliński, A. Galos, W. Korta, op. cit., p. 452. More on contemporary conservatism: T. Nipperdey, op. cit., pp. 313–319.

80 More about the then national movement in Germany: Ibid, pp. 300–313. Ernst-Wolfgang Böckenförde rightly points out that in Germany the approach to the issue of the nation was different from the French one. In Germany, the nation was an ethnic and cultural concept, nationality meant belonging to the so-called "German circle." In France, nationality was more of a political concept, meaning life in a specific state and political order. More: E-W. Böckenförde, *Die Einheit von nationaler und konstitutioneller politischer Bewegung im deutschen Frühliberalismus*, [in:] *Moderne deutsche Verfassungsgeschcichte (1815–1918)*, E-W. Böckenförde (ed.), Köln 1972, p. 27.

demanding access to positions in the state hitherto occupied by landed gentry and aristocracy.[81]

In the German Confederation, the first rebellion broke out in Baden, which was closest to France.[82] In mid-February 1848 the society of this state, influenced by the events in France, opposed the ruling. In the result of mass protests, the Baden regime was liberalized. Representatives of libertarian circles were allowed to rule, and freedom of press, speech or assembly were all introduced. The surprised German monarchs, now facing the threat of revolution, decided to make further concessions to the protesters to remain in power.[83] The end of the first stage of the revolution was marked by the gathering of leading German liberals, held in Heidelberg on 5 March 1848. There it was decided to convene the National Assembly in Frankfurt am Main.[84]

Assembled for the first time on 18 June 1848 in Frankfurt am Main, the all-German parliament was divided into three main parties.[85] The first was formed by conservatives, who wanted to preserve the current system of absolute monarchy. The strongest, in numerical terms, was the liberal party, postulating the widening of civil freedoms, liberalization of state systems and the introduction of constitutional monarchies. However the democrats, forming the most radical wing of the liberals, postulated the abolition of monarchy, referring to socialist slogans.[86] It must be stated that the Frankfurt Parliament did not live up to the expectations. It was an extremely slow decision-making body, a place for prolonged, and turbulent discussions. Its deliberations, which were frequently chaotic, and failing to meet their objectives, made it being perceived negatively throughout Europe.[87]

The main effect of the work of the Frankfurt Parliament was the adoption of the all-German constitution on 28 March 1849.[88] This act transformed

81 A. Dziadzio, op. cit., p. 183.

82 More about the course of the Spring of Nations in the German area: M. Wawrykowa, *Dzieje Niemiec 1789–1871*, Warsaw 1980, pp. 285–399.

83 T. Paluszyński, op. cit., p. 196.

84 Z. Zieliński, op. cit., p. 143.

85 More on the election to the Frankfurt Parliament: T. S. Hamerow, *Die Wahlen zum Frankfurter Parlament*, [in:] *Moderne deutsche Verfassungsgeschcichte (1815–1918)*, E-W. Böckenförde (ed.), Köln 1972, p. 215.

86 Z. Zieliński, op. cit., p. 143.

87 T. Paluszyński, op. cit., p. 201.

88 More about this constitution: J. Wąsicki, *Związek Niemiecki i Druga Rzesza Niemiecka 1848–1914*, Poznań 1989, pp. 196–207.

Germany into an empire with a bicameral parliament. In addition, the constitution spoke of the abolition of estate privileges, the introduction of freedom of speech, conscience, associations, and the accountability of the government to parliament.[89] It can be assumed that, by providing a broad catalogue of civil rights, it corresponded to the three most important slogans of the German revolution of 1848–49, i.e. freedom, equality and unity.[90] The German Emperor was the head the state, exercising executive power through the ministers he freely appointed and dismissed. The institution of ministerial countersignature was introduced for each legal act issued by the emperor. The emperor also had the right of legislative initiative to the bicameral parliament. The *Reichstag* consisted of the House of States (*Staatenhaus*), and the House of Commons (*Volkshaus*). Deputies were elected to the House of Commons in general and direct elections, and the House of States included the representatives of German states. The judiciary was separated from the administration and belonged to independent courts, the proceedings were open and oral, patrimonial courts were abolished. It must be stated, therefore, that the adopted constitution was to make unified Germany a state meeting the principles of constitutional monarchy and the idea of *Rechtsstaat*.[91]

The superior constitutional act entrusted the imperial crown to King of Prussia, Friedrich Wilhelm IV, who, however, not wanting to agree to renounce the freedoms of the absolute monarch, rejected this proposal.[92] As a result of the aforesaid, the revolution in Germany began to weaken. Both Prussia and Austria recalled their representatives from the Frankfurt Parliament, and revolutionary fighting began in individual German states, but it was quickly suppressed. The Spring of Nations in Germany came to an end, without bringing the expected results. The years following the outbreak of the Franco-Prussian war and the reunification of Germany by Otto von Bismarck were marked by the rivalry between Austria and Prussia for leadership in the process of unifying the German area.[93] It was a time when the Habsburg multinational monarchy was increasingly moving away from German affairs, and Prussia was becoming the leader of the unification process in Germany. In 1850 Friedrich Wilhelm IV granted it a constitution,

89 T. Paluszyński, op. cit., p. 201, Z. Zieliński, op. cit., p. 147.

90 A. Dziadzio, op. cit., pp. 183–184. More about the so-called “fundamental rights” in the Frankfurt Constitution: F. Ebel, G. Thielmann, *Rechtsgeschichte. Von der Römischen Antike bis zur Neuzeit*, Heidelberg 2003, p. 340.

91 A. Dziadzio, op. cit., pp. 183–184, 186.

92 T. Paluszyński, op. cit., p. 202.

93 More: Ibid., pp. 202, 207–222.

introducing democratic and liberal freedoms, which were to make Prussia more attractive among the societies of other German states.[94] Another consequence of the conflict between Prussia and Austria was the war that broke out between them in 1866.[95] Prussia's brilliant victory in this conflict was further confirmed by the peace concluded in Prague on 23 August 1866. Victorious Prussia was able to organize the northern and central parts of the German area under its dictate. To this end, they established the North German Confederation with its bicameral parliament and the chancellor, Otto von Bismarck. It was not long after that victorious Prussia imposed alliance treaties on Baden, Württemberg and Bavaria, that is, the remaining significant forces in southern Germany, which were Berlin's starting point for further integration of the country. The process of unification of Germany, as well as the decline of Robert von Mohl's life ended when Prussia won the war with France and proclaimed, on 18 January 1871 in Versailles, Wilhelm I as the hereditary emperor of the already united Germany.[96] The so-called "Wilhelmine Period" began.[97]

The historical context presented above is important from the point of view of the development of life, but also the thought of Robert von Mohl. In each era, its specific events and trends are reflected in the life and views of people living in it. Also von Mohl lived in a certain political, social and economic reality. What's more, he was not only a passive observer, but also a participant in dynamic political processes in Germany at that time. The nineteenth century was a century of developing new ideas, looking for the right way to organize the state in the face of the collapse of old relations, which materialized under the walls of the Bastille. Also von Mohl's achievements can be described as an attempt at finding new ways of understanding the state, society or the political position of the individual. In the light of the aforesaid, the broader historical context had to be introduced in the above subsection.

---

94 More: Ibid., pp. 209–210. More about the constitutional process in Prussia after 1850: F. Hartung, *Deutsche Verfassungsgeschichte vom. 15. Jahrhundert bis zur Gegenwart*, Stuttgart 1950, p. 257. H. Schulze, *Preußen als konstituionelle Monarchie 1850–1867*, [in:] *Handbuch der Preussischen Geschichte*, O. Büsch (ed.), Berlin, New York 1992, pp. 303–351.

95 More about this conflict: W. Czapliński, A. Galos, W. Korta, op. cit., pp. 510–516.

96 More about the Franco-Prussian war: Z. Zieliński, op. cit., pp. 159–162.

97 More about the Wilhelmine period: J. Wąsicki, op. cit., pp. 455–561. On the system of the Second Reich in the Wilhelmine period: J. Kostrubiec, *Nauka o państwie w myśli Georga Jellinka*, Lublin 2015, pp. 20–23.

1.2. The state in the views of selected German thinkers of the mid-nineteenth century

1.2.1. Karl Ludwig von Haller

Karl Ludwig von Haller was born Swiss, but because of the influence he had on it he was taken over by German science.[98] By its representatives, he is described as the leader of the restoration concept and a leading conservative in favour of bringing back the pre-revolutionary order.[99] Haller's conservatism affirmed feudalism, traditional forms of power, and represented the interests of landowners. It was a response to liberal ideas born in the result of the French Revolution. The conservative Haller therefore opposed the French Revolution, its ideas and consequences.[100] He emphasized that these in fact paved the road to rule of tyranny in France. This was to happen as a result of the conversion of former freedoms based on laws and customs, into a general freedom described by Haller as "meaningless philosophical theory"[101] which deprives everyone "from a beggar to a prince" of their rights.[102] By rejecting, what not only enlightenment, but also

98 Karl Ludwig von Haller (1768–1854). Swiss politician, lawyer and scholar. Professor at the Bern Academy. Converted from Protestantism to Catholicism. More on the life of K. L. v. Haller: E. Blöch, *Haller, Karl Ludwig von*, [in:] *Allgemeine Deutsche Biographie*, Bd. 10, Leipzig 1879, pp. 431–436, F. E. Reinhard, *Karl Ludwig von Haller. Ein Lebensbild aus der Zeit der Restauration*, Bachem 1915, K. v. Beyme, *Geschichte der politischen Theorien in Deutschland 1300–2000*, Wiesbaden 2009, p. 249. Haller's most important works include: K. L. v. Haller, *Handbuch der allgemeinen Staaten-Kunde*, Winterthur 1808, Idem, *Politische Religion oder biblische Lehre über die Staaten*, Winterthur 1811, Idem, *Restauration der Staatswissenschaften oder Theorie des natürlich-geselligen zustands, der Chimäre des künstlich-bürgerlichen entgegengesetzt*, Winterthur 1816, Idem, *Satan und die Revolution*, Luzern 1834.

99 M. Stolleis, op. cit., p. 144. More on restoration doctrine in the thought of Karl Ludwig von Haller: H. R. Liedke, *The German Romanticists and Karl Ludwig von Haller's Doctrines of European Restoration*, "The Journal of English and Germanic Philology," Vol. 57, No. 3 (Jul., 1958), pp. 371–393.

100 D. Avraham, *The Social and Religious Meaning of Nationalism: The Case of Prussian Conservatism 1815–1871*, "European History Quarterly," Vol. 38 (4), p. 527.

101 Cited in: K. v. Klemperer, *Germany's New Conservatism Its History and Dilemma in the Twentieth Century*, Princeton New Jersey 1968, pp. 25–26.

102 C. L. v. Haller, *Restauration der Staatswissenschaften oder Theorie des natürlich-geselligen Zustands, der Chimäre des künstlich-bürgerlichen entgegengesetzt*, 1 Bd., Winterthur 1820, p. XII.

Baroque and Renaissance brought in the philosophy of state, Haller drew primarily on medieval models, praising feudal relations.[103]

The most important work of this thinker is the *Restauration der Staats-Wissenschaft*.[104] The importance of this publication for the entire post-Napoleonic restoration movement is evidenced by the fact that the phrase "restoration" was adopted from its title.[105] One of the central claims of this work is the rejection of the concept of a social contract as a way for forming the state. According to Haller, the overthrow of the idea of contractualism was to restore the natural order in line with God's plan. So he rejected the concept of Jean Jacques Rousseau as well as theories concerning the existence of society as a political subject in the state.[106]

Haller opposed the claims that gave the human individual the ability to create political order and granted people full sovereignty. For him, the basis of human coexistence was the imperious relation. Due to the fact that people are not naturally given the same abilities by God, most of them must seek help and protection from more developed individuals.[107] According to Haller, relations of power are created in which the weak recognize their dependence on the stronger.[108]

In Haller's thought, the state and the political community emerged in a slow process of approaching each other and subjugation of the weaker by the stronger.[109] Therefore, the state as an institution should be based on the so-called "authority of the strong one" (*Herrschaft des Starken*), and not on the result of a social contract, which Haller considered to be an artificial concept, which was not based in reality.[110] The state, defined by Haller as the highest degree of natural,

---

103 *Doktryny polityczne XIX i XX wieku*, K. Chojnicka, W. Kozub-Ciembroniewicz (eds.), Kraków 2000, p. 142.

104 *Restauration der Staatswissenschaft*. More about Haller's main work: R. Roggen, *<Restauration> - Kampfruf und Schimpfwort Eine Kommunikationsanalyse zum Hauptwerk des Staatstheoretikers Karl Ludwig von Haller (1768–1854)*, Freiburg 1999, p. 18.

105 K. v. Beyme, *Geschichte der politischen Theorien in Deutschland 1300–2000*. . ., p. 249.

106 M. Stolleis, op. cit., pp. 144–145.

107 *Doktryny polityczne XIX i XX wieku*. . ., p. 140. A. Papuziński, *Filozoficzne dziedzictwo oświecenia a zrównoważony rozwój*, "Zeszyty naukowe Politechniki Śląskiej," seria: Organizacja i Zarządzanie z. 112, (2017), p. 311.

108 C. L. v. Haller, *Restauration der Staatswissenschaften oder Theorie des natürlich-geselligen Zustands, der Chimäre des künstlich-bürgerlichen entgegengesetzt*, Bd. 1. . ., pp. 355–356.

109 *Doktryny polityczne XIX i XX wieku*. . ., p. 141.

110 M. Stolleis, op. cit., p. 145.

private social and servant relations, could take two forms of system: monarchical or republican.[111] Haller derived the admissibility of a republican form from historical experience. It was supposed to show that a union of strong individuals on a corporate basis (resembling a company) would be possible, established in order to gain independence from other associations.[112]

Haller perceived the state based on the principle of monarchical power through the prism of private law relations, which were distinguished only by the presence of higher power and the monarch's freedom.[113] The ruler played the central role in such a state, and according to Haller it was an individual independent from anyone, whose independence resulted from the power and wealth that individual held. By the grace of God, the monarch received undivided power in a state which he should treat as so-called patrimonial property (*Patrimonialeige ntum*).[114] For Haller, the monarch is the owner of the state, who can rule it at his own discretion, without asking subjects for their consent or opinion. His actions should not be assessed in terms of their legality because he acts primarily in his own interest. However, he should respect the principle of justice in his actions.[115]

Haller also rejected the modern representation-based system, stating that state assemblies had only an auxiliary (advisory) function.[116] He was also alien to the dualistic concept of constitutional monarchy. The monarch had the right to demand service from others, but he did not serve anyone himself (so Haller also rejected the concept of the monarch as the first servant of the state, appearing primarily in the late Lutheran absolutism). It is also worth emphasizing that for Haller there was no concept of state objectives. The scholar was of the opinion that there was no such thing as community goals pursued by the state. What's

---

111 C. L. v. Haller, *Restauration der Staatswissenschaften oder Theorie des natürlich-geselligen Zustands, der Chimäre des künstlich-bürgerlichen entgegengesetzt,* Bd. 1…, p. 463.

112 Ibid., p. 474, *Doktryny polityczne XIX i XX wieku…*, p. 141.

113 K. v. Beyme, *Geschichte der politischen Theorien in Deutschland 1300–2000…*, p. 251.

114 C. L. v. Haller, *Restauration der Staatswissenschaften oder Theorie des natürlich-geselligen Zustands, der Chimäre des künstlich-bürgerlichen entgegengesetzt,* Bd. 1…, p. 473. M. Stolleis, op. cit., p. 145.

115 A. Benz, *Der moderne Staat: Grundlagen der politologischen Analyse*, München 2008, p. 46. *Doktryny polityczne XIX i XX wieku…*, p. 141.

116 M. Stolleis, op. cit., p. 145. C. L. v. Haller, *Restauration der Staatswissenschaften oder Theorie des natürlich-geselligen Zustands, der Chimäre des künstlich-bürgerlichen entgegengesetzt,* Bd. 2, Winterthur 1820, p. 338.

more, referring to the existence of such goals was dangerous for Haller, as it was to be an introduction and an excuse to seize power over citizens' property.[117]

It would be wrong, however, to admit that Haller considered the monarch's authority to be unlimited. So he did not take the view that the ruler only has rights and subjects have duties alone. In fact, he distinguished only a handful off duties of the subjects, including the obligation to pay taxes and serve in the military.[118] Referring to the relation between the ruler and the subject, it should be noted that Haller reserved his subjects the possibility of resisting, if the ruler violated their rights. The subject therefore had not only the right to move out of the state, but also the right to object, which Haller compared to defending private property against an external attack.[119] Haller should be considered a conservative thinker, who was ideologically embedded in the era of absolutism, as evidenced by his failure to address the issue of *Rechtsstaat*.

1.2.2. Friedrich Julius Stahl

Friedrich Julius Stahl is another thinker, politician and conservative scholar, whose thought is well worth presenting.[120] He was one of the most important Prussian state theorists and conservative politicians of the mid-nineteenth century. Wilhelm Füßl characterized Stahl's views as the opposite of the ideas brought out by the liberal thinkers of the time, such as von Mohl or Karl von Rotteck.[121]

---

117 Idem, *Restauration der Staatswissenschaften oder Theorie des natürlich-geselligen Zustands, der Chimäre des künstlich-bürgerlichen entgegengesetzt,* Bd. 1. . ., pp. 470, 473–474.

118 K. v. Beyme, *Geschichte der politischen Theorien in Deutschland 1300–2000*. . ., p. 250.

119 C. L. v. Haller, *Restauration der Staatswissenschaften oder Theorie des natürlich-geselligen Zustands, der Chimäre des künstlich-bürgerlichen entgegengesetzt,* Bd. 1. . ., p. 414.

120 Friedrich Julius Stahl (1802–1861), was born into a Jewish family in Würzburg. At the age of 17 he converted to Protestantism. He studied law at the Universities of Heidelberg and Erlangen. Professor of law at the University of Berlin. His most important works are: F.J. Stahl, *Die Philosophie des Rechts nach geschichtlicher Ansicht*, Heidelberg 1833, Idem, *Das Monarchische Prinzip, eine staatsrechtlich-politische Abhandlung*, Berlin 1845, Idem, *Die Revolution und die konstitutionelle Monarchie*, Berlin 1848.

121 D. Avraham, op. cit., p. 531. W. Füßl, *Professor in der Politik: Friedrich Julius Stahl (1802–1861)*, Göttingen 1988, p. 10.

A Jew by birth and a Christian (Protestant) by choice, he saw all power in human history derived from God's action. In Stahl's state doctrine, God, defined as both a personal and transcendent being, appeared as the highest reference point and the most important causative agent.[122] Relying on Christian ideology and God as the absolute of human existence led Stahl to reject all state-related ideas based on rationalism and the natural law. It concerns primarily the thinker's objection to the idea of the emergence of the state under a social contract.[123] Therefore, since the state was established by God, its headship was reflecting his essence and power. Its destiny is to follow God's instructions and plans.[124] Stahl distinguished the concept of so-called Kingship of God (*Gottesreich*) as a perfect state and the Moral Kingdom (*sittliche Reich*) as its temporal and imperfect dimension, which finds expression in law and political institutions.[125] The Moral Kingdom, which is a kind of Earthly equivalent of Kingship of God, should serve human purposes. The concept of the Moral Kingdom is an idea, which Stahl himself called superior to understanding his state doctrine. For Stahl, the Moral Kingdom was an indivisible principle based on ethical and intellectual motives that united people in a spiritual way.[126]

According to Stahl the most important characteristic of state is its morality, and the fact that it has to follow the broadly understood good. The state, perceived by Stahl as God's servant, was most of all the "close union of a large number of individuals subjected to supreme and sovereign power."[127] The divine destiny of the state was to manage and regulate all conditions and goals common to its inhabitants. According to Stahl, the state is the deepest embodiment of the human community, a unity constituting in itself all areas of human existence.[128]

The goal of the state based on religious and moral ideas was to formulate norms for the protection of the individual, personal freedom of citizens,

---

122 F. J. Stahl, *Die Philosophie des Rechts*, Bd. 2, *Rechts- und Staatslehre auf der Grundlage christlicher Weltanschauung*, Heidelberg 1854, p. 7.

123 W. Füßl, *Friedrich Julius Stahl (1802–1861)*, [in:] *Politische Theorien des 19. Jahhunderts Konservatismus, Liberalismus, Sozialismus*, B. Heidenreich (ed.), Berlin 2002, p. 184.

124 D. Avraham, op. cit., p. 531.

125 F. J. Stahl, *Die Philosophie des Rechts*, Bd. 2, *Rechts- und Staatslehre auf der Grundlage christlicher Weltanschauung*, Heidelberg 1845, p. 48.

126 F.J. Stahl, *The Philosophy of Law, The Doctrine of Law and State on the basis of the Christian world-view*, Book IV: *The doctrine of State and the Principles of State Law*, translated by Ruben Alvarado, Wordbridge Publishing 2009, p. 1.

127 Ibidem, p. 10.

128 Ibid., D. Avraham, op. cit., p. 532.

protection of property or family. The state cannot act arbitrarily.[129] That is why Stahl was in favor of the rule of law. It should be emphasized that the adoption of the *Rechtsstaat* idea by Stahl has hitherto been unheard of among the German conservatives. What's more, the concept of the rule of law in his view contained a clear demarcation with the concept of an absolutist police state. Therefore, one can say that the statement that Stahl is, next to von Mohl and Karl Theodor Welcker, one of the creators of the modern German idea of *Rechtsstaat*[130] is correct. According to Stahl, the state was established by God so that God's intended goals could be achieved. The law is implemented only and solely through the state. Both the law and the state are to shape the human race to live in an ethical world.[131]

Referring to the definition of the rule of law, Stahl formulated the following view:

> "The state should be a legal state, this is the slogan and a real motor for the development of our time. It should precisely define and firmly protect the paths and boundaries of its activity and the sphere of freedom of its citizens by law, and should not impose state methods directly, thus imposing moral ideas more than it belongs to the legal sphere, i.e. only for the necessary limitation. This is the concept of the rule of law, not in the sense that the state simply has a legal order without administrative tasks, or that it only protects the rights of individuals - it does not cover the purpose and content of the state at all, but only the manner and nature, in which they are to be implemented."[132]

We can conclude, from the above definition, that Stahl's concept corresponds to the later direction of legal positivism.[133]

Referring briefly to the issues of power in the works by Friedrich Julius Stahl, it should be pointed out that conservatism, in the period before the Spring of Nations in Germany, can be depicted by one slogan: monarchical principle (*das monarchische Prinzip*).[134] It is also the title of the 1845 work by Stahl. In the Prussian scholar's model of power, the monarch was the real head of state. Stahl

129 W. Füßl, *Friedrich Julius Stahl (1802–1861)...*, p. 185.

130 D. Grosser, *Grundlagen und Struktur der Staatslehre Friedrich Julius Stahls (Staat und Politik 3)*, Köln, Opladen 1963, p. 83.

131 F. J. Stahl, *The Philosophy of Law, The Doctrine of Law and State on the basis of the Christian world-view*, Book II: *Principles of Law*, translated by Ruben Alvarado, Wordbridge Publishing 2007, p. 24.

132 Quotation after: M. Zmierczak, op. cit., p. 44.

133 Z. A. Maciąg, *op. cit.*, p. 117.

134 W. Pöggeler, *Die deutsche Wissenschaft vom englischen Staatsrecht. Ein Beitrag zur Rezeptions- und Wissenschaftsgeschichte 1748–1914*, Berlin 1995, p. 68.

opposed the implementation of the system that already operated, e.g. in England, at that time, stating that the western political institutions, such as the sovereignty of the people, separation of powers or republic within the monarchic form were all alien to Germans.[135] In Stahl's model of power, the monarch was the actual head of the executive. A state-run parliament had only an advisory vote and the unique right to approve individual king's decisions. In order to secure the dominant position of the ruler, the entire administration, preparation of laws, and the right to appoint own government should be subject to him.[136]

Speaking of another important problem at the time, namely parliamentary representation, Stahl took a moderate position. He opposed both the demands of liberals, who saw parliament as the representation of all citizens of the state, and ultra-conservatives, who wanted to shape parliament according to feudal patterns.[137] Estates of the realm, in the understanding of Stahl, should therefore sit in parliament together and represent the common interest. Like many other conservatives and liberals, Stahl was in favor of a bicameral system, where both chambers should be organized by the principle of estate system. The so called *Standequalität* (the capacity to form part of the representative authority) was attributed, by Stahl, to only a minor portion of the nation. It was not vested in both proletarians, and capitalists without landed property. In conclusion, it should be noted that Stahl was guided by the rejection of the doctrine of sovereignty of the people, which, according to him, led to the rule of parliamentary majority. He believed that the government should be accountable only to the monarch. A bicameral parliament should be organized on basis of the estate system, but represent the common interest of the entire nation.[138]

With his doctrine, Stahl built the foundation for the constitutionalism in Prussia, which appeared relatively late there. His monarchical constitutionalism proved acceptable to conservatives.[139] According to Hans Boldt, Stahl enabled the demands of conservatives and liberals to be reconciled. This compromise consisted, on the one hand, in recognizing the system for representing the whole of the national interest (although maintaining a specific estate organization), and, on the other, strengthening the monarch's position.[140]

---

135 F. J. Stahl, *Das Monarchische Prinzip…*, pp. IV, 2, 44.

136 W. Füßl, *Friedrich Julius Stahl (1802–1861)…*, p. 187. D. Avraham, op. cit., p. 532.

137 W. Füßl, *Friedrich Julius Stahl (1802–1861)…*, p. 185.

138 K. v. Beyme, *Geschichte der politischen Theorien in Deutschland 1300–2000…*, p. 370–371.

139 M. Racky, *Die Diskussion über Gewaltenteilung und Gewaltentrennung im Vormärz*, Frankfurt am Main 2005, p. 41.

140 H. Boldt, *Deutsche Staatslehre im Vormärz*, Düsseldorf 1975, p. 196.

1.2.3. Adam Müller

For the purpose of the 19th century ideological landscape of Germany it is well worth to present the views of another thinker, representing the romantic philosophy of the state, namely Adam Müller.[141] The basic premise of this scholar's idea was the so-called theory of opposites (*Gegensatzlehre*). Müller based it on the theory of dichotomous opposites, from which unity was to arise. Therefore, he emphasized the differences in the state, e.g. between middle class and nobility, or secular and church institutions. According to Müller, the constantly uniting opposing positions of various subjects in the state and society were to generate a new unity of the late absolutism state.[142]

The Müller state gains a metaphysical dimension. The thinker defined the task of determining the scope of this concept as extremely difficult.[143] So even if a concept of state is created, it will quickly become outdated due to the fact that its subject, i.e. the state, is constantly evolving. Despite the difficulties in defining the concept of state, Müller is convinced that it is necessary for man.[144] Thus, the thinker compares the state to such essential things in life as a home. Organized institutions personified by the state are to help man carry, as Müller poetically states "all heavy loads that he must take on his journey of a lifetime."[145]

The scholar denied the claim that there was a time in the history of mankind in which there was no state, and its creation was the result of human will and wisdom. In Müller's views, we also find a rejection of the idea of a social contract, which in his opinion did not correspond to historical realities.[146] The state as a guarantor of order appeared already, when one man first made contact

---

141 Adam Heinrich Müller, (1779–1829), a philosopher, publicist and German politician, from a clerical Berlin family. Raised in evangelical faith, he later converted to Catholicism. He was an official in Tyrol and the Austrian ambassador in Leipzig. More on life of Adam Müller: P. P. Müller-Schmid, *Adam Müller (1779–1829)*, [in:] *Politische Theorien des 19. Jahhunderts Konservatismus, Liberalismus, Sozialismus…*, pp. 110–117. More on the phenomenon of political romanticism in Germany: A. Citkowska-Kimla, *Romantyzm polityczny w Niemczech. Reprezentanci, idee, model*, Kraków 2010, pp. 18–19.

142 *Doktryny polityczne XIX i XX wieku…*, p. 137.

143 A.H. Müller, *Die Elemente der Staatskunst…*, p. 20.

144 Ibidem, p. 29. A. Citkowska-Kimla, op. cit., p. 198.

145 A.H. Müller, *Die Elemente der Staatskunst…*, p. 30.

146 Ibidem, pp. 38, 147. K. v. Beyme, *Geschichte der politischen Theorien in Deutschland 1300–2000…*, p. 265.

with another, and then also the law appeared.[147] Referring to the role of the state, Müller stated:

> "The state is not only a manufacture, farm, insurance institution or mercantile company, it is a deep combination of all physical and spiritual needs, all physical and spiritual wealth, all internal and external life of the nation, into one great, energetic, turbulent and lively whole."[148]

Therefore, the state is something total: "(...) it is the totality of all human affairs and their union into one living whole."[149] However, as Peter Paul Müller-Schmid states, the state, as understood by Müller as this totality should be understood as the opposite of the absolute state, which through the despotism of the monarch, bureaucracy and unlimited power was not a total state in the sense of Romantic thought. In the sense of German Romanticism, totality does not mean subordinating all spheres of life to one area. Instead, it is expressed in the conviction that there is an organic unity of life that arose from its internal freedom but also its contradictions.[150]

Initially, Müller clearly advocated a monarchical system, believing that its important feature, in contrast to the republic, was its continuity and stability. Finally, he came to the conclusion that both the monarchical and the republican systems were impossible. A good political system required both republican and monarchical elements. The law should be stable and resistant to changing views in the society (monarchical element), but it should also be possible to conduct disputes between different groups in the state (republican element).[151]

The image of society emerging from the thought of Adam Müller can be called an image of pre-industrial and anti-capitalist one. The scholar praised farming as closest to nature.[152] He believed that the monarchical form was the original form of society. Müller attributed a special role to the nobility and aristocracy.[153] This estate should be privileged, but also have the most extensive duties. It was the nobility who were to be the guardians of tradition, representing the most important features and aspirations of the nation.[154] Müller's proposal,

147 *Doktryny polityczne XIX i XX wieku...*, p. 137.
148 A. H. Müller, *Die Elemente der Staatskunst...*, p. 37.
149 Ibidem, p. 48.
150 P. P. Müller-Schmid, op. cit., p. 125–126.
151 A. H. Müller, *Die Elemente der Staatskunst...*, pp. 175–180.
152 K. v. Beyme, *Geschichte der politischen Theorien in Deutschland 1300–2000...*, p. 266. More on Müller's vision of society: A. Citkowska-Kimla, op. cit., pp. 205–206.
153 A. H. Müller, *Die Elemente der Staatskunst...*, pp. 179, 183.
154 *Doktryny polityczne XIX i XX wieku...*, p. 138.

whose assumption was to alleviate the then strong conflict between the state and society, was to introduce a system based on estate organization, whose goal was to act for integration and unity. Therefore, unity in the state should be achieved through cooperation between the government and the elected representative body of the people. It should be emphasized at this point, that in his concepts Müller continued to support the old aristocracy and gentry, and their privileged position in the representative system.[155]

1.2.4. Karl von Rotteck

When considering the state thought of the liberal Robert von Mohl, one cannot ignore one politician and scholar, widely considered a crucial figure in early German liberalism. We are talking here about Karl von Rotteck, the author of *Staatslexikon* ("State Lexicon"),[156] which was then the main work of German liberals.[157] *Staatslexikon* expressed the most liberal ideas in the German area in the first half of the nineteenth century. This multi-volume publication, expressing above all the aspirations of liberal bourgeoisie from the south of Germany, included within its scope ideas relating to the liberalization of the legal system, respect for civil rights, the introduction of parliamentary representation and finally, the separation of powers.[158]

Referring to the origin of the state, von Rotteck stated that it is foremostly the so called sensual part of human nature that dictates social life.[159] He compared an individual living to a wild animal, unable to deal effectively with adversities of fate. According to him, these reasons prompted people to join in various social relationships. However, in view of the existence of such defects in people as, for example, selfishness or jealousy, the rational part of human nature dictates that community life should be an ordered life, so that it leads to general progress and development. This factor ensuring this order is to be the state and its law, acting

155 P. P. Müller-Schmid, op. cit., p. 127.

156 *Staatslexikon*.

157 Karl von Rotteck (1775–1840), German thinker, scholar and liberal politician. Professor at the University of Freiburg. His most important works include (in addition to the numerous editions of the *Staatslexikon*): C. v. Rotteck, *Allgemeine Geschichte vom Anfang der historischen Kenntniss bis auf unsere Zeiten,* Freiburg 1812–1827, Idem, *Lehrbuch des Vernunftrechts und der Staatswissenschaften*, 4. Bde, Stuttgart 1829–1835. More about von Rotteck's life and concepts: Z. A. Maciąg, op. cit., pp. 76–79.

158 M. Stolleis, op. cit., p. 160.

159 We are talking here about broadly understood, also involuntary human behaviour, which can be determined, for example, by various instincts.

on the basis of a social contract.[160] According to von Rotteck, the rule of law could also arise only in the result of a social contract. Thus, it can be seen that the scholar followed the path paved by Jean Jacques Rousseau.[161]

Trying to define the notion of the state, the scientist concluded that it was a combination of a certain number of human individuals remaining under legal authority, and this authority leads them to achieve common goals within the institution of the state. It is also worth noting that the scholar identified the state with society, calling the former a "society limited by contract,"[162] and an "association of settled people concluded for an indefinite period."[163]

According to von Rotteck, the most important goals of the state were to maintain legal order, ensure security in its territory, and support the general aspirations of people, which are easier to achieve through the use of collective (state) efforts.[164] The liberal thinker was alien to the concepts of the absolutist *Polizeistaat,* but unlike Humboldt, von Rotteck did not represent the understanding of the state as the so-called "night watchman state."[165]

Referring to the constitution of the state, it should be stated that its core in von Rotteck will be the concept of the so-called "collective will" (universal, general, *Gesamtwillen*),[166] expressed by general public. The collective will was to be a force specific to all citizens. It should also be manifested in the life of the state. Liberal von Rotteck argued for a democratic system and, moreover, for universal suffrage. According to him, the community life of people in the state will be effective only if they are allowed to participate in governance. Citizens' participation will therefore prevent the state from violating their rights and indicate it

160 C. v. Rotteck, *Lehrbuch des Vernuftrechts und der Staatswissenschaften*, Bd. 2, Stuttgart 1840, pp. 47–48.

161 K. Rotteck, *Rozprawa o konstytucji*, translated by H. Nowakowski, Lwów 1848, p. 42, after: M. Zmierczak, op. cit., p. 42. H. Brandt, *Karl von Rotteck (1775–1840),* [in:] *Politische Theorien des 19. Jahhunderts Konservatismus, Liberalismus, Sozialismus*. . ., p. 375.

162 C. v. Rotteck, *Lehrbuch des Vernuftrechts und der Staatswissenschaften*, Bd. 2..., pp. 47, 65.

163 Ibidem.

164 Ibidem.

165 K. v. Beyme, *Geschichte der politischen Theorien in Deutschland 1300–2000*. . ., pp. 313–314.

166 At that time also possible translation of the term "Gesammtwille" was "common will." F. Flügel, *A practical dictionary of the English and German languages in two parts*, Part II, Hamburg, 1861, p. 429

what goals it should support.[167] Von Rotteck also connected the idea of the rule of law with the idea of parliamentary representation. He believed that it was the realization of the idea of representation, which formed the precondition for the creation of the rule of law.[168]

Another determinant of the Karl von Rotteck doctrine, testifying to his liberal approach, was the concept of separation of powers. The power in the state should be divided between the mutually interacting: representative body, in form of the parliament; and the government together with the monarch.[169] These decision-making centres should also cooperate in making the most important decisions in the state. The areas of this cooperation were to be primarily legislation, but also political decisions such as declaring war. The government's exclusive competences were to include state administration, understood by von Rotteck as the implementation of legal acts provisions. In this area, the parliament could only have a controlling role, e.g. through the possibility of a "ministerial complaint" (*Ministerialanklage*).[170]

Von Rotteck advocated the direct election of deputies and the unicameral system.[171] It was always the duty of deputies in the parliament to speak and act on behalf of the common good, and to put the interests of the whole above any particular interests. The supreme law and order of representatives in parliament were therefore dictated by the general will of the nation. The goal of achieving universal good should guide not only the representative bodies, but also by the government.[172]

Referring to the role of the government, von Rotteck stated that its task was solely to fulfil the collective will, which is done either through legislation or through administration. Each action to fulfil the goals of the state was to be the fulfilment of collective will. As noted above, the government and monarch were, in von Rotteck's thought, to suppress too radical or erroneous demands of nations' representation. Here, the government and monarch are comparable to a judge, who can oppose parliament's decisions by means of a veto. It should

---

167 H. Boldt, op. cit., p. 157. C. v. Rotteck, *Lehrbuch des Vernuftrechts und der Staatswissenschaften*, Bd. 2. . ., p. 123.

168 K. Rotteck, *Rozprawa o konstytucji*. . .., p. 17, after: M. Zmierczak, op. cit., p. 42.

169 M. Stolleis, op. cit., p. 162.

170 Also "action against ministers," L. Vinx, *The Guardian of the Constitution. Hans Kelsen and Carl Schmitt on the limits of constitutional law*, Cambridge 2015, s. 106. The problem of ministerial responsibility was examined in Chapter V.

171 H. Brandt, *Karl von Rotteck (1775–1840)*. . ., p. 376.

172 C. v. Rotteck, *Lehrbuch des Vernuftrechts und der Staatswissenschaften*, Bd. 2. . ., p. 223.

be noted, therefore, that von Rotteck was an opponent of the perception of the monarch's position in its understanding by Benjamin Constant. The king was not meant to be the neutral authority (*pouvoir neutre*), but instead hold strong power to influence the situation in the state.[173] The monarch's political position resulted from von Rotteck's lack of full confidence in parliamentary bodies. The scientist was aware of the frequent divisions and profound differences in them.[174] In order to fulfil its task properly, the government had to be independent of the influence of representatives sitting in parliament. According to von Rotteck, such independence could also be guaranteed in a hereditary monarchy. Like most German moderate liberals, he argued for a constitutional monarchy, believing that democracy without control would quickly turn into despotism. This also led to the aforementioned rejection, by von Rotteck, of the concept of monarchical power, understood as *pouvoir neutre*.[175]

1.3. Life and work of Robert von Mohl

1.3.1. Family environment, childhood and youth

Robert von Mohl was born on 17 August 1799 in Stuttgart, the capital of the then Duchy of Württemberg. Both from his father's and mother's side, he came from well-respected Württemberg families.[176] His father Benjamin Ferdinand von Mohl (1766–1845)[177] came from a noble family whose roots date back to

173 More: Ibid., pp. 218–226.

174 K. v. Beyme, *Geschichte der politischen Theorien in Deutschland 1300–2000. . .*, p. 313.

175 H. Boldt, op. cit., p. 158.

176 E. Angermann, *Robert von Mohl 1799–1875 Leben und Werk eines altliberalen Staatsgelehrten*, Neuwied 1962, p. 19. On the life of Robert von Mohl: K-P Schroeder, *Vom Sachsenspiegel zum Grundgesetz. Eine deutsche Rechtsgeschichte in Lebensbildern*, München 2001, pp. 115–136. On von Mohl's family and childhood: J. Hähnle, *Die politischen Ideen Robert von Mohls. Ein Beitrag zur Geschichte des älteren süddeutschen Liberalismus*, Tübingen 1921, s. 4, A. Bosiacki, *Wstęp*, [in:] R. v. Mohl, *Encyklopedia Umiejętności Politycznych*, Warszawa 2003, pp. VII- XXXVII, H. Schulze, *Robert von Mohl. Ein Erinnerungsblatt dargebracht zur fünfhundertjährigen Jubelfeier der Ruperto-Carola*, Heidelberg 1886, p. 3.

177 More about the life of Benjamin Ferdinand von Mohl: F. Raberg, *Biographisches Handbuch der württembergischen Landtagsabgeordneten 1815–1933. Im Auftrag der Kommission für geschichtliche Landeskunde in Baden-Württemberg*. Kohlhammer, Stuttgart 2001, p. 574.

the early 17th century.[178] Robert von Mohl's father graduated from the elite *Karlsakademie*, and his professional career was associated with holding various offices in the official apparatus of the Kingdom of Württemberg.[179] Due to his short scientific career in the *Karlsakademie*, von Mohl's father also demonstrated a particularly keen interest in science, and in particular in history and various political disciplines.[180] It was he, who required both Robert and his brothers to publish various scientific publications from an early age. He devoted a lot of time to his children, paying special attention to their education.[181]

In contrast, his mother, Louisa Frederica, in the opinion of von Mohl himself, was a perfect "*Swabian Hausfrau*,"[182] devoted to her domestic duties and children. She took care not only of health and clean dress of her children, but also of their correct mental development. Mother instilled a strong sense of duty and punctuality in Robert and his brothers.[183] The mother's task and merit was also to educate her children from an early age in the ability to think independently and clearly, and to formulate statements. Von Mohl believed that it was thanks to his mother that he, and his brothers, developed the ability to formulate thoughts and conclusions very clearly, aptly and synthetically (for which he was well known in the academic community).[184]

The scholar described the marriage of his parents as good, even if their characters differed. His father was a fairly calm and phlegmatic man, while his

178 R. v. Mohl, *Lebenserinnerungen von Robert von Mohl 1799–1875*, Bd. 1, Stuttgat und Leipzig 1902, pp. 12–13. It should be emphasized that von Mohl was proud of his family connections with great German scholars; Johann Jakob Moser and his son Friedrich Karl (paternal grandmother of von Mohl was the sister of Johann Jakob Moser): Ibid., p. 8. More on family relationships with J. J. Moser: P. M. Ehrle, V. Schäfer (ed.), *Robert von Mohl (1799–1875) Austellung zu seinem 100. Todestag veranstaltet von der Universitätsbilbiothek und dem Universitätsarchiv Tübingen 4.-29. November 1975*, Tübingen 1975, p. 16.

179 Von Mohl's father was also known for literary and scientific activity, more: R. v. Mohl, *Mohl, Benjamin Ferdinand von,* [in:] "Allgemeine Deutsche Biographie 22" (1885), pp. 54–55, [Online-Version]; URL: https://www.deutsche-biographie.de/pnd117090158.html#adbcontent, [access date: 03/01/2018].

180 R. v. Mohl, *Lebenserinnerungen von Robert von Mohl 1799–1875*, Bd. 1…, p. 20. E. Angermann, op. cit., p. 19.

181 R. v. Mohl, *Lebenserinnerungen von Robert von Mohl 1799–1875*, Bd. 1…, pp., 21, 68, 77.

182 *Schwabische Hausfrau*

183 Ibidem, p. 27.

184 Ibid., p. 69, H. Schulze, op. cit., p. 5.

mother was an energetic and vivid person, which often led to quarrels between them.[185] They had a total of eight children, of which, unfortunately, only four sons reached adulthood.[186] Similarly to Robert, also the second oldest brother, Julius, born on 25 October 1800 devoted himself to scientific career. He was a famous orientalist and a member of the *College de France*, permanently residing in Paris. Another brother, Moritz, who was born on 9 February 1802, was an officer in charge of Customs Union affairs and a member of the Frankfurt Parliament. The last of four siblings was named Hugo and was born on 8 April 1805. He graduated in medicine, but he gained real scientific fame in the field of botany.[187]

Like his brothers, Robert von Mohl graduated from the twelve-year high school in Stuttgart, where he belonged to the best students.[188] He took particular interest in history, geography and modern languages.[189] Already in his youth, von Mohl's great reading passion and the passion for studying modern history were revealed.[190]

In 1817 von Mohl began his studies at the University of Tübingen. Despite the fact that he did not show much inclination to study law, he had to follow the choice made by his father, who for a long time wanted his eldest son to become a lawyer. Due to the low level of lectures at the Faculty of Legal Sciences of the University of Tübingen, he devoted a lot of time to library visits, where he tried to educate on his own.[191] His interest was focused on books devoted to history and the state, political matters.[192] After two years of study in Tübingen, in the spring of 1819 von Mohl moved to the University of Heidelberg to complete his studies there.[193] It was in Heidelberg that von Mohl met such outstanding scholars as

185 R. v. Mohl, *Lebenserinnerungen von Robert von Mohl 1799–1875*, Bd. 1. . ., p. 28. E. Angermann, op. cit., p. 21.

186 Two sisters and a brother passed away in their early childhood, while the last, youngest of the siblings Eduard, being less than 25 years old, committed suicide at Robert's house by shooting himself in the head with a pistol. R. v. Mohl, *Lebenserinnerungen von Robert von Mohl 1799–1875*, Bd. 1. . ., p. 29.

187 Ibid, pp. 31, 33–37. 39, 47.

188 This institution placed great emphasis on teaching Latin while giving up Greek altogether. Ibidem, pp. 73,75. E. Angermann, op. cit., p. 21.

189 J. Hähnle, op. cit., p. 5.

190 H. Schulze, op. cit., p. 11.

191 Ibid., pp. 85, 94. More: H. Schulze, op. cit. p. 12.

192 R. v. Mohl, *Lebenserinnerungen von Robert von Mohl 1799–1875*, Bd. 1. . ., p. 95.

193 Ibidem, p. 104. More about his stay in Heidelberg: E. Angermann, op. cit., p. 23.

Justus Thibaut and Karl Salomo Zachariae.[194] He returned home in the spring of 1821 meeting with his father's growing pressure to prepare a doctoral dissertation.[195] Thanks to Benjamin's efforts, his promotion took place in August 1821. The title of his dissertation in Latin was *Discrimen ordinum provincialium et constitutionis repraesentativae*,[196] and von Mohl was awarded doctorate in legal sciences.[197]

The period of youth and education was completed by a series of travels. According to the parents' assumption, after completing their studies, each of the sons received a certain amount of money to go on journeys, which were to ensure the completion and fulfilment of their education.[198] In the period from mid-September 1821 until April 1824, von Mohl travelled, among others, to Munich, Frankfurt or Göttingen, and then to Leipzig, Prague, Berlin and Paris.[199] His stays in Frankfurt, Göttingen and Paris were particularly important. In Frankfurt, he gained detailed knowledge of the law of the German Confederation. In addition to studying German law, he also focused on preparing publications on its justice system.[200] In 1822 he published the book *Public administration of justice of the German Confederation. The Journalistic approach*, dealing with the scope of jurisdiction of the union judiciary in the German Confederation, and allowed his father's wishes to be satisfied, enabling the young von Mohl to go to Göttingen.[201] In Göttingen, von Mohl focused on collecting library materials, as

194 Ibidem. Von Mohl considered Thibaut as "the ideal of a scholar." More about Thibaut and other professors from Heidelberg: R. v. Mohl, *Lebenserinnerungen von Robert von Mohl 1799–1875*, Bd. 1..., pp. 106–112.

195 Ibidem, p. 117.

196 Idem, *Dissertatio inauguralis sistens discrimen ordinum provincialium et constitutionis repraesentativae,* Tubingae 1821. More about the dissertation: Idem, *Lebenserinnerungen von Robert von Mohl 1799–1875*, Bd. 1. . ., p. 269.

197 Ibidem, p. 118. Ernst Meier stated that despite the fact that the thesis was written in bad Latin, it can be considered valuable in terms of its content. In the dissertation, von Mohl analyzed contemporary modern constitutionalism in relation to the state system prevailing in the Middle Ages: E. Meier, *Robert von Mohl*, "Zeitschrift für die gesamte Staatswissenschaft," Nr 34, 1878, p. 443.

198 R. v. Mohl, *Lebenserinnerungen von Robert von Mohl 1799–1875*, Bd. 1..., p. 119. H. Schulze, op. cit., p. 15.

199 R. v. Mohl, *Lebenserinnerungen von Robert von Mohl 1799–1875*, Bd. 1. . ., p. 120.

200 Ibidem, p. 121, 124. H. Schulze, op. cit., pp. 15–16.

201 R. v. Mohl, *Die Öffentliche Rechtspflege des Deutschen Bundes. Ein publicistischer Versuch*. Stuttgart und Tübingen 1822. Idem, *Lebenserinnerungen von Robert von Mohl 1799–1875*, Bd. 1. . ., p. 259, E. Angermann, op. cit., p. 25.

well as establishing scientific contacts, and participating in lectures by scholars such as Gustav Hugo and Karl Friedrich Eichhorn. From Göttingen he went to Paris, where in addition to improving his French speaking skills, he was to study the local government and administrative law.[202]

During his stay in Paris there was repeated pressure from his father for Robert to prepare another written statement. The effect of this was the publication of the *Federal State Law of the United States of America*,[203] which was also created thanks to the advice of the American consul in Paris, David Bailey Warden. As noted by Erich Angermann, this work allowed von Mohl to consolidate his position within the scientific community.[204] Its significance is also important for conclusions relating to the development of the scholar himself. It was in this publication that von Mohl dealt with the main issues related to the state for the first time: federal law, judicial review of legislation, and governments based on the principle of representative democracy. In addition, in this book von Mohl operated on the basis of positive law, trying to present its system rationally, which will also form a distinct feature of his later works.[205] It was during his stay in Paris that Mohl's liberal identification with the principles of the constitutional system developed in France, primarily by Benjamin Constant, which accompanied Mohl throughout his life, developed.[206] At the end of March 1824, the scholar had to leave Paris quickly to take a chair at the University of Tübingen.[207]

Before proceeding to the analysis of von Mohl's political and scientific activity, it is also worth to mention his 1830 marriage to Pauline, the daughter of a well-known Stuttgart physician dr. Gottlieb Benjamin Becher.[208] The marriage was a successful one. Von Mohl and his wife had four children.[209]

202 R. v. Mohl, *Lebenserinnerungen von Robert von Mohl 1799–1875*, Bd. 1…, pp. 127–129, 131.

203 Idem, *Das Bundes-Staatsrecht der Vereinigten Staaten von Nord-Amerika. Erste Abtheilung: Verfassungs-Recht*. Stuttgart und Tübingen 1824. Idem, *Lebenserinnerungen von Robert von Mohl 1799–1875*, Bd. 1…, pp. 260–261.

204 E. Angermann, op. cit., p. 27.

205 Ibidem.

206 H. Schulze, op. cit., p. 18.

207 R. v. Mohl, *Lebenserinnerungen von Robert von Mohl 1799–1875*, Bd. 1…, p. 138.

208 E. Angermann, op. cit., p. 32, J. Hähnle, op. cit., p. 7.

209 More about the children of von Mohl: R. v. Mohl, *Lebenserinnerungen von Robert von Mohl 1799–1875*, Bd. 1…, pp. 63–64. E. Angermann, op. cit., pp. 33, 74.

1.3.2. Scientific and academic activities

The scholar's scientific and academic activity began at the University of Tübingen, where he worked from 1824 to 1845.[210] The return to the provincial Tübingen from Paris, the capital of the world at that time, was as difficult as inevitable for von Mohl.[211] It was mainly due to efforts of his father, who held extensive contacts in governmental and university circles, that as early as 30 March 1824 he could be appointed an associate professor[212] of legal sciences at his *Alma Mater*.[213] The academic career of the scholar developed so quickly that in 1827 he obtained the position of regular professor,[214] but not at the Faculty of Law but at the "Faculty of Sciences of State" (*Staatswirtschaftliche Fakultät*), which was recently established in Tübingen (in 1817).[215]

Von Mohl began his teaching activity by lecturing in constitutional law of Württemberg,[216] which during his work in Tübingen remained the main axis of his activity. He also lectured on subjects called "Sciences of State Encyclopaedias,"[217] "Police Science,"[218] as well as secondary statistics.[219] Von Mohl prepared his lectures very diligently, continuously updating their content.[220] His classes (as well as scientific works) were characterized by high clarity, logic and solid substantive preparation. Despite the fact that he himself was not an extraordinary speaker, he enjoyed considerable popularity among students. This is evidenced, for example, by the fact that he began his lectures with eight listeners and then

---

210 R. v. Mohl, *Lebenserinnerungen von Robert von Mohl 1799–1875*, Bd. 1. . ., p. 143.

211 H. Schulze, op. cit., p. 19.

212 *außerordentlicher Profesor.*

213 R. v. Mohl, *Lebenserinnerungen von Robert von Mohl 1799–1875*, Bd. 1. . ., p. 145.

214 *ordentlicher Professor.*

215 At first he was not happy about it: Ibidem. For more on von Mohl's academic career: J. Hähnle, op. cit., p. 6. According to Wilhelm Bleek, the phrase *Staatswirtschaft* can be understood as synonymous with the word *Staatswissenschaft.* W. Bleek, *Die Tübinger Schule der gesamten Staatswissenschaft*, [in:] *Schulen der deutschen Politikwissenschaft*, W. Bleek, H. J. Lietzmann (eds.), Opladen 1999, p. 105.

216 *württembergisches Staatsrecht*. Fort the purposes of this work, the term "*Staatsrecht*" is translated into "constitutional law". Muret-Sanders, *Encyclopaedic English-German and German-English Dictionary*, 2nd Part, H. Bauman (ed.), Berlin 1910, s. 911.

217 *Encyklopädie der Staatswissenschaften.*

218 *Polizeiwissenschaft.*

219 R. v. Mohl, *Lebenserinnerungen von Robert von Mohl 1799–1875*, Bd. 1. . ., p. 147. H. Schulze, op. cit., p. 19, E. Angermann, op. cit., p. 34, J. Hähnle, op. cit., p. 6.

220 R. v. Mohl, *Lebenserinnerungen von Robert von Mohl 1799–1875*, Bd. 1. . ., p. 147.

quickly achieved an attendance of 50–100 people, which was quite extraordinary for the conditions of Tübingen.[221]

At the beginning of his scientific career, von Mohl also expanded his private library with extraordinary passion (he already had 6,000 items in it by 1835).[222] He also travelled frequently. This allowed him not only to break away from the small-town atmosphere of Tübingen, but also to study issues of interest to him in other countries. Major scientific escapades include his trips to Basel and Alsace (in 1836), where he studied the social problems of the emerging working class. A similar purpose was behind his spring 1840 trip to Belgium, where he met another well-known German scholar Heinrich Ahrens.[223] In 1842 von Mohl traveled to Italy, writing of which that it was the most pleasant time in his life.[224]

As far as didactic work was far from favourites of the scholar of Württemberg, the scientific activities were at their core, focusing his most important ambitions.[225] One should agree with the scholar himself, who (too modestly) did not consider himself the creator of the highest quality, but admitted that in many areas his works set new paths of thinking and were known for their uncommon logic and clarity of argument.[226] The most important publications created while working in Tübingen should undoubtedly include the *Constitutional law of the Kingdom of Württemberg*[227] and the *Police science according to the principles of the legal state*.[228]

The first of the above was in its time a pioneering position in Germany.[229] It presented the development of the particular law of a single German state in a precise and clear form. The Kingdom of Württemberg, which based its system on a constitution, was a very good object for systemic research. In this work von Mohl

221 Ibidem, pp. 147, 172, 223, 255. Idem, *Lebenserinnerungen von Robert von Mohl 1799–1875*, Bd. 2, Stuttgart und Leipzig 1902, p. 202, E. Angermann, op. cit., p. 34.

222 R. v. Mohl, *Lebenserinnerungen von Robert von Mohl 1799–1875*, Bd. 1..., pp. 149–151, E. Angermann, op. cit., p. 30.

223 R. v. Mohl, *Lebenserinnerungen von Robert von Mohl 1799–1875*, Bd. 2. . ., p. 365. More on travel to Belgium: Ibid, pp. 367–378.

224 More on his travel to Italy: Ibid, pp. 378–399.

225 Idem, *Lebenserinnerungen von Robert von Mohl 1799–1875*, Bd. 1. . ., p. 255. E. Angermann, op. cit., p. 34.

226 R. v. Mohl, *Lebenserinnerungen von Robert von Mohl 1799–1875*, Bd. 1. . ., p. 255.

227 Idem, Staatsr.Württem.1.1829, Idem, Staatsr.Württem.2.1831. The second edition was published in 1840 and 1846.

228 H. Schulze, op. cit., pp. 19–20.

229 More about the *Constitutional law of the Kingdom of Württemberg*: E. Angermann, op. cit., pp. 35–36, E. Meier, op. cit., pp. 448–449.

appeared as a monarchist, who was not advocating the theory of separation of powers, or liberalism like Karl von Rotteck. On the other hand, he was in favor of constitutional law and safeguarding the nation's fundamental rights.[230] He devoted a lot of attention to the separation of administrative law from constitutional law, speaking of the former one as "applying the constitutional principles to individual cases"[231] and "fulfilling the objectives of the state through the organs and institutions established for this end,"[232] which was generally recognized in German science.[233] This work was the first attempt to elaborate on a positive constitutional law and administrative law of a single German state, in a way exhaustive in both factual and literary manner, and all that in a very clear form, based on a logical system.[234] This made the young, thirty-year-old von Mohl, gain recognition in the scientific and clerical environment, and the work became almost an official commentary on the state activity in Württemberg, as well as a specific model for future studies.[235] Hermann Schulze called this item "a modern book in the best sense of this word[236]", and von Mohl himself noted that it was widely distributed for many years among Württemberg officials, members of parliament, and also ordinary citizens.[237]

The work entitled *Police science according to the principles of the legal state*[238] was also of great importance and publicity. Here again, von Mohl was the first to attempt to develop police science in accordance with the principles of the constitutional state of law.[239] Like the *Constitutional Law of the Kingdom of Württemberg*, also the *Police Science...* was based on lectures delivered by the scholar on this subject. The goal of von Mohl was to organize and systematize the whole range of issues related to the state's exercise of "internal

---

230 H. Schulze, op. cit., p. 23.

231 R. v. Mohl, Staatsr.Württem.2.1831, p. 4.

232 Ibidem.

233 E. Angermann, op. cit., p. 35.

234 Ibidem.

235 R. v. Mohl, *Lebenserinnerungen von Robert von Mohl 1799–1875*, Bd. 1. . ., s. 262, H. Schulze, op. cit., p. 24.

236 Ibidem.

237 R. v. Mohl, *Lebenserinnerungen von Robert von Mohl 1799–1875*, Bd. 1..., pp. 262–263.

238 Ibidem, p. 271. Idem, *Die Polizeiwissenschaft nach den Grundsätzen des Rechtsstaates, 2Bde,* Tübingen 1832, Idem, *Die Polizeiwissenschaft nach den Grundsätzen des Rechtsstaates, 2Bde,* Tübingen 1844, Idem, *Die Polizeiwissenschaft nach den Grundsätzen des Rechtsstaates, 2Bde,* Tübingen 1866.

239 H. Schulze, op. cit., p. 25. The following work is also of significance: R. v. Mohl *System der Präventiv-Justiz oder Rechtspolizei,* Tübingen 1834. Second edition, 1845. Third edition 1866 (from the second edition it formed part of the *Police Science...*).

administration,"[240] which the scholar referred to as "the police."[241] This need was all the greater because, according to von Mohl, police science was a lot more chaotic at that time, than the science of constitutional law was. In creating this work, he was guided by the following priorities: a clear and true definition of the subject and term of *Polizei*, and its proper location in the system of the state. In addition, von Mohl wanted the absolute elimination of everything that did not belong to the scope thereof. The undoubted merit and achievement of this work was the inclusion in the logically ordered system of science of the internal administration of a modern legal state for the first time ever.[242]

The works created in Tübingen also include the noteworthy 1837 monograph on *Responsibility of ministers in monarchies with the representation of the people, in legal, political and historical terms.*[243] This work concerned the minister's criminal liability for violation of applicable law in connection with the office held.[244] The creation of this work proves that von Mohl was able not only to write theoretical compendia, but also that he was a practicing lawyer.[245] At that time, von Mohl also published an *Opinion on Sir August d'Este's claims to the succession in the United Kingdom and Hanover.*[246] The collective works entitled: *Literature* of *Württemberg's entire law of the last century in a historical and critical perspective,*[247] and the *History of Legislation and Legal Order under King Wilhelm,*[248] are also noteworthy.

---

240 *innere Verwaltung.*

241 *Polizei.*

242 E. Angermann, op. cit., pp. 36–37. R. v. Mohl, *Lebenserinnerungen von Robert von Mohl 1799–1875*, Bd. 1. . ., p. 271.

243 Ibidem, p. 269. Idem, *Die Verantwortlichkeit der Minister in Einherrschaften mit Volksvertretung, rechtlich, politisch und geschichtlich entwickelt*, Tübingen 1837.

244 Idem, *Lebenserinnerungen von Robert von Mohl 1799–1875*, Bd. 1..., pp. 269–270.

245 Robert von Mohl's letter to Julius von Mohl of 6 March 1836, after: E. Angermann, op. cit., pp. 44–45.

246 R. v. Mohl, *Die Nichtigkeit der Ansprüche des Obersten Air Augustus d'Este auf Thronfähigkeit in Grossbritannien und Hannover. Gegen die Gutachten von Dillon, Klüber und Zachariä nachgewiesen*, Tübingen 1835. In this article von Mohl defended the thesis of the nullity of the marriage concluded between the son of Prince of Essex George III, Prince August Frederick with Lady August Murray, concluded contrary to the *Royal Marriages Act* of 1772. More: E. Meier, op. cit., p. 453.

247 R. v. Mohl, *Die Literatur des gesammten württembergischen Rechtes aus dem letzten Jahrzehnd, historisch kritisch dargestellt*, Stuttgart 1830. Idem, *Lebenserinnerungen von Robert von Mohl 1799–1875*, Bd. 1. . ., p. 275.

248 Idem, O. v. Sarwey, *Geschichte der Rechtsgesetzgebung und Rechtsordnung unter König Wilhelm*, Stuttgart 1841.

While working in Tübingen, von Mohl participated in publishing many scientific periodicals. In 1835 he joined the editorial board of the *Critical Review of Foreign Law and Jurisprudence*,[249] founded Karl Salomo Zacharia and Carl Joseph Mittermaier. In addition, he was a co-founder of the Tübingen *Journal for the entire science of state*, with the first volume printed in 1844.[250] Von Mohl also published in *Rau's Archives of Political Economy*.[251] We should devote our special attention to the article: *On the disadvantages of the factory industry system, relating to both workers and the welfare and security of the entire civil society*. It is important due to von Mohl's focus on studying the social problems of the contemporary working class.[252] The topic of workers was also discussed in the article: *Past, present and future of political economy*.[253]

The most important articles published *in the German Quarterly*[254] also include: *Universities in Germany, their current deficiencies and their healing*,[255] *On the establishment of faculties of sciences of state*,[256] *The representation system,*

---

249 *Kritische Zeitschrift für die Gesetzgebung und Rechtswissenschaft des Auslandes*. H. Schulze, op. cit., p. 30. List of all articles published by von Mohl in this journal: E. Meier, op. cit., pp. 436–438.

250 *Zeitschrift für die gesammte Staatswissenschaft*. H. Schulze, op. cit., pp. 30–31. All articles published in this journal were listed by Ernst Meier: E. Meier, op. cit., pp. 438–439. As von Mohl himself believed, the journal's task was to discuss and analyze all issues related to both the life of the state and society: R. v. Mohl, *Prospectus*, "Zeitschrift" für die gesammte Staatswissenschaft," Tübingen 5. Febr. 1843, p. 1. Similar translation of the title: DF. Lindenfeld, op. cit., p. 145.

251 *Rau's Archiv für politische Oekonomie.*

252 R. v. Mohl, *Ueber die Nachteile, welche sowohl den Arbeitern selbst als dem Wohlstande und der Sicherheit der gesammten bürgerlichen Gesellschaft von dem fabrikmässigen Betriebe der Industrie zugehen*, "Archiv der politischen Ökonomie und Polizeiwissenschaften," Bd. II, pp. 141–203.

253 Idem, *Die Vergangenheit, Gegenwart und Zukunft der politischen Ökonomie*, "Deutscher Vierteljahrschrift," H. 3, 1840, pp. 1–72.

254 *Deutscher Vierteljahrs Schrift.*

255 Idem, *Die deutschen Universitäten, ihre gegenwärtigen Missstände und deren Heilung*, "Deutscher Vierteljahrs Schrift," H. 2, 1839, pp. 1–37.

256 Idem, *Ueber die Errichtung staatswissenschaftlicher Fakultäten auf den deutschen Universitäten*, "Deutscher Vierteljahrs Schrift," H. 4, 1849, pp. 237–258.

its shortcomings and remedies. The political letters of an old liberal.[257] He also published in *Prussian Annals, the Journal of German Constituional Law and German Constitutional History, the Monthly Popular Journal* and the *Augsburg Universal Journal.*[258] Attention should also be paid to articles by von Mohl in *the Staatslexikon* (State Lexicon) of von Rotteck and Welcker (primarily on the subject of police),[259] as well as the *German State Dictionary* edited by Johann Caspar Bluntschli: *Act, Legislature, Legislation.*[260] What is also of importance are the articles *State novels,*[261] *The Historical and literary outline of the encyclopaedias of sciences of state*[262] as well as the *Review of the New Literature of the international law.*[263]

During the 22 years of his stay at the University of Tübingen, von Mohl worked not only as a teacher and writer, but also devoted himself to many organizational and administrative duties at this university. He was a member of the University Senate, one of the informal leaders of a group of young reformers, who worked to improve the university.[264] Mainly thanks to the efforts of von Mohl, it prepared annual reports on the condition of the university, which the king himself read with interest. This allowed to slowly gain monarch's support for reform ideas.[265] In the course of his activities in Tübingen, von Mohl served two

---

257 Idem, *Das Reprästativsystem, seine Mängel und die Heilmittel. Politische Briefe eines Altliberalen,* "Deutscher Vierteljahrs Schrift," H. 3, 1852, pp. 145–235.

258 *Preussischen Jahrbücher, Zeitschrift für deutsches Staatsrecht und deutsche Verfassungsgeschichte, Die Augsburger Allgemeine Zeitung.* E. Meier, op. cit., pp. 440–441.

259 R. v. Mohl, *Polizei,* [in:] *Das Staats-Lexikon, Encyklopädie der sämmtlichen Staatswissenschaften für alle Stände,* Bd. 10, C. v. Rotteck, C. Welcker (eds.), Altona 1848, pp. 692–721. R. v. Mohl, *Bevölkerung,* [in:] *Das Staats-Lexikon, Encyklopädie der sämmtlichen Staatswissenschaften für alle Stände,* Bd. 2, C. v. Rotteck, C. Welcker (eds.), Altona 1846, pp. 458–481.

260 R. v. Mohl, *Gesetz, Gesetzgebende Gewalt, Gesetzgebung,* [in:] J. C. Bluntschli, K. Brater (eds.), *Deutsches Staats-Wörterbuch,* Vierter Band, Stuttgart und Leipzig 1859, pp. 267–288. For more on von Mohl's publications in various periodicals: J. Hähnle, op. cit., p. 7.

261 R. v. Mohl, *Die Staatsromane,* "Zeitschrift für die gesamte Staatswissenschaft," Bd. 2, 1845, pp. 24–74.

262 Idem, *Literarhistorische Uebersicht über die Enzyklopädien der Staatswissenschaften,* "Zeitschrift für die gesamte Staatswissenschaft," Bd. 2, 1845, pp. 423–480.

263 Idem, *Übersicht der neueren völkerrechtlichen Literatur,* "Zeitschrift für die gesamte Staatswissenschaft," Bd. 3, 1846, pp. 3–93.

264 More: Idem, *Lebenserinnerungen von Robert von Mohl 1799–1875,* Bd. 1..., p. 174.

265 Ibidem, pp. 161.175–177. E. Angermann, op. cit., p. 42.

terms as chancellor (in 1835–1836 and 1841–1842),[266] at that time being one of the most influential people at the university.[267] In 1836 he also became the Head of the University Library,[268] which was in a state of general chaos at the time.[269] Thanks to his activities and reorganization, the library soon became one of the best-stocked and organized ones in all of Germany.[270]

After moving out of Tubingen, in 1847 von Mohl made a trip to England, whose purpose was primarily to study the political and legal institutions operating there. The result of the research was crowned in the publication of the article: *On different compisition of the representative system in England, France and Germany*.[271] This journey not only allowed him to realize the dream of visiting England, but first of all to get acquainted with its state and legal institutions, and in particular the parliamentary system.[272] Von Mohl visited not only London but also the universities of Cambridge and Oxford.[273]

In the result of his conflict with the public authorities of Württemberg von Mohl had to leave the University of Tübingen. In the spring of 1847, thanks to the efforts of the Baden minister Nebenius, as well as the economist Karl Heinrich Rau and Karl Mittermaier, von Mohl was appointed professor of sciences of state at the University of Heidelberg in the Grand Duchy of Baden.[274] The opportunity to work in Heidelberg not only dismissed the scholar's concern for ensuring the existence of his growing family, but also allowed him to participate in a wider and more international environment. Von Mohl's scientific activity in Heidelberg ended in 1861, when he was elected to the diplomatic service of Baden.[275]

266 R. v. Mohl, *Lebenserinnerungen von Robert von Mohl 1799–1875*, Bd. 1. . ., p. 145.
267 E. Angermann, op. cit., p. 43.
268 *Oberbibliothekär.*
269 R. v. Mohl, *Lebenserinnerungen von Robert von Mohl 1799–1875*, Bd. 1..., p. 152, E. Angermann, op. cit., p. 43.
270 Ibidem, p. 44. More about the role of von Mohl as library manager: P.M. Ehrle, *Robert von Mohl als Leiter der Tübinger Universitätsbibliothek (1836–1844)*, Tübingen 1875.
271 Robert von Mohl, *Über die verschiedene Auffassung des represäntativen Systemes in England, Frankreich und Deutschland*, "Zeitschrift für die gesamte Staatswissenschaft," Bd. 3, 1846, pp. 451–495.
272 Idem, *Lebenserinnerungen von Robert von Mohl 1799–1875*, Bd. 2..., p. 407.
273 More about travel to England: Ibidem, pp. 407–426.
274 Idem, *Lebenserinnerungen von Robert von Mohl 1799–1875*, Bd. 1..., p. 217. H. Schulze, op. cit., p. 36.
275 Ibidem. R. v. Mohl, *Lebenserinnerungen von Robert von Mohl 1799–1875*, Bd. 1..., p. 217.

In Heidelberg, von Mohl lectured subject relating to the sciences of state and law, German law and the police science.[276] He was remembered as a lecturer attaching great importance to the correctness of his language, using very clear argumentation.[277] It should be noted that in Heidelberg von Mohl was much less active in the field of university organizational activities than in Tübingen. It was connected with the fact of his involvement in the politics.[278] Already while working in Heidelberg, the scholar began publishing articles on issues of society. In 1851 he published the article entitled *Sciences of Society and Sciences of State*.[279] In 1853 he also wrote the article *Revision of Legal International Asylum Theory*.[280] In 1848, a work was also published in Heidelberg: *Proposals regarding the procedure of the Reichstag*..[281]

While working in Heidelberg he also published the *History and Literature of Sciences of State*,[282] the *Encyclopaedia of Sciences of State*[283] and the *Constitutional Law, International law, and Politics*.[284] The first of these works proves von Mohl's excellent knowledge of the subject literature related to the state. This work focused on many areas of state studies, apart from the German ones, also including the French and English ones. Despite covering such an extensive range, the work is extremely clear and orderly.[285] *History and Literature of Sciences of State* is also undoubtedly a monumental work, presenting all knowledge in a systematic and comprehensive way.[286]

The other great item, the *Encyclopaedia of Sciences of State* is primarily a collection of systematic views on issues that the scholar has dealt with throughout his life. Erich Angermann rightly called it the quintessence of von Mohl's views

276 Ibidem, pp. 217–218. E. Angermann, op. cit., p. 58.

277 H. Schulze, op. cit., p. 48.

278 R. v. Mohl, *Lebenserinnerungen von Robert von Mohl 1799–1875*, Bd. 1..., p. 254.

279 Idem, *Gesellschafts-Wissenschaften und Staats-wissenschaften*, "Zeitschrift für die gesamte Staatswissenschaft," Bd. 7, 1851, pp. 3–71.

280 Idem, *Revision der völkerrechtlichen Lehre vom Asyle*, "Zeitschrift für die gesamte Staatswissenschaft," Bd. 9, 1853, pp. 461–604. E. Angermann, op. cit., p. 77.

281 R. v. Mohl, *Vorschläge zu einer Geschäftsordnung des verfassungsgebenden Reichstages*, Heidelberg 1848.

282 *Die Geschichte und Literatur der Staatswissenschaften.*

283 *Enzyklopädie der Staatswissenschaften.*

284 *Staatsrecht, Völkerrecht und Politik.* H. Schulze, op. cit., pp. 48–49.

285 Ibidem, pp. 50–51.

286 R. v. Mohl, Geschicht.u.Lit.1, Idem, Geschicht.u.Lit.2, Idem, Geschicht.u.Lit.3. More on that work: Idem, *Lebenserinnerungen von Robert von Mohl 1799–1875*, Bd. 1..., pp. 275–279, E. Angermann, op. cit., p. 77, H. Schulze, op. cit., pp. 78–79.

on state and society.[287] Two goals have led the scientist in creating this work. First of all, he wanted to create a work that was an introduction to the subject. The second, addressed primarily to experts in the sciences of the state, was to present his own views on it, and critically analyze these presented by others.[288]

In the book *Constitutional Law, International law, and Politics*,[289] von Mohl answered all the burning questions of his contemporaneity. He based it not only on full objectivity, but also on great knowledge of literature and his own experience. He raised the issues of pros and cons of the constitutional monarchy and the representation system. He also referred to international law, asylum law, but also warfare. Finally, he focused on political problems, church-state relations, and educational activity of the state.[290] The success of this work, which also includes updated scholarly publications, exceeded his widest expectations.[291] It was widely distributed, and parts of it were even translated abroad (among others in the United States).[292] However, the following was not successful: *Legal and political considerations of a southern German on the reforms of the Confederation*.[293]

One of the scholar's latest publications is the *German Reich Constitutional Law. Legal and political considerations*.[294] This work concerned the public law of the newly created German Reich. In von Mohl's idea, it was not to be a systematic work elaborating on all issues, but a discussion of a set of selected key institutions.[295] The work that was based on the experience of sitting in the Reich parliament, were the *Critical remarks regarding the election to the German Reichstag*.[296]

---

287 E. Angermann, op. cit., pp. 81–82. R. v. Mohl, *Encyklopädie der Staatswissenschaften*, Erste Auflage, Tübingen 1859, Idem, *Encyklopädie der Staatswissenschaften*, Zweite Auflage, Tübingen 1872.

288 Idem, *Lebenserinnerungen von Robert von Mohl 1799–1875*, Bd. 1..., p. 283.

289 Idem, SVuP.1, Idem SVuP.2.1, Idem SVuP.3.2.

290 H. Schulze, op. cit., p. 57. More about the work: R. v. Mohl, *Lebenserinnerungen von Robert von Mohl 1799–1875*, Bd. 1..., pp. 279–281.

291 More: E. Angermann, op. cit., pp. 82–83.

292 R. v. Mohl, *Lebenserinnerungen von Robert von Mohl 1799–1875*, Bd. 1..., p. 280.

293 Idem, *Rechtliche und politische Eröterungen über die Bundesreformakte. Von einem Süddeutschen*, Erlangen 1863.

294 Idem, *Das deutsche Reichsstaatsrecht. Rechtliche und politische Eröterungen*, Tübingen 1873.

295 Idem, *Lebenserinnerungen von Robert von Mohl 1799–1875*, Bd. 1..., p. 265, E. Angermann, op. cit., p. 93.

296 R. v. Mohl, *Kritische Bemerkungen über die Wahlen zum deutschen Reichstage*, Tübingen 1874.

The scientific achievements of von Mohl should be considered significant for contemporary German science. This significance is further proved by the rank given to the 50th anniversary of his doctoral promotion.[297] Among the congratulations and letters of praise from all German universities, it is also worth mentioning that he received a honorary nobility from the Prince of Baden, as well as high ranking Prussian and Austrian state decorations.[298]

1.3.3. Political activity

The scholar's political activities began with his election to the parliament (*Landtag*) of Württemberg.[299] Unfortunately, the process of von Mohl's election to the Württemberg Legislature was marked by a conflict with the very influential Interior Minister Schlaner. Schlaner's beliefs in favour of a strong absolutist bureaucracy and the government's privileged position were inconsistent with von Mohl's election program.[300] The reason for the conflict and revolution in Württemberger's life was a letter he wrote on 5 September 1845 to a lawyer named Nagel in Balingen.[301] In this letter, von Mohl denied the accusation of being a candidate supporting the government. Furthermore, he listed many errors, including the beliefs and actions of Minister Schlaner.[302] To the surprise of von Mohl, the letter was published. He was treated by the then authorities as an act of insubordination of a state employee.[303] The consequence was the dismissal of the scholar from the university and a forced transfer to the position of government counsel to Ulm. After unsuccessful appeals, von Mohl decided to leave the state service (the professors were state officials in Württemberg)

297 More on that event: Idem, *Lebenserinnerungen von Robert von Mohl 1799–1875*, Bd. 1..., pp. 285–288.

298 Ibidem, pp. 286, H. Schulze, op. cit., pp. 73–74.

299 More about the activities of von Mohl in the Württemberg *Landtag*: E. Angermann, op. cit., pp. 51–53. On von Mohl's political activity also in: J. Hähnle, op. cit., pp. 7–10.

300 H. Schulze, op. cit., p. 33.

301 More: E. Angermann, op. cit. p. 51, letter from Robert von Mohl to a lawyer named Nagel in Balingen of 7 August 1845, printed in "Volks-Blatt" No. 277 Stuttgart 1 Okt. 1845 pp. 1109–1111. More: R. v. Mohl, *Lebenserinnerungen von Robert von Mohl 1799–1875*, Bd. 2. . ., pp. 3–5.

302 K. v. Beyme, *Einleitung*, [in:] R. v. Mohl, *Politische Schriften. Eine Auswahl*, K. v. Beyme (ed.), Köln und Opladen 1966, p. VIII.

303 H. Schulze, op. cit., p. 34, J. Hähnle; op. cit., p. 8.

and take up writing.[304] He regained his prestige in the spring of 1846, when he managed to obtain a mandate to the Württemberg *Landtag* from the Tuttlingen district. However, this activity cannot be classified as an outstanding one. As he admitted himself, the period of sitting in this parliament was too short, and he was just preparing to participate in the subsequent terms (which, as we know, never happened).[305]

Undoubtedly, Robert von Mohl's activities in the Frankfurt Parliament were much more significant. The atmosphere of Heidelberg and Baden differed from that prevailing in Württemberg. Baden liberalism, more well-grounded and developed than that in Württemberg, made Heidelberg one of those places, where progressive political programs for Germany were formulated. The *German Journal*[306] published in Heidelberg played a large role in the issue of further existence and unification of German states. It was in the pages of this Baden periodical that, for the first time, circles of South Germany formulated a conviction that the unification of Germany could only be accomplished by Prussia.[307]

For von Mohl, the first years in Heidelberg were marked not only by a long illness (pleurisy), but also by the outbreak of the 1848 revolution. We should emphasize the negative attitude of the scholar to these events. What he feared most was the escalation of violence, because he noticed that attempts to solve political problems often resulted in riots in the cities.[308] Von Mohl was also sceptical about the 1848 political situation in Germany. He saw the looming threat of anarchy and the impossibility of solving the problem of unification or the new organization of the German state. In addition, already in the mid of nineteenth century, he rightly predicted the threat of war with France.[309]

In his four articles published in the *German Journal*, von Mohl sketched his proposals regarding the system of the future, united German state. His ideas included, above all, postulates of basing the system on a bicameral parliament

---

304 Robert von Mohl, *Lebenserinnerungen von Robert von Mohl 1799–1875*, Bd. 2. . ., pp. 6–7. E. Angermann, op. cit., p. 53. More about the so-called Mohl's affair (*Mohlschen Affaire*): P. M. Ehrle, V. Schäfer (eds.), op. cit., pp. 63–67.

305 R. v. Mohl, *Lebenserinnerungen von Robert von Mohl 1799–1875*, Bd. 2..., pp. 12–14, E. Angermann, op. cit., pp. 53–54.

306 *Deutsche Zeitung*. H. Schulze, op. cit., p. 37. More on this topic: J. Hähnle, op. cit., p. 8.

307 H. Schulze, op. cit., p. 37.

308 Letter from Robert von Mohl to Julius von Mohl of 9 March 1848, after: R. v. Mohl, *Lebenserinnerungen von Robert von Mohl 1799–1875*, Bd. 2. . ., p. 31.

309 Letter from Robert von Mohl to Julius von Mohl of 1 May 1848, after: E. Angermann, op. cit., p. 60.

system, and electing a common ruler with the help of politically responsible ministers. The ideas of the *Rechtsstaat*, civil liberties and effective administration were also to form the core of the system.[310] When referring to the state that should play the role of leader in the process of unification of German lands, he initially turned towards Austria.[311] Later, however, he turned to Prussia. Although he did not like the Prussian junkers, he valued the Customs Union operating under the leadership of the Hohenzollern State. We can observe a gradual adaptation of the scientist to reality, in which it became clear to him that Austria was too weak to unite the Germans in one country. Ultimately von Mohl was in favour of Prussia, in his opinion the sole force capable of achieving unification.[312]

Von Mohl was elected to the Frankfurt National Assembly (*Nationalversammlung*) from the Württemberg district of Mergentheim-Gerabronn.[313] The scholar's strong sense of duty finds its confirmation in the following words he wrote to his brother: "God knows that I am not going to Frankfurt for pleasure, and all my private interests are in opposition to leaving my family and my affairs for longer period; but the matter is too important to pay attention to yourself."[314] He devoted the time to the debates, among others, to the preparation of the rules of procedure for the parliament, which were later adopted unanimously, though with minor changes.[315] What is of note is, first of all, the activity of the German liberal in the Constitutional Commission, where all the most important activities of the Frankfurt Parliament took place.[316] Apart from von Mohl, its members included scholars as Friedrich Dahlmann, Johann Droysen, Felix Lichnowsky or Hermann von Beckerath.[317] In the Frankfurt Parliament, von Mohl belonged to the centre-left club meeting at the *Württemberger Hof* hotel, which later gave rise to the more right-wing

310 P. Nordblom, *Robert von Mohl*, [in:] *Gelehrte in der Revolution. Heidelberger Abgeordnete in der deutschen Nationalversammlung 1848/49*, F. Engehausen, A. Kohnle (eds.), Ubstadt-Weiher 1998, p. 44.

311 H. Schulze, op. cit., p. 39.

312 E. Angermann, op. cit., pp. 60–61. On the reunification of Germany in the opinion of von Mohl also: J. Hähnle, op. cit., pp. 95–100.

313 R. v. Mohl, *Lebenserinnerungen von Robert von Mohl 1799–1875*, Bd. 2. . ., p. 31.

314 Robert von Mohl's letter to Julius von Mohl of 1 May 1848, after: P. Nordblom, op. cit., p. 41.

315 H. Schulze, op. cit., p. 39. P. Nordblom, op. cit., pp. 47–49.

316 R. v. Mohl, *Lebenserinnerungen von Robert von Mohl 1799–1875*, Bd. 2. . ., p. 32, H. Schulze, op. cit., p. 39.

317 Ibidem, pp. 39–40.

Augsburger Hof.[318] The scientist was alien to (above all leftist) radicalisms. He wanted to introduce a liberal, constitution and freedoms-based system, but also a system that would be accepted by monarchs.

The substantive abilities of von Mohl were appreciated on 9 August 1848, when he was appointed the Justice Minister of Reich (*Reichs-Justizminister*), which was part of the *Reichsministerium* - the Reich government, an office he held until 10 May 1849.[319] It should be noted, however, that he held the office of the minister of the state that was only to be created, functioning as an idea and having no special means to act.[320]

The service of von Mohl in the ministry ended with the rejection of the imperial crown by Friedrich Wilhelm IV. He was then replaced in his position by Heinrich von Gagern. Being tired of politics, he also gave up his seat in the Frankfurt Parliament, and returned to Heidelberg in the spring of 1849, where he could finally take up his favourite activity, i.e. scientific work.[321] The experience of Frankfurt and disappointment with practical politics meant that the scholar withdrew from public activities for several years (without running, for example, for a seat in the Erfurt Parliament). This time was filled with pessimism in relation to the political situation and waiting for new unrest and war.[322]

He returned to political activity in 1857, when von Mohl was elected to the Upper House of the[323] Parliament of Baden as a representative of the University of Heidelberg.[324] He held this office until 1873 (with a short break in 1861–1863).[325] Meetings of the Baden *Landtag*, with von Mohl holding the position of vice-speaker, and later the speaker, differed in their moderation and calmness from the lively, and often chaotic discussions in Frankfurt.[326] Von Mohl

318 Ibidem, p. 41.

319 R. v. Mohl, *Lebenserinnerungen von Robert von Mohl 1799–1875*, Bd. 2. . ., p. 32. On the activities of von Mohl in the ministry: J. Hähnle, op. cit., p. 9, P. Nordblom, op. cit., pp. 53–58.

320 R. v. Mohl, *Lebenserinnerungen von Robert von Mohl 1799–1875*, Bd. 2. . ., p. 74. H. Schulze, op. cit., pp. 41–42. On the role of von Mohl in the ministry more in: E. Angermann, op. cit., p. 65.

321 H. Schulze, op. cit., pp. 46–47.

322 E. Angermann, op. cit., p. 71, 84.

323 *Erste Kammer.*

324 H. Schulze, op. cit., p. 59, E. Angermann, op. cit., p. 85. More: R. v. Mohl, *Lebenserinnerungen von Robert von Mohl 1799–1875*, Bd. 2. . ., pp. 120–157.

325 Ibidem, p. 121, more on the activities of von Mohl in the Baden *Landtag*: Ibidem, pp. 122–156.

326 Ibidem, p. 120.

gained a strong position in this institution to such an extent that he very often had the casting voice on solving complicated issues in the legislative process. During this period, von Mohl also became a trusted associate of the Grand Duke of Baden, who consulted with him many of the most important state affairs. Finally, in 1861, he entrusted the scientist with the diplomatic office of the *badischen bundestags-Gesandten* (representative of Baden at the still-functioning Confederation Parliament),[327] which he held until 1865 (i.e. the withdrawal of Baden from the German Confederation). The scholar's diplomatic career was crowned with the acceptance of office of the ambassador of Baden to Bavaria (1866–1871).[328] He remembered this service as very pleasant (if not for any other reasons, mainly because of the interesting social life or rich library resources found in Munich).[329] It ended with Baden's accession to the German Reich.[330]

The 1866 Austro-Prussian war met with sadness and disappointment of the Württemberger, as it halted the unification process. The dream of the emergence of one state of all Germans, which was also manifested by von Mohl, did not come true until 1871. On 1 October 1871, he ended his diplomatic service and, having left Munich, took the office of the chairman of the Supreme Audit Office (*Oberrechnungskammer*) in Karlsruhe. This function, however, was only a sinecure, profitable but held without any particular satisfaction.[331]

The final stage of the scholar's political activity is marked by his election to parliament of the newly created German Reich. It is natural that as the author of the aforementioned *Constitutional Law of the German Reich* von Mohl wanted to participate in the life of this country in a practical way. So he became a member of the second *Reichstag*.[332] Like other liberals from Baden, von Mohl joined the national-liberal faction (although reluctantly, as he himself admitted).[333] Due to his age, he was no longer involved in fiery plenary debates, but he still devoted himself to various committees. For example, he was the clerk of the Upper Silesia electoral law. Despite the fact that he did not always agree with all the processes

327 H. Schulze, op. cit., p. 60, E. Angermann, op. cit., p. 86. More: R. v. Mohl, *Lebenserinnerungen von Robert von Mohl 1799–1875*, Bd. 2. . ., pp. 200–285.

328 Ibidem, pp. 200–201, p. 277, 307.

329 H. Schulze, op. cit., p. 67, E. Angermann, op. cit., p. 92. On von Mohl's diplomatic service: J. Hähnle, op. cit., pp. 9–10.

330 R. v. Mohl, *Lebenserinnerungen von Robert von Mohl 1799–1875*, Bd. 2. . ., p. 311.

331 Ibidem, p. 347.

332 H. Schulze, op. cit., p. 75.

333 E. Angermann, op. cit., p. 94. For example, Franz von Roggenbach, Karl von Grimm or Wilhelm Morstadt.

taking place in the united Germany (he was, for example, an opponent of universal suffrage), he still stated: "The New German Reich did not have a more ardent and sincere supporter than myself."[334] So he always supported the creation of a strong, united German state organism. He considered the leadership of Prussia in the new Reich to be justified because of its strength and size.

The end of von Mohl's political career is associated with increasing recognition (though not sympathy) for Prussia and its politicians. Although the main assumptions of Prussian policy were correct according to von Mohl, he opposed, for example, the conflict with the Catholic Church or confrontation with France.[335] His political career in the new German state was interrupted by an unexpected, but peaceful and dignified death. Robert von Mohl passed away in sleep on the night of 4 to 5 November 1875 in Berlin. An open book found with him testified that he was devoting himself to his greatest passion: reading.[336]

334 After: H. Schulze, op. cit., p. 75.

335 Robert von Mohl's letter to Julius von Mohl of 31 March 1873, after: E. Angermann, op. cit., pp. 92–93.

336 Ibidem, p. 94.

Chapter II Introductory concepts for the idea of state

2.1. Theory of the spheres and objectives of human life

The analysis of the perception of the state in the thought of Robert von Mohl should begin with the analysis of his concepts relating to the so-called "circles of life" or "spheres of life" (*Lebenskreisen*), in which the life of the human individual takes place.[337] Due to the purpose of the present publication, which includes presenting the Mohl's holistic vision of the state, it seems reasonable to discuss, albeit in abbreviated form, the remaining, apart from the state, loci of human activity distinguished by the scholar. This will not only form another proof of the comprehensive nature of Robert von Mohl's thought, but will also help to place the state within a specific and ordered conceptual system.[338]

Mohl's science of the spheres of human life begins with a statement saying that closer observation of various phenomena on Earth proves that every human being is among many different kinds of the so-called "circles of life." According to the scholar, each of these circles has different objectives, as determined by the aspirations of its members. Different types of relationships may occur between the respective circles. So they can mutually penetrate and intertwine, but what is very important, they are never mutually exclusive. The reason for the existence of more such life circles is, according to von Mohl, the fact that a human individual can, at the same time, strive to meet various objectives in life. For this end, he or she may need support from another circle, i.e. a different community of people.[339]

The concept of the spheres of human life and the distinction of their division appeared in Württemberger's thoughts as early as 1851, with the publication of the article entitled *Sciences of Society and Sciences of State*.[340] In this publication

337 More on the spheres of human life in terms of Robert von Mohl: H. Schmitz, *Die Staatsauffassung Robert von Mohls unter Berücksichtigung der verfassungsgeschichtlichen Entwicklung und des positivistischen Staatsdenkens*, Köln 1965, pp. 30–34, E. R. Huber, *Die deutsche Staatswissenschaft*, "Zeitschrift für die gesamte Staatswissenschaft / Journal of Institutional and Theoretical Economics," Bd. 95, H. 1. (1935), p. 10.

338 R. v. Mohl, *Encyklopädie der Staatswissenschaften*, Zweite Auflage..., p. 3.

339 Ibid.

340 R. v. Mohl, *Gesellschafts-Wissenschaften und Staats-Wissenschaften...*, pp. 3 – 71.

he pointed to the three basic spheres of human life, as found in every organized community, to which he included the "circles of individual lives" (*Lebenskreisen der einzelnen Persönlichkeiten*), the society (*Gesellschaft*) and the state (*Staat*).[341] In thinker's doctrine there appears the thesis stating that these particular circles are the most important in determining both social and state relations. In addition, he also distinguished the spheres of "family" (*Familie*), "tribe" (*Stamm*) and "interstate relationships" (*Staatengesellschaft*).[342] It should be noted, however, that in von Mohl's concept these circles were less significant for social and political relations.[343] The final concept of the categorization of spheres (circles) of human life is present in the second edition of the *Encyclopedia of Sciences of State* from 1872, where the circle of "municipality" (*Gemeinde*) was added to the six spheres that were already mentioned earlier.[344] Due to the subject and objectives of this work, the following subsections will present the circles of: individual, family, tribe, municipality and unions of states. The subsequent section will be devoted to the sphere of society, as it has large significance not only for von Mohl's thought, but also for proving the theses formulated here at the beginning. The sphere of the state as the main subject of the present analysis will be considered comprehensively in the third, fourth and fifth chapter.

As already noted, the first sphere of human life distinguished by von Mohl was the circle of a single individual. The scholar was convinced that all human beings were equipped with the same physical strength and mental abilities as to their kind. Diversity seems to be the key word for Mohl's understanding of the essence of the individual and its life.[345] We can see here not only the belief in large differences between people, but also drawing attention to the multitude of relationships in which they find themselves (for example, relations between a woman and a man, as well as relations between employers and employees). Von

341 Ibidem, Comments on the subject by Erich Angerman: E. Angermann, op. cit., p. 345.

342 R. v. Mohl, *Gesellschafts-Wissenschaften und Staats-Wissenschaften*..., p. 28.

343 Ibid. Same categorization also appears in the following works: *History and Literature of Sciences of State* and in the first edition of *Encyclopedia of Sciences of State*: Idem, Geschicht.u.Lit.1, p. 88, Idem, *Encyklopädie der Staatswissenschaften*, Erste Auflage..., p. 3.

344 Idem, *Encyklopädie der Staatswissenschaften*, Zweite Auflage..., p. IX. The phrase "*Gemeinde*" was translated into "municipality". Muret-Sanders, *Encyclopaedic English-German and German-English Dictionary*..., s. 426.

345 R. v. Mohl, *Encyklopädie der Staatswissenschaften*, Zweite Auflage..., p. 6. Idem, *Gesellschafts-Wissenschaften und Staats-Wissenschaften*..., p. 29. Similarly: Idem, Geschicht.u.Lit.1., pp. 89–90.

Mohl saw the source of these differences in natural conditions, which were independent from the individual, but also in the effects of historical and social processes.[346] In the perception of man by von Mohl, in his belief in the great diversity between people, one can see the influence of liberal thought, emphasizing both then and now on the individualism of the human being.'

The aforementioned diversity of human individuals is gaining additional significance for von Mohl. It forms the basis for people to adopt many different "life goals" (*Lebenszwecke*). Rooted in individualism, von Mohl argued that each person has its own life goal, which it must pursue. Such person always chooses the appropriate means to achieve this goal. Nevertheless we should note that among this great diversity the scholar managed to find one common, overarching goal. Referring to rationalism, he stated that the principle of "reasonable life of the individual according to the available options" is common to all individuals.[347] Importantly, however, in von Mohl the individual will never be able to achieve its life goal independently, and in order to fulfill it he or she must join with others. This state of affairs causes that for each individual there are both specific obligations and claims, which may be both religious, moral and legal in their nature.[348] The distinguishing feature of the individual in achieving its life goals is the fact that in this process he or she is guided by the so-called "permissible egoism" (*erlaubte Selbstsucht*), which manifests itself in the autonomous definition of tasks fulfilled within his or her sphere of life.[349]

Analyzing von Mohl's teaching regarding the life goals of the individual, it must be stated that in the beginning he did not classify them.[350] It was not until the first edition of the *Encyclopedia of Sciences of State* that the scientist formulated his theory of the purpose of the human individual.[351] According to von Mohl, the most important human goal (which he is morally obliged to accomplish) was to manage and maintain own life. This fact is extremely important, as it consequently raises the obligation for an individual to find means to achieve the goal of managing and maintaining life. In the result thereof, the individual is engaged in various types of relationships, joining with others to achieve the same

346 Idem, *Gesellschafts-Wissenschaften und Staats-Wissenschaften...*, p. 29.

347 Ibid, p. 30.

348 Ibidem.

349 More: Idem, *Encyklopädie der Staatswissenschaften*, Zweite Auflage..., p. 9.

350 It is neither found in the article *Sciences of Society and Sciences of State*, nor in the *History and Literature of Sciences of State*.

351 Idem, *Encyklopädie der Staatswissenschaften*, Erste Auflage..., pp. 6–9, Idem, *Encyklopädie der Staatswissenschaften*, Zweite Auflage..., pp. 7–9.

life goals. In determining, what life goals should be selected by individuals, von Mohl once again relied on individualism. Therefore, the sole factor that is able to determine the life aspirations of individuals are the conditions resulting from their needs and abilities. Therefore there is no authority capable of imposing anything on them in this regard.[352]

Referring to the categorization of life goals by von Mohl, it is worth paying attention to the scholar's view on the duality of human nature.[353] Striving to find the individual, most frequent goals, he referred to the sensual (emotional) and rational sides of human nature. For example, the goals dictated by the sensual dimension included getting food, clothes, securing housing, and enjoying.[354] So it is clear that in von Mohl's concept the sensual side of human nature responded to the needs, which can be called instinctive, and that are often driven not by man's free will but a specific impulse. The sensual dimension was opposed by the learned rational dimension, the so-called "rational being" (*vernünftigen Wesen*).[355] It is the rational part of human nature that is responsible for the more complex goals of higher order. They were, for example, the need to develop and acquire education. Man's goal as a rational being is also to shape a sense of morality, which is also linked to faith and religion. Finally, according to von Mohl, a rational person should strive to achieve the goal of developing a sense of beauty and good taste.[356]

We find proof of von Mohl's realistic approach in that he was well aware that the aforesaid division was an ideal one. In fact, few individuals were ever able to come close to it. Therefore, if people are not able to achieve all of the above objectives, then, guided by reason, they begin to separate important, indispensable things from those less important or unnecessary. This found its fruition in von Mohl's gradation of accomplishment of the respective life goals, as indicated below.[357]

So von Mohl defined the staying alive, mainly through preserving one's health, as the ultimate goal of human life. According to the scholar, this is the precondition for all other conditions. The second task should be reproduction,

352 Ibid, pp. 6–7.
353 Idem, Polizeiwiss.1.1844, p. 4.
354 Idem, *Encyklopädie der Staatswissenschaften*, Zweite Auflage. . ., p. 7.
355 Emphasizing rationalism is important in the context of the scholar's later statement that the rule of law is the result of a sufficiently high (rational) development of the population.
356 Ibid.
357 Ibid, p. 8.

which is the result of the need to maintain the species. The first goal that can be regarded as resulting from a rational nature, i.e. the appropriate moral and religious formation, appears no earlier, as third on this list. The fourth in the hierarchy of human goals was the development of science and mental development (as the main means to achieve other goals), and the fifth to develop a sense of aesthetics and good taste. However the ultimate, sixth goal of human life was to be its so-called "pleasant use," which the German thinker seemed to understand as the consequence of achieving all other goals. It should be remembered that von Mohl as a liberal thinker did not impose a specific order on the human individual to fulfill its life goals. On the one hand, he considered the order he presented to be corresponding with nature. It would therefore be unwise to oppose it. On the other hand, however, he allowed the individual to depart from the above order of goals.[358]

The subsequent discussed sphere of life is family.[359] The Württemberger defined it as "in fact only the multiplication of the individual 's strength"[360] and stated that it was "the first, simplest and most necessary union for human purposes."[361] This was due to the fact that a man living in isolation would never be able to achieve his goals of existence. And thus, for von Mohl, the family was a condition brought about by the nature of things, due to the need of human being (even at it lowest level of existence) for lasting relationships with other people.[362] The most important goal of the family, which for von Mohl meant the union of man and woman, was "the sexual community between its founders and the propagation of the human race."[363] Here we can see a clear focus on the reproductive function of the family. It is the most important for a scholar, but it does not occur alone. The family also serves to enable the person to live in an intimate sense of closeness and to achieve life goals together.[364] It is symptomatic of the

358 Ibid.

359 Remarks on the family of von Mohl: H. Schmitz, op. cit., p. 31. On the family in human life: E. Jarra, *Ogólna Teorja Prawa*, Warszawa 1922, pp. 79 – 81.

360 R. v. Mohl, Geschicht.u.Lit.1, p. 88.

361 Idem, *Encyklopädie der Staatswissenschaften*, Zweite Auflage . . ., p. 10.

362 Idem, *Encyklopädie der Staatswissenschaften*, Erste Auflage . . ., p. 11. Secondly, it should be noted that von Mohl did not agree with the view of Hobbes, Rousseau or Kant that there could once have been a "natural condition of man." More: comments by Adam Bosiacki: Idem, *Encyklopedia Umiejętności Politycznych*, t. 1 i 2, Warszawa 2003, p. 21.

363 Idem, *Encyklopädie der Staatswissenschaften*, Zweite Auflage . . ., p. 11.

364 Ibid., p. 11.

concept of family by von Mohl that the "permissible egoism" of individuals is moved to a higher level; the level of a family. Thus, every family in relations with other families is guided by egoism similar to the egoism of an individual and "turns to itself the whole outside world,"[365] considering itself to be at its centre. Due to the fact that the individuals participating in the family get rid of all their egoistic tendencies, either in whole, or at least a large part, the family is described by von Mohl as "the first and greatest school of morality."[366] As for the importance of the family for the institution of the state, according to Württemberger, both its spiritual and economic life were of great value to it.[367] Therefore, von Mohl granted the state the power to influence this sphere of life, e.g. through law. The Württemberger found an example of the proper influence of healthy family relations on the state in the situation in England at that time. In this country, "the moral foundations of family life are equally undoubtedly one of the main sources of strong civic sense and aptitude for establishing legal freedoms."[368] One of the negative examples was to be the family situation in the countries of the broadly understood east. The fact that there was polygamy and putting the man at the top of the family hierarchy was supposed to result, according to von Mohl, in the inclinations of these societies to absolute rule.[369]

The third most important sphere of human life, i.e. the tribe (*Stamm*),[370] was seen by von Mohl as:

> "A greater number of people and families of common descent, and therefore considering themselves related, who, due to common physiological features and history, share common customs."[371]

According to the German liberal, the tribe should be considered as an intermediate field between the individual, the family, and the more developed areas of human life. This sphere, derived from a common ancestor, is the result of the continuous and slow growth of one family, the establishment of their own families by the children of the original family. At that time, the tribe did not represent

365 Idem, Geschicht.u.Lit.1, p. 88.

366 Ibid, p. 12.

367 Ibid., p. 89.

368 Idem, *Encyklopädie der Staatswissenschaften*, Zweite Auflage . . ., p. 13.

369 Ibid., pp. 13–14. More about the understanding of law in Islamic culture: M. Sadowski, *Islam religia i prawo*, Warszawa 2017.

370 More about the tribe in von Mohl: H. Schmitz, op. cit., p. 31.

371 R. v. Mohl, *Gesellschafts-Wissenschaften und Staats-Wissenschaften*. . ., p. 28. The same definition appears in the *History and Literature of Sciences of State*: Idem, Geschicht.u.Lit.1, p. 89. On the tribe in von Mohl: E. Angermann, op. cit., p. 350.

much importance for von Mohl, due to the development of civilization and the emergence of nations as subjects of political processes. The tribe ceased to play an important role in the process of achieving human goals, but in von Mohl's assessment it formed a peculiar basis for the historical shaping of specific attitudes of individuals.[372]

Importantly, in the idea of von Mohl the tribe does not appear in a top-down fashion, but spontaneously, as a result of the need to pursue common interests. The basis of the tribe's sphere are therefore the historical and social processes. In view of the above, according to von Mohl, life of the tribe does not require to be taken into any specific organizational framework, because it is primarily psychological. For the German scholar, the most important feature of human tribal life is the community of origin, which generates a number of specific consequences. It concerns primarily the consequences of physical (similar appearance) and mental (similar views on specific issues) nature. It is these factors that are to lead to the gradual differentiation of a tribe from the others.[373]

For von Mohl, the tribe was also an entity that could be described as imperishable, which resulted from the constant inflow of its newborn members.[374] However, one must note the scholar's view that, in fact, the tribe "does not take a separate position in life."[375] This is because, on the one hand, the tribe is realized in its internal relations through the state (if it exists independently, then it will form a state at some point), or when mixing with other tribes it reveals itself as so-called "social moment" (*gesellschaftliches Moment*). Then, belonging to a larger whole, it builds a larger social circle, i.e. the society.[376] To conclude the analysis of the tribe, it should be noted that von Mohl did not identify the concept of that with race or nation.[377] Speaking of race he stated:

---

372 R. v. Mohl, *Encyklopädie der Staatswissenschaften*, Zweite Auflage . . ., pp. 17–18. The issue of relationships between the concept of tribe and nationality will be discussed later in the work.

373 Ibid, pp. 15–16.

374 Ibid, p. 16.

375 Idem, *Gesellschafts-Wissenschaften und Staats-Wissenschaften*. . ., p. 28.

376 Ibidem, p. 29. Moreover, von Mohl speaking of the tribe noticed that it could lead to a kind of grouping, intensive growth of "race properties," which would lead to the development of nationality as "diversity in the unity of mankind": Idem, *Encyklopädie der Staatswissenschaften*, Zweite Auflage . . ., p. 16.

377 Ibid, p. 18: "A tribe cannot be mixed with the concept of race or the concept of nationality."

> "The term race is understood as diverse, permanent varieties of the human kind that differ in their entire body structure, namely skin color, face angle, hair type, etc."[378]

According to the thinker, the race defined in this way may break up into larger numbers of tribes that will be divided among themselves despite having a common group of basic features. It should also be emphasized that the tribe itself can, according to von Mohl, arise from a merger of two different races.[379] As for the nation, which is "nothing other than the subject of the state"[380] for the Württemberger, it differed from the tribe in two ways. First of all, a single nation could consist of several, very different tribes. Secondly, the nation, according to von Mohl, was characterized by features other than tribal features, such as living in a common state.[381]

The next circle of human life resulting from the classification by von Mohl is the municipality (*Gemeinde*).[382] Comments relating to it are important because it is an entity frequently subject to complex relations with the state. In his earlier works (primarily the *History and Literature of Sciences of State*) von Mohl did not define it as a separate circle of human life, stating that it was only a creation, whose task was to fulfill the duties for the state. It can be concluded that he perceived the municipality in two distinct ways. First of all, as an administrative unit of the state, performing its tasks. Secondly, as a group of people representing common interests by reason of their residence.[383] When it comes to the very genesis of the municipality, according to the German scholar, it appeared among populations reaching a higher level of civilization. The municipality is created by people who feel the need to organize their lives in a given territory.[384]

Von Mohl referred to relations between the municipality and the state in one of his first works, that is, the *Constitutional Law of the Kingdom of Württemberg*. There he distinguished three types of relations between the state and the municipality. The first, the scholar named the "government system" (*Regierungssystem*), is characterized by the perception of municipalities by the state only as administrative units without any autonomy. Thus, the state here arbitrarily manages

378 Ibid.
379 Ibid.
380 Idem, Geschicht.u.Lit.1, p. 89. The issue of the nation is discussed below, in chapter three.
381 Idem, *Encyklopädie der Staatswissenschaften*, Zweite Auflage . . ., p. 18.
382 Remarks by Erich Angermann and Helmut Schmitz on the concept of municipality in Robert von Mohl: E. Angermann, op. cit., pp. 348–349, H. Schmitz, op. cit., p. 32.
383 R. v. Mohl, Geschicht.u.Lit.1, p. 89.
384 Idem, *Encyklopädie der Staatswissenschaften*, Zweite Auflage . . ., pp. 19–20.

municipal expenditure and income. At the other extreme is the so-called "system of independence" (*Selbstständigkeits-System*), where the state sees municipalities as independent entities, governing according to their own rules, and without any external supervision. Von Mohl also highlighted the intermediate type, where the state attempts to combine and soften the features of the first two systems. He based it on the state's respect for the independence of municipalities in managing local problems. However, the state also has the right to use the municipalities to pursue its own interests.[385]

As the analysis below demonstrates, it is this third path that the Württemberger opted for. On one hand, von Mohl understood the municipality as the lowest organizational unit in the country, also forming a unit of its administration. On the other hand, the municipality was a special kind of community for him. The scholar bestowed it with the right to create its own regulations, often having a significant impact on the lives of residents. What we notice in Württemberger's view is the opposition to perceiving the municipality solely as an administrative unit of the state. He respected the existence of municipalities also as a special kind of territorial communities, connecting their inhabitants on the basis of their shared interests.[386] The liberalism of the scholar finds its confirmation in the fact, that he did not perceive the autonomy of municipality as something negative, or a threat to the state. He was of the opinion that all the above-mentioned processes and characteristic features of municipalities are independent from state institutions, and thus stand outside its competencies. It can therefore be argued that the autonomy of the municipality from the state was not harmful to von Mohl due to the scope of tasks it should carry out. The tasks were described by the scientist as "facilitation of the daily life,"[387] which can be described as managing all mundane matters of life in a small, territorial community of people.

The last sphere discussed in this subsection will be the "unions of states" (*Staatenverbindungen*), or "higher state unions."[388] Von Mohl had a dual perception of these. Firstly, as federal states (*Bundestaaten*) or associations of states (*Staatenbunden*), and secondly as associations arising from international law relations.[389] The first statement by von Mohl referring to the sphere of unions of states was the opinion that the emergence of states as subjects of law and politics

385 Idem, Staatsr.Württem.2.1831, pp. 101–102.
386 Idem, Geschicht.u.Lit.1. . ., p. 95.
387 "*Erleichterung des täglichen Verkehres*": Ibid.
388 "*höhere staatliche Einheiten*."
389 R. v. Mohl, Geschicht.u.Lit.1, p. 89.

was not yet the *apex* of the civilizational development of humanity. Outside the sphere of the state, he noticed tasks exceeding the capabilities of a single state organization. There can be various reasons for this. First, it is the fact that some neighboring countries are not able to sufficiently support the implementation of specific life goals of their inhabitants. Therefore, for the scholar, one reason for the development of relations between states is the "insufficiency" (*Unzulänglichkeit*). The German scholar distinguished two types of responses to this weakness of states. It will be either the creation of federal states (*Bundestaaten*), which he defined like today's federal states, or the organization of associations of states, which are similar to today's international organizations.[390]

2.2. The concept of society in the thought of Robert von Mohl

2.2.1. Attitude to the contemporary understanding of society

As already demonstrated in the previous subsection in the concept of von Mohl the society (*Gesellschaft*) was one of the spheres (circles) of human life. The scholar noticed that the so-called "social question" (*Sozialerfrage*, *Gesellschaftsfrage*) had major implications for his understanding of the state.[391] This makes a more detailed discussion of the science of the sphere of society in a separate subsection highly justified. Such action is all the more justified because, as will be demonstrated in chapter five, von Mohl's concept of society is associated with the idea of a parliamentary system of representation.

The analysis of the concept of society and all that is associated with it in the thoughts of Robert von Mohl requires a brief presentation of the views of the German scholar on the achievements of past and contemporary authors. This will not only show that von Mohl was well acquainted with scientific literature, but also, by indicating the assessment of the concept of specific thinkers, he was able to signal the principles of his social thought.

It should be noted that von Mohl's had an overwhelmingly critical attitude towards both past and contemporary authors dealing with the concept of society.[392] The German scholar was of the opinion that past representatives of science understood the state's relations in two ways. On the one hand, they were only to analyze the position of the individual in the state and the relationships that it had as a participant in it. On the other hand, they focused on analyzing

390 Idem, *Encyklopädie der Staatswissenschaften*, Zweite Auflage . . ., pp. 41–44.
391 E. Angermann, op. cit., p. 329.
392 Idem, *Gesellschafts-Wissenschaften und Staats-Wissenschaften*. . ., p. 6.

power, as the most important factor in the state. Based on the aforementioned scientific fields, focusing on the state, the whole science about its objective, power, civic rights and the scope and essence of state organs was to be created.[393] The most important of the mistakes that the German scholar accused the contemporary science of was focusing only on concepts related to the objective of the state. These concepts were intended only to properly explain the processes of its creation and to indicate the best of its forms and institutions. As a consequence, representatives of the current doctrine were limiting their research on the state, on the one hand, to the issues of the individual and its rights and obligations towards it, and on the other, to dealing solely with the relations occurring in it, ignoring the broadly understood area of human life, or the society in the thought of von Mohl.[394]

In the thought von Mohl we observe the view that up to and including Kant's works, one cannot speak of treating the concept of society as an independent subject of research. So he took the position that it was impossible to find even a single work in subject literature that would capture the spheres of human life outside the scope of the state and try to explore them as a whole.[395] It was not until the end of the eighteenth and the beginning of the nineteenth century, and the events accompanying them, that a slow process of scientific dealing with society was initiated. Occasionally, letters began to appear describing the need and fact of social life of people (their territorial coexistence, the diversity of their characteristics, and the needs arising from this type of relationships).[396] However, this fact did not change the scholar's view that "(...) even Kant and his numerous and abundant successors in the law of nature, did not recognize social organisms, anywhere in their entire study of the legal purposes of the state and the theory of the social contract for its formation. Only individuals and the state are discussed by them."[397]

We can only partially agree with the above thesis formulated by the German scholar. It is impossible to ignore the fact that the set of facts, that we would today call people's social life, was the subject of considerations already in the times

---

393 Ibid, pp. 11–12.

394 Idem, Geschicht.u.Lit.1, p. 73.

395 Idem, *Gesellschafts-Wissenschaften und Staats-Wissenschaften. . .*, p. 15.

396 Von Mohl points here to individual works, e.g.: P. Ch. Reinhard, *Versuch einer Theorie der gesellschaftlichen Menschen*, Leipzig 1797, or F. Bucholz, *Hermes oder über die Natur der Gesellschaft*, Tübingen 1810. After: R. v. Mohl, Geschicht.u.Lit.1, p. 74.

397 Ibid, p. 77. Similarily: Idem, *Gesellschafts-Wissenschaften und Staats-Wissenschaften. . .*, p. 16.

of ancient Greeks.[398] One cannot fail to pay attention to the sociological reflection seen in Plato, Aristotle's discussion of *homo politicus*, or Saint Augustine, who based it on a social community of (Christian) values.[399] Also renaissance authors, like Jean Bodin, were familiar with references to the complicated community of people (society) subjected to absolute and sovereign power. It would also be a mistake to omit the social aspects of the works of Thomas Hobbes and John Locke.[400] There is no doubt, however, that it were the times of great, revolutionary changes and Enlightenment ideas in the eighteenth and nineteenth centuries, that constituted an impulse for a separate perception of society. However, as Jerzy Szacki notices, confirming in a way what von Mohl was talking about: "The pursuit of the Enlightenment thinkers to constitute the science of society did not lead to the creation of anything that could be called enlightenment sociology. One cannot speak of such sociology, because the learned reflection on society has not yet fully separated itself from philosophy, historiography, jurisprudence, political economy, literature and politics (…) ".[401] To sum up the assessment of the German scholar's view, it should be stated that it was not until the eighteenth and nineteenth centuries that a separate, scientific understanding of society was born. However, this does not change the fact that in the case of earlier authors, one can also see observation and reflection on the community existence of people.

In discussing the achievements of the precursors of the concept of society, von Mohl devodet particular criticism to Jean Jacques Rousseau, who in his opinion, as the author of the world famous *Social contract*, at the same time remained completely alien to ideas relating to the society. According to von Mohl, Rousseau, who focused on the theory of social contract, was the one who associated the creation of the state solely with the will of individuals. Rousseau's rights and obligations were to be based solely on a contract with individuals.[402] There is no doubt that in Rousseau's thought the main position is occupied by the concept of a social contract, consisting of a contract for the emergence of a political body (state), and the subsequent contract of submission to sovereignty. It would be wrong, however, to say that the notion of society does not exist at all

398 J. Szacki, *Historia myśli socjologicznej*, Warszawa 2002, p. 21.
399 Ibid, pp. 24–25, 27–33, 41.
400 Ibid, pp. 53–54, 66–69.
401 Ibid, p. 78.
402 Robert v. Mohl, Geschicht.u.Lit.1, p. 77.

in Rousseau's work.[403] Moreover, according to the author of *The Social Contract*, a person can only fully develop in society.[404] The interpretation problem that von Mohl may have suffered could be due to the fact that Rousseau comes to identifying the state with society (community).[405]

One of the earlier authors, whose notion of society was noteworthy for the Württemberg scholar, was August Ludwig von Schlözer.[406] Von Mohl even described him as a "brilliant man," who already in the eighteenth century was able to show the right way to perceive the issue of society.[407] It was in the Schlözer's concept of Metapolitics (*Metapolitik*) that von Mohl saw the origins of the concept of society.[408] He thought the very term Metapolitics was unfortunate, but believed that von Schlözer was surprisingly right believing in existence of the internal need for permanent "formation of people" (*Gestaltungen der Menschen*), focused around the common interests and needs of their members. According to von Mohl, Schölzer was a scholar, who was 60 years ahead of his time, contributing to the little popularity and even less understanding that his ideas enjoyed.[409]

In addition to assessing the perception of society in the past, von Mohl also analyzed the achievements of contemporary authors in this field. The most important and common achievement was to clearly recognize the existence of society as a subject different than, and even independent of the state.[410] As in the case of the assessment of authors from the past, von Mohl has clearly criticized his contemporaries. He stated that, despite good intentions and often having great abilities: "so far, special works on society have not led to a proper

403 J. Szacki, op. cit., p. 95. Cz. Porębski, *Umowa społeczna według Jana Jakuba Rousseau*, "Etyka" 22, 1966, p. 217.

404 J.J. Rousseau, *Umowa społeczna*, trans. A. Peretiatkowicz, Kęty 2002, p. 169. M. Baranowska, *Jana Jakuba Rousseau refleksa o naturze* człowieka, [in:] P. Fiktus, H. Malewski, M. Marszał (eds.), *"Rodzinna Europa": europejska myśl polityczno-prawna u progu XXI wieku*, Wrocław 2015, p. 169.

405 M. Baranowska, op. cit., p. 70.

406 More on this subject also in: A. L. v. Schlözer, *Allgemeines Staatsrecht und Staatsverfassungslehre*, Göttingen 1793, pp. 31 -78. More on August Ludwig von Schlözer: A. Wolff-Powęska, *Niemiecka myśl polityczna wieku oświecenia*, Poznań 1988, pp. 184 -188, J. Stagl, *A History of Curiosity The Theory of travel 1550–1800*, Abingdon 1995, pp. 244–269.

407 R. v. Mohl, Geschicht.u.Lit.1, p. 82.

408 Ibid. On this topic also: E. Angermann, op. cit., p. 331.

409 R. v. Mohl, Geschicht.u.Lit.1, p. 82.

410 Ibid, p. 77.

knowledge of its exact subject, and even more so to the formation of its recognized, proper and elaborated science."[411]

The authors of new studies on the problem of society were divided by scholar, who believed that they belonged to three different currents of thought. The first (exemplified by their greatest number) was planning the reconstruction of societies functioning among the peoples of Christian civilization, and setting itself the task of "designing and demanding plans for new real life organizations."[412] Von Mohl qualified to this group, first of all, the entire output of socialist and communist literature, which according to the scholar was giving science a great impulse to deal with social issues, but brought about false results.[413] According to von Mohl, socialist and communist thinking about property issues meant that the science of society emerging from it was falsified, which led him to the conclusion that observing society from the socialists' point of view "would never bring anything solid."[414]

To the second group of contemporary authors dealing with society, according to von Mohl included "historical writers and critics of socialist writings and plans."[415] Referring to their achievements, he noticed that in the process of criticizing leftist ideas, representatives of this group succeeded in creating their own social concepts. However, they also failed to avoid the error of perceiving the society from purely economic perspective. Von Mohl named Lorenz von Stein as the creator of this group, who in his understanding of society was not to go beyond the perception of it only through the prism of economic relations.[416]

It should be noted that von Stein's assessment by von Mohl was accurate. Speaking about society, Lorenz von Stein stated that individuals living in marriage and a family are forced to perform tasks appropriate not only for themselves but also for the these two. According to von Stein, the individual fulfills this task based on its own property, and in particular through work. It was property, an economic factor, that for Stein was the factor that "has the right to make the order of the community permanent, as the participation in a well-general

---

411 Ibid, p. 78. Similarly: Idem, *Gesellschafts-Wissenschaften und Staats-Wissenschaften...*, p. 19.

412 Idem, Geschicht.u.Lit.1, p. 78.

413 Ibid.

414 Ibid, p. 80.

415 R. v. Mohl, Geschicht.u.Lit.1, p. 80.

416 Ibid. Similarly: Idem, *Gesellschafts-Wissenschaften und Staats-Wissenschaften...*, p. 21. More about the concept of society by Lorenz von Stein: E. v. Philippovich, op. cit., p. 152–154, E. Grünfeld, *Lorenz von Stein und die Gesellschaftslehre*, Jena 1910.

process of life defines life tasks and, also in part, the views on the lives of individuals."[417] The above approach was supposed to lead von Stein to take a too narrow starting point, similar to that presented by leftist thought, and result in failure to discover the whole truth about the concept of society.[418] It should be noted, however, that one of von Stein's merits (of which von Mohl also spoke) was the recognition of the emergence of a new social class in the form of the proletariat, which he considered "perhaps the most important fact in the whole new life of the society."[419]

The third set of thinkers specified by the German scholar consisted of those, who in their study of relations of individuals with the state were to come to the conclusion that there is a form of human co-existence that is independent of the state, i.e. the society, and created their own philosophical systems related to it. However, according to von Mohl, the results of the work of this group of authors were not satisfactory, because they did not achieve the goal (which was the scientific study of the issue of society) in a comprehensive way.[420] Von Mohl included in this group primarily Georg Frierdrich Wilhelm Hegel, whom he assessed in two ways.[421] On one hand, he appreciated Hegel's introduction to the canon of the sciences of the very concept of society and the definition of it as a entity separated from the state. On the other hand, von Mohl disagreed with the Hegelian definition of society as a creation founded between individuality (family in case of Hegel) and the state, which is a group of families living next to each other and pursuing their goals mutually. According to von Mohl, Hegelian "civil society" (*bürgerliche Gesellschaft*), defined as "the multitude of families living side by side and serving each other in achieving their goals,"[422] it was not a real concept and, what is very important, was not an organism functioning outside the state.[423] For von Mohl, what Hegel called the society was in fact a system

417 L. v. Stein, *Der Socialismus und Kommunismus des heutigen Frankreichs*, Leipzig 1848, p. 23.

418 R. v. Mohl, Geschicht.u.Lit.1, p. 81.

419 L. v. Stein, *Der Socialismus und Kommunismus des heutigen Frankreichs*. . ., p. 47.

420 R. v. Mohl, Geschicht.u.Lit.1, pp. 78, 81.

421 Ibid, p. 82. More about society in Hegel: G. W. F. Hegel, *Grundlinien der Philosophie des Rechts, Naturrecht und Staatswissenschaft im Grundrisse*, Berlin 2017, pp. 147–186, R-P. Hortsmann, *Hegels Theorie der bürgerlichen Gesellschaft*, [in:] *G. W. F. Hegel: Grundlinien der Philosophie des Rechts*, L. Siep (ed.), Berlin/Boston 2017, pp. 189–208, P. S. Załęski, *Neoliberalizm i społeczeństwo obywatelskie*, Toruń 2012, pp. 49 – 59.

422 R. v. Mohl, *Gesellschafts-Wissenschaften und Staats-Wissenschaften*. . ., p. 18.

423 Idem, Geschicht.u.Lit.1, p. 82.

of yet underdeveloped and unjustified claims relating to the human community, the personification of which was called the state. According to von Mohl in a society understood in Hegelian terms there was constant mutual mixing in the relations of individuals, social relations and state institutions. In addition, the state was also deprived of its institutions and the goals that did not belong to it.[424]

According to von Mohl, Friedrich Julius Stahl also belonged to the third group,[425] whom, at least in the discussion of social issues, he believed to be "brilliant and prudent."[426] Stahl's teaching on the so-called "elements of the state" (*Elemente des Staates*), which were to comprise municipalities, estates and communities was of particular importance to von Mohl. For the Württemberger, the fact that these elements were governed, according to Stahl, by their own rules, rules that were different than those resulting from the state, was of great importance in this concept. However, according to von Mohl, Stahl could not to be completely right, for he only gave these elements a complementary function to the state, which was intended to dominate them.[427] Summing up Stahl's teaching, von Mohl stated: "Instead of admitting that the task of the state is to meet society's goals and improve its natural imperfections, he recognized the society as a sphere serving the state."[428]

According to von Mohl, Heinrich Ahrens and Italian Giuliano Ricci, were closest to the truth about "sciences of society."[429] For Ahrens, society was "the result of people's natural tendency to connect and associate."[430] Much like Aristotle, Ahrens believed that man is characterized by natural inclinations to social life, because man is the sole earthly being to feel that it cannot achieve his development without the help of other individuals.[431] Society was defined by Ahrens as "An association of a certain number of people who joined in a voluntary manner to achieve a preset, common goal by joining their activities."[432] Thus, the society was understood by Ahrens as a unified whole of all spheres of life serving the attainment of life goals.[433] The above belief resulted in the

---

424 Idem, *Gesellschafts-Wissenschaften und Staats-Wissenschaften...*, p. 18.
425 Idem, Geschicht.u.Lit.1, p. 85.
426 Ibid.
427 Ibid.
428 Ibid, p. 86.
429 More about society by Heinrich Ahrens: DF Lindenfeld, op. cit., p. 182.
430 H. Ahrens, *Das Naturrecht oder die Rechtsphilosophie nach dem gegenwärtigen Zustande dieser Wissenschaft in Deutschland*, Braunschweig 1846, p. 345.
431 Ibid.
432 Ibid, p. 346.
433 E. Grünfeld, op. cit., p. 193.

goal of society, which was “individual and social pursuit of the goals of people’s nature.”[434]

In his work entitled *Del Municipio considerato come unità elementare della città e della nazione italiana*[435] Giuliano Ricci held, in the opinion of von Mohl, an excellent discussion of relations between social circles in relation to human life and above all in relation to the state. Ricci listed seven such circles, which he called units (*unità*). These included family, tribe, caste, corporation, science, district and municipality. Mohl thought it was right that Ricci recognized independent and organized areas of human existence. At the same time he accused him that the spheres he distinguished did not belong to the same species. Therefore, the proper definition of the essence of social circles (and thus also society) cannot, according to von Mohl, be based on various entities, that are partially alien to each other. These entities were not considered by Ricci as an organic whole, and their essence was not opposed to the essence of the state or the human being - stated von Mohl.[436]

Summing up the research on the nature of society, the German scholar stated: “Thus, research on the concept of society has not, to this date, led to a sufficient result, nor did the wild plans of the socialists or the observations of critics following them; (...).”[437] It should be assumed that by performing such a thorough analysis of the perception of the issue of society, von Mohl proved not only great knowledge, but also tried to justify the need for this analysis by himself. Based on the criticism of the ideas of other thinkers referring to society, it is already possible to indicate the directions in which the German liberal will follow. He will perceive the society as, first and foremost, an equity that does not equate with both the state and the sphere of life of individuals. The principle of society was to be its separateness, it should be governed by its own rules, that are specific for it alone. Importantly, for von Mohl, the society could not be exclusively based on economic relations, on questions of ownership and property. The scholar will perceive them much more widely, trying to look at society through the prism of most of the reference points of human existence.

---

434 H. Ahrens, *Das Naturrecht oder die Rechtsphilosophie nach dem gegenwärtigen Zustande dieser Wissenschaft in Deutschland*. . ., p. 346.

435 G. Ricci, *Del Municipio considerato come unità elementare della città e della nazione italiana*, Livorno 1847.

436 R. v. Mohl, *Encyklopädie der Staatswissenschaften*, Erste Auflage . . ., p. 5.

437 Idem, Geschicht.u.Lit.1, p. 88. Idem, *Gesellschafts-Wissenschaften und Staats-Wissenschaften*. . ., p. 23.

2.2.2. The concept of society

In *History and Literature of Sciences of State*, analyzing the notion of society, von Mohl formulated the following view[438]:

> "Recently, it was clearly recognized that the community life of people in no way takes place exclusively in the state, and that between the sphere of a single personality and the organic unity of life of the nation [state-ed. aut], there is a certain number of spheres of life, which also aim at community subject, and which do not arise from the power of the state or with its help, and if they already exist in it, they are of utmost importance for its prosperity."[439]

In addition, the German scholar made a very interesting opinion regarding the condition that, at that time, prevailed in considerations about society:[440]

> "So the word society resounded. Some say it with deep concern, while others say it is a toxic threat; it serves as the key word for quarrels both in the stands of speakers and in the taverns; (...) In life and science its concept, special essence, need, present and future are revealed, bringing about a completely new state of consciousness, action and thinking. What was unclear at first, manifested itself as absurd, gains more and more of its property and natural rights, and is now ever better understood."[441]

It should be recognized that, using the above statements, von Mohl accurately conveyed the spirit of the modern age. He correctly recognized that the state is not the only sphere in which collective human relations function. He rightly noticed the emotions and peculiar ferment that overwhelmed Germany in the mid-nineteenth century, associated with the emergence of modern society on its territory.

As far as the definition of the sphere of society is concerned, first of all, von Mohl based his empirical thinking on the following:

> "As experience demonstrated, in all the more numerous and more civilized peoples, numerous homogeneous relations are formed, which result in the permanent formation of individual components of human population."[442]

---

438 On society in von Mohl's thought: F. Jonas, *Geschichte der Soziologie*, T. 2, Reinbek bei Hamburg 1968, pp. 117–119.

439 R. v. Mohl, Geschicht.u.Lit.1, p. 70.

440 More about the situation regarding social issues at the time: D. F. Lindenfeld, op. cit., pp. 180–181.

441 R. v. Mohl, *Gesellschafts-Wissenschaften und Staats-Wissenschaften. . .*, pp. 6–7.

442 Idem, *Encyklopädie der Staatswissenschaften*, Zweite Auflage . . ., p. 27.

According to von Mohl, the focal point of these relations between people was a definite, lasting and important interest, which made the individual people, who shared it, group and act to accomplish it. The effect of such relationships is not only the formation of common customs and "life views" (*Lebensansichten*), but also the emergence of more or less elaborated and aware social organisms. It should be noted that in von Mohl's assessment, these relationships between people had to arise naturally, based on shared relationships and interests, and they could never be enforced (for example, by the state). These social communities may be small, for example limited to a specific professional group in the respective territory. They can also form huge organizations to which von Mohl counted the great religions. Participation in these communities was not exclusive, that is, every person could participate in more or fewer such communities (as they might wish to pursue the realization of their various interests). Von Mohl called all these types of communities of interests operating in a given country the society.[443]

When talking about examples of such communities, one should pay attention to the then common interests, as von Mohl said, of "employment and possession relations."[444] Von Mohl as one of the first in contemporary Germany noticed and began to analyze the so-called "social issue," dealing with issues related to the emerging working class. He distinguished the communities, linked common position and interests, of employees, entrepreneurs, capitalists (owners of great property), as well as various types of breeders, tenants and farmers.[445] Focusing on the "population working in factories" (*fabrikarbeitenden Bevölkerung*)[446] von Mohl stated that this community of millions of people, often exceeding the borders of a single state, was able to develop a community of mode and similar life views and interests. It was also characterized by community in its position towards other social groups.[447] For the German scholar, the social group of factory workers appeared as a completely new element, independent of the laws of the state, and until then regulated in a superficial manner only.[448]

443 Ibid, pp. 27–28.

444 Idem, *Gesellschafts-Wissenschaften und Staats-Wissenschaften...*, p. 40.

445 Idem, Geschicht.u.Lit.1, p. 96.

446 Erich Angermann put forward the correct thesis that it was von Mohl's dealing with workers' problems that enabled him to see the creation of society: E. Angermann, op. cit., p. 329.

447 R. v. Mohl, *Gesellschafts-Wissenschaften und Staats-Wissenschaften...*, p. 40.

448 Geschicht.u.Lit.1, p. 96. Mohl elaborated extensively on the labor issue (*Arbeiterfrage*) in *Constitutional Law, International law, and Politics*: Idem, SVuP.3.2., pp. 509–604.

We find the evidence that von Mohl was a scholar partly rooted in the time of absolutism as he has distinguished the estate of the realm communities as part of the society.[449] According to the German scholar the examples of communities of estate included: aristocracy, clergy, middle class and peasantry, but also the caste systems of ancient India. However, the evolution of his views is evidenced by the fact that in later works (primarily in the *Encyclopedia of Sciences of State*) he gave up the use of the term "estate" (*Stand*) in favor of the concept of "social circle." Thus, one can see the departure of von Mohl from the conceptual apparatus embedded in the eighteenth century in favor of the new, nineteenth-century terms. This seems to be justified due to the slow departure of societies from the estates of the realm system.[450]

The von Mohl's concept referring to social circles is further characterized by the freedom of their creation. The scholar has left space for the activities of free individuals, who can merge on the basis of faith in the same religion, or education. In fact, it was not important for von Mohl to enumerate all possible interest groups. However, it was more important to find the principles that accompany the formation of social communities.[451] These rules, which prove a formal approach to the issue of society, form the key to its perception by von Mohl.

Rules and factors that influence the creation of social communities are mentioned for the first time in the article *Sciences of Society and Sciences of State*. The factors that, based on his life experience, von Mohl found to be crucial in the creation of social communities will be: living together and living next to each other, the formation of elites, for example in the form of nobility, the similarity of work performed and property relations.[452] It should be noted, however, that von Mohl's definition of the above features was dynamic in its nature. Already in his *History and Literature of Sciences of State* he emphasized that social relations must first of all be characterized by their durability, wide range and momentous significance. However, the most important factor raised by von Mohl seems to be the common interest. What should distinguish social communities of interest from the state should be the lack of their formal organization and the fact that being part of one community cannot limit participation in another.[453]

On this topic also: E. Pankoke, *Sociale Bewegung - Sociale Frage - Sociale Politik Grundfragen der deutschen "Socialwissenschaft" im 19. Jahrhundert*, Stuttgart 1970.

449 R. v. Mohl, Geschicht.u.Lit.1, p. 94.

450 E. Angermann, op. cit., p. 348.

451 R. v. Mohl, Geschicht.u.Lit.1, p. 97.

452 Idem, *Gesellschafts-Wissenschaften und Staats-Wissenschaften...*, p. 50.

453 Idem, Geschicht.u.Lit.1, pp. 97–98.

The broadest and most complete explanation of the factors underlying social communities can be found in the *Encyclopedia of Sciences of State*. For von Mohl, the first factor with significance for the creation of social communities was the "community of nationality and language" (*Gemeinschaft der Nationalität und der Sprache*). It was important for creating a sense of community between the specific tribes, and even races. It creates a sense of separateness from other groups. The result of the interaction of the community of nationality and language is "spatial separation" and the resulting creation of different needs and customs.[454]

Another determinant of the creation of social communities of interest was "common descent from historically distinguished or legally privileged families" (*Die gemeinschaftliche Abstammung von geschichtlich ausgezeichneten oder rechtlich bevorzugten Familien*). According to the Württemberger, a social circle based on this principle may be the result of sheer pride related to the common origin of its members, but these members may also be strongly connected to preserve certain privileges belonging to them by reason of their birth. Such social circles may cover the territories of many countries, as long as there are reasons for that, of both historical and legal nature. Communities based on this principle feel their strong separation from the lower strata and are united by their common customs. To some extent, they are also connected by a community of similar activities undertaken, or, finally, kinship. One cannot forget about the most important factor in the Mohl's concept of society, namely the community of interests.[455]

Another reason for the creation of social communities is "joint personal meaning" *(die gemeinschaftliche persönliche Bedeutung)*. According to von Mohl, social communities based on this principle were communities of people of a similar social position. They will be, for example, members of the political elite, united by similar education, significant wealth and position in the state (importantly, the scholar did not require noble birth here). They present a community of interests and positions, in particular in their relations with the masses. The English gentry served von Mohl as an example of such a social circle.[456]

The fourth factor was the "equal occupation" (*Gleiche Beschäftigung*).[457] Castes in India or Ancient Egypt were perceived by von Mohl as the historical examples of "communities of employment." Von Mohl also defined the bourgeoisie,

---

454 Idem, *Encyklopädie der Staatswissenschaften*, Erste Auflage . . .,pp. 20–21.
455 R. v. Mohl, *Encyklopädie der Staatswissenschaften*, Zweite Auflage . . ., p. 29.
456 Ibid, pp. 29–30.
457 Ibid, p. 30.

peasants, factory owners, and merchants, as circles of common employment, albeit with looser relationships. For the German thinker the fact of common employment formed a reason for the creation of common customs and life attitudes. People functioning in similar employment were to notice that their prosperity depends on similar factors, which led to the creation of a strong community of interests between them.[458]

"Joint relations of ownership and acquisition" (*Gemeinschaftliche Verhältnisse des Besitzes und Erwerbes*) are extremely important for the creation of a community of interests, and thus also a social community. This factor was understood by von Mohl in two ways. First of all, it is a community of "magnitude of ownership." Individual property classes (the affluent, the middle class, and the poor) have always produced completely separate groups, often hostile towards each other. The magnitude of possession and the resulting inequalities between individual groups were usually to result in diversity in adopting life attitudes and formulating various claims directed to the community.[459] As with previous factors, the impact of similar ownership creates a sense of solidarity between members and fosters the appearance of a specific interest. Type of possession, which von Mohl understood primarily by the ownership of real estate and movable property, was another significant factor. The scholar was of the opinion that ownership of real estate contributes to the development of a tendency towards stability and aversion to political change in the owners. On the other hand, movable property (first of all the monetary capital) was, for von Mohl, a catalyst for "cosmopolitanism," continuous movement and undertaking new initiatives.[460]

The sixth factor is the "community of religion" (*Die Gemeinschaft der Religion*). Von Mohl stated: "shared faith and worship is the most significant interest for most people."[461] On the other hand, the very nature of religion has a great impact not only on spiritual matters, but also on the economic situation. In addition, for the Württemberger, community of religion and nationality were the natural conditions because: "A relationship that corresponds to nature is when, in at least one nation with a substantially equal level of civilization, everyone belongs to the same religion."[462]

458 Ibid.
459 Ibid, p. 30–31.
460 Ibid, p. 32.
461 Ibid.
462 Ibid.

Given the purpose of this publication, it seems highly justified to discuss the relationship between society and the state in the thought of Robert von Mohl. The most important difference between the state and society (consisting of a large number of communities of interest) is therefore the scope of the goal they set themselves to achieve. The state that von Mohl describes as "the realization of the idea of the unification of the nation" (*Verwirklichung des Einheitsgedankens im Volke*), manifests itself not only through its authority and its institutions, but also through various activities aimed at helping to achieve various goals, as seen through the prism of the state.[463] Social communities, on the other hand, always have the task of achieving only the fragmentary goal that is characteristic to them. In addition, social communities are independent of the will of the state and are based on natural relationships between the people. In von Mohl's view, even the smallest state institution must always be conditioned by the actions of the state authority defining the rights, subject and scope of its activities.[464] The scholar's liberalism is further proved by his conviction that every capable society, not just the state, has the right to organize itself. However, one cannot forget that according to von Mohl the state still holds a superior position in relation to social structures. This is because he granted it the right and obligation to influence those social communities, whose activities are incompatible with the interests of the majority, as well as with recognized private interests. Therefore, the state has the right to oppose and stop the development of such social initiatives that would threaten the legal order and stability of the community. Moreover, the state also has the right to use certain communities to pursue its own goals.[465] As David Lindenfeld rightly points out, what distinguished the state from society by von Mohl was the fact that the state was to ensure the unity of diverse individualities and collectivities, while the society was simply a collection of a larger number of communities.[466]

The assessment of Mohl's social doctrine forms a difficult task, due to its ambiguity. It should be noted that the development of von Mohl's social concept proves the scholar's gradual shift towards social liberalism. The first works by von Mohl devoted little or no space to society.[467] His initial work, therefore, does not clearly focus on the concept of society and the study of its independence from

463 Idem, Geschicht.u.Lit.1, pp. 99–100.
464 Ibid, p. 100.
465 Ibid. Idem, *Gesellschafts-Wissenschaften und Staats-Wissenschaften*. . .,. pp. 47–49.
466 D. F. Lindenfeld, op. cit., p. 182.
467 E. Angermann, op. cit., p. 334.

the state. It was partly the result of von Mohl's identification with the liberal, atomistic perception of the state, which led him to adopt the vision of society as a more or less systematized sum of the citizens of the respective state.[468] However, the later achievements of von Mohl on social issues are assessed by German (and even Polish) science as significant for the definition of this concept. Von Mohl, perceiving society as a field located between the individual and the state,[469] is considered by Hans Freyer (along with Lorenz von Stein and Heinrich Riehl) to be one of the most important representatives of German sociology of the nineteenth century.[470] On the other hand, Zygmunt Balicki stated: "It was only Lorenz Stein, Robert v. Mohl, Rudolf Gneist, and especially Wilhelm Riehl, who created the concept of society and even a separate *Gesellschaftswissenschaft*."[471] Eckart Pankoke considers the *Sciences of Society and Sciences of State* article as groundbreaking for the history of social sciences in Germany. Therefore, von Mohl's merit was undoubtedly the "discovery" of the concept of society, as a sphere located between the sphere of the individual and the state, and in principle functioning independently of both of them.[472] Much like Ahrens (linked to him by use of the theory of social circles) and von Stein (with whom he shares his interest in the source of social life), von Mohl should be considered as one of those, who contributed to the dissemination of knowledge about society as an area outside the sphere of the individual as well as the sphere of the state.[473] Relations between society and the state, indicating the supremacy of the state, but also its subsidiary actions are also extremely important.

It should be added, however, that the idea of Robert von Mohl's society is characterized by many ambiguities and inconsistencies. This is due to the fact that he was a precursor, constantly seeking for the right shape of the concept of society. There are many indications that von Mohl was not entirely sure of his

---

468 Ibid. The atomistic concept, which distinguished only the state on the one hand, and on the other hand the individual was so deeply rooted in German philosophy (e.g. by Kant or Fichte) that the nineteenth-century ideas proclaiming the existence between the above spheres of other independent circles were gaining a scale of a scientific discovery: E. v. Philipovich, op. cit., p. 157.

469 E. R. Huber, op. cit., p. 10.

470 H. Freyer, *Gegenwartsaufgaben der Deutschen Soziologie*, "Zeitschrift für die gesamte Staatswissenschaft / Journal of Institutional and Theoretical Economics" Bd. 95, H.1 (1935), p. 117.

471 Z. Balicki, *Metody Nauk Społecznych i ich rozwój w XIX stuleciu*, Warszawa 1903, p. 27.

472 E. Pankoke, op. cit., p. 120.

473 E. Grünfeld, op. cit., p. 191.

views. This is evidenced, e.g., by the specific terminological inconsistency. He described society as "a component of the common life of humans"*(Bestandtheil des menschlichen Zusammenlebens)*, "one of the common human formations" (*eine der allgemienen menschlichen Lebengestaltungen*), or simply "the circle of life" (*Lebenskreis*). All these phrases are very abstract, and seem to be artificial, which suggests that von Mohl himself was not sure about the precise definition of the society as such.[474] The abovementioned instability of the rules defining social communities, or the initial inclusion of the municipality in them, and its subsequent separation, also point to instability in von Mohl's social doctrine. One cannot resist the impression that von Mohl perceived (in contrast to Ahrens) the society in a narrow manner, excluding, for example, the family and assuming certain set of factors leading to its creation. It is also worth paying attention to the lack of identity between the concepts of society and tribe in von Mohl. His tribe was a community of people based strongly on common descent. Kinship, but also the similarity of physiological features and historical experiences were the central binders of tribal communities. However, the main catalyst for creating social groups was the community of interests. This may have resulted from common descent, but it was not a factor considered necessary.

From the point of view of sociology, von Mohl should be assessed as a precursor and a thinker standing between epochs. Erich Angermann rightly included him among those who, among the emerging "sciences of society," were just laying the foundations for new theories rather than elaborating their final form.[475] Undoubtedly, it is important to remind that von Mohl's state will be a sphere separated from the society (albeit supposed to support it). Society and the concept of common interest will also play important roles in von Mohl's teaching on the representation system.

2.2.3. The system of "sciences of society"

The analysis of the system of "sciences of society" (*Gesellschaftswissenschaften*)[476] found in the thought of Robert von Mohl is, for the purposes of the present

474 E. Angermann, op. cit., p. 365.

475 Ibid, p. 368.

476 More about von Mohl's development of the system of sciences of society: K. Lichtblau, *Die Stellung der Soziologie innerhalb der geistes- und sozialwissenschaftlichen Disziplinen*, "Soziologie" 2010, nr 39, z. 3, p. 283, Idem, *Zwischen Klassik und Moderne Die Modernität der klassischen deutschen Soziologie*, Wiesbaden 2017, pp. 10–11, H. L. Stoltenberg, *Kurzer Abriß einer Geschichte der deutschen Soziologie*,

publication, significant in three different ways. First of all, its discussion will form one of the proofs of demonstrating the predisposition, which is particularly present in case of von Mohl, to systematize the discussed matter. Secondly, its presentation will complete the picture of the concept of society, as discussed above. Thirdly, the presentation of the sciences of society system and its brief description will form a good starting point for the analysis of the system of sciences of state, as performed in the subsequent chapter.[477]

For a thinker guided by empiricism in his research, observing facts and drawing conclusions from them, the derivation of a separate system of sciences of society appeared to be the logical and necessary consequence of the emergence of the very concept of society in science. The German scientist set himself the goal of defining scientific disciplines relating to the essence of society, its formation and development, and the laws to which it was subjected. Von Mohl wanted the scientific approach to society to be separated from other fields of science, dealing with the analysis of other relationships of human life together, and to be perceived from every point of view of interpersonal relations.[478] Similarly to the concept of society itself, in relation to the development of the system of sciences of society one can observe scholar's contestation of previous achievements, which were not to lead to any positive effect. He also took the view that only once the society and its issues were presented as one whole, with all its relations and properties, would its major significance for humanity be revealed. Describing the society in a scientific way also had another purpose for von Mohl. Namely, it was to provide tools for proper understanding of contemporary social issues and their swift resolution.[479] The scholar was aware that the introduction of a completely new scientific discipline would destroy the current perception of this problem. However, he was characterized by determination and a focus on

---

"Weltwirtschaftliches Archiv" 1930, t. 32, p. 62. Duk-Yung Kim, *Georg Simmel und Max Weber*, Wiesbaden 2002, pp. 41–42

477 This is due to the fact that (as will be demonstrated), the Mohlian concept of sciences of society is based on the sciences of state developed by von Mohl earlier (it should be noted that Erich Angermann was very critical of the above): E. Angermann, op. cit., pp. 365–366.

478 R. v. Mohl, *Gesellschafts-Wissenschaften und Staats-Wissenschaften. . .*, p. 52.

479 Ibid, p. 53. Von Mohl did not explicitly specify what these dangers are, but the earlier analysis of his achievements in the field of labor and social issues allows us to conclude that this concerns the dangers arising from the flaws of the industrial system and the formation of the proletariat.

the goal which, as noted before, was the scientific description of society in all aspects.[480]

Moreover, the separation of sciences of society was also to have a positive effect in relation to the sciences that study the human individual, as well as in relation to the sciences related to the state. The scientist, who at that time was valued for his ability to clearly define the examined matter, wanted to give a real dimension to the objective scope of sciences of state and sciences of society. In his opinion, giving them a scope that corresponds to reality would not only make them more transparent, but would allow countries to be managed more rationally. The separation of sciences of society was therefore to bring particularly significant effects on the scope of sciences dealing with the state. These effects were to be twofold. First of all, the natural consequence was to deprive the system of sciences of state of entire great disciplines and to transfer them to the system of sciences of society. Secondly, the material scope of sciences of state already developed was also to change.[481]

The ideas presented above guided von Mohl seeking a systematic and separate development of sciences of society.[482] However, the course of action selected by the German scientist was also characterized by a set of methodological assumptions. The first of them assumed that "also society can be understood and scientifically described on the basis of holistic, diverse points of view, from which relations of people's common life can be observed at all."[483] However, the second methodological assumption was that the development of sciences of society is allowed on the basis of two methods: the so called organic one; "which, in the order of the relevant system, discusses the individual points always comprehensively according to the above relations [of the community life of people: ed. aut.], and as a result describes them scientifically, one by one."[484] And the method of "externally and logically ordered comparison, into an exhausted whole, of disciplines resulting from established viewpoints."[485] Von Mohl decided to opt for the latter method. Based on the above methodological assumptions, the German

480 Ibid.

481 Ibid, p. 65.

482 More on the issue of separating sciences of society from sciences of state: H. Peukert, *Das Tradierte Konzept Der Staatswissenschaft*, Berlin 2005, pp. 32–38.

483 R. v. Mohl, *Gesellschafts-Wissenschaften und Staats-Wissenschaften...*, p. 55.

484 Ibid, pp. 55–56.

485 Ibid, p. 56.

scientist presented his original scheme for the division of sciences of society, which he defined as comprehensive and externally ordered.[486]

Dogmatic sciences of society

General sciences of society
Science of social law
  Philosophical social law
  Positive social law

Social ethics
  Philosophical social ethics
  Applicable, i.e. religious social ethics

Social Policy

Historical sciences of society

History of society and its circles
Society statistics

Due to the subject of this work, which focuses on the understanding of the state by Robert von Mohl, the description of the respective sciences of society will be presented in a summary form, with the purpose of preparing the basis for the analysis of his system of sciences of state.[487]

---

486 Ibid. It should be noted that the aforementioned Lorenz von Stein understood sciences of society differently than von Mohl. He wrote about it in the following way: "It is possible to research every system of interests in a clear, complete and systematic manner; and this knowledge built on the concept of society and developed by its principle is nothing but the first field of sciences of society. It, and nothing else, is the foundation of this science, which is destined to absorb all fields of the so called sciences of state shortly": L. v. Stein, *Geschichte der Sozialen Bewegung in Frankreich von 1789 bis auf unsere Tage*, 1 Bd., Leipzig 1850, p. XLII. It should be remembered, however, that in his work entitled *System der Staatswissenschaft* Lorenz von Stein changed his approach and made sciences of society the second part of the broadly understood study of the state: "The second part of the study of the state is the study of society." More on that: Idem, *System der Staatswissenschaft*, 1 Bd., Stuttgart und Tübingen, 1852, pp. 21 -22, E. Angermann, op. cit., p. 366, E. R. Huber, op. cit., pp. 8–10.

487 This pattern appears in von Mohl in the *Encyclopedia of Sciences of State*: R. v. Mohl, *Encyklopädie der Staatswissenschaften*, Erste Auflage . . ., p. 45, Idem, *Encyklopädie der Staatswissenschaften*, Zweite Auflage . . ., pp. 50–51. A similar pattern, but treating general sciences of society separately (not as dogmatic science) is presented in the article *Sciences of Society and Sciences of State*: Idem, *Gesellschafts-Wissenschaften und*

It is not difficult to notice that the first division used by von Mohl was a division into sciences related to the dogmatics of the subject, as well as sciences related to its history and the presentation of specific facts (statistics). The first of the dogmatic sciences was the "general sciences of society," perceived by the scholar as a discipline with the task of introducing the subject under consideration.[488] The very need to distinguish general science, similarly as in case of sciences of state, resulted from the methodological assumption that each scientific concept needs "to build a general science about the essence, purpose and limits of the phenomenon." Therefore, von Mohl wanted to build a general enough base to make it a proper introduction for the more elaborate considerations.[489]

As far the both approaches to the science of social law (the philosophical and positive) are considered, they should, according to von Mohl, be developed in three directions. First, towards the internal relations of society, i.e. the relationship between individual social circles, and the relationship of those circles with their members. Secondly, the legal relations of society in relation to individuals foreign to it. Thirdly, legal relations of the society with the state. The science of social law was understood by von Mohl as a science dealing with the comprehensive presentation of all legal relations to which a particular, individual social circle is subject. In his opinion, this gave rise to the need for, e.g. for "law of estates" (*Recht der Stände*), "church law" (*Recht der Kirchen*) or "municipal law" (*Recht der Gemeinden*).[490]

The thinker drew attention to the large significance of isolating the aforesaid fields for the entire systematics of legal sciences. He was aware that it could not lead to a situation in which there would be double regulations (public and private law) referring to the same entity (the same social sphere). However, all formal doubts concerning the doubling of regulations were to disappear with the process of recognizing society as a separate entity, not including the state or the individual.[491] Can this view be considered correct? Surely not. It seems that

---

Staats-Wissenschaften. . ., pp. 56 – 57, Idem, Geschicht.u.Lit.1, pp. 103–104. More on this topic: M. Stolleis, op. cit., p. 174, E.R. Huber, op. cit., pp. 11–12.

488 R. v. Mohl, *Gesellschafts-Wissenschaften und Staats-Wissenschaften*. . ., p. 56, Idem, *Encyklopädie der Staatswissenschaften*, Zweite Auflage . . ., p. 51.

489 Idem, *Gesellschafts-Wissenschaften und Staats-Wissenschaften*. . ., p. 58. A similar methodological assumption will be formulated in relation to the "general theory of the state" (*Allgemeine Staatslehre*).

490 Ibid, pp. 56, 59, Idem, *Encyklopädie der Staatswissenschaften*, Zweite Auflage . . ., p. 51.

491 An example was the church law. More: Idem, *Gesellschafts-Wissenschaften und Staats-Wissenschaften*. . ., p. 60.

it is based on an overly general assumption about the emergence of a separate sphere of society, and its effects on the systematics of the discussed field of science. Therefore, the researcher may get the impression that von Mohl has made a copy of his division of sciences of state and transferred it, without reflecting on that, to the realm of sciences of society.

Referring to the field of social ethics, he drew attention primarily to its specific spread to other scientific fields, and the use it made of them. First of all, it is about (desirable according to von Mohl) absorption of religious morality. The German liberal was of the opinion that it was impossible to examine society completely, without discussing it from a religious point of view. Von Mohl also stated that the religious analysis of society should be accompanied by the moral (philosophical) analysis. In other words, he sought to combine these two sources into one whole, based on religious, but also philosophical and moral principles.[492]

The separation of another scope, i.e. social policy,[493] which was to take over the entire large branch of political economy (*Nationalökonomie)* was for von Mohl an extremely momentous event, and the purpose of it did not require justification. This science was to study the means to achieve the goals of a particular social circle.[494] Similarly, as in the case of politics perceived from the perspective of the state, it was based on the assumption that "every human relationship can, and must, be understood also from the point of view of prudence and purposefulness."[495] Therefore, it was very important to examine the ways, in which specific social circles come to reach their goals.

According to the Württemberger, the "historical sciences of society" i.e. history and statistics of society, also did not require any proof of justification. What is characteristic for von Mohl's thought is the separation of these disciplines as referring to facts. Their goal was to obtain complete knowledge about society as a separate entity disconnected from the sphere of the state.[496]

The above concept of the systematics of sciences of society (similarly to the concept of society discussed earlier) met with criticism of contemporary science. The most famous and vivid example of this was the polemic of the Prussian scholar and politician Heinrich von Treitschke. The presentation of his different

492 Ibid, p. 61.
493 Von Mohl developed his views on social policy in the work *Constitutional Law, International law, and Politics*: Idem, SVuP.3.2, pp. 475–656.
494 Idem, *Gesellschafts-Wissenschaften und Staats-Wissenschaften...*, p. 56. On the issue of social policy in von Mohl: E. v. Philipovich, op. cit., p. 156.
495 R. v. Mohl, *Gesellschafts-Wissenschaften und Staats-Wissenschaften...*, p. 62.
496 Ibid, p. 65.

views will allow us to highlight the characteristics of von Mohl's approach to social but also to state issues.[497] Von Treitschke, standing on the ground of the Hegelian tradition of accepting the identity of the concepts of state and society,[498] opposed von Mohl's ideas, calling for the separation of sciences of society from the area of science relating to the state.[499] It should be noted, however, that the above-mentioned opposition did not mean that von Treitschke completely rejected the need to examine social issues in general. He believed that they should be analyzed on the basis of the correctly understood science of the state.[500] Referring to the system of sciences of society according to Robert von Mohl, his main opponent stated: "a brief look at the system of sciences designed by von Mohl demonstrates that it is unsustainable."[501]

Von Treitschke, while assessing individual elements of the Mohl system, focused primarily on the criticism of the concept of separate social law, which in his opinion should form part of the constitutional law. One should agree with von Treitschke, who draws attention to the enigmatic nature of von Mohl's statement in relation to social law. Furthermore, in his view, social law had to be ordered and supervised by the state, as was the case with private law.[502] Society (consisting of circles with different, often conflicting interests) cannot be regulated by legal relations between particular social groups.[503] At this point, we need a state with its uniform force, as well as universal aspirations. Therefore, von Treitschke represented the position that the state must regulate relations between particular groups within the society.[504]

---

497 More: E. Angermann, op. cit., pp. 380–382, M. Reif, *Public Sociology? Nicht mit uns!*, [in:] *2015: Routinen der Krise - Krise der Routinen. Verhandlungen des 37. Kongresses der Deutschen Gesellschaft für Soziologie in Trier 2014*, S. Lessenich (ed.), p. 1684. On von Treitschke's views on the vision of von Mohl: H. Tyrell, *History and sociology - the First Century From Ranke to Weber*, "Inter Disciplines. Journal of History and Sociology," Vol. 1, No.1 (2010), pp. 105–106.

498 K. v. Beyme, *Politische Theorien im Zeitalter der Ideologien 1789–1945,* Wiesbaden 2002, p. 194.

499 E. N. Megay, *Treitschke Reconsidered: The Hegelian Tradition of German Liberalism*, "Midwest Journal of Political Science," Vol. 2, No. 3 (Aug., 1958), p. 308.

500 Von Treitschke noted: "Is it impossible to present all these social circles in a scientific discipline? No, (. . .)": H. v. Treitschke, *Die Gesellschaftswissenschaft ein kritischer Versuch*, Leipzig 1859, p. 71. E. Angermann, op. cit., p. 380.

501 H. v. Treitschke, op. cit., p. 68.

502 Ibid.

503 Von Treitschke pointed out: "(...) no law arises from the existence of mutually opposite, alien and independent interests": Ibid.

504 Ibid.

In his science of social morality, von Treitschke attributed a large role to religious institutions and churches,[505] which were to take care of annihilating sin in those places where it occurs. The role of the state is to recognize these efforts, but only if they do not violate the legal order.[506] The social policy in Mohl's understanding was also unacceptable for von Treitschke. The von Mohl opponent believed that the assumption that "every social circle pursues different tasks"[507]; cannot be reconciled with von Mohl's understanding of politics as "science of achieving goals." An example was to be the Catholic Church's behaviour in relation to various estates, which "serves only church purposes, it is the policy of the Church, and not the society."[508] In concluding his argument on social history, von Treitschke said: "If we want to show more than just an external, mutual sequence of different things, the most important thing is to show the mutual interaction of social circles on the state."[509]

According to Heinrich von Treitschke, there were only two possibilities for scientific description of society and its circles. The first option was to rely on the spirit of the nation by demonstrating how it manifests itself in the life of the state. The easiest way to achieve this was to describe the facts. It should be emphasized that von Treitschke always set the state as the focal point of this process, as a base for the actions of the nation, which he identified with the notion of society. According to von Treitschke, the second way to describe social relations was to demonstrate how often the divergent efforts of a particular nation require a unifying ordering entity (state), contribute to its creation, are regulated and react to it. The idea of this scholar was based on a strong connection between the state and the national factor. According to him, it was not possible to describe nation and state separately.[510] Therefore, if the nation is to achieve its goals through the state, it is not possible to separate its scientific analysis from the analysis of the state.

We find the reply of von Mohl to the views of von Treitschke in the second edition of the *Encyclopedia of Sciences of State*, where he assessed his visions as "a great misunderstanding."[511] Responding to criticism, von Mohl put forward the view that it was not his goal to entirely separate the society from the state.

505 Also von Mohl drew attention to the religious aspect of this teaching.
506 Ibid, p. 69.
507 Ibid.
508 Ibid.
509 Ibid.
510 Ibid, pp. 71, 72.
511 R. v. Mohl, *Encyklopädie der Staatswissenschaften*, Zweite Auflage . . ., p. 51.

He was only interested in recognizing that the concepts of state and society are not synonymous, and thus give the society an independent scientific dimension. Justifying his thesis, von Mohl cited, for example, "long since scientifically described" circles of an individual and family, "which can be applied by any other science."[512]

Referring to the effects of separation of sciences of society from sciences of state, he once again voiced the need to give the right scope to the sciences of the state. The way to achieve that, was to separate the sciences of society from it. In von Mohl one can also find disagreement with the methods of scientific presentation of society presented by von Treitschke. He criticized, above all, the failure to present it from a dogmatic point of view, which in his opinion was to result in an incomplete presentation of the issue of society. The objection against inclusion of the sciences relating to the society in the state sciences also does not come as a surprise.[513]

The objection of selective treatment of the matter of society should also be raised. Von Mohl, whose methodological assumption was always to cover the entire subject (whether state or society) criticized the approach of von Treitschke. He stated: "Nobody thinks about including all geography or all statistics in sciences of state, which, after all, have a diverse impact on their results, and for the same reason one does not think about including all private law in them."[514] According to von Mohl, sciences of society should not be treated differently. In addition, von Mohl rightly pointed out that "the description of a society solely from a state perspective, even if its scope was correctly defined, would be unilateral and incomplete."[515] Württemberger's reply ends with the following sentence: "Whoever does not deny the idea and fact of the existence of society, must recognize and demand its proper scientific description."[516]

Without focusing on who was right in the above dispute, it must be stated that both von Treitschke and von Mohl did not avoid mistakes. History proved that von Treitschke's wrong assumption was the postulate of the state absorbing all sciences of society. Still, already at the end of the nineteenth century, Georg von Mayr will oppose von Mohl's view of the separate perception of the state and society. He will support the view of von Treitschke stating that the state and

512 Ibid.
513 Ibid, p. 52.
514 Ibid.
515 Ibid.
516 Ibid.

society are not opposing concepts. He will consider the society as something general, that encompasses all kinds of human socialization, including a strong and formal state that is stable in its organization.[517]

The Mohl's concept of the sciences of society system also received unfavorable assessments in the eyes of modern science. Erich Angermann stated that the concept of sciences of society by the German liberal did not lead to modern sociology, perceived in the narrow sense as a special science about all interpersonal relations. It also did not go in the direction of social sciences in today's meaning, as a limited whole consisting of individual disciplines devoted to the common life of people.[518]

It is impossible not to notice (especially after getting acquainted with the systematics of sciences of state) that Mohl's systematics of sciences of society was a schematic copy of the systematics of the former. One of the main accusations towards the German scholar is therefore his extensive schematic, in a way hampering and limiting the final effect.[519] David Lindenfeld came to similar conclusions, even advancing the thesis that "Mohl's approach to defining the new science reflected his classificatory mentality – as well as the difficulty experienced by an older generation in accepting shifts of paradigms."[520]

It proves difficult to disagree with critical views in this regard. The systematics of sciences of society according to von Mohl contained errors and understatements, referring even to the separation of social law, and it certainly required further development. Von Mohl himself seemed not quite sure of his systematics of sciences of society. A very short description of its individual parts can be found only in the article *Sciences of Society and Sciences of State*, while in the *History and Literature of Sciences of State* and both editions of *the Encyclopedia...* he abandoned these descriptions altogether.

---

517 G. v. Mayr, *Begriff und Gliederung der Staatswissenschaften Zur Einführung in deren Studium*, Tübingen 1910, p. 5, Idem, *Statistik und Gesellschaftslehre*, Freiburg 1895, § 1 & 11. Also on differences between von Treitschke and von Mohl regarding the notion of society: O. H. v. d. Gablentz, *Der Kampf um die rechte Ordnung*, Köln und Opladen 1964, pp. 111–112.

518 E. Angermann, op. cit., p. 367.

519 Ibid, pp. 365–366. Erich Angermann assessed the Mohl system of sciences of society as a mistake. Werner Sombart was also critical of the Mohl system of sciences of society: W. Sombart, *Die Fehlurteile Robert von Mohls und Paul Barths über den Begriff der Soziologie*, [in:] *Hauptprobleme Der Soziologie Erinnerungsgabe Für Max Weber*, I Band, M. Palyi (eds.), München und Leipzig 1923, pp. 5–6.

520 D. F. Lindenfeld, op. cit., p. 181.

The system of sciences of society by von Mohl, therefore, must be treated in the same way as the concept of society he derived it from. Despite the imperfections, it should be noted that von Mohl was one of the first scholars in Germany to address the issue of developing separate sciences of society. Therefore, it should be stated that his merit was to give an impulse, which began a movement resulting in further research on this issue.[521] Erich Angermann thus rightly stated that it was von Mohl who initiated the process of overcoming the narrow, doctrinal approach requiring to look at scientific relations through the prism of either the state or the individual.[522] We find confirmation of the innovative and even groundbreaking nature of von Mohl's work in the field of social sciences, in the opinion of Ernst Rudolf Huber, who, assessing the article *Sciences of Society and Sciences of State*, stated: "It is right to state that German sociology has its source in this very article."[523]

2.3. The genesis, concept and systematics of "sciences of state"

The analysis of the concept and shape of the system of sciences of state in Robert von Mohl's thought should be preceded by some comments and explanations regarding the translation of the phrase *Staatswissenschaften* adopted for the purpose of this publication. It should be noted that today the German word *Staatswissenschaften* is translated as "political sciences." Despite this, we decided to translate the phrase *Staatswissenschaften* as "sciences of state," which we did for the following reasons.

It should be noted that the translator of the Polish edition of the *Encyclopaedia...* Antoni Białecki, referring to the subject of the *Encyclopaedia...* spoke about sciences regarding everything that relates to the state.[524] He signalled that the subject of the concept of *Staatswissenschaften* was the state as such. David Lindenfeld also comes to a similar conclusion. Referring to the historical

521 W. Dilthey, *Gesammelte Schriften I. Band, Einleitung in die Gesiteswissenschaften*, Göttingen, 1990, p. 24, F-X. Kaufmann, *The idea of Social Policy in Western Societes: Origins and Diversity*, "International Journal of Social Quality" vol 3 number (2), Winter 2013, p. 20. So, Eckhart Pankoke rightly states, saying: "Mohl's program to supplement the outdated <sciences of state> with the new <sciences of society> is an early testimony to the recognition of sociology as a special science of social processes": E. Pankoke, op. cit., p. 120.

522 E. Angermann, op. cit., pp. 382–383.

523 E. R. Huber, op. cit., p. 12.

524 A. Białecki, *Translator's note to the Reader*, [in:] R. v. Mohl, *Encyklopedia Umiejętności Politycznych*. . ., p. 1.

(nineteenth-century) meaning of the phrase *Staatswissenschaften*, Lindenfeld defines it with the English expression the "sciences of state."[525] The same translation was adopted in F. Flügel's *A practical dictionary of the English and German languages in two parts.*[526] On the other hand, the 1874 *German-Polish Dictionary of Legal and Administrative Terms* and 1911 Muret Sanders Dictionary adopt the phrase "political sciences."[527]

It can and should therefore be assumed that the two forms of translation of the phrase *Staatswissenschaften* may be used interchangeably. The options are relying on the first form, derived from the historical and contemporary dictionary definitions, or adopting a translation that takes into account the subject of the sciences (as did the aforementioned David Lindenfeld). Due to the scope of work covering Robert von Mohl's thought related to the state, we opted for the latter solution. This resulted in a translation of the phrase *Staatswissenschaften* as "sciences of state." This is justified even more because (as the analysis below demonstrates) von Mohl sought to compose a system of sciences related to the state, while politics (*Staatskunst*) formed only a part of it.

The phrase *Staatswissenschaft* first appeared in German science in the 18th century. German science considers the year 1763 as the turning point, after which the use of this expression became generally accepted. This was the year that the first edition of the aforementioned work by August Ludwig von Schlözer entitled *Allgemeines Staatsrecht und Staatsverfassungslehre* was published. Its first chapter was entitled *Einleitung in die Staatswissenschaft.*[528] However, as Suzanne Schüttermeyer rightly notes, the roots of disciplines relating to the nature and functioning of the state reach much deeper in German science. The impulse for the development of sciences of state was, among others, the Reformation and

---

525 D. F. Lindenfeld, op. cit., p. 1.

526 F. Flügel, *A practical dictionary of the English and German languages in two parts*, Part II, Hamburg, 1861, p. 899–900.

527 *Niemiecko-Polsko Słownik Wyrazów Prawniczych i Administracyjnych*, Kraków 1874, p. 267. Muret-Sanders, *Encyclopaedic English-German and German-English Dictionary*. . ., p. 911.

528 A. L. v. Schlözer, *Allgemeines Staatsrecht und Staatsverfassungslehre*. . .,. E. R. Huber, apart from the work by von Schlözer, also included in the so called The "Old sciences of state" (*Alte Staatswissenschaft*) the Mohl's *History and Literature of Sciences of State*, the multi-volume work of von Rotteck and Welcker the *Staatslexikon*, as well as the Hegelian *Elements of the Philosophy of Right*, More: C. v. Rotteck, C. Welcker, *Staats-Lexikon oder Encyklopädie der Staatswissenschaften*, 1 Bd., Altona 1834, G. Hegel, *Zasady filozofii prawa*, trans. A. Landman, Warszawa 1969. On this topic also: ER Huber, op. cit., p. 2.

the resulting need to educate professional state personnel, whose task was to be, among others, the promotion of the Protestant religion. Over the years (also under the influence of absolutism), there emerged sciences, the centre of which was the state, and the arrangement of its activities so that it was capable of providing its citizens with wealth and prosperity in all aspects of their existence.[529]

The nineteenth century brought a rise of state sciences in Germany.[530] In many German states, the times of Napoleonic domination left a strong bureaucratic apparatus, controlling a large number of areas of life. In many of them at the beginning of the nineteenth century there was a need to develop a system of sciences that would provide properly trained staff to support such an extensive state administration.[531] This was also the case, among others, in the homeland of Mohl. In Württemberg, following the Napoleonic period, there was a strong need to consolidate and professionalize administration in a state that adopted the constitutional monarchy system.[532] The above was one of the reasons behind the Royal Decree of 17 October 1817 establishing the "Faculty of Sciences of State" (*Staatswirtschaftlichen Fakultät*)[533] in Tübingen. From that moment the German science dates the rise of the entire "Tübingen school of entire sciences of state" (*Die Tübinger Schule der gesamten Staatswissenschaft*). The spiritual and

---

529 More: S.S. Schüttemeyer, *The Current State of Political Science in Germany*, [in:] *The State of Political Science in Europe*, H.-D. Klingemann (ed.), Opladen/Farmington Hills 2007, pp. 163–186. On the development of sciences of state in the 18th century on the example of the University of Halle: A. Rüdiger, *Die Staatswissenschaft an der Universität Halle im 18. Jahrhundert*, Tübingen 2005. On the History of sciences of state from Antiquity to Modern Times: F. Bülau, *Encyklopädie der Staatswissenschaften*, Leipzig 1856, pp. 2–5.

530 More on the history of sciences of state at German universities: V. Hentschel, *Die Staatswissenschaften an den deutschen Universitäten im 18. und frühen 19. Jahrhundert*, "Berichte zur Wissenschafts-Geschichte," 1 (1978), pp. 181 – 200, D. F. Lindenfeld, op. cit., p. 6.

531 More: Ibid, pp. 89–94. One should agree with David Lindenfeld, who comes from German nineteenth-century state sciences in an earlier cameral science program (*Kameralwissenschaft*), developing after the 1648 Peace of Westphalia. At the end of the 18th century, one of the currents of this program focused on the analysis of the state (as the central reference point) in legal, political, statistical and historical terms. More: Ibid, pp. 11–33.

532 More: Ibid, p. 94.

533 W. Bleek, op. cit., p. 106.

intellectual father of the faculty in Tübingen was Friedrich List,[534] but Robert von Mohl was also remembered as its *spiritus rector*.[535]

The Württemberger belonged to this group of German scholars, which was in favour of creating separate faculties of state science at German universities.[536] Their task was to provide a general theoretical basis for education for officials so that they perform their functions in the most professional and effective manner, thus ensuring the achievement of the objectives of the state.[537] Von Mohl's work on the methodology of state sciences and his organizational talent ensured him respect of the academic community.[538] One of the scholars' merits was the creation of the aforementioned *Zeitschrift für die gesamte Staatswissenschaft* journal at the University of Tübingen, which was supposed to focus publications from the broadly understood field of sciences of the state, society, economics, etc.[539]

The system of state sciences in the thought of Robert von Mohl was based on the basic methodological assumption saying that:

> "All human relations can be described in a scientific way, that is, their essence can be thoroughly studied, the laws to which this essence is subjected to discovered and formulated, and eventually that conclusions can be made, relating both to theory and practice. In addition, all historical knowledge should also be taken into account [related to the subject - author's note]"[540]

This principle was also to apply to relations covering the collective life of people in the state.[541] Relations between individuals, within family, tribe and nation,

---

534 Friedrich List (1789–1846) - was a German economist recognized today as one of the precursors of the German school of economics. More: ME Hirst, *Life of Friedrich List and selections from his writings*, London 1909.

535 W. Bleek, *Die Tübinger Schule der gesamten Staatswissenschaft...*, p.107. More about the role of von Mohl in this faculty: Ibid., Pp. 107–113, Idem, *Geschichte der Politikwissenschaft in Deutschland*, München 2001, pp. 121–129.

536 More about the need to establish separate faculties of state science in the opinion of von Mohl: R. v. Mohl, SVuP.3.2, p. 220.

537 Ibid, pp. 228–229. K. v. Beyme, *Einleitung...*, p. XXIII.

538 W. Bleek, *Die Tübinger Schule der gesamten Staatswissenschaft...*, p.107.

539 On the history of the periodical *Zietschrift für die gesamte Staatswissenschaft* and the role of von Mohl in it: H. Sauermann, *Die gesamte Staatswissenschaft im Spiegel dieser Zeitschrift*, "Zietschrift für die gesamte Staatswissenschaft/ Journal of Institutional and Theoretical Economics," Bd. 134, H.1, März 1978, pp. 1–6.

540 R. v. Mohl, *Encyklopädie der Staatswissenschaften*, Zweite Auflage..., p. 48.

541 Referring to scientific dealing with the state, von Mohl said: "Dealing with the state in a systematic way from both a legal and political point of view has been part of higher education from the earliest times. This is proved by Plato and Aristotle, Cicero,

social relations, state-individual relations, were also be the subject of scientific study.[542] Based on this assumption, von Mohl sought to comprehensively describe the state as a subject of science. He expressed the view that the scope of state sciences under the slogan "All state sciences and only the state sciences" (*alle Staatswissenschaften und nur Staatswissenschaften*), should include only disciplines in which the state is the main reference point. At the same time it should avoid these areas, where the state was not playing the most important role.[543] Therefore, before we proceed to discussing the system of state sciences presented by von Mohl, it is worth paying attention to the analysis of sciences that, in his opinion, should not belong to its scope.

According to von Mohl disciplines such as private law (both the natural, "philosophical," and the constitutional), faith and morality, both of individuals and families, principles of "prudence" of individuals, and the aforementioned sciences of society were all beyond the scope of correctly understood state sciences.[544] These exclusions also concerned "political economy" (*Nationaökonomie*) except for the field of revenue and expenditure of the treasury, and "financial science" (*Finanzwissenschaft*), and also partly the "science of culture" (*Kulturwissenschaft*).[545] It should be remembered, however, that these disciplines, despite their fundamental exclusion from the scope of state sciences, were in von Mohl's concept, form of its auxiliary sciences. They could provide a lot of basic information regarding functioning in the state, for example this concerning various social circles.[546]

Moving on to discussing the division of the system of state sciences, it should be noted that in Robert von Mohl's thought its development was related to the development and analysis of the role of encyclopedic representation of specific circles of science. It was on the canvas of the analysis of the subject of the encyclopedia, and in particular the encyclopedia of sciences related to the state, that von Mohl made his own division of state sciences, which was published in one

---

Machiavelli, Bodin, Hugo Grotius, Hobbes and Locke, Puffendorf, Wolf, Montesquieu, J.J. Moser and Putter.": Idem, SVuP.3.2, p. 220.

542 Idem, *Encyklopädie der Staatswissenschaften*, Zweite Auflage . . ., pp. 48–49.

543 Ibid, p. 50. Similarly: Idem, *Literarhistorische Uebersicht über die Encyklopädieen der Staatswissenschaften*. . ., p. 425.

544 More comments on the perception of "philosophical law" in further part of our study.

545 Idem, *Encyklopädie der Staatswissenschaften*, Zweite Auflage . . ., pp. 50, 58. Similarly: Idem, *Literarhistorische Uebersicht über die Encyklopädieen der Staatswissenschaften*. . ., p. 427.

546 Idem, *Encyklopädie der Staatswissenschaften*, Zweite Auflage . . ., p. 50.

of his most important works, i.e. the *Encyclopedia of Sciences of State.*[547] The fact that it was in the encyclopaedic study that von Mohl descrived the system of state sciences once again proves that the German scholar had a special penchant for classifying and systematizing the area of knowledge he dealt with.

The importance the Württemberger attributed to encyclopaedic studies, is evidenced by his opposition to the then-popular underestimation of encyclopaedic studies by science and their use as primarily a teaching aid.[548] Von Mohl represented a different approach. He believed that it was only through a properly prepared, universal encyclopaedic publication, that the real impact of a particular branch of knowledge could be revealed. The encyclopaedia, being for him a complete and practical overview of contemporary information in the field of science, had many advantages.[549] First, it was supposed to best analyze individual scientific disciplines in a proportionate manner, and according to their level of development. For the scholar, it was important because it was to avoid unjustified excessive focus on one topic without the other being neglected. Secondly, the main feature of the encyclopaedic approach was the opportunity to present a specific discipline of knowledge from the point of view of all the relationships it is governed by. The idea of a complete presentation of the subject of science (in this case the state) forms the characteristic feature of the concept of the German liberal.[550] To sum up, guided by his penchant for systematization, it was in encyclopaedias that von Mohl found a means to properly and completely present the scope of the subject being studied. This also undoubtedly applied to state sciences.

The scholar distinguished two main methods of encyclopaedic representation of a specific science. The first of these was the so-called "External ordering of

547 One should agree with Georg von Mayr, who presented the view that in German areas in the first half of the nineteenth century, state sciences developed precisely on the basis of encyclopaedic studies created at that time.: G. v. Mayr, *Begriff und Gliederung der Staatswissenschaften. Zur Einführung in deren Studium...*, pp. 23–24.

548 R. v. Mohl, *Literarhistorische Uebersicht über die Encyklopädieen der Staatswissenschaften...*, p. 423.

549 Ibid, the Encyclopaedia referring to a particular science was defined by von Mohl as: "a complete overview of the total scope and content of all its parts [of a given science - author's note]": Idem, *Encyklopädie der Staatswissenschaften*, Zweite Auflage ..., p. 53. Friedrich Bülau saw similar advantages of encyclopaedias (and encyclopaedias of state sciences in particular):: F. Bülau, op. cit., pp. 1–2.

550 R. v. Mohl, *Literarhistorische Uebersicht über die Encyklopädieen der Staatswissenschaften...*, p. 423.

matter" (*äußere Ordnung des Stoffes*). It consisted in the analysis of individual branches of a respective knowledge, presented in a brief way, but based on its entire scope, and then presenting them as a logical whole. For von Mohl the main advantage of this first method was that it allowed to avoid a one-sided approach to the researched object, i.e. provided a postulate to examine it from all possible reference points.[551]

The second encyclopaedic method was the "organic presentation of matter" (*organische Darstellung des Stoffes*), adopted by the scholar in his system of state sciences.[552] Based on this method, the entire scope of a given science should be presented by analyzing its individual parts (subjects) and their interrelationships. The effect of this approach is to discuss each individual subject from multiple reference points. Von Mohl saw the advantage of this method primarily in enabling a general view of the overall scope of science, which was also to facilitate the perception of knowledge.[553]

Von Mohl presented the view that the encyclopaedia of state sciences, presenting their system properly, should focus only on disciplines relating to the state, and only on them.[554] As in the case of sciences of society, the proper definition of the subject of state sciences was extremely important for von Mohl. It referred primarily to the efficiency and purposefulness of the state and its institutions.[555] In the light of the above, it can be concluded that von Mohl's system of state sciences was firstly characterized by proper definition of the subject (dealing only with the state and its relations). Secondly, its feature was to be versatility, that is, consideration of all relations and processes occurring in the state from all possible points of view (law, morality, politics). The scholar's ambition was that everything proper to the state could be analyzed in a holistic way, based on parts of this system. This was to guarantee a comprehensive analysis of the subject.[556]

Similarly to general comments on the encyclopaedia, von Mohl distinguished two methods of encyclopaedic approach to the sciences of the state. The first consisted in the "external ordering of matter" consisting of individual disciplines

---

551 Idem, *Encyklopädie der Staatswissenschaften*, Zweite Auflage . . ., pp. 53–55.

552 A. Białecki, op. cit., p. 8.

553 R. v. Mohl, *Encyklopädie der Staatswissenschaften*, Zweite Auflage . . ., pp. 54, 55.

554 Idem, *Literarhistorische Uebersicht über die Encyklopädieen der Staatswissenschaften*. . ., p. 425.

555 Idem, *Encyklopädie der Staatswissenschaften*, Zweite Auflage . . ., p. 50.

556 Idem, *Literarhistorische Uebersicht über die Encyklopädieen der Staatswissenschaften*. . ., p. 430.

into a logical and compact whole. The scope of each of the disciplines should be briefly summarized.[557] The second was the method of "organic presentation" of the entire circle of science. Based on this method, individual science subjects were analyzed based on their remaining in mutual relations. According to von Mohl, this method was to guarantee that every single discussed subject or fact would be subjected to comprehensive scientific investigation from the point of view of various disciplines.[558] In his system, von Mohl adopted the latter method.[559] His concept of state sciences, in accordance with his practical approach, was to reflect reality, and the changes occurring in it, as accurately as possible. So in his works, Von Mohl focused more on offering practical solutions to issues of reality than on theoretical considerations and formulation of experimental theories.[560] Based on the above assumptions, he made his own division of state sciences, the scheme of which is as follows:

Dogmatic sciences of state:

General theory of the state
Public law:
Constitutional law:
Philosophical constitutional law
Positive (applicable) constitutional law

International law:
Philosophical international law

---

557 Idem, *Encyklopädie der Staatswissenschaften*, Zweite Auflage . . ., p. 54.

558 Ibid. For example, von Mohl included the already mentioned works of August Ludwig von Schlözer and Hegel as one of the works guided by the method of "external ordering." Among the works guided by the alphabetical method, he included the *Staatslexikon* by von Rotteck and Welcker or *Deutsches Staatswörterbuch* by Bluntschli and Brater.: A. L. v. Schlözer, *Allgemeines Staatsrecht und Staatsverfassungslehre. . .*, G.W.F. Hegel, *Grundlinien der Philosophie des Rechts, oder Naturrecht und Staatswissenschaft im Grundrisse*, Berlin 1820, C. von Rotteck, C. Welcker, *Staatslexikon oder Encyklopädie der Staatswissenschaften. . .*, After: R. v. Mohl, *Encyklopädie der Staatswissenschaften*, Zweite Auflage . . ., pp. 64–67.

559 A. Białecki, op. cit., p. 8. Antoni Białecki defined the method of "external ordering" as a method based on a separate presentation of each branch of state science about (e.g. constitutional law and international law). He saw the organic method as a method dealing not with individual, separate branches of science, but developing separate issues from a legal, philosophical, political point of view, etc.: R. v. Mohl, *Encyklopedia umiejętności politycznych ...*, p. 59.

560 D. F. Lindenfeld, op. cit., p. 96.

Positive (applicable) international law

State ethics
Politics

Historical sciences of state:

Political history
Statistics[561]

Based on the analysis of the above classification of state sciences, the opinion of Georg von Mayr, qualifying von Mohl to those systematics, who were guided by the narrow and literal meaning of state science, as voiced over 50 years after the classification was published, must be considered correct. This meant that von Mohl focused only on the relations and properties of the state. This trend was characteristic and widespread among the trends prevailing in German sciences concerning the state in the first half of the nineteenth century.[562]

The first and most important division of state sciences made by von Mohl consisted in the distinction between the "dogmatic sciences of state" (*dogmatische Staatswissenschaften*) and the "historical sciences of state" (*geschichtliche Staat swissenschaften*).[563] The basic principle distinguishing these two great areas of knowledge in von Mohl's thought was the belief that the "historical state sciences" referred only to facts (occurring in the past or in a given period of time). In other words, dogmatic sciences in Mohl's systematic can be described as the more abstract, focusing on the search for proper definitions, principles and solutions relating to the state. On the other hand, the historical sciences were to

561 Scheme: R. v. Mohl, *Encyklopädie der Staatswissenschaften*, Zweite Auflage . . ., p. 59. K. v. Beyme, *Einleitung*. . ., p. XIV.

562 G. v. Mayr, *Begriff und Gliederung der Staatswissenschaften Zur Einführung in deren Studium*. . ., p. 19. The systematics adopted by Bluntschli: J. C. Bluntschli, *Staatswissenschaft*, [in:] *Deutsches Staats- Wörterbuch*, J. C. Bluntschli, K. Brater (eds.), Bd.10, Stuttgart/Leipzig 1867, pp. 152–154.

563 Idem, *Encyklopedia umiejętności politycznych...*, p. 52. Idem, *Literarhistorische Uebersicht über die Encyklopädieen der Staatswissenschaften*. . ., p. 430. It should also be remembered that the scope of state sciences is determined by von Mohl by separating sciences of society (as discussed earlier). Idem, *Gesellschafts-Wissenschaften und Staats-Wissenschaften*, "Zeitschrift für die gesamte Staatswissenschaft" 1851, v. 7, p. 57. The division into dogmatic and historical sciences was present in von Mohl from the publication of the article *Literarhistorische Uebersicht über die Encyklopädieen der Staatswissenschaften*.

provide solely the knowledge based on dry facts pertaining to specific situations that were occurring or occurred in the state.

Within the Mohl's system the dogmatic sciences were designed to analyze relations and events occurring in the state based on the belief that every man in his state existence is subject to three types of principles. They formed the basis for consideration relations in the respective state. For von Mohl, these were firstly the rules of law. Secondly, moral rules (the so-called "state ethics" of *Staatsittengesetz, Staatsmoral*), based on the conviction that maintaining moral principles in human life should also extend to its existence within the state. Thirdly, the principles of politics understood by the scholar as a science of prudent and wise implementation of objectives of the state.[564] A separate dogmatic discipline was, like for example in Johann Caspar Bluntschli, the so-called "General theory of the state" (*Allegemeine Staatslehre*).[565]

Moving on to discuss individual dogmatic parts of state science, we should first focus on the general theory of the state.[566] Speaking of it, von Mohl stated:

> "Admittedly, if a particular institution or action is required of the state, such a demand should be justified from the point of view of law, morality or purpose, resulting in three complete sciences based on these three principles; but because of the fact that life in the state is not subject to only one type of regulation, its general essence cannot be sufficiently, and without forced stretching, described in one of the above theories, but it requires a broader foundation instead. This general representation of the nature of the state is described by the general science of it."[567]

Thus, the emergence of general theory of the state was a consequence of von Mohl's methodological conviction that the analysis of all individual disciplines relating to the state should be preceded by a general presentation of its essence, purpose and boundaries.[568] It was therefore logical to present the basic concepts, in the beginning in a comprehensive study, so that they form the basis for more elaborate considerations.[569]

---

564 Idem, *Encyklopädie der Staatswissenschaften*, Zweite Auflage . . ., pp. 55–57. A. Białecki, op. cit., p. 8. Similarly: R. v. Mohl, Geschicht.u.Lit.3, p. 352.

565 Idem, *Encyklopädie der Staatswissenschaften*, Zweite Auflage . . ., p. 63.

566 Importantly, initially von Mohl did not classify general state theory as a separate dogmatic discipline. Yet in both the first and the second edition of the *Encyclopaedia*. . . it is classified as a dogmatic science.: Idem, *Literarhistorische Uebersicht über die Encyklopädieen der Staatswissenschaften*. . ., p. 430.

567 Idem, *Encyklopädie der Staatswissenschaften*, Erste Auflage . . ., pp. 56–57.

568 Idem, *Gesellschafts-Wissenschaften und Staats-Wissenschaften*. . ., p. 58.

569 Thus, von Mohl stated that "the full and therefore proper presentation of the general foundations of the state requires taking into account the statements arising

Therefore, the task of general theory of state was to provide a basis for grouping concepts from all the three dogmatic areas in order to expose the more complex relations in the state. The initial discussion of independent and comprehensive general science of the phenomenon (in this case the state) was to avoid a limited and one-sided approach. In addition, separating general science allowed, in von Mohl's assessment, first of all, for beginners to enter individual disciplines more easily, and second, for critics to assess the correctness of the entire scientific approach.[570] It should be remembered, however, that general science was not understood by Württemberger as "a pointless and groundless mixture of all kinds of statements in the field of various state sciences, or a talk about the subject characterized by clichés it applies."[571] It was supposed to be, by all accounts, a scientific presentation of the subject under discussion within concise boundaries corresponding to the general approach.[572]

We should now ask the question about the relationship between Mohl's understanding of general science of the state and the definition of the concept of science in general. When talking about the definition of science, one should first pay attention to its ambiguity. Both Tadeusz Kotarbiński and Stanisław Kamiński presented their belief in the multidimensionality of this concept.[573] Stanisław Kamiński defined science as, most generally "a kind of mental or mental-physical activity."[574] Tadeusz Kotarbiński introduced the so-called functional and static understanding of science. In the functional sense, he perceived science as a complex of research and ancillary activities, and in the other as the complex of known truths.[575] In conclusion, Kotarbiński stated that "(...) science is all that is worthy of being the subject of intellectual teaching in higher education, and only in higher education, as a separate specialty."[576] Does the Mohl's *Allgemeine*

---

from all three disciplines": Idem, *Encyklopädie der Staatswissenschaften*, Zweite Auflage…, p. 63.

570 Idem, *Gesellschafts-Wissenschaften und Staats-Wissenschaften…*, p. 58.

571 Ibid.

572 Ibid.

573 S. Kamiński, *Nauka i Metoda. Pojęcie nauki i klasyfikacja nauk*, Lublin 1992, p. 12.

574 Idem, p. 13.

575 T. Kotarbiński, *Elementy teorii poznania, logiki formalnej i metodologii nauk*, Warszawa 2003, p. 573, Z. Kowalewski, *Historia nauki i naukoznawstwo. Zarys kierunków rozwoju i zmian organizacyjnych Zakładu Historii Nauki i Techniki*, "Kwartalnik Historii Nauki i Techniki" 15/3, 1970, p. 471.

576 T. Kotarbiński, *Sprawność i błąd: (z myślą o dobrej robocie nauczyciela)*, Warszawa 1960, p. 47.

Staatslehre exhibit the features mentioned above? Undoubtedly yes. After all, it was a range of knowledge resulting from mental activity that contained the so-called "truths known" and was the result of research activities. Thus, one can speak of fulfilling both the functional and static approach to science according to Kotarbiński. In addition, the general subject of state science was taught at German universities both in the nineteenth century and today. Thus the condition from the definition of science by Tadeusz Kotarbiński is met.

Public law was another scope recognized by the Württemberger. Von Mohl divided it into two basic branches, namely constitutional law and international law. He perceived both of them through their "philosophical" (which can be compared with natural law) and positive (binding) aspects. In von Mohl's thought the need to legally regulate the relations of the joint life of people and states is dictated by two reasons. First of all, legal regulations bring order to people's lives, without which it is difficult to achieve the objectives of even a single state. Secondly, the introduction of public law principles is necessary because not all people always act in the right way of their own free will. Therefore, the joint existence of people in the state must be included in a certain externally arranged order to which every citizen will subdue and which, in special cases, will be able to resort to coercion.[577] The legal order must function both in the state and in relations between individual state (hence the need for international law). The conviction that the order of law in the state as well as the order of international law should originate from competent authorities (who have the legitimacy to publish and maintain it) forms the specific sign that the postulate of the rule of law was superior in Württemberger's doctrine.[578]

With regard to constitutional law, both in its "philosophical" and binding aspect, we observe the evolution of views of the scientist. In one of his earlier works, i.e. in the *Constitutional Law of the Kingdom of Württemberg*, he defined the notion of constitutional law (*Staatsrecht*) as a complete scientific representation of those legal relationships that emerge through the state and underlie it, are connected with it and are related to it, and in a certain way accented and developed by it.[579] The task of constitutional law as a creation covering all entities existing in the state is to deal with, and regulate only the internal life of the state

577 R. v. Mohl, *Encyklopädie der Staatswissenschaften*, Zweite Auflage . . ., p. 56.

578 Erik Jayme rightly points out, saying that von Mohl's concepts relating to international law are still pending in-depth research: E. Jayme, *Internationales Privatrecht, Ideengeschichte von Mancini und Ehrenzweig zum Europäischen Kollisionsrecht*, Heidelberg 2009, p. 89.

579 R. v. Mohl, Staatsr.Württem.1.1829, s. 23.

as an enclosed and territorially limited entity.[580] In the thought of von Mohl the scope of constitutional law regulation is divided into two great parts: firstly, one referring to all rights and obligations that apply to individuals, social communities or entire strata of the population in the state, and secondly, limited only to those principles that regulate state relations.[581]

The above assumptions result in the division of constitutional law due to the entity to which it applies. These will be so-called "legal claims of the head of state" (*Rechtsforderungen des Staatsoberhauptes*), i.e. requirements related to the implementation of the state's objectives that can be imposed on its citizens. The head of state as an entity being, in the science of von Mohl, responsible for achieving the objectives of the state, must have the power not only to issue legal regulations, but also to enforce them so that the objectives of the state can be achieved. The sovereign position of the head of state was also reflected in the duty of its subjects (residents of the state) to obey and respect it, but also to cooperate in achieving state objectives. Constitutional law also includes "legal claims of the subjects against the state" (*Die rechtlichen Forderungen der Unterthanen an den Staat*). Von Mohl noted that since the objective of the state is to support the achievement of the life goals of a particular nation, then the nation as well as its individual elements also have the full right to demand such actions from the state. The addressee of claims of subjects functioning in the nation is the head of state as the personification of its essence and the entity having the ability to implement specific collective actions.[582]

In the science of Robert von Mohl, constitutional law is divided into two approaches to his subject: "philosophical" and obligatory (positive). "Philosophical constitutional law" is defined as:

> "(...) an ordered set of legal principles that define the rights and obligations of all participants of the state as such, as long as these principles relate to the internal life of a single state on one hand, and on the other, as long as they logically and necessarily stem from the state in general and its single species and form in particular"[583]

580 Idem, *Encyklopädie der Staatswissenschaften*, Zweite Auflage . . ., pp. 174– 176.

581 Ibid, pp. 174–175. Von Mohl stated: "The creation of a proper division requires the adoption of a dual nature: firstly, to extend it to all rights and obligations that both individuals and entire classes and social circles have in relation to collective life in the state, on the other hand, to limits it to these rules only, which relate solely to state relations."

582 Ibid, p.175.

583 Ibid, p. 174. The expression "participants in the state" used in this quote by von Mohl can be translated as "citizens." However, one should remember about the lack

Therefore, it is a science arising from and referring to the essence of a particular species of state.[584] As a law based solely on the principles of reason, it is not subject to codification. It can be defined as a creation based on the principles of logic and common sense, and not resulting from any legal principles.[585] In contrast to applicable law, "philosophical law" is characterized by deriving legal principles from the essence of the state and from its species and forms.[586] Unlike the norm of statutory law, a specific norm of "philosophical constitutional law" applies due to the so-called reasonable and rational "internal need" (*innere Notwendigkeit*) without external coercion that characterizes the positive law. Another difference between "state philosophical law" and applicable law, is in von Mohl, the scope of regulations resulting from their essence. The "philosophical law" is therefore more abstract and more extensive, while the applicable law is more detailed and deals with complex issues. Within the thought of von Mohl, "philosophical constitutional law" can be compared and identified with the concepts of natural law. What is sought here is a set of rules based on the belief that there are unchanging, elementary standards, the validity of which is independent of the receipt of sanctions by the state. In this case, the nature from which von Mohl derived certain principles is the nature of a particular species and forms of state. The "philosophical constitutional law," just like natural law concepts, is based on solid ideas and sets of obligations resulting from the natural conditions of a given phenomenon.[587]

---

of consistency and terminological uncertainty of the scholar in this aspect. More comments on this subject can be found in the second subsection of chapter four.

584 The topic of diversity of states is discussed in chapter three.

585 Ibid, p. 188. Idem, Staatsr.Württem.1.1840, p. 87. It is legitimate to conclude that in philosophical terms the law overlaps, in von Mohl's teaching, with the essence of natural law. More about the problem of natural law: M. Łuszczyńska, *Prawo natury a prawo stanowione- dwa antagonistyczne ujęcia filozofii prawa*, "Annales UMCS Sectio G (Ius)," 2005–2006, vol LII/LIII, pp. 87–108, R. Wojtyszyn, *Szkoła prawa natury od Hugona Grocjusza do Johna Locke'a*, "Studia Erasmiana Wratislaviensia Wrocławskie Studia Erazmiańskie, Zeszyt Naukowy Studentów, doktorantów i pracowników naukowych Uniwersytetu Wrocławskiego," 2007, pp. 49–63.

586 R. v. Mohl, *Encyklopädie der Staatswissenschaften*, Zweite Auflage . . ., p. 176. Von Mohl makes a detailed assessment of the history of "philosophical constitutional law," dividing it into three main periods: antiquity, the Middle Ages and modern times (*Neuere Zeit*). More: Ibid, pp. 178–188. Explanation of the terminology used by the scholar, concepts such as species or form of state is provided in subsection four of chapter three.

587 More on this topic: M. Łuszczyńska, *Prawo natury a prawo stanowione – dwa antagonistyczne ujęcia filozofii prawa*. . ., pp. 92, 94. S. Wronkowska, Z. Ziembiński,

The division of "philosophical constitutional law" is determined by its scope, focusing in von Mohl, on the essence of the state itself and its "species." Thus, "philosophical constitutional law" is divided into two main components: "general philosophical constitutional law" (*allgemeines philosophisches Staatsrecht*) analyzing the most general principles of the state applicable to all its individual species, and "particular philosophical constitutional law" (*besonderes philosophisches Staatsrecht*), which aims to discuss specific, individual species and forms of states.[588]

In von Mohl's assessment, the "philosophical constitutional law" was of great significance in providing people with knowledge about the state.[589] It says us what obligations arise for an individual from being a subject or a citizen in a particular species of state. Since man "cannot live outside the state, on the contrary he must live in a specific state relation appropriate to its degree of civilization,"[590] then he should have knowledge about what kind of limitations his freedom and self-determination will be subject to in a given species of the state. "Philosophical constitutional law" also allows us to assess the correctness of implementation of basic ideas in the respective states.[591]

For von Mohl the principles resulting from "philosophical constitutional law" were also of great importance for the functioning of the state itself. He assigned it the function of anterior identification of gaps in the current legislation and directing it to changes. "Philosophical constitutional law" could also be used to criticize constitutional law and thus give impetus to its improvement. According to von Mohl, the use of principles expressed in "philosophical constitutional law" can also serve to explain the questionable principles of constitutional law. Philosophical law is also important in determining the actual will of the legislator. Therefore, when the interpretation (understood here as the desire to determine the content of behavioural patterns or the result of this process) does not bring a clear result, one should apply the principles arising from the nature of

Zarys Teorii Prawa, Poznań 2001, pp. 59–60. Also the current problems arising in the terminology applied in this field cannot be ignored. More about the distinction between the concepts of the law of nature, the laws of nature, and natural law and natural laws: M. Łuszczyńska, *Prawo natury a prawo stanowione – dwa antagonistyczne ujęcia filozofii prawa...*, pp. 94, 97–98

588 R. v. Mohl, *Encyklopädie der Staatswissenschaften*, Zweite Auflage ..., pp. 177, 199. Similarly Idem, Staatsr.Württem.1.1840, pp. 23–24.

589 Idem, *Encyklopädie der Staatswissenschaften*, Zweite Auflage ..., p. 188.

590 Ibid.

591 Ibid, p. 189.

a particular legal institution, as appropriate for the respective species of state, supposing that the legislator also wanted to follow these principles.[592] The last advantage of "philosophical constitutional law" is increasing the legal awareness of citizens regarding mutual legal claims. Legal awareness created in this way, permeating the masses, protects the state against government's misinterpretation of its objectives.[593]

Although "philosophical constitutional law" gathered principles that were of great importance for the state, they were defined by von Mohl as non-detailed principles. In addition, they did not have the attribute of absolute applicability, and thus could not be enforced. Consequently, "philosophical constitutional law" was not enough to regulate relations prevailing in the state in a comprehensive manner.[594] Therefore, there was a need to establish a positive (applicable) law, defined as: "a systematic presentation of legal principles established by the competent authority, ordering the internal life of one, several or all states that exist in reality."[595]

The first feature of positive constitutional law is its origin in the so-called "Competent authority" (*zuständige Auctorität*). Which entity will be considered capable of legislating and enforcing laws, will depend on the species of the state (referred to as "philosophical constitutional law"). Thus, in von Mohl, also a deity acting with the help of its priests in a theocratic state form the "competent authority." It can also be the people as a sovereign in democracy, or finally it can be a monarchical ruler. The positive lawmaking process is closely related to the species the state belongs to.[596] Positive state law should also cover all legal principles in force in the respective state. Its subject were, for von Mohl, not only the

---

592 Ibid, p. 190. Von Mohl noted: "Something that can only increase the value of <the philosophical constitutional law> for a politician, the fact is that in addition to the possibility of using it as a direct source of law, it can often be used as a means of facilitating the acquisition of comprehensive knowledge about a specific issue in the state, thus enabling and encouraging criticism and finding gaps in it": Idem, Staatsr.Württem.1.1840, p. 88. More about the concept of interpretation of law: A. Kalisz, L. Leszczyński, B. Liżewski, *Wykładnia Prawa, Model Ogólny a Perspektywa Europejskiej Konwencji Praw Człowieka i Prawa Unii Europejskiej*, Lublin 2011, p. 13.

593 R. v. Mohl, *Encyklopädie der Staatswissenschaften*, Zweite Auflage . . ., p. 190.

594 Ibid, p. 382.

595 Ibid. When it comes to elaborating on the constitutional law of several states, von Mohl placed the condition that these states, in order to function together in this combination, should have historical kinship, kinship of nationalities, and a similar "views on life" (*Lebensauffassung*): Ibid, p. 383.

596 Ibid, p. 384.

"organization principles" (*Verfassung*) relating to the state, but also to its administration (*Verwaltung*).[597] The above statement requires observing the fact that von Mohl is following the creation of separate branches of state (public) law, i.e. constitutional and administrative law.

Similarly, as in the case of "philosophical constitutional law," just as in the case of the applicable law, possessing knowledge about it has certain advantages. First, its thorough scientific study is a guide for residents of the state and provides knowledge about their rights and obligations in the said state. Such knowledge is acquired not only by the citizens of the state, its individual social classes, but above all by the rulers. Thorough knowledge related to the science of applicable constitutional law allows us not only to solve problems related to the functioning of the state. It also makes it possible to popularize legal awareness among individuals and the general population of the state. Raising these advantages by von Mohl should be seen as a progressive and liberal postulate. The scientist wanted the legal awareness among all inhabitants of the state to be as high as possible. In his opinion, this could hinder possible abuse of power or neglect of their duties by those in power. It should be noted that these assumptions of von Mohl were not only theoretical. Many of his works, primarily the *Constitutional Law of the Kingdom of Württemberg* and the *Encyclopaedia of state sciences*, were also aimed at popularizing legal awareness among the people.[598]

We should also indicate the sources on which the applicable constitutional law may be based. Von Mohl distinguished four of them. The first is written law, then customary law, analogy and the last "philosophical constitutional law." Written law will be the subject of our discussion of law in rule of law, so its analysis will be omitted at this point. As for customary law is considered, von Mohl followed the generally accepted scientific definition saying that these are legal norms considered by all residents of the state or their specific group to be binding, although they do not come from legal authority and have not been published. The source of customary law is "widespread legal conviction,

597 More about the creation of a separate administrative law (*Verwaltungsrecht*) in German areas: M. Stolleis, op. cit., pp. 258–265. R. v. Mohl, *Encyklopädie der Staatswissenschaften*, Zweite Auflage . . ., p. 383. Idem, Staatsr.Württem.1.1829, pp. 23–24. *Constitutional law of the Kingdom of Württemberg* is recognized as one of the first works postulating the separation of organizational (constitutional) and administrative law: D.F. Lindenfeld, op. cit., p. 113. On the difference between *Verfassung* and *Verwaltung* in the science of von Mohl: H. Schmitz, op. cit. pp. 44–45, and in subsection four of the fourth chapter.

598 R. v. Mohl, *Encyklopädie der Staatswissenschaften,* Erste Auflage . . ., pp. 379–381.

established and proven by common practice."[599] Customs can also be of great significance in constitutional law, because not all state issues requiring resolution can always be brought within the framework of acts of law.[600] Von Mohl also noticed the role of analogy in the process of applying the law.[601] The use of legal analogy results from the adoption of the principle that the legislator, as a logically acting entity (i.e. one withing to create a compatible and internally coherent legal system) would regulate a certain legal issue (which it neglected to regulate) in the same way, as similar situations it already regulated. Von Mohl's condition for allowing an analogy is the lack of explicit regulation on the part of the legislator regarding the particular problem, and the characterization of this problem with features that are significantly similar to those of the issues already regulated by law.[602] The understanding of analogy adopted by von Mohl is similar to the concept of *analogia legis* in the contemporary theory of law, i.e. the application of a law regulating a certain factual state (X) to a factual state (Y) after establishing its similarity with the former.[603]

The last source of legal norms (if it is impossible to find a written norm, customary and analogy-based one) is to derive the applicable constitutional law from the principles of the general essence of the state or "philosophical constitutional law." Due to the fact that positive constitutional law does not always comprehensively regulate specific issues in the state, there is a need to turn precisely in the direction of philosophical law.[604] The legal principle arising from "philosophical constitutional law" will be based on the nature of a particular species and form of state. Therefore, the basis of legal reasoning is the general idea on which the very state is based.[605]

---

599 Idem, *Encyklopädie der Staatswissenschaften*, Zweite Auflage . . ., p. 390. More about the problem of customary law in von Mohl's thought: subsection three of the fourth chapter of the work.

600 Ibid, pp. 390–391. On contemporary understanding of customary law: G.F. Puchta, *Das Gewohnheitsrecht*, Erlangen 1828.

601 More about legal analogy in the thought of von Mohl: W. Pauly, *Der Methodenwandel im deutschen Spätkonstitutionalismus, Ein Beitrag zu Entwicklung und Gestalt der Wissenschaft vom öffentlichen Recht im 19. Jahrhundert*, Tübingen 1993, p. 71.

602 R. v. Mohl, *Encyklopädie der Staatswissenschaften*, Zweite Auflage . . ., pp. 391–392.

603 M. Hotel, A. Rychlewska, *Analogia jako metoda prawnicza*, "Kwartalnik Prawo-Społeczeństwo-Ekonomia," 2/2015, p. 32.

604 R. v. Mohl, Staatsr.Württem.1.1840, p. 87.

605 Idem, *Encyklopädie der Staatswissenschaften*, Zweite Auflage . . ., p. 392. Idem, Staatsr. Württem.1.1840 pp. 87 -88.

In ending our considerations regarding the "philosophical" and applicable constitutional law, it is also worth paying attention to the relations between them and the priority of their validity. This is even more important as it will testify to the primacy of the rule of law in von Mohl's thought. The German scholar categorically stated that it was not acceptable to put the principles of "philosophical" law over applicable law.

There is no doubt, therefore, that von Mohl (as one of the creators of the concept of the rule of law) was in favour of the primacy of applicable (written) law over "philosophical" law. On the other hand, however, both types of rights do not have to be in conflict with each other. This is due to the fact that a feature of a law enacted in a particular state should also be the rationality that forms the basis of "philosophical" law. However, whenever there is a conflict between the norms of these two types of rights, for example, when the actual legal relations do not allow the realization of a reasonably justified objective in the state, then both the "philosophical" and binding law remain valid.[606] It would be an abuse to give "philosophical constitutional law" an advantage over statutory law in the event of their mutual contradiction. However, according to von Mohl, this cannot be a reason for completely ousting the "philosophical constitutional law" from the life of the state and its citizens.[607] In von Mohl's thought, it is impossible not to observe, one can say, the eternal conflict between statutory law and natural law. As Małgorzata Łuszczyńska emphasizes, already in ancient Greece we can observe the creation of a division into rights created by man and such rights that do not depend on his activities. The dispute arising from this division, of course with varying intensity, continues to this day.[608]

Another branch of dogmatic state sciences distinguished by von Mohl was the international law (*Völkerrecht*), also in the "philosophical" and applicable

---

606 Idem, *Encyklopädie der Staatswissenschaften*, Zweite Auflage . . ., pp. 176–177. Von Mohl stated: "It is not necessary for a contradiction between these two types of laws ["philosophical" and positive - author's note] to occur, because what has been passed may, or even should be in accordance with the dictates of reason."

607 Ibid, p. 191.

608 M. Łuszczyńska, *Prawo natury a prawo stanowione – dwa antagonistyczne ujęcia filozofii prawa. . .*, pp. 88, 91. More on the relationship between natural law and constituted in historical terms: M. Maciejewski, *Odniesienia między prawem naturalnym i prawem stanowionym w wybranych doktrynach filozoficznych, politycznych i prawnych*, [in:] *Pozytywizm prawniczy i szkoła prawa natury – tradycje sporu i jego współczesne implikacje*, P. Kaczmarek, Ł. Machaj (eds.), Wrocław 2010, pp.9–27.

aspects, referring to relations between states.[609] The emergence of international law appears to the Württemberger as a necessary consequence of the coexistence of many states, side by side,[610] referring to relations between mutually independent and independent states.[611] Due to the fact that in relations between individual states there is no external authority that can impose compliance with specific norms, there is a need for the functioning of international legal norms.[612]

For von Mohl, the "philosophical international law" was based on the general principles of reason and logic, referring to relations between individual states, but importantly, they were supposed to be states belonging to European civilization.[613] "Philosophical international law" (like the constitutional law of this kind) was not mandatory. Its binding force was based on the general principles and achievements of European civilization. According to von Mohl, it set a specific "ideal objective," and served to provide rational guidance in those situations, where there are no currently applicable norms.[614]

One should also notice the similarity in the justifications for the existence of "applicable European law"[615] and applicable constitutional law. Due to the fact that the "philosophical" law consists of abstract and non-mandatory norms: "also in this case there is a need for universally recognized norms that originate from and are maintained by an external authority."[616] The applicable international law differed from its state counterpart in that the latter came from the authority having the tools to enforce its observance, while the applicable international law,

609 R. v. Mohl, SVuP.1., pp. 586–587. About positive and "philosophical" international law: H. Schmitz, op. cit., pp. 74–76.

610 More about the development of international law in the opinion of von Mohl: SVuP.1., pp. 579–778.

611 Ibid, p. 587.

612 Idem, *Encyklopädie der Staatswissenschaften*, Zweite Auflage. . ., p. 403.

613 Ibid. Von Mohl believed that at the then level of human development it was impossible to speak about the existence of general norms of international law, applicable to the whole world. More: Ibid. On international philosophical law also in: K. H. L. Pölitz, op. cit., pp. 28–30.

614 R. v. Mohl, *Encyklopädie der Staatswissenschaften*, Zweite Auflage . . ., p. 404. Similarly, the "philosophical international law" was percieved by Bülau: F. Bülau, op. cit., p. 396.

615 It should be remembered that von Mohl included United States as one of the countries of European civilization. He also predicted that Australia would also follow them in the near future. R. v. Mohl, *Encyklopädie der Staatswissenschaften*, Zweite Auflage . . ., p. 471.

616 Ibid, p. 468.

in the absence of such authority, based its validity only on the voluntary consent of states, so there is no adequate force to enforce its standards.[617]

According to von Mohl the sources of international law in force in European civilization include treaties and customary law.[618] He divided the treaties between states into universal ones, i.e. those concluded by most or all European countries (von Mohl quotes the example of the Final Act of the Congress of Vienna), and specific, or more universal agreements concluded between a number of larger or smaller states.[619] Interestingly, the fact that many separate treaties concluded between different states are based on similar principles formed, for the Württemberger, a confirmation of the common roots of international law in European civilization.[620]

The custom as a source of applicable international law was responsible for the creation, among European countries, of legal principles that function either as a mere "international courtesy" (*internationale Höflichkeit*), or as voluntary mutual concessions. Their observance, however, is seen as the duty of every civilized state.[621] Miloś Već rightly states that von Mohl's attachment to the value of "European civilization" testifies to his belonging to this group of scholars dealing with international law that associated it with abstract values.[622] One should also agree with Stefan Kroll that the study of international law in his approach departs from the pure legal positivism. Therefore, international law is based in von Mohl on both a philosophical and a positive basis.[623] It is also worth pointing out that, according to von Mohl, international law refers to the joint existence and relations between individual states, which makes it similar to public international

617 Ibid.

618 On the concept of European international law: G. F. Martens, *Versuch über die Existenz eines positiven Europäischen Völkerrechts und den Nutzen dieser Wissenschaft*, Göttingen 1787.

619 Friedrich Bülau spoke about "practical European international law" (*praktische europäische Völkerrecht*): "The practical European international law is a joint concept referring to the same binding rules of legal relations between states among the peoples of European civilization": F. Bülau, op. cit., p. 440.

620 R. v. Mohl, *Encyklopädie der Staatswissenschaften*, Zweite Auflage . . ., pp. 469–470.

621 Ibid, p. 470.

622 M. Vec, *From Invisible Peace to the Legitimation of War: Paradoxes of a Concept in Nineteenth Century International Law Doctrine*, [in:] *Paradoxes of Peace in Nineteenth Century Europe*, T. Hippler, M. Vec (eds.), Oxford 2015, p. 35.

623 S. Kroll, *The Illiberality of Liberal International Law: Religion, Science, and the Peaceful Violence of Civilization* [in:] *Paradoxes of Peace in Nineteenth Century Europe*. . ., p. 244.

law in its today's understanding. He did not, however, develop an idea that could today be compared with the private international law.

State ethics (*Staatsittenlehre*) forms another branch of dogmatic sciences of state in the thought of Robert von Mohl.[624] Its separation resulted in the scholar's assumption that there is also the need to study the state also from the point of view of moral principles. Relations in the state (for example, the organization of its administration), referring to the organized common life of people living in it, had to be, according to the German scholar, regulated alongside legal principles, also according to the rules of morality.[625]

In contrast to the principles of constitutional law (but also the principles of politics, which will be discussed later), the principles of state morality result from the moral, spiritual tasks of man in the state, and are derived from human conscience. The need to introduce the science of state morality is born, as man is not only subject to the laws sanctioned by the state but also to the laws of "higher nature" (*höheren Gesetze*). In addition, the existence of this teaching justifies the fact that not all actions of the state and individuals in the state can be enforced by legal coercion. Therefore, since the individual is obliged to follow the principles of reason and morality in its various life relations, it should also adhere to these principles in relation to its participation in the state. It amounts to acting (whenever the state does not apply legal coercion) according to the principles of morality.[626] Therefore, state ethics refers to those actions, attitudes (whether of state authority or citizens), which cannot be enforced by means of coercive measures, but which should result from the principles of logical, ethical reasoning.[627]

---

624 On the science of state morality in von Mohl: H. Schmitz, op. cit., pp. 58–62. Von Mohl was in favor of popularizing the scientific interest in developing state morality: K. v. Beyme, *Einleitung...*, p. XIV.

625 R. v. Mohl, *Encyklopädie der Staatswissenschaften*, Zweite Auflage . . ., pp. 504–505. Idem, Geschicht.u.Lit.1, p. 116.

626 Idem, *Encyklopädie der Staatswissenschaften*, Zweite Auflage . . ., pp. 56–57.

627 Ibid, p. 505. It is worth noting that the philosophy of law in today's understanding is based, among others, on the idea of justice. One cannot ignore the relationships that characterize the philosophy of law and moral philosophy. Małgorzata Łuszczyńska rightly points to the resulting strong connection between law and morality. More on that topic: M. Łuszczyńska, *Filozofia prawa: w poszukiwaniu tożsamości*, "Studia Iuridica Lublinensia" 16, 2011, pp. 173, 176. More on relations between statutory law and the equity category: L. Leszczyński, *Kategoria słuszności w wykładni prawa*, "Studia Iuridica Lublinensia," vol. XV, 1, 2011, pp. 45–46.

The emergence of the science of state ethics implements the postulate derived by von Mohl to perceive the state in a holistic, comprehensive manner, i.e. from all the possible points of view. So what is relevant are not only legal principles (as discussed earlier) or policy principles, but we also need science that focuses on the requirements set by moral principles.[628] Therefore, the task of state ethics was to protect authorities and officials, or citizens, from fulfilling only such obligations that are imposed on them solely by law. According to von Mohl, the law set the basic, minimum requirements, while state ethics was required because residents of the state should also be required to fulfil higher obligations, not only under duress or fear of sanctions.[629] The difference between law and morality and their mutual essence in von Mohl's thought finds its perfect illustration in the example of a citizen's existence in the state. There is no doubt that the regulations of law requires a citizen only to act or cease acting according to their principles. Morality, on the other hand, sets requirements for the citizen to go much further, as the scholar noted: "Morality requires him [citizen- ed. aut] that, provided it is appropriate, he would voluntarily contribute to the promotion of the common good, have the courage to counter dangers and overcome evil, and make a voluntary sacrifice at the time of defeat and danger."[630] What seems crucial here is the voluntariness of citizen's actions. What we see in Württemberger's thought is the firm conviction that the law will never be able to regulate comprehensively all the factual conditions of the state. Thus, appealing to morality is the key for him to tie his citizens closer to the state and persuade them to act in its favor.

Attention should also be paid to the aspect concerning the relationship between law and morality in the state. The main difference between statutory law and moral principles is the state's ability to use coercion to enforce the former. There is no doubt that a citizen of a given state, who is after all, subject to legal norms, is obliged to comply with the resulting orders and bans. From the moral point of view, on the other hand, a citizen is obliged to act voluntarily, often making personal sacrifices for the common good. Therefore, the principles of morality require the "participant of the state" to act rationally in his life and to respect and, if necessary, support the rational aspirations of others.[631]

---

628 R. v. Mohl, *Encyklopädie der Staatswissenschaften*, Zweite Auflage . . ., p. 507. The science of state morality was considered by von Mohl to be a underdeveloped discipline. More about von Mohl's attitude to current political ethics literature: Idem, Geschicht.u.Lit.1, pp. 43–44.

629 Idem, *Encyklopädie der Staatswissenschaften*, Zweite Auflage . . ., p. 508.

630 Ibid.

631 Ibid, pp. 505–506, 508.

In principle, von Mohl was of the opinion that legal and moral principles are not in contradiction, moreover, the task of morality is to respect and support the law as the means of maintaining order in the state. The sole possibility of a collision between legal and moral obligations in a state is a situation, in which a certain legal norm introduces a rule incompatible with "purely reasonable will and action." On one hand, obeying such a norm is usually sanctioned, and the potential failure to do so may have negative consequences, while on the other hand there are norms of human conscience ordering non-compliance.[632] The Württemberger took the position that in case of doubt of a moral nature, one should comply with the law. Such a view results from the belief that maintaining and observing the legal order as a condition of the highest importance for social life forms, of itself, a moral order. Robert von Mohl, however, left a possibility that can be compared to the institution of civil disobedience. He believed that if there was a situation in which a single citizen was in no way able to reconcile the order or legal prohibition with the norm of their own conscience, then he or she should not comply with the legal order, and treat the resulting sanctions as so-called "inevitable evil" (*unvermeidliche Uebel*).[633] In this case, the state authority is burdened with moral obligation to prevent such collisions from continuing to recur and, if necessary, to pardon a citizen who opposes the regulations of such law.[634]

The last dogmatic state science distinguished by von Mohl was politics, also known as "state art" (*Staatskunst*).[635] The separation of this discipline resulted from the scholar's belief that "the collective actions of people in a state must comply with the principles of purposefulness and prudence."[636] It is not enough, therefore, to apply only legal and moral principles to actions in the state. Actions must still be "rational" (*verständig*), i.e. based on the principles of common sense,

632 Ibid, p. 506.

633 Ibid, p. 507.

634 Ibid. Speaking of state ethics, von Mohl drew attention to the achievements of Niccolo Macchiavelli. Idem, Geschicht.u.Lit.1, p. 44. More on civil disobedience: L. Sobkowiak, *Obywatelskie nieposłuszeństwo*, [in:] *Encyklopedia politologii*, t.1, W. Sokół, M. Żmigrodzki (eds.), Kraków 1999, p. 425. The concept of imposing, on authorities, the obligation to establish legal norms consistent with the principles of morality is also found in works of Immanuel Kant. More on this topic: M. Chmieliński, *Moralność a prawo w doktrynie polityczno-prawnej Immanuela Kanta*, [in:] *Moralność i władza jako kategorie myśli politycznej*, J. Justyński, A. Madeja (eds.), Warszawa 2011, pp. 239–253.

635 On politics in von Mohl: H. Schmitz, op. cit., pp. 76–79, W. Bleek, *Geschichte der Politikwissenschaft in Deutschland...*, p. 123. K. v. Beyme, *Einleitung...*, p. XV.

636 R. v. Mohl, *Encyklopädie der Staatswissenschaften*, Zweite Auflage . . ., p. 57.

purpose and rationality.[637] Every idea and intention relating to the state should be implemented in it in the right way and at the right time, because even the best plan (in accordance with law and morality) will fail if it is not implemented properly. The task of the politics is therefore the appropriate, prudent conduct of state management processes.[638] The above assumptions allowed the German scientist to define politics as: "Science about the means, by which the objectives of the state are realized to the fullest possible extent."[639]

Politics, which for von Mohl was a field of knowledge dealing with finding the right means to achieve the objectives of the state, was of great importance to him. For the state, a complicated apparatus, which complexity increases with the development of the civilization of the nation that inhabits it, needs a science that will determine what measures should be taken to achieve the objectives adopted by that nation best.[640] The importance of politics, i.e. choosing the right means to achieve these objectives is enormous, because, for example, adopting the wrong means can lead not only to the delay in achieving the goal, but even to its foiling. The division of politics in the concept of von Mohl is dictated by the scope of activity of the state entity. The first division will therefore concern the policies of "internal life of the state" and "external life of the state." Internal policy will again be divided into "organizational" (*Verfassungspolitik*) and administrative (*Verwaltungspolitik*) policies.[641] On the other hand, external policy will focus on securing the state and achieving its objectives on the international stage.[642] An

637 The art of governance was associated in the German science with the term *Klugheit* (cleverness, wisdom, prudence): DF Lindenfeld, op. cit., p. 1.

638 R. v. Mohl, *Encyklopädie der Staatswissenschaften*, Zweite Auflage . . ., p. 57.

639 Ibid, p. 543. Similarly: Idem, Geschicht.u.Lit.3, p. 341. It should be noted that the Mohl's definition of politics, despite the fact that it differs from others its wording, in fact had a subject scope coinciding with the definitions of other scientists at that time. Heinrich Luden understood politics as the science of "the behavior of those in power," and Friedrich Bülau explicitly spoke of politics as the science of achieving the goals of individual states: H. Luden, *Handbuch der Staatsweisheit oder der Politik*, Jena 1811, pp. 36–37, F. Bülau op. cit., p. 267. It will also be reasonable to conclude that von Mohl's understanding of politics is similar to that of Aristotle. The Greek thinker also described politics as practical activities related to the designation and implementation of specific tasks of the state. Aristotle, *Etyka Nikomachejska*, trans. D. Gromska, Warszawa 1982, pp. 3–9. More: W. J. Korab-Karpowicz, *Historia Filozofii Politycznej od Tukidydesa do Locke'a*, Kęty 2010, pp. 72–73.

640 R. v. Mohl, Geschicht.u.Lit.3, p. 349.

641 Idem, *Encyklopädie der Staatswissenschaften*, Zweite Auflage . . ., pp. 542–543.

642 Ibid, p. 702.

important view of von Mohl, influencing the systematics of politics and public sciences in general is that "police science" (*Polizeiwissenschaft*) does not constitute a separate field next to administrative policy, but forms part of it.[643]

Worth mentioning is von Mohl's teaching on the relationship of law and morality to politics. The German scholar presented the view that there could be no contradiction between the principles of law and morality and political principles. Logic dictates to observe, that since the tasks and goals of the state are indicated by law and morality, the science of their implementation (politics) cannot assume that we should adopt means to achieve these objectives that are not leading to them.[644] Of course, one can imagine a situation in which norms of law and morals would establish certain binding rules on one hand, and on the other would be deliberately violated for the purpose of obtaining immediate benefits (for example by state authorities). The result would be a contradiction between the state organism and itself, as well as chaos among state officials and its citizens who would not know how they should act. A contradiction between the principles of law and morality and the principles of politics would mean that the state could not demand specific behaviors from citizens, setting a bad example of a contradictory activity.[645]

Robert von Mohl did not accept concessions or allow for the possibility of political actions contrary to the law or morality. Also if the temporary balance of profit and loss would be beneficial. According to von Mohl, immoral policy will always have negative consequences and lead to losses that outweigh the unfairly attained benefits.[646] Therefore, one should note the idealistic approach of the scholar to this issue, which stands in contradiction to the principles derived more than three hundred years earlier by Niccolo Machiavelli.[647]

643 Idem, *Encyklopädie der Staatswissenschaften,* Erste Auflage . . ., p. 543.

644 Idem, *Encyklopädie der Staatswissenschaften*, Zweite Auflage . . ., p. 546. Speaking about the conflict between law, morality and politics, von Mohl stated: "If there is a conflict between law, morality and politics, either one of these relations is based on a false basis, or there an error occurred in the final conclusion. The whole task is therefore to find this error and thus bring harmony; indeed, there is not a contradiction and it cannot be such.": Idem, Geschicht.u.Lit.3, p. 352.

645 Idem, *Encyklopädie der Staatswissenschaften*, Zweite Auflage . . ., p. 546.

646 Ibid, pp. 547–548. On the relation of politics to morality in von Mohl: K. v. Beyme, *Einleitung...*, p. XV.

647 On the assessment of Macchiavelli by von Mohl: R. v. Mohl, Geschicht.u.Lit.3, p. 354. More on Nicollo Machiavelli's understanding of ethics: A. Gugnin, T. Pliszek, *Instytucjonalny wymiar etyki w ujęciu Niccolo Machiavellego*, "Nierówności społeczne a wzrost gospodarczy," z. 15, 2009, pp. 120–126. A comprehensive review and assessment

According to von Mohl, the relations between law, morality and politics were governed by three principles of utmost importance. The first was that if a certain act was appropriate from a legal, moral and political point of view, it should be absolutely carried out. The second stated that if a given action in a state (politically justified) is neutral from the point of view of law and morality (they neither require it nor prohibit it), it can be applied, provided it is really necessary. However, if there is a collision between political action and the principles derived from legal norms, it should be absolutely abandoned.[648] Von Mohl, however, provided for three exceptions to the above principles: the first in which the law of a particular individual conflicts with the achievement of the general objective and is materially measurable (with money); then the collision should be removed by paying the individual appropriate remuneration (compensation), for example in return for expropriation. The second exception will be emergency situations, such as saving the state, where the state objectives prevail over the rights of the individual, even when the losses cannot be compensated.[649] The third principle stated that since maintaining the "impeccable legal order" forms the most important task of the state, in a situation where a given law is contrary to the general legal order it should be allowed, and it is recommended not to apply it, and later to amend or cancel it.[650]

Robert von Mohl should be considered one of the most important German scholars in politics at the time. Among other things, he should be credited with making politics emerge as an independent discipline that explores the means to achieve state objectives. Like many of his contemporaries, he understood politics as a field of state science, with the task and subject of finding rational means to achieve objectives, as set primarily by law but also by morality.[651]

The second, full-fledged part of the system of state sciences in the thought of Robert von Mohl were the disciplines whose task was to describe factual events, i.e. "history of the state" (*Staatsgeschichte*) and "statistics" (*Statistik*), forming parts of the "historical state sciences" (*Geschichtliche Staatswissenschaften*). The task of historical sciences was to provide knowledge related to the realities of the life of the state both in the past (history of the state) and the present (statistics).

---

of Macchiavelli's concept was presented by Jan Malarczyk: J. Malarczyk, *U źródeł włoskiego realizmu politycznego: Macchiavelli i Guicciardini*, Lublin 1963.

648 R. v. Mohl, *Encyklopädie der Staatswissenschaften*, Zweite Auflage . . ., pp. 548–549.

649 Two separate rules appear in the first issue of the *Encyclopedia*. . ..: Idem, *Encyklopädie der Staatswissenschaften*, Erste Auflage . . ., pp. 546–547.

650 Idem, *Encyklopädie der Staatswissenschaften*, Zweite Auflage . . ., pp. 549–550.

651 W. Sacher, op. cit., p. 14. D. F. Lindenfeld, op. cit., p. 114.

The function of the state history, based on knowledge of the past history of the state was the analysis of the so-called "general state life" (*das gesammte staatliche Leben*), and to provide information on what paths did its existence take in response to general or specific events. On the other hand, the purpose of statistics was to present, in a structured manner, certain actual conditions in the state at a single moment.[652] Both the history of the state and statistics in von Mohl thought remain in a strong relationship, which is best illustrated by his recognition as apt the assertions by August Ludwig von Schlözer, stating: "History is moving statistics, and statistics is history stopped in its run."[653]

The historical and statistical approach to the state were as important to von Mohl as the perception of it from the dogmatic point of view. The purpose of historical state sciences was to make the individual aware of the character and specifics of the state relations in which it finds himself. This makes the individual fully understand the tasks it faces in its life, and forecast the most likely course of events in relation to the state, or even the entire humanity. In view of the fact that life in the state was the most important dimension of human existence on earth (although not the sole one), in order to find the "right answer to the mystery of our existence" one should possess skills relating to the history of the state and its statistics.[654] The importance of historical sciences for dogmatic sciences is illustrated by the following quote:

> "The theory of the science of the state, the scope of which is not supplemented by the use of history and state statistics, will be incomplete and may not cover all the abundance of conditions of human life. - Science that does not take into account knowledge of real events occurring in a given phenomenon [state- author's note] also brings the danger of formulating incorrect rules applying to it."[655]

The last advantage of historical sciences, which are based on and analyze the facts, will be that they enable all to assess whether specific theoretical goals (set, for example, by law belonging to dogmatic sciences) work in reality. So they allow to explain the consequences of applying specific theories, and the effectiveness of

652 R. v. Mohl, *Encyklopädie der Staatswissenschaften*, Zweite Auflage ..., pp. 55, 725. Similarly: Idem, *Literarhistorische Uebersicht über die Encyklopädieen der Staatswissenschaften*..., p. 425.

653 Quote after: Idem, *Encyklopädie der Staatswissenschaften*, Zweite Auflage ..., pp. 750–751.

654 Ibid, pp. 725–726.

655 Ibid.

their lives. In addition, by pointing to discrepancies between facts and theoretical assumptions, they can also indicate errors in dogmatic sciences.[656]

The history of the state (*Staatsgeschichte*) is a science which, in von Mohl's mind, breaks down into so-called "the history of the internal state life of certain peoples" and "the history of the interaction of co-existing states, i.e. the history of political systems."[657] The history of the state seen from an internal point can be based on the so-called "universal-historical" approach (*welthistorischer Auffassung*), where it presents the history of all civilized peoples from the beginning of their existence, describing the entire history, or focus on one fragment of time. The internal history of the state may also present the history of one nation or several related tribes. The form for its elaboration can be, for example, monographs presenting either the general history of a certain state institution among all peoples possessing it, or existing only in one particular state. Internal history can also be compiled on a biographical basis, showing, for example, by describing the life of an eminent politician, all specific political changes.[658]

Examination of the so-called "relations internal history," according to von Mohl, allowed a more or less detailed review of concepts related to a particular state. This not only provides important information about it, but also allows conclusions to be drawn regarding its further development. The analysis of individual state institutions makes it possible to describe the effectiveness of their operation, detect the errors committed and avoid them in the future.[659]

"History of political systems" (or history in the external sense) represents a narrower scope than history in internal terms, because it does not refer to the whole of human life, nor can it be compiled in such different ways as internal history can. The task of the external history of state life was to be a general analysis of the entire political system, the advantage of which is to provide information on the current fate of specific states and to compare them. It can also present a selected political system of a given country in a detailed form. According to the Württemberger, the knowledge resulting from such an analysis can provide information on the errors and appropriate motions of another state and allows different states to draw on this experience as a result of providing conclusions regarding its future planned activities.[660]

656 Ibid, p. 727.
657 Ibid, p. 730.
658 Ibid, pp. 730–731.
659 Ibid, pp. 731–732.
660 Ibid, pp. 732, 734.

Speaking about the justification for the existence of statistics, von Mohl noted:

> "As long as states and their officials exist, there is a practical need for a thorough understanding of their [country's - author's note] state of affairs. (...) Wherever they did not wish to rule in an irrational way and, based on chance or at least on high uncertainty, at all times information was collected for the head of state about the state of his own country and foreign countries. (...)"[661]

Statistics belonging to historical science deals with the presentation and description of specific facts. Due to the fact that the reasons for the emergence and persistence of specific situations in reality should be explained by the history of the state or by dogmatic sciences, the task of statistics is only to show actual facts without attempting to assess them. By providing insight into specific, objective information, statistics allow not only to draw conclusions as to the causes of specific phenomena, but also to determine their natural principles. This means that it is of great importance both for those who rule the state, but also for the general knowledge of citizens about it.[662]

Defining the statistics, von Mohl stated that it did not have to present facts referring only to the present, because it could as well deal with the presentation of historical factual conditions.[663] The purpose of the statistics is to present facts related to the state but also to "social facts." It would seem, therefore, that the German scholar has broken his principle saying that the subject of state sciences should be the state alone. It should be stated, however, that he adhered to his next rule of faithful reflection of reality by science. Therefore, on one hand, von Mohl noticed that statistics relating to state life should be limited only to the presentation of the so-called "state peculiarities" (*Staatsmerkwürdigkeiten*). On the other hand, however, he was aware that at that time statistics had adopted a direction of development, which caused it to cover various issues not strongly related to the state, focusing on the mental and physical characteristics of people.[664] Therefore,

661 Idem, Geschicht.u.Lit.3, p. 643.

662 Ibid, p. 645. Speaking about the objectives of statistics, the scientist stated: "In itself, statistics has nothing to do with explaining the reasons, why certain things went this way, and it is rather the task of other sciences, e.g. history, politics or economics.": Ibid, p. 646.

663 Idem, *Encyklopädie der Staatswissenschaften*, Zweite Auflage ..., p. 746, 750. Frierdrich Bülau, aslo spoke about statistics as the science of contemporary condition of states: F. Bülau, op. cit., p. 250. On the understanding of statistics at that time also: A. L. v. Schlözer, *Theorie der Statistik*, Göttingen 1804, K. G. A. Knies, *Die Statistik als selbständige Wissenschaft*, Kassel 1850. More about the 19th century development of statistics in the German territories: DF Lindenfeld, op. cit., pp. 131–133.

664 R. v. Mohl, Geschicht.u.Lit.3, p. 644.

von Mohl comes to the conclusion that some facts in the field of social relations should also be included into the scope of statistics. Such action was to allow giving specific depth to information related to the state due to the fact that, in the opinion of the German scholar, it was impossible to understand the essence of the state without analyzing its social relations. It should be remembered, however, that state statistics should not present facts about all social relations, but focus on those that are directly related to the life of the state.[665]

We should also remember that the German liberal considered it a mistake for the statistics to describe only such content that would only be represented by numbers and to exclude information written with use of words. For the Württemberger both numbers and words were equally valid in presenting specific facts. It was important to present the given fact or circumstance in the most comprehensive, yet also the most convenient way, so that the information provided by it could be best used for efficient management of the state.[666]

The scholar's distinction of a separate field of historical state science certainly proves that he wanted to cover the entire scope of knowledge relating to the state. Thus, not only the ideas and legal regulations of dogmatic sciences, but also the knowledge relating to dry facts found a place in the Mohl's system of state sciences. What's more, the disciplines of dogmatic and historical sciences do not function in isolation. On the contrary, they seem to complement each other. The role of historical sciences seems to be particularly important here, as they provide information enabling proper implementation of the state's objectives in relation to dogmatic sciences.

665 Idem, *Encyklopädie der Staatswissenschaften*, Zweite Auflage . . ., pp. 749–750.
666 Idem, Geschicht.u.Lit.3, pp. 647–648.

Chapter III The idea of the state and its diversity.

3.1. The origin of the state

The spheres of human life discussed in chapter two, such as family, tribe or society, functioned in Robert von Mohl's doctrine as the formations enabling the individual to effectively achieve life goals that would otherwise be impossible to attain on its own. In addition to facilitating the implementation of increasingly complex tasks and objectives, the existence within these communities provided man with the opportunity to climb to ever higher levels of mental and civilization development. The complexity of these levels was directly proportional to the complexity of these communities.[667]

For von Mohl, there was no doubt that the abovementioned spheres of life are necessary and even indispensable for individuals, as they beneficially affected their existence. However, they are characterized by features that will first distinguish them from the state, and secondly will condition its creation. The most important difference between the state and communities such as family, tribe or society was, according to German liberal, the way they were brought to life. According to von Mohl, these communities were created naturally. This was to be determined by the fact that they are not established (and regulated) by so-called "external authority" (*äußere Auctorität*), which can be compared to power, or political suzeranity.[668] The above necessitates us to emphasize the impermanence of these life spheres. On the basis of the issues presented in the second chapter, for example, society in von Mohl's concept can be considered a limited and accidental structure, i.e. one that spontaneously forms, without top-down control. As mentioned earlier, individual "social circles" gather their members on the principle of community of interests. These interests can be variable, but also opposite. Therefore, various types of conflict will always appear in the heart of the society, often preventing people from living peacefully and achieving their individual goals.[669]

---

667 Idem, *Encyklopädie der Staatswissenschaften*, Zweite Auflage. . ., p. 38.

668 H. Schmitz, op. cit., p. 34. It is worth noting that, for example, for Jean Jacques Rousseau, the family is the oldest and the sole natural "of all societies": J. J. Rousseau, op. cit. p. 12.

669 R. v. Mohl, *Encyklopädie der Staatswissenschaften*, Zweite Auflage . . ., pp. 38–39.

In the view of von Mohl, what determines the need for a state was primarily the insufficiency of the more primary spheres. This incompleteness should be seen as a lack of power, i.e. a factor capable of constantly removing any violations of the principles of coexistence between people. According to von Mohl, the sole entity capable of ordering human life and demarcating its various spheres was the state.[670]

To sum up, all the aforementioned spheres of human life are characterized primarily by lack of order. As spontaneous creations, they are not subject to predetermined and enforceable rules. Such a state of affairs may cause that conflicts will arise between individuals and their groups, which will result in impediment or failure to achieve life aspirations. As a result of this, the need for a state is revealed, understood by von Mohl as a creation which, being uniform and equipped with force instruments, captures and organizes in its essence all the individuals, families, tribes and social communities of the respective nation.[671]

The task of the state, like other spheres of human life, is to provide support in achieving the existential objectives of individuals. The distinguishing feature of the state in Robert von Mohl's thoughts is its uniformity and the power at its disposal. However, the scholar did not have an absolutist approach to the state. One of the most important claims about the state should be considered the belief that its goal is not to replace or eliminate all the naturally shaped spheres of life. Its task is most certainly to supplement them.[672] Thus, the state reveals itself here only as one of the institutions (admittedly the strongest), which is to serve the realization of life goals by individuals. We find evidence of the rationality of Mohl's approach to the state in the rejection of all concepts assuming its connection with factors of a transcendent and higher nature (for example, divine influence). Contrary to the already mentioned Friedrich Julius Stahl, von Mohl did not think it right to recognize the state as a natural "manifestation of the divine world order."[673] It should be noted, however, that despite this opposition, based

670 Ibid.

671 Ibid, p. 39. On this topic: H. Schmitz, op. cit., p. 35.

672 R. v. Mohl, *Encyklopädie der Staatswissenschaften*, Zweite Auflage . . ., p. 40.

673 Ibid, p. 41. Von Mohl will also oppose the organic theory of the state, comparing its individual parts with members of the human body. Such a view, as presented, for example, by Johann Caspar Bluntschli, is called an irrational "toying" (*Spieleri*), and it is considered illogical to make comparisons of completely different things (i.e. man and state): Ibid. Remembering Johann Caspar Bluntschli, it is also worth noting that referring to the difference between the state and the Church, he will remain on the basis of references to the world of human nature. He compares the first the

on historical experience, he will still recognize the existence of theocracy and the emergence of states based on religious ideas.

Knowing the justification for the existence of the state, one should look at the ways in which it first emerged, as distinguished by von Mohl. The theory of the emergence of states is another proof of Württemberger's rationality and adherence to the principles of empiricism. The main premise of views on the formation of states is the belief in their diversity. In the *Constitutional Law of the Kingdom of Württemberg* the scholar presented an interesting view that there will be as many ways of establishing a state as there will be the species of it. It is impossible to imagine that a theocratic state was created on the basis of a social contract, and the legal state as a result of the so-called "Divine order."[674] In addition, historical experience and observation of reality show diversity in the formation of states. Some will be formed in the result of the development of a particular tribe, and the aforementioned theocracies will be based on the principles of a religion. Finally, states may also form as a result of the population clustering around a prominent individual.[675] In von Mohl's thought, therefore, all views of scholars who consider only one specific way of state creation as the sole possible one, are negated. So the Württemberger opposed both the views based on the creation of the state solely on the basis of an agreement and the vision represented, for example, by Stahl, proclaiming the formation of states solely in the result of activities of transcendent forces.[676]

When analyzing the ideas related to the formation of the state in von Mohl, it should first be stated that the scholar tried to answer the question of what may be the so-called "legal" ways for its creation. In other words, what ways of establishing the state can be considered fair and right not only from the point of view of law but also that of morality. The creation of a state in a "legal" way is extremely important because, according to von Mohl, it is a prerequisite for ensuring the durability of its system, as well as its acting in a lawful manner in individual situations. A state that does not arise in a "legal" way will be affected by something like a primary defect. Guided by legal reasoning, the scholar noted that something that arose in an unlawful manner, for example, could not have

so-called "Masculinity" and the Church to the so-called "Femininity": J. C. Bluntschli, *Psychologische Studien über Staat und Kirche*, Neumünster bei Zürich 1844, pp. 7–10.

674 R. v. Mohl, Staatsr.Württem.1.1829, pp. 5–6.

675 Idem, *Encyklopädie der Staatswissenschaften*, Zweite Auflage. . ., p. 90. H. Schmitz, op. cit., p. 38.

676 R. v. Mohl, *Encyklopädie der Staatswissenschaften*, Zweite Auflage. . ., pp. 97–98.

legally binding effects. That is why the emergence of "legal" ways of establishing the state was so crucially important.[677]

The thesis about Württemberger's liberal attitude finds further confirmation in his distinction and affirmation of the principle of contractualism as the "legal" path for the emergence of a state.[678] In von Mohl's thought, the establishment of a state under a contract can take place in two ways. The first is the situation in which the agreement for the creation of the state is concluded by all those who wish to establish it. This agreement is concluded consciously and decides on all the details of the functioning of the newly created statehood. The second way for contracting the creation of a state is by joining a larger or smaller number of units already associated in one way or another with particular existing power. On the path of slow evolution, on the basis of separate contracts, individual communities are bonded, and eventually they become a single whole.[679] One cannot fail to notice that in the latter way of establishing the state on the basis of the agreement he presented a scholarly view similar to the conservative Karl Ludwig von Haller. For von Mohl, however, this way of establishing the state was characteristic of the patrimonial state. The Württemberger also criticized the fact that Haller did not highlight other ways for forming the state.[680]

According to von Mohl, the social contract was a legitimate ("legal") way for the emergence of states. In addition, it provided evidence that the state could arise through an "explicit agreement of comrades."[681] Interestingly, von Mohl did not rule out a situation, where it is not all members of the nation that conclude the agreement, but only those who hold power. The case in which a state arises with the participation of all members of a given nation was for the scholar a *signum temporis* of the epoch, in which he lived. The reason for this was, inter alia, popularization of the idea of the rule of law, which for the Württemberger was related to the perception of the entire nation as an entity in the state, having

677 Ibid, pp. 91–92.

678 Ibid, pp. 93, 95. More about the concept of a social contract: J. J. Rousseau, op. cit., pp. 18–20, M. Łuszczyńska, *Umowa społeczna jako fundament życia zbiorowego*, "Studia Iuridica Lublinensia" 21, 2014, pp. 43–54. M. Maciejewski, *Zarys dziejów kontraktualistycznych koncepcji genezy społeczeństwa i państwa,*[in:] *O źródłach państwa i władzy politycznej*, A. Wielomski, C. Kalita (eds.), Biała Podlaska 2011, pp. 140–163.

679 R. v. Mohl, *Encyklopädie der Staatswissenschaften*, Zweite Auflage. . ., p. 95.

680 Ibid, pp. 78, 101.

681 Ibid, p. 93.

certain rights in it.[682] Creation of the United States was, according to von Mohl, an example of the establishment of the state as part of a contract.[683]

In von Mohl's doctrine, however, social contract is not the sole proper way to create a state. As already indicated, history and experience constituting the scholar's reference points for his claims demonstrated that the state can also be formed on the basis of a population joining under the orders of a specific tribal ruler, or on the basis of a religious idea. A social contract is, therefore, just one of the various ways in which the state was formed.[684]

In addition to the agreement, von Mohl distinguished its establishment by the so-called "Legitimate authority" (*berechtigte Auctorität*), which can adopt two forms. First, it can be understood as a religious authority.[685] The condition for the emergence of a state on this principle is the existence of a strong faith in the nation. A specific people must not only believe in a given religion, but also be firmly convinced of its special role in the so-called "Divine plan." This state of affairs will justify forming the state on a religious basis. However, it should be remembered that functioning on this principle will logically imply that such a state may only adopt the theocratic form of the system.[686]

When discussing the emergence of the state on the basis of religion, one should once again emphasize von Mohl's objection to its treatment as a "universal image of God's Kingdom."[687] The establishment of religion as the only reference point

---

682 Ibid, p. 101. Idem, SVuP.2.1, p. 313.

683 On the other hand, for von Mohl the rise of California (Republic of California) was an example, where all the population participated in the establishment of the state on the basis of an agreement. According to the scholar, the inhabitants of California had not only the right but also the moral obligation to establish an organism that would organize their life together. However, it should be remembered that the Republic of California existed for a very limited time only.: Ibid, p. 317. More on this subject: Idem, *Nordamerikanisches Staatsrecht*, "Kritische Zeitschrift für Rechtswissenschaft und Gesetzgebung des Auslandes," Bd. 27, 1855, pp. 294–302, F. Tuthill, *The History of California*, San Francisco 1866, pp. 152–175.

684 R. v. Mohl, *Encyklopädie der Staatswissenschaften*, Zweite Auflage..., pp. 85–87.

685 Ibid, p. 95. H. Schmitz, op. cit., p. 39.

686 R. v. Mohl, *Encyklopädie der Staatswissenschaften*, Erste Auflage..., p. 96. Among the nineteenth-century writers who saw God's power in the formation of the state, there is also the Frenchman Joseph de Maistre. More about the theistic theory of the emergence of the state: J. W. Garner, *Introduction to Political Science a treatise on the origin, nature, functions, and organization of the state*, New York, Cincinnati, Chicago 1910, pp. 87–91.

687 "*Abbild des allgemeinen Gottesreiches.*" Stahl and de Maistre did just that.

for the state was, for von Mohl, an irrational narrowing of its essence. Despite opposing views, the scientist appears here primarily as a realist, stating that just as respectable are the views of peoples focusing on material goals of life, it may be equally legitimate to perceive the state and temporal life through the prism of religion. So he admitted the existence of "Christian theocracy," however, denying the view that this is the only possible system of the state.[688] What is also worth noticing, is that not only the Christian religion failed to gain the appreciation of the scholar, as basis for forming a state. In principle, von Mohl was of the opinion that the state should never be subjected to one (sole valid) philosophical theory, stating: "the atrophied and wrongful compulsion of secular philosophy is as unbearable, as a religious dogma."[689]

The second example of the creation of a state through "legitimate authority" will be its creation through "fatherly authority" (*väterliche Auctorität*).[690] This situation applies in von Mohl to the transformation of lower forms of collective life of people (in this case a tribe) in higher forms, i.e. the state. If a specific tribe, centred around a patriarchal leader, develops enough to require a more efficient organization, it may turn into a state. The key factor here, in addition to the sufficiently high level of development, is the agreement of the ruler or those in power so far. According to von Mohl, they are the ones holding the right and the task of determining the organization of the state. In essence, therefore, it is a way similar to a social contract concluded only by a specific, power-wielding group. It is not difficult to guess, although the scholar did not express it explicitly, that this way should refer to the patriarchal state.[691]

It is also worth noting the errors, as highlighted by von Mohl, that can be committed in the formation of the state. First of all, what does not correspond to the idea of the legal formation of the state is, when entities establishing a state organization, by force, without the consent of a specific people or nation, force them to enter the structures of a particular state. Von Mohl's liberal approach is proved in his belief that the state cannot be based on violence, which in his opinion would be morally wrong. Another situation of unlawful foundation of a state will be a condition that can be compared to an institution of error in civil law. Therefore, it will be inappropriate if in the process of establishing a state one of the parties will be accidentally or deliberately convinced of an essence or

688 R. v. Mohl, *Encyklopädie der Staatswissenschaften*, Zweite Auflage. . ., pp. 83–84, 89–90.
689 Ibid, p. 85.
690 H. Schmitz, op. cit., p. 39.
691 R. v. Mohl, *Encyklopädie der Staatswissenschaften*, Zweite Auflage. . ., p. 96.

a form of the state differing from the actual one. Another mistake will be non-compliance with the *pacta sunt servanda* principle, i.e. non-compliance with the contract that has been agreed. The ultimate mistake would be to include the accomplishments of life objectives of one part of the nation, while omitting the requirements of the remaining part.[692]

However, one cannot ignore the fact that von Mohl also allowed a kind of validation for the process of erroneous founding of the state. Therefore, he recognized the possibility of fixing it so that it could continue to operate. The above inconsistency once again demonstrates, how highly did the scholar value the state itself. It was more appropriate for him to correct even serious errors, so that the structure of the state could continue to operate, than to follow unreflectively and fundamentally the principles accompanying its formation.[693]

The last concept referring to the emergence of states was von Mohl's admission that, despite committing the abovementioned "primary errors," such as the use of violence or the resistance of the nation, the state may come into existence in a lawful manner. This will be the case, when the use of violence or action in the face of resistance of the population was the sole way to "create the whole nation in such a state in which it could achieve the life goals determined by the level of its civilization."[694] The pragmatism of the scholar is clearly noticeable. He assumed that some external force is able to impose a certain form of organization on the nation, in a situation where the nation itself is unable to organize or opposing it. Nevertheless two conditions had to be met to establish a state in this manner. Firstly, von Mohl postulated that the nation in question should be affected by "physical violence" (*physiche Gewalt*) that would hinder or prevent it from climbing a higher level of development. This could be, for example, a despot, a country that exploits its colony, or groups that present retrograde views. Secondly, the peaceful attempts at changing the organization of the nation to bring it to a higher level of development should prove ineffective. Thus, presenting the view that physical violence can only be overcome by other physical violence, the Württemberger stated, that the creation of a state in conditions of violence is justified only when there is no other possibility to achieve a specific goal.[695] Examples of such state formations were, for von Mohl, the processes of

692 Ibid, pp. 93, 94, 98. On errors that are possible in establishing the state: H. Schmitz, op. cit., p. 38.
693 R. v. Mohl, *Encyklopädie der Staatswissenschaften*, Zweite Auflage…, p. 94.
694 Ibid, p. 96.
695 Ibid, p. 97.

often violent, armed separation of colonies from metropolitan states, where only the establishment of one's own state would be sufficient to achieve the life goals resulting from the civilizational development of its inhabitants.[696]

Summing up the teachings of von Mohl on the origin of the state, it should be said that they are immersed in empiricism. It also testifies to the scholar's tear between epochs. Empiricism is proved by basing on historical experience, and observation of reality. The functioning of von Mohl on the border of eras is evidenced by pointing to the ways of the emergence of states known from earlier times. Although he seems to be a supporter of the social contract as part of the rule of law, he does not forget about the other, more primary ways for establishing a state. Furthermore, he appears as a pragmatist. He believed that there are situations in which the use of coercion to create a state is justified. What we observe here is also the impact of the aforedescribed political situation of German area. After all, Prussia appeared in it as a state able to unite the German nation, often by means of forced solutions.

Speaking about the genesis of the state, von Mohl followed the paths already indicated by earlier thinkers. We are talking here about Jean Jacques Rousseau or John Locke. Like Locke, he was empirical. The creation of the state was also associated with the occurrence of conflicts and the incompleteness of the original human groups. The possibility of conflicts between natural communities in von Mohl may resemble the so-called John Locke's state of nature. The state appears as a factor protecting from the state of war, and in von Mohl it also regulates conflict situations between individuals.[697] Referring to the concept of a social contract it is again connected with the thought of Jean Jacques Rousseau. Similarities can also be traced to the thoughts of Thomas Hobbes. Von Mohl used the concept of natural human groups that are not sufficient to control conflicts between people. Therefore, there is a need for the state to exist as a factor capable of preventing conflicts, also through coercion. It should be remembered, however, that unlike Hobbes, von Mohl did not treat the state as the necessary evil.[698]

---

696 Von Mohl stated: "only a state of its own corresponds to life goals derived from a higher level of civilization," Ibid., p. 102.

697 J. Locke, *Dwa traktaty o rządzie*, trans. Z. Rau, Warszawa 2015, pp. 328–329. On the concept of the emergence of the state and social contract in the mind of John Locke: Z. Rau, *Umowa społeczna w doktrynie Johna Locke'a*, [in:] *Umowa społeczna i jej krytycy*, Z. Rau, M. Chmieliński (eds.), Warszawa 2010, pp. 127–151.

698 R. v. Mohl, *Encyklopädie der Staatswissenschaften*, Zweite Auflage…, p. 79, T. Hobbes, *Lewiatan czyli materia, forma i władza państwa kościelnego i świeckiego*, trans. Cz. Znamierowski, Warszawa 2005, pp. 253–259.

3.2. Definition of the state and evolution of its concept

Speaking of the significance of the definition of the state, its objective and elements, one cannot ignore the evolution which, during more than fifty years of von Mohl's scientific career, did his understanding of the state undergo.[699] In the *Constitutional Law of the Kingdom of Württemberg*, speaking of the state, von Mohl stated that it was "The embodiment of those establishments that are located in a given territory in relation to the ordered community life of a specific human mass (nation)."[700] It is impossible to resist the impression that this definition is quite narrow. However, it lists the main designations of the state, which will remain unchanged in the future. First of all, therefore, it will be the sum of specific "establishments" (institutions).[701] These institutions must refer to a specific community of people (i.e. have an appropriate subjective scope), and be characterized by territorial limitation. Therefore, already in the early period of his work, von Mohl found the population and territory to be the basic elements of the definition of the state. The scholar's definition of state was similar in his *Police science according to the principles of the legal state.* In its first edition, the state is the most comprehensive and most important institution of "the order of the common life of a nation in a given area."[702] However, in the second edition

---

699 On the concept of the state and its evolution in von Mohl: H. Schmitz, op. cit., pp. 35–38, B. Stöcker, *Die Gemeinwohltheorie Robert von Mohls ale ein früher Ansatz des sozialen Rechtsstaatsprinzips*, München 1992, pp. 122–123, R.-J. Grahe, op. cit., pp. 65–70.

700 R. v. Mohl, Staatsr.Württem.1.1829, p. 3.

701 It is worth pointing out the explanation of the phrase "establishment" (*Einrichtung*) adopted by von Mohl. The scholar was of the opinion that the word best and most extensively describes the entire "content or parts of the state organism," which is characterized by great diversity in relation to their form and purpose. He opposed, for example, the use of the words 'laws' or 'legal norms,' which he considered parts of the state, but not the only ones.: Idem, *Encyklopädie der Staatswissenschaften*, Zweite Auflage. . ., p. 72. Johann Caspar Bluntschli also used the expression *Einrichtung* in a similar sense: J.C. Bluntschli, *Allgemeine Staatslehre*, Stuttgart 1886, p. 13. The word *Einrichtung* in both the nineteenth century and today is translated from German as an "establishment" or "institution": *The Oxford-Duden German dictionary*, W. Scholze-Stubenrecht, J.B. Sykes (eds.), Oxford 1994, s. 236. *Niemiecko-polski słownik wyrazów prawniczych i administracyjnych*. . ., p.91. W. Skibicki, *Słownik terminologii prawniczej i ekonomicznej, niemiecko-polski*, Warszawa 1993, p. 132.

702 R. v. Mohl, Polizeiwiss.1.1832, p. 5.

of this work, the state is also "the order of the nation's common life in a specific area," but already subject to "the supreme authority."[703]

A more interesting and increasingly expanded understanding of the state appears in von Mohl in 1855. In the *History and Literature of Sciences of State*, the state is the "organism of institutions" located in a specific space and referring to living together. However, what is important, the state is also a factor that unites people, for the implementation of common objectives, by means of "collective will" and "collective power."[704] It is extremely important that the state appears here as a necessary unity without which people "cannot survive."[705]

Von Mohl included his most elaborate definition of the state in the *Encyclopaedia of sciences of state*. Its creation coincided with the scholar's dealing with the so-called "Social issue" (*soziale Frage*) and "workers issue" (*Arbeiter Frage*).[706] In the *Encyclopaedia*... von Mohl not only notices the existence of society, but also gives it specific tasks concerning the support of its inhabitants. In view of the above, the state in the first edition of the *Encyclopaedia*... is:

> "(...) the permanent, uniform organism of these establishments, which, driven by collective will, as well as maintained and carried out by collective power, are intended to support the allowed life objectives of a specific and territorially limited nation, from the individual up to entire society."[707]

However, the definition that we will adopt as the basis for consideration of the Mohl's concept of the state will be the one that appeared at the end of the scholar's life, in the second edition of the *Encyclopaedia*...:

> "The state is a permanent, unified organism of these establishments, which, run by collective will, as well as maintained and carried out by collective power, are intended to support the existing, allowed life objectives of a specific and territorially limited nation, from the individual to society, as long as not they are able to attain these objectives with use of their own forces, and these objectives are the subject of a common need.[708]

When discussing individual elements of the definition of the state, one should firstly pay attention to the requirement of its permanence. A permanent state is a state protected against chaos and its negative effects. According to von Mohl, the need for a state organization is eternal, because the state always exists, albeit

703 Idem, Polizeiwiss.1.1844, p. 5.
704 Idem, Geschicht.u.Lit.1, p. 90.
705 Ibid, p. 91.
706 E. Angermann, op. cit., p. 123.
707 R. v. Mohl, *Encyklopädie der Staatswissenschaften*, Erste Auflage. . ., p. 65.
708 Idem, *Encyklopädie der Staatswissenschaften*, Zweite Auflage. . ., p. 71.

in various forms. The necessity of the existence of the state will appear as long as there exist people, who need support in realizing their life intentions.[709] Being a permanent entity, the state will be able to guarantee protection and help in achieving these life objectives.[710]

Another important feature of the state is its uniformity (uniformity or indivisibility of state power will be one of von Mohl's main postulates). If the state is to guarantee, above all, "order, security and suitability" (*Ordnung, Sicherheit und Verhältnißmäßigkeit*), then it must function under an indivisible power. It is in the unified organism of the state that the individual aspirations of the nation are combined.[711]

The guarantor of order and lack of conflict, and at the same time the feature of state understood by von Mohl as the "organic unity" (*eine organische Einheit*) is its direction and shaping by the so called "collective will" (*Gesammtwillen*). For the state must be directed and maintained in unity by "the undeniable supreme will."[712] "Collective will" will always occur wherever the inhabitants of the state will legitimize a certain power (authority), as capable of governing the state or recognize that its action will not violate their general agreement. Therefore, "collective will," according to von Mohl, does not always mean reconciling the will of all residents of the state. An individual in the state is obliged to subdue itself to the "collective will." It should be noted, however, that the degree of its influence on the affairs of individuals will be different in different species of states.[713]

The next element of Mohl's understanding of the state is the existence of "Collective power" (*Gesammtkraft*). Its appearance results from fact that the strength of individuals is not enough to remove external obstacles standing in the way of achieving life objectives.[714] "Collective power" is therefore a combination of forces of individuals living in the state. Its task is not only to remove obstacles that are not removable by individual forces, but also sometimes to force individuals acting in a "unreasonable" way to respect the rules that are in place

709 Ibid, pp. 71–72

710 H. Schmitz, op. cit., p. 36.

711 R. v. Mohl, *Encyklopädie der Staatswissenschaften*, Zweite Auflage…, p. 72. For more about the uniformity of the state: C. Rössler, *System der Staatslehre, A. Allgemeine Staatslehre*, Leipzig 1857, pp. 1–3.

712 R. v. Mohl, *Encyklopädie der Staatswissenschaften*, Zweite Auflage…, p.73. B. Stöcker, op. cit., p. 123.

713 R. v. Mohl, *Encyklopädie der Staatswissenschaften*, Zweite Auflage…, p. 73. Idem, Geschicht.u.Lit.1, p. 93.

714 More about collective strength ("*Gesamtkraft*"): B. Stöcker, op. cit., p. 123.

in the said state.[715] The sole force capable of forcing individuals to submit to the fulfillment of "logically necessary" things (*logisch Nothwendige*) is precisely the "collective power."[716]

It was real and obvious for von Mohl that the state, in certain situations, can and must limit the will of the individual. However, this limitation should be directed against such actions that are irrational or anti-social. Such action was not understood by the scholar as evil, but as "great felicity."[717] As long as there exist, in a particular community of people, irrational individuals, violating universally accepted principles of coexistence, there must be a force (authority) that will limit these behaviours, so that one individual does not violate the rights of the other.[718]

It is extremely important for the scholar to recognize what kind of goals of human life should be supported by the state. First of all, the state can support only the "allowed" goals of human life. Von Mohl pointed out that the entity whose task would be to support prohibited goals, would itself become illegal. It should be noted, however, that the defined and allowed life goals of a given nation and its individuals were dependent on the degree of development at which it is located.[719] Such an opinion was already expressed by von Mohl in the *Constitutional Law of the Kingdom of Württemberg*.[720] Therefore, one general goal of the state cannot be determined, not because it is an "aimless" organism, but because human nature is so rich and multi-faceted that it generates the necessity for existence of many different objectives of the state.[721] The Württemberger, focusing on individualism of individuals, was guided by a liberal approach. He opposed attempts to find and establish one timeless, ultimate objective (or group of goals) appropriate for each nation.[722] On the other hand, however, the above opinion did not prevent von Mohl from distinguishing between groups of the most common life goals of individuals. He did not approve the imposition of any

715 R. v. Mohl, *Encyklopädie der Staatswissenschaften*, Zweite Auflage. . ., p. 73.
716 Ibid. H. Schmitz, op. cit., p. 37.
717 R. v. Mohl, *Encyklopädie der Staatswissenschaften*, Zweite Auflage. . ., p. 79.
718 Von Mohl used the word *Gewalt*, which in German means "force," but also power. Ibid, p. 73.
719 Ibid., pp. 73–74.
720 Idem, Staatsr.Württem.1.1829, p. 3.
721 Idem, *Encyklopädie der Staatswissenschaften*, Zweite Auflage. . ., p. 74. Von Mohl made a similar statement in *History and Literature...*, saying that these goals will be different in different countries: Idem, Geschicht.u.Lit.1, p. 92.
722 R. v. Mohl, *Encyklopädie der Staatswissenschaften*, Zweite Auflage. . ., p. 74.

abstract objective on the state or a group of people living in it, but he was able to admit that often large groups of people follow similar intentions in their lives.

What is certain, however, is that what goals dominate a particular nation will depend on the degree of its development. Nations standing at a low level, of the so-called "civilization" (*Gesittigung*) will be guided by priorities other than developed nations. Experience demonstrates that for some nations, where religion will play the most important role, the goal of salvation will be crucial. Others will adopt temporal objectives, while still others will formulate no goals at all, taking life as it is. The state only has to recognize these goals and be able to support them.[723]

Since man (as already discussed in chapter two) is a sensual-rational individual, these features will also affect the goals of the state. Therefore, the character traits of individuals that dominate in a particular nation will also give the objective and character to the state.[724] Von Mohl said that the "psychological character of the nation" (*Der psychologische Character des Volkes*), is, in the long run, always identical to the political nature of its state.[725] Therefore, it will be legitimate to compare the nation to nature, and the state to the form that a given nation takes.[726] As a form of the nation's existence, the state should take over its goals and help in achieving them. Otherwise, there will be either a sudden or gradual change in the institutions of the state, or oppression difficult for the people to bear.[727]

When discussing the issue of state goals, it is also worth taking a look at von Mohl's views on the question of what it is absolutely not intended for. First of all, the state is not formed to implement the so-called "The objective of humanity" (*Menschheitszweck*). According to von Mohl, it is impossible to deduce a single,

723 Idem, Polizeiwiss.1.1844, p. 3. Idem, Polizeiwiss.1.1832, pp. 3–4. Idem, *Encyklopädie der Staatswissenschaften*, Zweite Auflage. . ., pp. 74–75. The issue of supporting the life goals by the state was raised in the fourth chapter within the framework of the analysis of the principles of police operation in the state. The word *Gesittigung* can be translated as "civilization." Muret-Sanders, *Encyclopaedic English-German and German-English Dictionary*. . ., s. 439. More on the term *Gesittigung*: O. H. v. d. Gablentz, *Einführung in die Politische Wissenschaft*, Köln und Opladen 1965, pp. 321–322.

724 Idem, Staatsr.Württem.1.1829, p. 4.

725 Ibid. Similarly: Idem, Polizeiwiss.1.1832, p. 5. J. Hähnle, op. cit., p. 12. A similar view was also presented by Johann Caspar Bluntschli saying: "the spirit of the nation (...) is the spirit of the state": J. C. Bluntschli, *Allgemeine Staatslehre*. . ., p. 19.

726 R. v. Mohl, Staatsr.Württem.1.1829, p. 4.

727 Idem, Polizeiwiss.1.1844, p. 5.

human-specific goal. Such action would always be at the expense of other tasks. Tasks, life goals that are adopted by specific nations must be adapted to the aforementioned degree of their development. It would not be appropriate to impose the implementation of a specific task on nations, whose level of development does not yet correspond to it. Certain peoples must come to the higher order tasks in a gradual, evolutionary manner.[728]

In von Mohl we find the criticism of the seemingly very correct view that the state serves the "overall happiness" of all its inhabitants.[729] Von Mohl formulated numerous objections to the thesis presented by Francis Bacon (in his *New Atlantis*), Christian Thomasius (in: *Foundations of the Law of Nature and Nations*) or Jeremy Bentham[730] (who advocated the view that social institutions make sense in so far, as they benefit the individual, and thus society). First of all, he was of the opinion that it was impossible to define what happiness the state should care for. He rightly stated that happiness is a concept far too abstract, difficult to define. If happiness is understood as a state in which all citizens of the state are satisfied with their lives, then this situation is impossible to achieve. It is impossible to please everyone and everywhere with the same means. To sum up, it is impossible for the state to achieve happiness for all individuals.[731]

In addition, von Mohl pointed out the mistaken belief that achieving happiness is the only calling of people on Earth. Man fulfils certain tasks in his existence and if he achieves happiness then it is a desirable situation. However, the meaning of human life is not to achieve happiness. He also stated that giving the state the task of achieving human happiness can be dangerous. There is always the risk that actions aimed at achieving evil goals will be masked by the

---

728 Idem, *Encyklopädie der Staatswissenschaften*, Zweite Auflage..., pp. 82–83.

729 H. Schmitz, op. cit., p. 37. More about Mohl's assesment of Bacon: R. v. Mohl, Geschicht.u.Lit.1, p. 189.

730 More about this author: Idem, Geschicht.u.Lit.3, pp. 590–635. Von Mohl included Bentham among one of the most progressive thinkers in the field of sciences of the state, but he considered his utilitarianism inappropriate, stating that "human nature has far more properties than just the feelings of pleasure and torment": Ibid, p. 632.

731 Idem, *Encyklopädie der Staatswissenschaften*, Zweite Auflage..., p. 80. According to Jeremy Bentham's principle of utilitarianism, the goal of the state was to ensure the greatest possible happiness for the largest possible number of its inhabitants. More: G. M. Ekeløve-Slydal, *Jeremy Bentham's Legacy: A Vision of an international Law for the Greatest Happiness of All Nations*, [in:] *Philosophical Foundations of International Criminal Law: Correlating Thinkers*, M. Bergsmo, E. J. Buis (eds.), Brussels 2018, p. 433. D. Roberts, *Jeremy Bentham and the Victorian Administrative State*, "Victorian Studies," Vol. 2, No. 3 (1959), pp. 194–195.

idea of achieving universal happiness. Therefore, it should be stated that von Mohl appears here as an opponent of all concepts of the state relating to the achievement of universal well-being as the goal of the collective life of the population. Von Mohl accused socialists, communists and authors of various political utopias, who proclaimed these theses, not only of detachment from reality, but also of disregarding human freedom, stating that the fulfilment of their intentions would lead to its complete destruction.[732]

The "legal objective" (*Rechstzweck*) was not also the sole and exclusive goal of the state.[733] According to von Mohl, this trend was initiated by Samuel Pufendorf,[734] and developed by Kant, and he considered it inappropriate. For von Mohl, conceiving the state as an institution dealing solely with the protection of law demonstrated disregard for the essence of its nature.[735] Guarding the legal order is an important task of the state, maybe even the most important one, but it is also only a precondition for fulfilling its more important tasks. Therefore, the law is treated by von Mohl only as an instrument for achieving more important goals set for the state, i.e. supporting the population. Even the most comprehensive protection of the legal order by the state will not meet the needs that exist in every nation. For von Mohl the examples of state objectives that reached beyond the mere protection of the legal order included all activities consisting in, for example, removing the consequences of natural disasters, improving transport or education. These views of von Mohl were opposed by another contemporary German liberal, Karl Salomo Zachariae, who claimed that the state had two goals, practical (only to protect the law) and natural (which was supposed to be supporting the general education of the population).[736]

Returning to the definition of the state, one should indicate its subsequent element, i.e. the nation. Later in the present work we will discuss the issue of nation in a broader manner. However, at this point it should be noted that for the purposes of his definition of the state von Mohl understood the nation as a human community that is defined, territorially limited and thus distinguished from others. It was not necessary for him that the nation should be understood by the descendants of one tribe, meaning one nationality (despite the fact that

732 R. v. Mohl, *Encyklopädie der Staatswissenschaften*, Zweite Auflage…, pp. 81, 87.

733 On the disagreement of von Mohl with this view: E. Angermann, op. cit., pp. 107–113.

734 More about Pufendorf's state: R. Zippelius, *Geschichte der Staatsideen*, München 1994, pp. 132–136.

735 R. v. Mohl, *Encyklopädie der Staatswissenschaften*, Zweite Auflage…, pp. 81, 88.

736 Ibid, pp. 81–22, 88.

the situation of only one nationality inhabiting the state was considered favourable by the thinker).[737]

Since a nation is understood as a territorially limited community, the logical consequence is that the state itself should cover a specific territory.[738] At this point, it is worth devoting a moment to the question of the territory of the state, especially since the territory was recognized by von Mohl as one of the foundations of its life.[739] In the opinion of the German liberal, a people without a specific territory would only be a "wandering horde" (*herumziehende Horde*), and it is extremely difficult, or even impossible for a state without territory to fulfil its tasks.[740] Territory, next to the population and ownership, is the most important factor affecting the overall well-being of the state. According to the German scholar, the most important aspects of the territory's impact on the life of the state organism were its size, boundaries, shape it has, location (including access to the sea) and fertility of the land in which it is located.

Holding a vast territory in absolute, i.e. objective sense, and not in relation to other states, has many advantages for a state. It allows, for example, to protect against hostile raids.[741] So von Mohl seems to be in favour of broadening the territorial expansion of states, which should hold as large territories, as only

---

737 Ibid, p. 76. Johann Caspar Bluntschli, in a similar position to von Mohl, stated that "One can speak of the state when it comes to crossing the circle of a single family, and there occurs the unification of a specific group of people (namely families, men, women and children)": J. C. Bluntschli, *Allgemeine Staatslehre*. . ., p. 15.

738 R. v. Mohl, *Encyklopädie der Staatswissenschaften*, Zweite Auflage. . ., p. 76. On the importance of the territory for the state: E. Jarra, op. cit., pp. 90–93.

739 R. v. Mohl, *Encyklopädie der Staatswissenschaften*, Zweite Auflage. . ., p. 567. Similarly: Idem, Geschicht.u.Lit.3, p. 358.

740 Idem, *Encyklopädie der Staatswissenschaften*, Zweite Auflage. . ., p. 130. Bluntschli had a similar opinion: J. C. Bluntschli, *Allgemeine Staatslehre*. . ., p. 15. J. W. Garner, op. cit., p. 69. The view of the indissolubility of the state and territory is also present in the pages of the *Staatslexikon* of Welcker and von Rotteck, where it is also stated that the political nature of the nation depends on the shape of its territory: J. Held, *Territorium,* [in:] *Das Staats-Lexikon*, Dritte Auflage, Vierzehnter Band, K. Welcker (eds.), Leipzig 1866, p. 100.

741 It is worth pointing to Russia as an example of a country with a large area and extensive borders. On the one hand, this factor allowed the Russians to use their strategic depth in the event of hostile invasions, on the other, the defense of extensive borders required the involvement of large financial and human resources. More: J. Bartosiak, *Rzeczpospolita między morzem a lądem. O wojnie i pokoju*, Warszawa 2018, pp. 201–300.

feasible. The only limitation of territorial expansion are possible negative effects that may appear when the state reaches excessive dimensions. The ever growing territory may hinder the administration of the state, which is why governments should avoid excessive enlargement, which may cause problems.[742] For the scholar, an example of a state where at one point greatness became a burden, and not a source of power, was the Roman Empire.[743]

One of the most important factors related to the state's territory is the exact marking of its borders. This is the basis for maintaining order in the internal arena, but also in international relations, because it protects the "natural area of the nation's activity."[744] It is noteworthy that von Mohl noticed the positive value of natural boundaries. Natural borders (mountains, rivers, etc.) will not only determine the range of occurrence of a particular nation, but also create geographical obstacles for potential attackers.[745]

However, location can have a dual impact on the well-being of the state. First of all, it determines the climate in which the state functions. The climate determines not only on the nutrition of the population, but also on the entire lifestyle it will demonstrate. Climate disadvantages (frost, floods, etc.) can affect the development of trade and the general welfare of the state. Von Mohl noticed, however, that the climate is not a decisive factor, and thanks to proper organization it is possible to overcome its negative effects. In other words, the scholar did not deny the presence of the influence of the climatic factor on a particular nation, but according to him it did not form the decisive factor of absolute importance.[746] In this context, attention should also be paid to the assessment made by von Mohl of Montesquieu's concepts relating to the impact of climate

---

742 R. v. Mohl, *Encyklopädie der Staatswissenschaften*, Erste Auflage…, p. 564. John Stuart Mill thought the same, stating that there is a limit to the extent of the state guaranteeing good management from one central place. More: J. S. Mill, *Considerations on Representative Government*, London 1861, p. 310. R. v. Mohl, *Encyklopädie der Staatswissenschaften*, Zweite Auflage…, p. 567.

743 Ibid, pp. 131,135.

744 Ibid, pp. 569–570. More on the importance of borders for the state: J. W. Garner, op. cit., pp. 71–72. R. v. Mohl, *Encyklopädie der Staatswissenschaften*, Zweite Auflage…, p. 130.

745 Idem, *Encyklopädie der Staatswissenschaften*, Erste Auflage…, 1859, pp. 564–565. More about the importance of natural borders for countries and their nations: B. Haselsberger, *Decoding borders. Appreciating border impacts on space and people*, "Planning Theory & Practice," 2014, Vol. 15, No. 4, pp. 505–526.

746 Idem, *Encyklopädie der Staatswissenschaften*, Zweite Auflage…, pp. 131,135. Similarly: Idem, Geschicht.u.Lit.3, p. 360. Bluntschli also extensively spoke about the

on the organization and policy of specific nations. The Württembergee agrees with Montesquieu's view on the impact of climate on the politics of nations. However, this agreement is not complete because von Mohl did not consider Montesquieu's statements that peoples living in a hot climate were like anxious old men, in contrast to peoples living in a cold climate, which were to be characterized by courage.[747] In addition, von Mohl seemed to argue with Montesquieu, citing many national cultures that retained their characteristics regardless of the climate. He spoke here about the Anglo-Saxons (who were given a special esteem by the scholar) who preserved their political culture regardless of where they were in the world. A similar example for him was the presence of French influence in Louisiana and in Canada.[748]

Observing the development, and being fascinated by Anglo-Saxon culture, von Mohl also came to the conviction that one of the key territorial factors guaranteeing the prosperity of the state its access to the open sea. The scholar was of the opinion that he is not only a source of wealth and a driving force of intellectual development, but even that "a country that does not have an access to the sea will never reach a significant position in the world."[749] In addition, an additional factor is the possession of various types of rivers and waterways, which by connecting with the sea will facilitate transport and trade, contributing to wealth.[750]

Significant factors also include the "geometric shape" (*geometrische Figur*) of the state territory. Von Mohl argued that the shape of the state should be closest to the circle, which should facilitate its management and communication. This

---

influence of the climate on the state and the political nature of specific nations J.C. Bluntschli, *Allgemeine Staatslehre*. . ., pp. 255–260.

747 R. v. Mohl, *Encyklopädie der Staatswissenschaften*, Zweite Auflage. . ., p. 134. Montesquieu stated: "The peoples in hot countries are fearful, as are the elders; peoples in cold countries are as brave as young people": Montesquieu, *O duchu praw*, trans. T. Boy-Żeleński, Kraków 2003, p. 210.

748 R. v. Mohl, *Encyklopädie der Staatswissenschaften*, Zweite Auflage. . ., p. 135. More about the impact of the climate on the population in Montesquieu's thought: Montesquieu, op. cit., pp. 209–221.

749 R. v. Mohl, *Encyklopädie der Staatswissenschaften*, Zweite Auflage. . ., p. 132. Friedrich von List stated similarly: "He who has no access to the sea is cut off from the good things of this world, he is the stepson of our Lord God" quoted after: S. Sławski, *Dostęp Polski do morza a interesy Prus Wschodnich*, Gdańsk 1925, p. III. On the disadvantage of countries without access to the sea, cf. S. Vasciannie, *Land-locked and geographically disadvantaged states*, "Commonwealth Law Bulletin," 2005, 31:1, pp. 57–68.

750 R. v. Mohl, Geschicht.u.Lit. 3, p. 358.

is, inter alia, entails to avoid creating various types of enclaves and exclaves that impede state administration.[751] The territory should therefore be as homogeneous and as compact as possible. However, this did not stop the thinker from stating that states should lead colonial expansion, which, through exploitation of overseas possessions by metropolises, brought only benefits.[752]

The last element of the definition of the state is the belief that it is only intended to support specific objectives of the nation's life, and not to fulfil them.[753] In a situation where the state begins to fulfil them for its inhabitants, there occurs an unlawful restriction of individual freedom. In addition, these tasks will never be effective. The state will never be able to accumulate enough funds to meet all needs.[754] According to von Mohl, the human individual has "both the right and the obligation to live in an independent manner and achieve its own goals accordingly."[755] Only where the individual does not have the strength, does it have the right to be assisted by "higher human groups," including the state.[756] It should also be remembered that life goals, whose implementation is to be supported by the state, must be goals whose requiredness is universally recognized.[757]

To assess the general perception of the state in the science of von Mohl, it must be said that in many places these ideas are far from novelty. His views on the state include many concepts already present in literature. He also based his observations on reality and historical experience, which further proves his empirical approach. Speaking about the objectives of the state, he followed in the footsteps of Montesquieu (like Montesquieu he applied the empirical method), which made the purpose of the state dependent on the level of development of its nation and the conditions in which it existed.[758] This view should be considered very rational and true.

However, following the footsteps of Jean Jacques Rousseau, von Mohl spoke about the "collective will," although it must be admitted that in his teaching this concept is vague. Nevertheless, justice must be given that also in Rousseau's thought the concept of "universal will" is not explicitly explained, and may also

---

751 Idem, *Encyklopädie der Staatswissenschaften*, Zweite Auflage…, pp. 132, 570.

752 Ibid, p. 566.

753 H. Schmitz, op. cit., p. 37. Similarly: B. Stöcker, op. cit., p. 123.

754 R. v. Mohl, *Encyklopädie der Staatswissenschaften*, Zweite Auflage…, p. 77.

755 Ibid, p. 83.

756 Ibid.

757 The theory of so-called "common needs" is discussed in chapter four under the description of the tasks of state administration.

758 E. Angermann, op. cit., pp. 119–120.

raise doubts.[759] It can be considered that von Mohl believed the existence of "collective will" of the precondition for functioning of the state. In the conditions of the "collective will," the inhabitants of the state are convinced that the authorities are guided by the common good and therefore acquire their legitimacy to act. Collective will, guaranteeing "common consent" can therefore be identified, in von Mohl, with the interest of the general community of which Rousseau speaks.[760] The collective power of von Mohl should be understood as a combination of forces of individuals inhabiting the state, which offer their forces to it, to better fulfil its functions, which is to bring them benefits.[761] Similarities with Rousseau's views can also be seen in the question of size of the state. The creator of the concept of social contract believed that it should not be too extensive so as not to impede its administration, but it should also not be too small so as not to be able to support itself.[762]

One cannot forget the many similarities that connect von Mohl's ideas with the concept of the state by another German liberal, Johann Caspar Bluntschli.[763] Like von Mohl, Bluntschli believed that the goal of the state cannot be only the purpose of safeguarding the legal order and that it is an organism that unites individuals. Bluntschli also shared the view that the territory of the state is inseparable, and that the spirit of the nation influences the so-called spirit of the state. What makes von Mohl different from Bluntschli is the fact that the latter

759 J. Grygieńć, *Jana Jakuba Rousseau koncepcja woli powszechnej. Czym jest, po co jest i dlaczego nie działa jak powinna?*, "Dialogi polityczne," 3–4/2004, sp. 19. Similarly: J. Bacławski, *Wola powszechna i jej stabilność według koncepcji J.J. Rousseau*, "Przegląd filozoficzny – Nowa Seria," R. 21: 2012, Nr 4 (84), p. 183. On the contemporary meaning of the common will: M. Łuszczyńska, *Umowa społeczna jako fundament życia zbiorowego. . .*, p. 49. More about common will in Rousseau: J. Grygieńć, *Wola powszechna w filozofii politycznej*, Toruń 2012, pp. 55–96, D. Pietrzyk-Reeves, *Republikańska koncepcja umowy społecznej Jana Jakuba Rousseau*, [in:] Z. Rau, M. Chmieliński (eds.), op. cit., pp. 157–165.

760 J. Grygieńć, *Jana Jakuba Rousseau koncepcja woli powszechnej...*, p.25. J.J. Rousseau, op. cit., p. 26.

761 The "collective force" in von Mohl seems to be similar to the concept of "united force" used by Locke: J. Locke, *List o tolerancji*, Warszawa 1963, p. 49. More about Locke's concepts related to, among others, social contract: Z. Rau, op. cit., pp. 127–151.

762 J. J. Rousseau, op. cit., p. 41.

763 More about the purpose of the state according to Bluntschli: J. C. Bluntschli, *Allgemeine Staatslehre. . .*, p. 367.

perceived the state as the likeness of the human body, stating that the state is the "image of the human body."[764]

Heinrich von Treitschke, as in the case of the concept of society, proved to be an invaluable supplier of criticism of von Mohl's concept of state.[765] He accused von Mohl of fundamental mistake, which was the adoption of a concept of state that was too narrow. According to this opponent, the state is not only an "organism of institutions grouping people in unity," but a uniform, external form of life of a given nation. According to von Treitschke, the definition by von Mohl was "void" by not linking it with the concept of a nation.[766] There is a clear difference in the perception of the concept of nation by both Treitschke and von Mohl. In the Württemberger's definition of the state there is place for the concept of a nation, however understood as the general population of the state. For Treischke, the nation as an ethnic community was to play the crucial role in the state.

It should be noted that this comparison perfectly demonstrates the two trends of liberalism in Germany. Unlike von Treitschke, von Mohl was rooted in Western European tradition, which perceived the state as a means to achieve certain objectives. Von Treitschke, on the other hand, saw the state in the sense of German Romanticism, where the ethnic community came first. Like Stahl, he perceived it as a higher order being, governed by its own principles. Erich Angermann rightly stated that the concept of state by von Mohl was much more rational and substantive.[767] For the Württemberger the state appeared to be one of the final effects of the development of human life circles.[768] The state is therefore a necessary complement to such spheres as family, tribe, etc.. It appears to von Mohl as a "superstructure" grouping all individual interests.[769] What is also of utmost importance is that the essence of the state is subsidiarity. It is to work only when the forces of individuals are not enough to meet the challenges in achieving life goals.

---

764 Idem, *Psychologische Studien über Staat und Kirche...*, p. 22. Bluntschli raised: "The state is an image of man. The image of the state organism is the image of the human organism."

765 E. Angermann, op. cit., p. 375.

766 H. v. Treitschke, op. cit., pp.73–74.

767 E. Angermann, op. cit., pp. 377–378.

768 H. Schmitz, op. cit., p. 94.

769 R.-J. Grahe, op. cit., pp. 66–68.

3.3. Population of the state

3.3.1. The state and the significance of its inhabitants

As already mentioned in the previous subsection, the population living in a given country was understood by von Mohl as one of its basic factors. It is for the population that the state exists, and the people are its "main content and the sole purpose."[770] In addition, it is the various characteristics of the population that lives in a given country that have the decisive impact on most of its institutions.[771] It is also worth noting that when speaking of the general population of the state, the scholar interchangeably used the words *Volk* or *Nation*, which both denote the nation in his thoughts. On the contrary, he understood the concept of nation as all, i.e. "those participating in the state" (*Theilnehmer des Staates*) or its inhabitants.[772]

The first undoubtedly progressive, at least for its time, statement of von Mohl was his belief that all inhabitants of a state must belong to the nation in its political sense. Any restriction on belonging to a nation, for example only to the nobility, was understood by him as highly unfair. In the view of von Mohl a system, which would exalt only one social class, regardless of whether it is the upper class (nobility) or the lower class (proletariat), inhibits the development of the state and is inappropriate. Therefore, if the state is understood as unity, then, according to the scholar, all both poor and rich, people of high and low birth, have to belong to that unity.[773]

---

770 R. v. Mohl, Geschicht.u.Lit. 3, p. 413. Similarly: Idem, *Encyklopädie der Staatswissenschaften*, Zweite Auflage…, p. 573, Idem, *Bevölkerung*, [in:] *Das Staats-Lexikon, Encyklopädie der sämmtlichen Staatswissenschaften für alle Stände*, Bd. 2, C. v. Rotteck, C. Welcker (eds.), Altona 1846, p. 458.

771 R. v. Mohl, Geschicht.u.Lit. 3, p. 413.

772 Idem, *Encyklopädie der Staatswissenschaften*, Zweite Auflage…, p. 127. The concept of nationality and the subject of the difference between the concepts of *Volk* and *Nation* will be subject to our consideration in the next section. At this point, it should only be stated that the word "*Nation*" for von Mohl will be identified more with the word *Volk*, which is a political community. It is worth noting that the emergence of the modern concepts of nation and citizen is undoubtedly associated with social processes, which culminated in the French Revolution. More on this topic: A. Zahorski, *Trzy syntezy Wielkiej Rewolucji Francuskiej: Albert Mathiez, Georges Lefebvre, Albert Soboul*, "Przegląd Historyczny," 55/1, 1964, pp. 22–45. K. Trzciński, *Początki nowożytnego obywatelstwa w Europie – obywatel państwa i katalog jego praw w dokumentach Rewolucji Francuskiej*, "Studia Europejskie," 2/2005, pp. 74–81.

773 R. v. Mohl, *Encyklopädie der Staatswissenschaften*, Zweite Auflage…, pp. 127–129.

The inhabitants of a given state, as one of its most important elements, have a considerable impact on its shape and functioning, and this in numerous aspects. Von Mohl included the following factors related to the population to those that affected the state: the population inhabiting it, its origin (also in the national sense), the degree of its civilization development, physical features and abilities, as well as its social shape and stratification.[774]

Referring to the influence of the population on the state, as was the case with the issue of its territory, von Mohl distinguished the impact of the total (absolute) number of population, and the relative ratio (taken into account in relation to specific conditions) of the number of inhabitants in relation to space available in the state.[775]

According to von Mohl a large absolute number of population had both negative and positive impact on the internal life of a state. For example, the positive effects of a large number of inhabitants included the possibility of gathering a large army. Another positive factor, which also testifies to von Mohl's liberalism, was the advantage of creating strong public opinion. The higher the absolute number of the population, the stronger will be the public opinion functioning within it.[776] However, one should not forget about the negative aspects of having a large absolute population in a state. According to von Mohl, a large number of residents will prevent the functioning in the so-called state of "pure people's rule," or democracy in which all residents would participate. In addition, a country with a large population may not be able to meet all their demands and its administration may prove difficult. These disadvantages did not overshadow the benefits that the state drew from having a large total population. In view of the above, it must be stated that von Mohl appears to be a supporter of a state having a large absolute population, primarily as a factor determining its power in external relations.[777]

The Württemberger listed many more advantages and disadvantages of a large or small relative population (i.e. the population in relation to the area of the state).[778] A situation in which a small population inhabits a relatively large area, and so in modern language, the population density is low, generates both

---

774 Ibid, p. 128.

775 Ibid, p. 574.

776 Ibid.

777 Ibid, pp. 574–575.

778 An example of a country, where the majority of both good and bad effects of the population of the state in relation to its territory can be observed was, for von Mohl, the United States. Idem, *Encyklopädie der Staatswissenschaften*, Zweite Auflage. . ., p. 582.

advantages and disadvantages. In such a state there is no question of the lack of availability of arable land, everyone able to work will be able to provide themselves with adequate food, fuel, etc. Since everyone will also be able to provide most of their livelihoods themselves, they will not be threatened by monopolies of any kind.[779] However, it should not be forgotten that low population density will also have detrimental effects on the economic development of such a state. The division of labor is difficult because, as already mentioned, each resident must take care of himself to meet all his life needs.[780] The low population density hinders the development of industry and communication, factories do not find enough employees, whose work in turn is highly valued.[781] In other words, according to von Mohl, there is a fear that so-called "sources of wealth of the state" (*Reichstumsquellen des Landes*) will not be used appropriately. People will interact less often with each other, which will also result in a lower level of intellectual development. One cannot forget about the difficult administration of such a state.[782] The government will not be able to provide enough educated officials, so the impact of statutory laws and law in general will be weak.[783]

Von Mohl, looking for the golden mean, inclined to the postulate that the state should have a relatively large population, but not large enough to hamper its functioning. This would require more effort from residents to secure their livelihoods, and real estate may be more expensive. However, the development of industry will be facilitated by the availability of workers, who will not own land. Communication of the population, and the division of labor will also prove easier. A relatively large population will also support the development of education (there is a large number of people generating demand for this type of services), which will contribute to the overall growth of the nation's civilization. Cities will also undergo faster development. They can constitute centres of civilizational influence, which will also cause an increase in the state's strength in the international arena.[784]

In conclusion, von Mohl inclined again to the statement that the size of the state's population should be in proper relation to the territory it occupies. Proper, i.e. one that enables the most optimal development in every respect. If this

---

779 Idem, Polizeiwiss.1.1866, p. 98. Similarly: Idem, *Bevölkerung...*, p. 468.

780 Idem, Polizeiwiss.1.1866, p. 98.

781 Idem, *Encyklopädie der Staatswissenschaften*, Zweite Auflage..., p. 575, Idem, Polizeiwiss.1.1866, s. 99.

782 Ibid, pp. 98, 100, 575. Similarly: Idem, *Bevölkerung...*, p. 469.

783 Idem, Polizeiwiss.1.1866, p. 100.

784 Ibid, pp. 100–101.

relationship is appropriate, it will not only support the economic and spiritual development of the state, but there will be no threats arising, that von Mohl listed in numerous of his writings, i.e. the rebellion of the population and the rise of the proletariat.[785] The state should therefore be populated, but not overpopulated, so that all means of subsistence and support for the population do not conflict with its number.[786]

It should also be remembered that the scholar reserved the state the possibility of influencing the population, both when it was too large and also when it was too small. Both too small and too large a population can have negative effects for the state.[787] The task of the state is therefore to help citizens where, for example, the terrain prevents the free development of population relations. The state administration must constantly monitor and respond to population changes. If it is threatened by overpopulation or is already overpopulated, it must act to eliminate this poor state of affairs, for example by encouraging emigration. The state must act in the same way if the population is insufficient. Once the population ratio is correct, the state must endeavour to keep it this way.[788]

The "spiritual formation of its inhabitants" (*gesitige Bildung der Bevölkerung*) will also be extremely important for the state, its shape, and prosperity.[789] The higher the moral, spiritual and civilizational level of the population, the greater the complexity and artistry of the institutions of the state in which they reside.[790] This factor is important, because it determines what life goals the population will pursue, and therefore what benefits will be expected from the state.[791] If the state is organized in a way that does not correspond to the degree of development of its inhabitants, it will be a source of their constant dissatisfaction, because it will not meet the requirement to meet the specific needs of the nation. The political system of the state must therefore correspond to the level of development of its nation, otherwise the nation will rebel against the state.[792]

785 Idem, *Encyklopädie der Staatswissenschaften*, Zweite Auflage…, p. 576, Idem, Polizeiwiss.1.1866, p. 118.

786 Idem, *Bevölkerung...*, p. 470.

787 Idem, Polizeiwiss.1.1866, p. 119.

788 Ibid pp. 120–121. More on state actions to increase the population: Idem, Polizeiwiss.1.1866, p. 130–152. More on measures to reduce the population: Ibid, pp. 152–174. More about how the state can increase and decrease population: Idem, *Bevölkerung...*, pp. 475–481.

789 Idem, *Encyklopädie der Staatswissenschaften*, Zweite Auflage…, p. 578.

790 Ibid, p. 579. Similarly: Idem, *Bevölkerung…*, p. 459.

791 Idem, *Encyklopädie der Staatswissenschaften*, Zweite Auflage…, p. 578.

792 Ibid, p. 579.

Speaking about another factor of the population, i.e. the "physical attributes" (*körperliche Beschaffenheit*) of the population, he stated that the state should strive for the physical strength of its inhabitants to be expanded, but also take care of their health (the entire "medical police" *Medicinalpolizei* was to serve this purpose). Von Mohl approached this issue pragmatically. Sick and weak residents will not present any benefits for the state, but will generate costs instead. Therefore, it is far more rational to prevent health problems than to combat them later.[793]

Social stratification (*Gesellschaftliche Bildung*) is also a population factor affecting the prosperity and shape of the state.[794] What is of utmost significance in this respect is the aspect of dividing the nation into the so-called "Professional classes" (*Beschäftigungsclassen*). According to von Mohl, the appropriate quantitative ratio between individual occupational classes formed the source of prosperity and peace in the state.[795]

The above analysis confirms the thesis about the crucial importance of the population for the prosperity of the state in the thought of Robert von Mohl. The state appears here as an entity created for the well-being of its population. It constantly monitors, and should also be able to interfere in population relations, wherever the situation requires it. Von Mohl favored the most populous state possible, but in a sustainable way. Giving the key dimension to the importance of the population for the state will justify the granting of special powers exercised by its police apparatus. What we are talking here about is, among other, helping residents in medical conditions.

3.3.2. State and nationality

As already noted in the previous subsection, in von Mohl the concept of "nation" for which he used interchangeably the terms *Volk* (which can also be translated as a people) and *Nation* (nation) was associated with the total population of the state.[796] So it was not a vision of nation in its present sense, where it is understood

793 Idem, *Encyklopädie der Staatswissenschaften*, Zweite Auflage…, pp. 579–580. More on *Medicinalpolizei*: Idem, Polizeiwiss.1.1866, pp. 174–307.

794 Tenże, *Encyklopädie der Staatswissenschaften*, Zweite Auflage…, p. 580.

795 Idem, *Bevölkerung*…, p. 462.

796 More on differences in the perception of the concept of the nation by Germans, Anglo-Saxons and other cultural and scientific circles: E.K. Francis, *The Nature of the ethnic group*, "Journal of American Sociology" 52, No 5 (March 1947), pp. 393–400.

as a structure of community of language, history, etc..[797] This does not mean, however, that the scholar did not notice this issue. The so-called. The "question of nationality" (*Nationalitätsfrage*) was noticed, and moreover von Mohl devoted much attention to its in-depth analysis.

The issue of the importance of nationality (*Nationalität*) for the state and state sciences was considered by von Mohl at that time to be one of the most important problems requiring in-depth analysis. This state of affairs generated the formation of great nation-states, as well as the division of national groups between other states (the example that the scholar quotes was the situation of the Polish, Hungarian or Italian nations). In addition, nationality issues also began to appear under international law, and were developed from the point of view of legal and natural rights that result from the existence of nations.[798]

Analysis of the issue of nationality and its impact on the state in Robert von Mohl's thought should begin with a return to the issues already mentioned in chapter two, namely the perception of race and tribe. Until the very end of his scientific activity, the scholar remained in the position that the mankind is divided into races, and these again into individual tribes. Belonging to a particular race manifested itself for the most part in external factors, such as skin and hair colour (which can be equated with today's understanding of human races). Tribal affiliation, however, was for von Mohl a more symptom of traits arising from the human mind, among which language formed one of the most important.[799]

In von Mohl's thought, it is the concept of the tribe that will be linked to the issue of nationality. It can even be assumed (as the analysis below demonstrates) that the nation in today's understanding will more or less correspond to what von Mohl will call a tribe in the nineteenth century, although he did not express it anywhere *explicitly* (which again indicates the uncertainty of the scholar, operating in a new area of science). This is also evidenced by the fact that while in the early periods of creativity, for von Mohl, tribal origin seemed to be synonymous with national, then later (including in the second edition of the *Encyclopaedia...*) among the factors creating nationality he included factors that were not characteristic of the tribe, such as for example, economic or state factors.[800]

---

797 On the modern understanding of the terms *Volk* and *Nation*: R. Lötzsch, *Was ist ein Volk und was eine Nation?*, "UTOPIE kreativ," H, 103/104 (Mai/Juni) 1999, pp. 15–30.

798 R. v. Mohl, SVuP. 2.1., pp. 333, 335.

799 Idem, *Encyklopädie der Staatswissenschaften*, Zweite Auflage. . ., p. 576. Similarly: Idem, SVuP. 2.1., pp. 337–338. The view that the most important distinguishing feature of nationality was also presented by Constantin Roessler: C. Roessler, op. cit., p. 532.

800 Fr. J. Neumann, *Volk und Nation*, Leipzig 1888, pp. 3–4.

Speaking about the concept of nationality, von Mohl stated that these are all spiritual as well as physical characteristics that distinguish one people from another. They can be expressed in physical characteristics, but the abstract spiritual factor is much more important. According to von Mohl, one of the most important factors distinguishing specific components of the mankind was language, as developed in a slow process by each community.[801] In addition to language, the Württemberger also included, among the nationality factors distinguishing one nationality from another, the level of civilization development and the community of historical events. He also saw the climate, common heroes, territory as well as religion, as the factors that could impact shaping the nationality. Nationality consists of all the above-mentioned features. However, von Mohl did not combine the concept of nationality with the concept of state. He even thought that an organized state organism does not have to be a feature of a given nationality, because on the one hand we can meet many nationalities living in one country, and on the other, we can meet nationalities divided between different states.[802]

One of the extremely important factors affecting the state is what race and tribe the nation inhabiting them will belong to.[803] Humankind is characterized by the similar so-called "spiritual inclinations" (*geistige Anlagen*) such as the ability to think, sense of morality, imagination or the ability to feel joy or sadness. On the other hand, there are differences in strength of particular tendencies among specific races and nationalities, which affect their state and political institutions. For example, in a situation where a given tribe is characterized by prudence, respect for the law and reluctance to superficiality, it may, according to the scholar, operate under conditions of democracy, universal suffrage or freedom of association, without fear of abuse of these institutions.[804] On the other hand, tribes that will be characterized by "knightly bravery" (*ritterliche Tapferkeit*), focusing on honorary issues, tendency to change, and aversion to strangers, should, for example, function under various types of military state forms. The same with piety dominating certain people, which will cause and even force the merger of the state and the church organizations.[805] The political task of the

801 R. v. Mohl, SVuP.2.1., p. 338. We can clearly see the impact of relations at that time in German lands, where the German people were described as primarily a language community.

802 Ibid, p. 339

803 More about the understanding of the diversity of human race at that time: J. C. Nott, R. Gliddon, *Types of mankind*, Philadelphia 1854.

804 R. v. Mohl, SVuP. 2.1., p. 338. Idem, *Bevölkerung*. . ., p. 459.

805 Ibid.

state is to closely track the qualities of a particular nation and adapt its political institutions to them. The state must therefore follow the level of education and development of a particular nation. Furthermore, von Mohl said: "Concepts of the state that treat it only as a tool to implement individual plans of their rulers, and the population only as a source to provide spiritual and material means to implement these plans, do not deserve the attention of science, deserving resistance in real life."[806]

At the beginning of dealing with issues of population and nation, in an article about the population of the state published in the famous *Staatslexikon* of von Rotteck and Welcker, von Mohl stated that it is extremely difficult to answer the question whether there are races and tribes in the world that will simply be unable to organize in higher state organisms.[807] On one hand, he distances himself from the views that some races, by their very nature, do not have the capacity to form higher (e.g. state) organizations and are only intended to serve the "superior" races.[808] On the other hand, there is no doubt for him not only that there are great differences in the "spiritual forces" of different races, but also that not all possible state institutions will suit all tribes (nationalities) and races.[809]

When it comes to the direct influence of nationality on the state, von Mohl distinguished its two aspects. First of all the fact of national homogeneity will be of significance to the state (i.e. whether the population of the state consists of one or several nationalities), and whether a given nationality inhabits just one state, or is distributed among different state. For von Mohl, there was no doubt that the "tribal community" of the population was a very beneficial situation for the state. It is very beneficial for the state to be inhabited by one nationality, and very importantly, one living only in that state.[810] Overlapping of a given nationality with national borders will positively affect its internal strength, causing even stronger bonding of the ethnic community and development of its intellectual level. The common history, language, customs and generally "jointly created civilization," forming a uniform population make it easier to agree on the general shape of the state and the general directions it should take. This will result in easier administration and functioning of the state.[811] There will be no dispute as

806 Ibid, p. 460. Idem, SVuP. 2.1., p. 340.

807 Idem, *Bevölkerung...*, p. 459.

808 Idem, *Encyklopädie der Staatswissenschaften*, Zweite Auflage..., p. 576.

809 Ibid, p. 576. Similarly: Idem, *Bevölkerung...*, p. 459.

810 Idem, *Encyklopädie der Staatswissenschaften*, Zweite Auflage..., p. 576. Idem, *Bevölkerung...*, p. 460.

811 Idem, *Encyklopädie der Staatswissenschaften*, Zweite Auflage..., p. 577.

to the appearance of the country's political institutions, which will further facilitate legislation and all formal aspects of its conduct. In such a homogeneous structure, a sense of community will be strong, which will also be important for relations with other nationalities.[812] It is obvious that in the absence of national homogeneity in the state, these beneficial features will be hindered in their development. Language differences will cause divisions in the state and problems in its administration.[813] On the other hand, the presence of a nationality, which has been separated from its homeland will undoubtedly cause instability, conspiracy and even war with the state it lives in.[814]

It is extremely important for von Mohl to see that nationality can be a source of legal claims, both in positive and "philosophical" (equivalent to natural) laws. As far as positive law is concerned, of course, these are various types of privileges of minorities in the system of a state, such as the option of education in their own language, or a separate administrative structure or organization of the army. The scholar also took the position that if a minority presented a lower level of civilization than the dominant majority, it did not give the majority the right to use its dominant and more developed position to violate the rights of minorities.[815]

What seems more important for von Mohl are the general norms of law, he calls "philosophical" that refer to nationalities. The scholar emphasized that the effect of the issue of nationality on the political science scene was to create the view that each individual nationality has the right to create a separate state. This view states that nationality is something older and superior to the state. Von Mohl found much right in this view. As mentioned before, nationally unified states are developing harmoniously and are free of anxieties related to the lack of homogeneity.[816] On the other hand, however, there is no overestimation of the role of the nationality factor in the state by von Mohl. There is no doubt that the population was the most important factor in it (after all, the state is an organism created "from people and for people"). However, it would be inappropriate to ignore other factors. The state consists not only of people, but also of territory. In addition, the number of its population is equally important for the state. As stated above, the state must have an adequate population and territory capable of making it function properly. Thus, von Mohl appears as a supporter

812 Idem, *Bevölkerung…*, p. 460.

813 An example for von Mohl was Austria at the time: Idem, *Encyklopädie der Staatswissenschaften*, Zweite Auflage…, p. 584.

814 Idem, *Bevölkerung…*, p. 460.

815 Idem, SVuP. 2.1, pp. 346–347.

816 Ibid, p. 349.

of homogeneity of the state, but certainly not at all costs, at the expense of, for example, the effectiveness of its operation or the ability to defend its territory. Nationality has no doubt a great influence on the state but it cannot dominate it.[817]

And since the best situation for the state is when it consists of one nationality (one tribe), then it must strive to achieve it. In the *Staatslexikon*, von Mohl noted that the state must first use every legally allowed opportunity to attain such a condition.[818] It must perform the "melting" (*Verschmelzung*) of foreign, minority nationalities, as quickly as possible, with the main nationality of the state[819] (for "every interference with a foreign element in the state is burdensome and debilitating for the life of the state and nation").[820] However, von Mohl was not uncompromising in his postulate, because he did not advocate, for example, a forced ban on using the minority language or cultivating their own habits. The state's action to this end is intended to convince the national minority to assimilate with the ruling majority. Under no circumstances, however, can this be performed with use of violence. It must be gradual and evolutionary activity based on encouragement, not coercion. So he was more in favor of mixing nationalities by gentle means, such as promoting the teaching of the majority language, mixing soldiers in garrisons, and facilitating the deepening of relations between nationalities. For von Mohl the Slavs from the left bank of the Elbe who became German, or residents of Wales or Cornwall belonging to the English nationality were examples of such an unification.[821]

It is also possible to merge states composed of separated parts of the same tribe into one organism. As already mentioned, this is a desirable action for von Mohl, but he saw many difficulties in joining many separated parts of the tribe into one state (we can clearly see references to the situation of the German lands here). What may interfere are, e.g., interests of those in power in smaller states. There may also be a problem with the new capital, where former offices must be relocated, etc.[822] The solution to the conflict of interests between the desire to merge the nationality into one state and the particular interests of smaller states was, for von Mohl, the creation of federal states. The last solution may be the joint, state existence of a greater number of different national tribes (or parts thereof) without a clear dominant element. Here, for the consistency of the state,

817 Ibid, pp. 350, 352, 354.
818 Idem, *Bevölkerung. . .*, p. 461.
819 Idem, SVuP.2.1, p. 364.
820 Ibid.
821 Ibid, p. 365. Idem, *Bevölkerung. . .*, p. 461.
822 Idem, SVuP.2.1, pp. 354, 356.

a certain "connecting element" must be selected. It can be the promotion of a common language, common ideals, common culture, etc.[823]

Mention should also be made of von Mohl's extremely pragmatic approach to the national issue in the united German Reich. It is perfectly illustrated by his opinion on the issue of the Grand Duchy of Poznań and Alsace-Lorraine. This case was for the scholar the residence in the German Reich of parts of the nationalities that were completely foreign to the Germans, i.e. Poles in the east and the French in the west. According to von Mohl, there could be no question of "losing Poznań" and not only because it was a region associated with German border regions, but also because of the strong German element living there. He was in favor of the Germanization of those areas, which may have been long "but it will definitely succeed."[824] In view of the above, von Mohl considered state organization of Poland separated from the Reich impossible. Moreover, von Mohl did not agree with concessions to Poles, but also to the French. According to the scholar, this would be a sign of weakness, without hope of gratitude from these peoples. Therefore, all freedom aspirations and signs of disobedience were to be strongly suppressed by law.[825] Thus, von Mohl clearly shows the historical context and the impact of the German unification process. The scholar advocated a homogeneous country and celebrated the advantages of homogeneity.

To sum up the above argument, it should first be stated that von Mohl is a scholar (alongside e.g. Heinrich Ahrens) who does not formulate a clear distinction of the concepts of *Nation* and *Volk*. Unlike, e.g., Zachariae or Bluntschli, he did not focus on the proper separation of the meaning of these terms.[826] Antoni Czubiński also drew attention to the blurred separation of the concepts of *Volk* and *Nation* in modern times. It should be noted that the concept of *Volk* is more general, and older than the concept of *Nation*, which was taken over in German

---

823 Ibid., pp. 357, 368–370. Switzerland can be mentioned as an example of such an organism.

824 Idem, *Das deutsche Reichsstaatsrecht, Rechtliche und politische Eröterungen...*, p. 125.

825 Ibid, pp. 125, 128.

826 Fr. J. Neumann, op. cit., pp. 1–3. Speaking of *Nation* and *Volk*, Ahrens stated that "in essence these terms are synonymous": H. Ahrens, *Naturrecht oder Philosphie des Rechts und des Staates*, Zweiter Band, Wien 1871, p. 333. On the issue of the nation in Joseph von Held: J. Held, *Staat und Gesellschaft vom Standpunkte der Geschichte der Menschheit und des Staats*, Erster Theil, Leipzig 1861, pp. 531–563.

from Latin. *Volk* should be understood as the whole of the population of the state, i.e. people, society and nation.[827]

The above differences in views perfectly reflect the atmosphere of that era in Germany, and the resulting uncertainty, trembling and disputes arising from the unification process. The views of von Mohl and the aforementioned thinkers are certainly connected by their understanding of the language, level of civilization and cultural community (also expressed in the literature of the nineteenth century) as one of the foundations for creating a sense of national community.[828] When analyzing von Mohl's concepts, one should definitely pay attention to a certain discrepancy between the views of the scientist in the different periods of his work. In the mid-nineteenth century the Württemberger appears as a pragmatic liberal. He believes that the "nationality factor" is important in the life of the state (although not strictly prioritized), what is more, it distinguishes a number of natural rights stemming from nationality. However, at the end of his life, after the reunification of Germany, von Mohl appears as a pragmatic nationalist. The interest of the new German Reich is more important to him than the abstract ideas of respecting national rights (in this case of the French and Poles). He was in favor of Germanization, even forced. This proves the evolution of the views proclaimed by von Mohl, the transition from idealism (in the early period of his creativity) to later pragmatism, manifesting itself especially in assessing the situation in Germany at that time.

3.4. Theory of the "species and forms of states"

The previously presented views of von Mohl highlighted his belief that the goals that individual human beings set as well together their various communities are determined by the level of civilizational development at which they stay. This paradigm is also present in the Württemberger's teaching about species and types of states. The species was the basic unit of division of states in the science of von Mohl. It was based on distinguishing the most basic features resulting

827 A. Czubiński, *Rozwój poczucia narodowego i dążeń do zjednoczenia narodowego w krajach niemieckich w dobie kapitalizmu (1776–1945)*, [in:] *Pojęcia "Volk" i "Nation" w historii Niemiec*, A. Czubiński (ed.), Poznań 1980, p. 26.

828 These factors were particularly important for the Germans in the unification process. B. Piotrowski, *O romantycznej wizji narodu niemieckiego uwag kilka*, [in:] *Pojęcia "Volk" i "Nation" w historii Niemiec...*, p. 195. More on development of nationalism and the notion of a nation in German history: O. Dann, *Nation und Nationalismus in Deutschland 1770–1990*, München 1996.

from the objective and the level of development of the population of the respective state. However, the form of state can be understood as its so-called subspecies, separated from the species due to the presence of certain, characteristic features.[829]

In the beginning of his scientific activities, in the first edition of the *Constitutional Law of the Kingdom of Württemberg*, von Mohl did not seem to be entirely certain, whether it was possible to create a closed catalogue of individual species of states. Since it proved impossible to define all the life aspirations of certain peoples, it will also be impossible to describe all the species of states that will suit them. Mohl states that every nation has a chance to create its own, particular species of the state, corresponding to the life goals it follows.[830] However, the German scientist, who was guided in his research with empiricism, also came to the conclusion that historical reality and life experience provide examples of the existence of specific, so to say "popular" species of states (*Staatsgattungen*).[831]

In his *Constitutional Law of the Kingdom of Württemberg*, von Mohl distinguished four basic, species of states, differing in terms of their objectives and nature. These will be a species of patriarchal state (*patriarchalische Staatsgattung*), theocratic state (*theokratische Staatsgattung*), legal state (*Rechtsstaats-Gattung*) discussed in the subsequent chapter, and the despotic state (*despotische Staatsgattung*).[832] Each species of the state will be characterized by the existence of equal goals of human life and a specific level of civilization, which will again determine the objectives of the state that are proper for that particular species. Theocracy will correspond to the "religious direction" of the nation's life, the patrimonial state is based on private law, and patriarchal on family relations. "Sensual-rational" nature will be at the root of the rule of law, while in despotia the goals and level of development of the nation will be "miserable and dwarfed."[833] However, one cannot forget that in von Mohl each species will

829 R. v. Mohl, Geschicht.u.Lit.1, p. 123. The analysis of species of states in the thought of Robert von Mohl was also carried out by Józef Nowacki: J. Nowacki, *Państwo prawne w typologii państw Roberta von Mohla*, [in:] *Przybliżanie przeszłości. Księga pamiątkowa ofiarowana Profesorowi Czesławowi Głombikowi z okazji czterdziestolecia pracy nauczycielskiej*, J. Bańka (ed.), Katowice 1998, pp. 123–125.

830 R. v. Mohl, Staatsr.Württem.1.1829, p. 6.

831 Ibid, p. 7. Friedrich Schmitthener also relied on historical experience in examining the degrees of development of the countries: F. Schmitthenner, *Zwölf Bücher vom Staate, oder systematische Encyklopädie der Staatswissenschaften*, Dritter Band, Giessen 1843, p. 26.

832 R. v. Mohl, Staatsr.Württem.1.1829, pp. 7–10.

833 Idem, Polizeiwiss.1.1844, p. 5. Similarly: Idem, Polizeiwiss.1.1832, p. 5.

divide into "forms" (*Arten der Staatsgattungen*), which should be understood as "subspecies" based, as already mentioned, on the similarity of their most important features. What is more, it should be remembered that during its historical existence, the state may adopt various species, for example European countries, passing according to von Mohl from the medieval species of theocracy or patrimonial state to higher levels of their development.[834]

Like many other views of the Württemberger, also the science of species and forms of states gained its ultimate shape in the *Encyclopaedia of state sciences.* This work also has a liberal view of the great diversity of life goals of certain peoples. All the time he was guided by empiricism and analysis of the reality and the history of occurrence of various types of states.[835] He also critically referred to the classification of states solely on the basis of their system, ignoring their essence or species. Therefore, von Mohl did not accept the division by Friedrich Jakob Schmitthener, who did divide the states only into monarchies and republics, or the Bluntschli classification, distinguishing four basic forms of the state in the form of ideocracy (with its ultimate type, i.e. theocracy), democracy, aristocracy and monarchy.[836] Von Mohl did not agree with the view presented by Welcker (and later also supported by Bluntschli), comparing certain species of states to the stages of human life and the age at which he is. The scholar similarly did not accept the division into correct and incorrect regimes, as presented by Aristotle.[837]

Ultimately, in the second edition of the *Encyclopedia of Sciences of State*, von Mohl distinguished the following species of states: patriarchal states (*Patriarchalische Staaten*), theocratic states (*Theokratieen*), patrimonial states (*Patrimonialstaaten, Patrimonialherrschaften*), "classical" or antique states (*classische oder antike Staaten*), modern rule of law (*Rechtsstaat der Neuzeit*) and despotic states (*Despotieen*).[838]

The species of the patriarchal state is based in the science of von Mohl on the so-called "sensual-childish view of life" (*sinnlich-kindlichen Ansicht vom Leben*),

834 Idem, *Encyklopädie der Staatswissenschaften*, Zweite Auflage…, pp. 103–104. Idem, Staatsr.Württem.1.1829, pp. 9–10.

835 Idem, *Encyklopädie der Staatswissenschaften*, Zweite Auflage…, p. 103.

836 Ibid, p. 110. J. C. Bluntschli, *Lehre vom modernen Staat*, Erster Teil, *Allgemeine Staatslehre…*, pp. 379–380. On the differences in understanding of the state in the Middle Ages and in modern times: Idem, *Über den Unterschied der mittelalterlichen und der modernen Staatsidee*, München 1855.

837 R. v. Mohl, *Encyklopädie der Staatswissenschaften*, Zweite Auflage…, p. 111.

838 Ibid, pp. 104–108.

referring to the simplest pleasures and needs of human existence. In this case, the state is juste a huge "private association" (*Privatverein*), manifesting itself either as a constantly growing family or as a relationship based on ownership. Members of the people see themselves as members of a particular family, or are bound by material relationships. In this case, the head of state is either the "father of the tribe" (*Staamvater*) or the landowner. The relations of this species of state are based not only on law, but mainly on customs.[839] The species of patriarchal state can take on two forms, depending on the factor on which it is based. In the first, when the state is based on family relations, it is created by the process of group of families growing into a state organism. The leader of the original tribal group becomes the leader of the state.[840] In the second, the state relies on material relations. Every member of the state operates with its ruler also in private-legal relations. On the basis on the diversity of these relationships there emerge the estates of the land.[841]

The patriarchal state is based on the principle of "fatherly power" (*väterliche Gewalt*). The principle of this power is to order the life of the tribe. For von Mohl, this species of state organization is lowest in the hierarchy, and it is based on the lowest and undeveloped human civilizations. It is very close to the natural social communities.[842] The species of patriarchal state will be most suitable for underdeveloped peoples (both in economic and in social terms), still guided by tribal principles of life in general, and where religious principles are still weak or nonexistent. Such a state, which is characterized by "such a simple and weak establishment" (*so einfache und so wenig kräftige Einrichtung*), can only operate in small territories, within a small population. It does not develop administration or higher forms of state institutions, because it has no funds, and there is also lack of people with appropriate education.[843]

Another species of the state, the theocracy, is based on the faith of the people in the creation of a state organization by God and their belief that the divine being is the initiator of all events in the state.[844] The basis of this species is the

839 Idem, Staatsr.Württem.1.1829, p. 7. On this kind of state in von Mohl: H. Schmitz, op. cit., pp. 47–48.

840 R. v. Mohl, Staatsr.Württem.1.1829, p. 12. Karl Salomo Zachariae also speaks of a similar species of state: K. S. Zachariae, *Vierzig Bücher vom Staate*, Bd. 2, Stuttgatt und Tübingen 1820, pp. 160–179.

841 R. v. Mohl, Staatsr.Württem.1.1829, p. 12.

842 Idem, *Encyklopädie der Staatswissenschaften*, Zweite Auflage. . ., p. 104.

843 Ibid, pp. 301, 303–304.

844 R. v. Mohl, *Encyklopädie der Staatswissenschaften*, Zweite Auflage. . ., p. 104. About this species of state by von Mohl: H. Schmitz, op. cit., pp. 48–49. We should note here

belief of its inhabitants that life on Earth should be considered in religious terms. Earthly existence is only the preparation for eternal life, the spiritual stands above the sensual, the eternal above the earthly, and religious organizations stand above the state. All state institutions are characterized by their reference to religion, it can be said that the ultimate oracle in state matters is God, expressed also through the clergy. In addition to the law, the basis for the state's operation is also morality based on religious principles.[845] In this state there are religious norms, and the most important one is the divine command, which must not be opposed. It is also worth noting that for von Mohl, theocracy may also arise in other denominations, and not only on the basis of Christianity.[846]

Thus, regardless of the religion, in each case the theocratic state is based and arises on the basis of a people with strong faith, which could also be further supported by conviction about some special historical role that the God envisaged for that people.[847] Interestingly, it was theocracy that von Mohl considered the most stable species of all. He derived this belief from the logical consequence that as long as faith in people is strong, this state will function stably and invariably.[848] On the other hand, he believed that theocracy was based on "the darkness of reason, the unilateral formation of feelings, and inexorable intolerance."[849] Therefore, theocracy will hold only where there is strong faith in people, where it does not exist, or wherever it begins to weaken, the system of such state begins to falter.[850] So if faith is damaged, then the whole state may destabilize.[851]

Similarly to the patriarchal state, the theocratic state is also divided into two form. It will either be a "pure, indivisible theocracy" (*reine oder ungetheilte Theokratie*) or a "dualistic theocracy" (*dualistische Theokratie*). In the first form, where the power belongs to a king-priest in one person, political and religious

---

that in England, as late as in 17th century, Robert Filmer presented the belief of the divine origin of rights of the monarch. He thus opposed democracy and spoke for the omnipotent position of king in the state. More: R. Filmer, *Patriarcha or the Natural Power of Kings*, London 1680. T. Tulejski, *Sir Robert Filmer. Sam przeciwko wszystkim! Część II*, "Studia Prawno-Ekonomiczne," t. CII, p. 145.

845 R. v. Mohl, Staatsr.Württem.1.1829, pp. 7–8.

846 Idem, *Encyklopädie der Staatswissenschaften*, Zweite Auflage. . ., pp. 312, 317.

847 Ibid, p. 311.

848 Idem, Staatsr.Württem.1.1829, p. 10.

849 Ibid.

850 Interestingly, von Mohl noticed that in order to preserve its position and existence, theocracy could change in such conditions into a despotic state driven by coercion: Idem, *Encyklopädie der Staatswissenschaften*, Zweite Auflage. . ., p. 317.

851 Idem, Staatsr.Württem.1.1829, p. 10.

matters are combined. The constitution of this state can be the directly adopted holy book, and the temples serve as public offices.[852] In the second form, clerical matters are in the hands of clergy, and temporal matters are in the hands of the laity.[853] Worldly matters are directed by lay people with a certain degree of freedom, but always according to the divine law.[854]

While theocracy is based on faith, the species of the patrimonial state is based in von Mohl on the concentration of individual components of the state organism around one "power" (*Macht*). In return for protection, care and assistance in achieving their life goals, individuals subdue to this power and have to obey it.[855] It is worth mentioning that von Mohl distinguished three forms of patrimonial state. Firstly, based on the ruler's land property, secondly divided among the companions of the ruler, who in return must provide him with military assistance, and thirdly, the form in which a particular city municipality rules.[856]

The factors conditioning the creation of such a state are the existence of relatively developed property relations and the resulting need to protect private property. Those in possession (most of all of land) are starting to look for ways to legally secure their property. To this end, they puts themselves under the protection of the said force, a power that is able to protect it. Such a power can be vested in a single man (feudal lord) or a collective organization such as a city municipality. What also characterizes the patrimonial state will be the diversity of legal position of individuals, who are under the protection of "power," resulting, for example, from the privileges granted to specific estates.[857]

The civilization of people living under the patrimonial state is undoubtedly higher than in the patriarchal state. Agriculture and crafts develop, and people rely primarily on private-legal relations. However, such a state is not developed enough to create institutions of a higher level of development, such as educational institutions. The power behind the force, which in a patrimonial state

852 Idem, *Encyklopädie der Staatswissenschaften*, Zweite Auflage. . ., pp. 313, 316.

853 Idem, Staatsr.Württem.1.1829, p. 14.

854 Idem, *Encyklopädie der Staatswissenschaften*, Zweite Auflage. . ., pp. 104–105, 313, 316–317.

855 R. v. Mohl, *Encyklopädie der Staatswissenschaften*, Zweite Auflage. . ., p. 105. Von Mohl considered the "military feudal states" (*militärische Lehenstaat*) - based on war obligations, a separate form of patrimonial state. On this kind of state by von Mohl: H. Schmitz, op. cit., p. 48.

856 R. v. Mohl, *Encyklopädie der Staatswissenschaften*, Zweite Auflage. . ., p. 310.

857 Ibid, pp. 304–305.

could be, for example, a prince, is compared by von Mohl to private property. The prince himself acquires this power in various ways (whether through inheritance or marriage, but also purchase, etc.), and is not elected by the people.[858]

The higher level of development of the patrimonial state in relation to the patriarchal state is evidenced by the fact that subjects may demand actions justified by law from their ruler. Furthermore if a duty does not rest on the rulers, they can themselves, create on their own organizations to meet their specific goals.[859] In the patrimonial state there are also some founding stones of "citizens' rights" of its inhabitants. Von Mohl listed, for example, the right to lodge a complaint with the ruler (by specific groups), or the ruler's ability to assign his rights to residents. In the context of the considerations contained in chapter four, it should be noted that von Mohl perceived the patrimonial state as a state strictly based on legal positivism.[860] The source of all kinds of actions and claims in this country can only be a contract, law, and not, for example, abstract philosophical principles. The power of the patrimonial state goes only as far as the law allows it.[861]

The species of state distinguished by the Württemberger in the later period of his scientific activity was the classical state. This species of state occurred in antiquity and was represented by Greek and Roman civilizations. Its main task was to connect the existence of all of its citizens as closely, as feasible. The individual was to unite with the total so that it would give up its pursuit of its particular goals. For in the classical state, according to von Mohl, the prosperity of the community and the public was more important than the prosperity of the individual.[862] What will make the classic state similar to the species of rule of law, as discussed in the subsequent chapter is the fact that it can be based on a monarchical, aristocratic and democratic system. Nevertheless, what distinguishes the

858 Ibid, p. 305.

859 Ibid, pp. 306–307.

860 We are talking here about legal positivism, i.e. a trend of thinking about law in which its perception is detached from morality. What matters above all, is the formal aspect of the law, so the law is everything that has been sanctioned in accordance with the adopted procedure. More about the legal positivism: S. Wronkowska, Z. Ziembiński, op. cit., pp. 48–58.

861 Ibid, p. 308. An analysis of this species of the state was also carried out by Bluntschli: J. C. Bluntschli, *Patrimonialstaat und patrimoniale Staatsidee* [in:] *Bluntschli's Staatswörterbuch in drei Banden*, E. Löning (ed.), Dritter Band, Zürich 1872, pp. 34–36.

862 R. v. Mohl, *Encyklopädie der Staatswissenschaften*, Zweite Auflage…, pp. 105–106. About this species of state by von Mohl: H. Schmitz, op. cit., p. 49.

classical state from the modern state (in von Mohl it will be the state of rule of law) is the fact that in the classical state the general and the community were the most important, while what counts in the "modern legal state" is the "atomic egoism" (*atomistischer Selbstsucht*).[863]

The most important principle of the classical state is to create the fullest possible community life, because only in such a life does the individual achieve the highest level of its development. The principle of the classical state is, therefore, the fullest and most intimate union of individuality with the state. What counts are the community and statehood, whose condition affects the life of the individuals. An individual in the classical state must therefore abandon its individual desires and submit them to the interests of the totality. This stretches to all spheres of its existence, even to the right to life (the scholar gave the example of sick children who had to be abandoned when they were not valuable to the state). The state is responsible for raising the children. Citizens cannot present views contrary to the state, and are obliged to military service.[864]

On the other hand, however, a citizens receive a number of political rights from the state. They can take part in managing the state and demand protection from it. Man in the classical state is a servant of the state, and the possible prosperity of the state must be understood as the well-being of the individual. One can say that the individual is there to ensure prosperity for the state. In the ancient classical state, there is no room for the legal existence of foreigners, while slaves are its indispensable element.[865]

The last state species discussed here will be despotism. In a despotic state, the people are perceived exclusively as simple tools in the hands of a strong individual ruling the state. It is based on a master-slave relationship. What governs the state is solely the will of its despotic ruler. The principle of the institutions and operation of the state is fear used by despots to achieve their goals. There is no question here of following the development of some higher ideas.[866] In a despotic state it is also difficult to talk about specific, various forms, because they depend only on the ruling despot.[867] In such a state the ruler's will is the

863 R. v. Mohl, *Encyklopädie der Staatswissenschaften*, Zweite Auflage…, pp. 106, 113.

864 Ibid, pp. 319–320.

865 Ibid, pp. 320–321.

866 Idem, Staatsr.Württem.1.1829, p. 9. The despotic state was understood similarly to von Mohl by Johann Caspar Bluntschli: J.C. Bluntschli, *Despotie*, [w:] *Bluntschli's Staatswörterbuch in drei Bänden*, E. Löning (ed.) Erster Band, Zürich 1869, pp. 471–472.

867 R. v. Mohl, Staatsr.Württem.1.1829, p. 19.

law, and the direction of general action is the direction selected by him.[868] Despotism, also called by von Mohl "coercion power" (*Zwangsherrschaft*), is based on coercion. A despotic ruler has no obligation to care for the subjects. A despotic state should not be compared with an absolute monarchy. Despite the fact that in the "unlimited kingdom" there are no legal instruments limiting the king's authority, it is, according to von Mohl, obliged to act for the realization of life goals resulting from the given species of the state and education of the population.[869]

The law in a despotic state is always the will of the head of state, one that was already expressed and was not yet revoked. There are no legislative procedures in place, the only legislative action is the despot's expression of will. According to von Mohl, religious provisions may form the only limitation of the despot's will, in certain situations protecting the residents against the arbitrariness of the ruler (von Mohl provides the provisions of the Koran, sometimes protecting against the arbitrariness of Muslim rulers, as an example here).[870] Similarly all the officials in the state are subject exclusively to the will of the ruler, they are his personal servants, and are obliged to carry out only his instructions. There is also no independent judiciary. Since despotism requires unrestricted obedience from subjects, it must have the appropriate power. It is the "physical violence" (*physiche Gewalt*) and fear that form the basic means of governance in a despotic state. The state must therefore have sufficiently numerous and obedient armed forces, capable of suppressing any resistance. Subjects of a despotic state do not have any rights. The ruler and his authorized officials are the lords of their life and death. They can dispose of the subjects' property. Everything is regulated by the opinion and will of the ruler. He may allow the submission of complaints or consultations with his subjects, but this is only his will.[871]

In order to assess the concept of the German thinker referring to the species and forms of states, it should be noted that it is built in a rational, and thoughtful way. Von Mohl tried to analyze historical reality, searching for actual conditions characterized by set, repeated characteristics. The science of species and forms of states is not only inscribed in the ways of their formation, as distinguished by

868 Idem, *Encyklopädie der Staatswissenschaften*, Zweite Auflage…, p. 108.
869 Ibid, pp. 376–377.
870 Ibid, pp. 378–379, 381. More about law in Islam: M. Sadowski, *Islam*…, Warszawa 2017.
871 R. v. Mohl, *Encyklopädie der Staatswissenschaften*, Zweite Auflage…, pp. 379–380.

von Mohl, but also based on the crucial belief concerning the role of the civilizational level of the population. We also cannot forget that the aforementioned species of states constitute a historical background for the species discussed in the subsequent chapter, i.e. for the rule of law.

Chapter IV The legal state in theory and action

4.1. The legal state: the genesis and meaning of the concept

Considerations referring to the concept of the rule of law in Robert von Mohl's thought should begin with the presentation of his genesis of this idea.[872] Von Mohl is considered to be one of the first scholars, who based their vision of the rule of law on thorough historical and doctrinal research.[873] The analysis of the genesis of the rule of law in the thoughts of this liberal thinker is not intended solely to prove the substantive depth of his considerations. It will also create a backgroud for his original vision of this idea.

Von Mohl traced the beginnings of the idea of rule of law back to the times of Reformation. In his opinion, with the advent of this process, rationalism first appeared in thinking about the state.[874] Its main merit was to overcome the medieval way of thinking about the state, which according to the Württemberger was based on scholasticism (which in turn he perceived as an obstacle to the development of the *Rechtsstaat* idea).[875] However, it seems that the impact of the Reformation on the creation of the idea of the rule of law should not be overestimated. One can agree with the claim that it could give some impetus to changes, to break with the old order, especially with the influence of religion on the state. However, from the point of view of the emergence of this idea this was far from decisive, if only because of the difference, of almost three hundred years, separating these historical phenomena.

Hugo Grotius was the first thinker included by von Mohl to the group of precursors of the *Rechtsstaat* idea.[876] The German liberal argued that the barbaric wars, in which Christianity had plunged, lead Grotius to abandon the "dogma" of indisputable religious principles, and convinced him of the need to regulate relations between states, based on new principles.[877] It was the great work of

872 On the genesis of the rule of law in the thought of Robert von Mohl: Z. A. Maciąg, op. cit., pp. 82–90.

873 Ibid, p. 82.

874 As it will be proved, it is rationalism and a reference to common sense that will form, for von Mohl, the key factors conditioning the emergence of the *Rechtsstaat* idea.

875 R. v. Mohl, Geschicht.u.Lit.1, pp. 227–229.

876 G. Gozzi, *Rechtsstaat and individual rights in German constitutional theory*, [in:] *The Rule of Law History, Theory and Criticism*, P. Costa, D. Zolo (eds.), Dordrecht 2007, p. 237.

877 R. v. Mohl, Geschicht.u.Lit.1, p. 229. Z. A. Maciąg, op. cit., p. 82.

the Dutch philosopher entitled *On the Law of War and Peace* that, according to von Mohl, paved the way for a new way of understanding the state. It should be emphasized that von Mohl attached great importance to the concept of human rationality in Grotius. He presumably demonstrated that the individual is characterized by the so called need for rational life, i.e. living with other individuals in a peaceful and ordered manner. A manifestation of this rationality was the belief in the need to create a state on the basis of social contract.[878] In addition to basing the state on the rational approach of the individuals to their existence, von Mohl found several other claims of Grotius, which he considered to be the foundations of the *Rechtsstaat* idea. It should be indicated that the state only forms means to achieve human goals (and not an end in itself), there is the conviction that there is a need to limit its activities and to base them on the principles of appropriateness and necessity.[879]

The English: John Locke and Algeron Sidney are another thinkers mentioned by von Mohl, who were to contribute to the idea of the rule of law. In their case, the Württemberger drew attention to both the view about the citizen's obedience to the law and the idea of negative freedom. For von Mohl the important liberal view of Sidney was the conviction that the people do not exist for state, but state for the people. Therefore, it is the people who have the right to organize and change the state according to their plans. Much like Locke and Sidney, von Mohl also emphasized that legitimacy to rule can only be acquired through a contract.[880] It is worth noting that William Godwin, who in his work *An Inquiry Concerning Political Justice*[881] postulated the introduction of democratic rule in the state based on the inalienable subjective freedom of the individual, was, according to von Mohl, among the precursors of the idea of the rule of law on English ground.[882] At this point, however, it is difficult to agree with von Mohl, after all, William Godwin is considered one of the fathers of anarchism, which cannot be combined with the idea of *Rechtsstaat*.[883] However, it

878 R. v. Mohl, Geschicht.u.Lit.1, p. 229. The trait of rationality clung to the *Rechtsstaat* idea from the very beginning of its development. German scholars such as Karl Theodor Welcker or von Aretin believed that the rule of law as a way of organizing a community of people stems from their rational approach to life. More: G. N. Bhat, *Recovering the Historical Rechtsstaat*, "Review of Central and East European Law," 32, 2007, p. 67–69.

879 R. v. Mohl, Geschicht.u.Lit.1, p. 230.

880 Ibid, pp. 231–232.

881 W. Godwin, *An Inquiry Concerning Political Justice*, Vol. 1–2, London 1793.

882 R. v. Mohl, Geschicht.u.Lit.1, p. 232.

883 A. Heywood, *Ideologie polityczne. Wprowadzenie*, Warszawa 2008, p. 201.

seems that von Mohl wanted to emphasize Godwin's belief in the rationality of human beings, which will also form the basis for Mohl's understanding of the rule of law. Speaking about the genesis of the rule of law, von Mohl devoted attention to Jeremy Bentham, considering him "one of the most penetrating and brave thinkers of all times and nations." Although he did not agree with it, he emphasized Bentham's postulate that the state should ensure the fullest possible happiness for the largest number of people living in it.[884]

In addition to Grotius, the Württemberger devoted attention to the genesis of the idea of the rule of law to the Dutchmen Ulrich Huber and Baruch Spinoza. In the former, attention is devoted to the process of establishing the state on the basis of a social contract, the man is led to by his social nature. It should be emphasized that von Mohl, while admiring Huber's views, he in fact joined the critics of Thomas Hobbes, who thought that people are calling the state out of a purely selfish desire to defend their interests, in the so-called "war of all against all."[885]

Also in France, the German scholar found some sources of the idea of the rule of law. He attached the greatest importance to the achievements of Montesquieu and Jean Jacques Rousseau. According to von Mohl, the merit of Montesquieu was the synthesis of three major theorems. The first of them stated that the spiritual characteristics of the population and the geographical conditions of the country have an impact on the rights and institutions of the state. The second said that various forms of state suit different peoples because of their nature. According to von Mohl, the third achievement was the theory of the separation of powers. For the German liberal, "rule of law with divided powers" will be one form of rule of law as a species. According to von Mohl, the concept of social contract, which was manifested in the highest form in Jean Jacques Rousseau, laid the foundations for the *Rechtsstaat* idea. In addition to the creation of the state on the basis of a voluntary contract, von Mohl also recognized the equality and freedom of individuals, as well as the sovereignty of the people, as important features of Rousseau's state doctrine.[886]

Speaking about his native area, von Mohl came to the conclusion that in German lands the development of the *Rechtsstaat* idea was based on the concepts

884 R. v. Mohl, Geschicht.u.Lit.1, p. 233.

885 Ibid., p. 234. Z. A. Maciąg, op. cit., p. 82. On the opposites of the concepts of social contract in Hobbes and Huber: A. Fukuoka, *The Sovereign and the Prophets, Spinoza on Grotian and Hobbesian Biblical Argumentation*, Leiden 2018, pp. 311–343.

886 R. v. Mohl, Geschicht.u.Lit.1, p. 237.

of Hugo Grotius. As the precursors of the rule of law concept he listed: Samuel Pufendorf, Christian Thomasius and Christian Wolff. It is worth mentioning that all these thinkers considered a contract to be the basis for the functioning of the state.[887] However, von Mohl accused German philosophers of paying too little attention to issues related to the rights of subjects, primarily in terms of securing them against abuse by the authorities (the ruler).[888] This statement is important from the point of view of the events of the German Spring of Nations (in which von Mohl took part). At that time, by determining fundamental rights, efforts were made to strengthen the legal position of individuals relative to those in power.

It is not surprising that in German lands, considerable merit for formulating the entire so-called *Rechtsstaatsgedanke* von Mohl finds in the teachings of Immanuel Kant. Once again we can see the reference of the Württemberger to broadly understood rationality. Kant's merit was to base the state and law on so called "practical reason."[889] According to von Mohl, it was Kant's reasonable, rational human nature that was the basis for joining people in states. On the other hand, the idea of a rule of law is a system of scientific assertions that are to be the rule for states that existed at the time, but in a philosophical dimension it was to demonstrate values with a transcendent value.[890] What von Mohl also perceived as merit of Kant was the understanding of the state based on exploring the essence and strengthening of individual rights.[891]

What proves important in the context of the later ideas of von Mohl relating to the objectives of the rule of law is his attention to Wilhelm von Humboldt. In his considerations he raised the postulate (as it turns out, extremely similar to Mohl's) that the purpose of a rational man is the "comprehensive and harmonious education of all individual forces."[892] Humboldt also stated that freedom is a prerequisite for achieving self-realization.[893] As already mentioned, according

887 Ibid, p. 240. M. P. Thompson, *Locke's contract in context*, [in:] *The social contract from Hobbes to Rawls*, London and New York 2005, pp. 80–85.

888 R. v. Mohl, Geschicht.u.Lit.1, pp. 240–241.

889 Ibid, p. 241. Z. A. Maciąg, op. cit., p. 84.

890 R. v. Mohl, Geschicht.u.Lit.1, p. 241.

891 For more about the purpose of Kant's state: P. Koslowski, *Staat und Gesellschaft bei Kant*, Tübingen 1985, pp. 26–38.

892 W. v. Humboldt, *Ideen zu einem Versuch, die Gränzen der Wirksamkeit des Staats zu bestimmen*, Breslau 1851, p. 9. Więcej na ten temat: M. Chmieliński, *Dwa niemieckie indywidualizmy...*, pp. 69–72.

893 W. v. Humboldt, op. cit. p. 9, R. v. Mohl, Geschicht.u.Lith.1, p. 242.

to Humboldt, the state should limit its activities to only to the necessary things, leaving the individuals the widest possible field of activity. As Maciej Chmieliński notes, this minimum, when it comes to state actions, is the protection against an external enemy and punishment of criminals.[894]

Johann Friedrich Herbart was another German thinker who, in the opinion of von Mohl, held merits for the development of the idea of the rule of law. Von Mohl drew attention to his belief in the need to establish the state by collective (universal) will and its rational purpose. What was extremely important for von Mohl in Herbart, and what also made him stand out from earlier German thinkers, is the belief that the state does not have one specific purpose. On the contrary, the task of the state in Herbart was to support all morally acceptable goals for the realization of which people form states (a very similar view to that of von Mohl).[895] In the context of the observations made in the second chapter, it should be noted that von Mohl considered Herbart's view of the existence and shape of society to be true. Herbart understood it in a very similar way as did von Mohl, i.e. as a collection of various types of groups serving the purposes of the individuals associated in them.[896] According to von Mohl, the work of Karl Christian Friedrich Krause also contributed to the creation of the rule of law in Germany. According to the Württemberger, Krause's rational approach was to be based on the belief in the necessity of establishing a state on the basis of a social contract and on the postulate of separation of powers.[897]

The above analysis allows to state that the formulation of concept of the rule of law according to Robert von Mohl was preceded by his thorough research in the field of political and legal thought. It should also be noted, however, that the Württemberger placed little emphasis on analyzing the political realities of his time, focusing primarily on the creators and their concepts related to the idea of the rule of law.[898] Nevertheless there is no doubt that the aforementioned genesis of the idea of the rule of law already allows for the definition of some

894 M. Chmieliński, *Polityczna wizja społeczeństwa w poglądach Wilhelma Humboldta*, [in:] *Przez tysiąclecia: państwo-prawo-jednostka*, t. III, A. Lityński, M. Mikołajczyk (eds.), Katowice 2001, p. 143. W. v. Humboldt, op. cit., p. 39. J. Isensee, *Subsidiaritätsprinzip und Verfassungsrecht, Eine Studie über das Regulativ des Verhältnisses von Staats und Gesellschaft*, Berlin 2001, pp. 50–51.

895 R. v. Mohl, Geschicht.u.Lit.1, p. 244.

896 Ibid. More on Herbart's understanding of the state and society: J. F. Herbart, *Allgemeine Practische Philosophie*, Göttingen 1808, pp. 312–327.

897 R. v. Mohl, Geschicht.u.Lit.1, p. 244.

898 Z. A. Maciąg, op. cit., p. 87.

of its features, which will later be seen in the Mohl's perception of *Rechtsstaat*. Therefore, the rule of law should be characterized by the principle of agreement of free and equal individuals, establishing the state on the basis of a contract. The statement that authorities exist for the people, and not the people for the authorities, also has a liberal overtone. Instead, authorities should be guided by the common good. The goal of the rule of law state should therefore be to meet the needs of the people living in it, in terms of security (and not only legal), and support in the development and achievement of their life goals. The individuals living in a rule of law state are free, their freedom can be limited only by factors arising from the needs resulting from their coexistence with other individuals in the state organism. Important, in view of later considerations regarding the tasks of the state administration, is von Mohl's conviction about the functioning in the state of a social structure consisting of voluntary communities, whose objective is to fulfil specific tasks.[899]

Turning to discussing the meaning of the concept of the rule of law in Robert von Mohl's thought, it should be noted that it appears rather early in its development. Already in the *Constitutional Law of the Kingdom of Württemberg*, next to such species of the state as listed in the previous subsection; theocracy, patrimonial state or despotism, he distinguished the so-called "species of rule of law" (*Rechtsstaats-Gattung*).[900] It was this species of state, which differed radically from the others, and was analyzed by von Mohl in the most thorough and comprehensive manner. Thanks to his synthesis of the idea of the rule of law, von Mohl permanently entered the canon of German and European political and legal thought of the 19th century. Despite the fact that the term *Rechtsstaat* was already known thanks Johann Wilhelm Placidus, prior to the activities of von Mohl, the German science agrees that it is thanks to him that this name was popularized and permanently entered the terminology of law and politics.[901] Von Mohl, on the other hand, reached the heights of the *Rechtsstaat*[902] concept.

However, before the scholar's views on the issue of the definition of the rule of law and the purpose, which should guide it, we should raise the issue

899 Similarly on this topic: Ibid, pp. 88–89.

900 R. v. Mohl, Staatsr.Württem.1.1829, p. 8.

901 J. Fernandez-Villaverde, *Magna Carta, the rule of law, and the limits on government*, 'International Review of Law and Economics,' 47 (2016) 22–28,' p. 26.

902 U. Bermbach, *Liberalismus*, [in:] *Pipers Handbuch der Politischen Ideen,*I. Fetscher, H. Muenkler (eds.), Bd. 3, München 1986, p. 355. On the concept of the rule of law by von Mohl: *Der europäische Rechtsstaat, 200 Zeugnisse seiner Geschichte*, J. Brand, H. Hattenhauer (eds.), Heidelberg 1994, pp. 97–98.

of rationality as a factor that shapes this species of state. It is basing it on the so-called "rational principle," or organization of the state in accordance with the demands of rationality, that for von Mohl forms first and initial feature of the *Rechtsstaat* concept, distinguishing it from other species of state. Von Mohl took the position that the prerequisite for the emergence of states belonging to the species of the rule of law is that individuals living in the respective nation achieve a sufficiently high level of civilizational development. This development is to manifest itself primarily in that the inhabitants of a given country base their lives on the principles of rationality and the common sense understanding of the world. Properly developed individuals, reaching the "rational" understanding of the world and their existence, therefore give up the belief that mortal life is only a preparatory process for eternal life (as is the case, for example, in theocracy). According to von Mohl, a man who is guided in his life by the principles of rationalism concludes that the sole rational goal of his life on Earth is to develop in the most comprehensive manner possible.[903] Therefore, the development and training of individual personality and its abilities appears as the sole purpose of the existence of individuals.

It can be assumed that the above-mentioned specific way of understanding existence, represented by rational individuals, is, in von Mohl, oriented individualistically, as it concerns the development of individual abilities and forces.[904] The above assumption is the key to understanding the concept of the rule of law in Robert von Mohl, because it will condition the acceptance of the principle that it is freedom (of the citizen) that is the most important principle of the *Rechtsstaat*. He understood freedom above all as an opportunity to take all actions enabling an individual to develop in a comprehensive way.[905]

Under this freedom, a rational individual, striving to achieve his or her life goals, must sometimes accept limitations (with a rational or a legal basis). Therefore, it cannot take actions that would be irrational, oppose its nature and essence, nor can it violate the rights of other individuals.[906] Based on the above reasoning, we can clearly see the how much von Mohl remained under the influence of the classical educational ideal, as known from German idealism. In von Mohl one can see not only the influence of German idealism, but also the

---

903 R. v. Mohl, *Encyklopädie der Staatswissenschaften*, Zweite Auflage. . ., pp. 325–326, Idem, Polizeiwiss.1.1844, pp. 6–7.

904 J. Hähnle, op. cit., p. 15.

905 K. v. Beyme, *Einleitung*. . ., p. XVIII. R. v. Mohl, Polizeiwiss.1.1844, p. 8.

906 E. Angermann, op. cit., p. 121.

optimistic, early liberal, characteristic of German middle-class people, belief in the power of human reason and the autonomy of individuals.[907] In Mohl's understanding of the individual, there is a clear opposition to absolutist concepts. Instead of a limited individual, subordinated to the state, what we observe in von Mohl is an independent individual that rationally exercises its rights and freedoms.[908]

With regard to the concept of the rule of law in Robert von Mohl, it should be emphasized that there is a definite difference between this species of state and the species listed in the previous chapter.[909] It will differ from both the patriarchal and patrimonial states in its objective (discussed in a moment). What distinguishes it from theocracy is the belief that faith is only one aspect of human existence in the state. Furthermore, the aspect of faith in the rule of law will be subject to restrictions, primarily by generally applicable laws. The *Rechsstaat* will differ from the classical state in that its goal will be to achieve life satisfaction of individuals and their social circles, and not, in the first line, by the abstractly understood general population of a given state. By its very essence, the rule of law differs from a despotic state directed not at the good of individuals and their communities, but at the good of the ruling.[910] In the classification of species of states by von Mohl, the rule of law occupies the highest position, as a being based on rationality and forming the effect and proof of the high civilizational development of the community that creates it.[911]

Regarding the justification and the process of establishing the rule of law, it should be pointed out in Robert von Mohl's thought that it differs little from the concepts regarding the creation of the state in the general sense (as discussed in chapter four). To demonstrate the full idea of the Mohl's rule of law, it is worth to, at least briefly, follow the process of the emergence of the rule of law, as indicated by the scholar, against the background of general theory of the state. As with the general concept of the state, one can see here an individual who, noticing that his forces are not sufficient to achieve his goals, joins with others in increasingly complex social structures, culminating with a state. According to von Mohl, there are two ways rule of law can emerge. As a supporter of contractualism, he pointed out that it could arise in the result of the conclusion of a social contract

907 B. Stöcker, op. cit., pp. 34–35.
908 H. Schmitz, op. cit., p. 110.
909 Ibid, p. 50.
910 R. v. Mohl, *Encyklopädie der Staatswissenschaften*, Zweite Auflage. . ., pp. 106–107.
911 Ibid, p. 326.

by certain individuals (see the example of California, already cited). The rule of law state can also manifest itself as an effect of the civilizational development of its inhabitants (through an evolutionary process).[912] Authorization to act is gained through "general agreement" and its strength is "the joining of all individual forces for its protection."[913] In order for the rule of law to be able to act for the benefit of individuals, each of them must, according to von Mohl, give some of their power to the state so that a state power arises out of it, granting it enough strength to perform its tasks.[914]

The analysis of the purpose of the rule of law in the Robert von Mohl doctrine should begin with the symptomatic statement that he did not, in fact, consider the name "*Rechtsstaat*" as appropriate to define this idea.[915] For von Mohl, the use of only the word '*Recht*' or 'law' in the name was misleading, resulting in the conviction that the purpose of a state operating on the basis of the *Rechtsstaat* idea would only be to protect the law. According to a German scholar, the second half of the state's activity, which was broadly understood by the police (*Polizei*), was neglected here. Despite the fact that von Mohl finally opted to keep the name *Rechtsstaat* (accepting it as already functioning in circulation), he never got rid of doubts whether this species of the state should not be called "*Rechts- und-PolizeiStaat*" ("Legal and police state"), or maybe at all, referring to its rationalist basis -"*Verstandes-Staat*"- ("rational state").[916]

Based on the above-mentioned doubts of the scholar regarding the role of the rule of law, one should examine his definition of its objective. In one of his most important works, *Police science according to the principles of legal state*, von Mohl said:

912 Ibid, pp. 325–326.

913 Idem, Staatsr.Württem.1.1829, p. 8.

914 Idem, Polizeiwiss.1.1844, p. 8. E. Angermann, op. cit., pp. 129–130.

915 The specific uncertainty of German science regarding the meaning of the term *Rechtsstaat* is well reflected in the quote from Otto Mayer: "The word [*Rechtsstaat*-author's note] came when the case was already pending. This term was meant to mean something that did not exist, or at least was not ready, (...)": O. Mayer, *Deutsches Verwaltungsrecht*, Bd. I, Leipzig 1895, p. 61.

916 R. v. Mohl, Staatsr.Württem.1.1829, p. 11. A. Bosiacki, *Egalitaryzm a elitaryzm w klasycznej koncepcji państwa prawnego w Niemczech XIX wieku*, [in:] *Księga pamiątkowa dedykowana Profesorowi Romanowi A. Tokarczykowi*, t. V, Z. Władek, A. Bereza (eds.), Lublin 2014, p. 22. G. Dietze, *Staatsrecht und Rechtsstaat*, [in:] K. v. Beyme (ed.) *Theory and Politics, Theorie und Politik, Festschrift zum 70. Geburtstag für Carl Joachim Friedrich*, Haag 1871, pp.547–548.

> "The rule of law can have no other purpose than to organize the collective life of the nation in such a way that each member is aided and supported in the most free and comprehensive exercise use of all his powers possible."[917]

In the above definition of the purpose of the rule of law, one can clearly see a reference to the previously described aspirations of individuals operating in the state. The rule of law is nothing more than an instrument to provide individuals, first of all order, and secondly support in the pursuit of their intentions. However, one cannot help the impression that the above definition of the rule of law's objective seems to be quite general, which determines the need for an in-depth examination of its scope. According to von Mohl, the purpose of the rule of law is to enable, protect and support individuals as well as their social groups in the development of their strengths (abilities) and in achieving the goals resulting from the rational understanding of the essence of human existence. Therefore, it should be stated that from the essence of the legal state in von Mohl results its duty to protect and support the comprehensive development of individuals striving to achieve their life goals.[918]

The aforementioned purpose of the rule of law will determine two great areas of its activity, which are limited to safeguarding the legal order and supporting individuals and their communities. For von Mohl, there is a belief that individuals may encounter two types of obstacles in the process of achieving their life goals. The first are the unlawful and unfair activities of other individuals. Removing this kind of obstacles corresponds to the first part of *Rechtsstaat* 's activity, i.e. maintaining legal order, guaranteed by the activity of justice (*Justiz*).[919] According to von Mohl, maintaining the legal order, manifested, among others in the enforcement of generally applicable law, is not only a value in itself (after all, "the sanctity of all laws" was for von Mohl the most important rule of the rule of law), but also a prerequisite for all its further activities.[920] In order to perform the task imposed on it the Mohl's *Rechtsstaat* must operate within a specific legal order. All its actions must be justified and take place within the limits of generally applicable law.[921]

---

917 R. v. Mohl, Polizeiwiss.1.1844, p. 8.

918 Idem, Polizeiwiss.1.1866, pp. 4–5.

919 Idem, Staatsr.Württem.1.1829, p. 8.

920 Idem, *Encyklopädie der Staatswissenschaften*, Zweite Auflage…, pp. 325–326. K. Sobota, op. cit., pp. 313–314.

921 R. v. Mohl, *Encyklopädie der Staatswissenschaften*, Zweite Auflage…, p. 106.

Another type of obstacles that stand in individuals' way of achieving their life goals, determining the second, perhaps the most important aspect of *Rechtsstaat*'s activity in von Mohl, will be the obstacles resulting from the impact of the so-called "force majeure." This phenomenon should be understood as various external factors that an individual cannot overcome by itself. These obstacles are overcome by the rule of law state through its police apparatus (*Polizei*).[922] What constitutes the essence of the rule of law's police activity is its subsidiarity. For von Mohl, one of the most important principles of the rule of law is the freedom of citizens. Under this freedom, citizens must move within limits of reason and law. This postulate results in the belief that the rule of law is only a means to achieve goals, and that it cannot enter all spheres of life.[923] Thus, it can support citizens in achieving their life goals (take care of their well-being) only when they are unable to do it themselves.[924]

The concept referring to the support of individuals and their goals shows a certain departure of von Mohl from the principles of individualism of individuals. Well, the rule of law state is not intended to support any individually defined goals, even if they were rational.[925] According to von Mohl, it would be impossible to meet this assumption. In its activities it must take into account only the so-called "general view of the nation on life,"[926] resulting from general life aspirations and the level of civilization development of the inhabitants of the respective country.[927]

The idea of the rule of law in von Mohl, which is a state that protects the law and cares for the well-being of citizens, shows a clear distance between the scholar and the views not only of Kant or Frédéric Bastiat, but also German

---

922 Idem, Staatsr.Württem.1.1829, p. 8.

923 Idem, Polizeiwiss.1.1844, p. 8.

924 Idem, Staatsr.Württem.1.1829, p. 8, Idem, *Encyklopädie der Staatswissenschaften*, Zweite Auflage. . ., pp. 325–326. It is noteworthy that the constitution of the German Reich of 16 April 1871 stated, in its preamble, that one of its goals is concern for the welfare of the German Nation. According to von Mohl, the "scholary" example of the *Rechtsstaat* idea was precisely the provision of the German Reich Constitution stating that the "eternal union" was established "for the protection of territory under its law, as well as for the welfare of the German Nation.": *Verfassung des Deutschen Reiches, gegeben Berlin den 16. April 1871*, L v. Roenne (ed.), Berlin und Leipzig 1882, p. 1. R. v. Mohl, *Das deutsche Reichsstaatsrecht, Rechtliche und politische Eröterungen*. . ., pp. 26, 39.

925 Idem, *Encyklopädie der Staatswissenschaften*, Zweite Auflage. . ., p. 511.

926 Idem, Polizeiwiss.1.1844, p. 7.

927 Ibid.

thinkers such as Karl Heinrich Ludwig Poelitz or Sylvester Jordan, who considered the rule of law solely from the point of view of the purpose of protecting the law, bypassing its goal of supporting individuals (i.e. speaking the language of that times - its "police" purpose).[928] According to von Mohl, the erroneous view of the solely "legal" purpose of the state confirms the answer to the rhetorical question: "Who would want and could live in such a state that functions only as a judiciary without allowing any police assistance?."[929] The difference between the concept of the rule of law in von Mohl and Friedrich Julius Stahl (described in chapter one) should also be noted. The latter, called the creator of the formal concept of the rule of law, focused primarily on defining the rule of law as a mode of action that is based on laws. He did not give the idea of *Rechtsstaat* a deeper material dimension, as von Mohl did.[930]

The issue that requires to be addressed when discussing the Mohl's concept of the rule of law is the belief of the scholar that its functioning does not depend on the form of government it adopts. Therefore, any way of organizing state power can be applied in a rule of law state. The sole condition is that the state authority should be able to achieve the tasks that are imposed on the rule of law.[931] According to von Mohl, any shape of state power that would guarantee the achievement of two overarching goals of the rule of law, i.e. protection of the law and support for the achievement of individual goals is thus possible. The adoption by the rule of law of a particular form of government was therefore only a matter of adapting each of them in the best possible way to the prevailing conditions.[932]

Therefore, just as in case of the classical state, also the rule of law adopts different kinds in Württemberger's thought. It can be a "pure" democracy (direct democracy) and a representative democracy.[933] It can also take an aristocratic or monarchical form. A monarchical rule of law can be either an absolute monarchy, a monarchy limited by estates of the realm, a monarchy limited by

928 Idem, Staatsr.Württem.1.1829, p. 11. Frenchman Frédéric Bastiat, an unprecedented critic of socialism, believed that the state should focus on protective functions guaranteeing property, justice and security. More: L. Dubel, *Idea "minimum państwa" w koncepcjach Frédérica Bastiata*, "Annales Universitatis Mariae Curie-Sklodowska, Sectio G (IUS)," Vol. LIX, 2, p. 9.

929 Idem, Polizeiwiss.1.1866, p. 5. Z. A. Maciąg, op. cit., p. 79.

930 Ibid, p. 115.

931 R. v. Mohl, *Encyklopädie der Staatswissenschaften*, Zweite Auflage…, p. 326.

932 Ibid, p. 332.

933 Idem, Staatsr.Württem.1.1829, pp. 14–15.

the representation of the people, and finally the so-called "state with divided powers."[934] It should be remembered, however, that the issue of what political system will be adopted by a given legal state, although important, does not change the essence of its species. For example, in a rule of law functioning as a monarchy, the ruling individual has no right to change the objective of the rule of law according to his own preferences. Therefore, the aims and basic principles of the rule of law remain unchanged.[935] Robert von Mohl considered the belief that only democracy is the proper and legitimate form of the rule of law to be erroneous. He emphasized that the rule of law is mainly about achieving the collective objectives of the people, while the form of its government is only a means subordinate to this goal. So if, as he said, as long the objectives of the state can also be achieved with various other forms of government, then these forms can also be called the rule of law.[936]

To sum up the considerations related to the genesis and essence of the concept of the rule of law, it should be stated, firstly, that in von Mohl this idea originates from rationalist thought about the state, which was characteristic for early German liberalism.[937] Von Mohl, who introduced the concept of *Rechtsstaat* to the general discussion, but also Karl Theodor Welcker or another German liberal Johann Christoph von Aretin, all saw the rule of law not as a special form of regime or government, but as a separate species of state. The basis of such state is reason, which characterizes, most of all, the individuals that create it.[938] For von Mohl, both the entire nation and its individual members must find the realization of their life goals in the state. The most important rule of the state of rule of law is the freedom of citizens, which manifests itself primarily in the unrestricted development and achievement of goals by individuals. However, this

934 Ibid, pp. 15–18. Idem, *Encyklopädie der Staatswissenschaften*, Zweite Auflage…, pp. 107–108, 332.

935 Ibid, p. 333.

936 Z. A. Maciąg, op. cit., p. 98.

937 More about the creators of early German liberalism: H. Ottoman, *Geschichte des politischen Denkens*, Bd.3: *Neuzeit*, Stuttgart 2008, pp. 93–99.

938 E.-W. Böckenförde, *Staat, Gesellschaft, Freiheit, Studien zur Staatstheorie und zum Verfassungsrecht*, Frankfurt am Main, 1976, p. 66. Welcker, like von Mohl, spoke of a "state of reason" ("*Staat der Vernunft*"), and Aretin of a state "(…) in which power is exercised according to a reasonable common will directed at the general good." What Aretin understood under "general good" was the widest possible freedom and security of all members of society.: J. Ch. v. Aretin, *Staatsrecht der constitutionellen Monarchie*, Leipzig 1838, p. 156.

development must take place within the limits of reason and law, and the idea of the common good underlying the rule of law.[939]

German science agrees that Robert von Mohl and his concept of the rule of law are the culmination of an early, primarily material-oriented idea of the *Rechtsstaat*. It was a successful combination of the following aspects: formal, focused on legal security, and material, focused on justice in the broader sense.[940] The activity of the state gains a material dimension by means of borders extending to virtually all areas of public, economic and cultural life. The formal principle is evidenced by the fact that the state should always be basing on laws in its proceedings in these matters.[941] Therefore we should adopt as fact, that the concept of rule of law in von Mohl has both material and formal dimension. It seems that he has tried to take a middle direction, in which the state will be limited by certain legal forms, but nevertheless it remain an active entity.[942] *Rechtsstaat* is for von Mohl a rational state, founded on the principle of freedom, first and foremost the freedom of the individual, yet not including its life in an unlimited way. It deviates from the boundless goal of promoting prosperity (known from the police state), in favour of removing obstacles that individuals face, and cannot remove themselves.[943] Since the rule of law is only to supplement the individual, its will, and its activities, it should be concluded that the individual stands in the center of the Mohl's *Rechtsstaat*. Nevertheless von Mohl noted that the will of the individual cannot dominate the interest of the society in general. In addition, especially when considering the principles for operation of police in the state, von Mohl will find many exceptions and situations, in which the individual will have to subordinate itself to them.[944] On the other hand, the most important goal of an individual in the rule of law is the most comprehensive and individual development of the "modern" man possible. From this follows the dual

939 B. Stöcker, op. cit., p. 37.

940 I. Maus, *Entwicklung und Funktionswandel der Theorie des bürgerlichen Rechtsstaats*, [in:] *Der bürgerliche Rechtsstaat*, M. Tohipidur (ed.), Frankfurt am Main 1978, p. 13. On the rule of law by von Mohl: J. Meierhenrich, *The Remanants of the Rechtsstaat, An Ethnography of Nazi Law*, Oxford 2018, pp. 75–79.

941 B. Stöcker, op. cit., p. 49.

942 Ibid, p. 51.

943 U. Scheuner, *Der Rechtsstaat und die soziale Verantwortung des Staates: Das wissenschaftliche Lebenswerk von Robert von Mohl*, "Der Staat" Vol. 18, No.1 (1979), pp. 17–18.

944 H. Schmitz, op. cit., p. 109.

task of the rule of law, firstly the support of people's rational goals and, secondly, maintaining legal order.[945]

In fact, von Mohl's teaching about the rule of law was nothing but a reflection of views of the state and society that corresponded to the spiritual and economic interests of the early German bourgeoisie. First of all, freedom, both in the spiritual and economic dimension. Secondly, the liberal concept of self-responsibility, which in von Mohl was not just an empty postulate. Self-responsibility, however, did not mean the rejection of any state aid. It could provide it, yet was not allowed to impose it.[946] The rule of law in early German liberalism departs from all abstract, transcendent approaches to its goals. The state will no longer be an institution created by God, but a community created to pursue the goals and well-being of individuals. The starting point for the state is an independent, free and equal individual and its life goals, and supporting it forms the task and source of legitimacy of the state.[947]

The tasks of the rule of law should, on the one hand, consist in maintaining the legal order throughout the entire scope of state power, and on the other, supporting rational human goals, but only if and only to such an extent that the resources of individuals and the smaller social groups supporting them would not suffice them to achieve them. In this way Mohl formulated the principle of subsidiarity. In this aspect, however, he differed, e.g. from Humboldt, in that he expanded the scope of state activities to all rational goals and aspirations of individuals, and did not narrow them down only to ensuring security. Thus, he combined both of the main objectives of the state, legal security of the individuals and their pursuit of rational goals. He associated the current understanding of the rule of law, formulated by extreme liberals, with the positive values of the police state.[948] So one should agree with Erich Angermann, who thought the vision of von Mohl was more in line with reality.[949] A state organization where the individual will not only be protected against injustice but such, where it will be supported by welfare in the broader sense thus seems more realistic.

---

945 P. v. Oertzen, *Die soziale Funktion des staatsrechtlichen Positivismus*, Frankfurt am Main 1974, p. 98.

946 E. Angermann, op. cit., p. 127.

947 E.-W. Böckenförde, *Staat, Gesellschaft, Freiheit, Studien zur Staatstheorie und zum Verfassungsrecht*. . ., p. 67.

948 Z. A. Maciąg, op. cit., p. 91.

949 E. Angermann, op. cit., p. 126.

4.2. The legal state and the individual

In the previous subsection, we proved that the rule of law in the thought of Robert von Mohl cannot be understood solely as a state safeguarding the legal order. In case of this thinker *Rechtsstaat* is an idea that brings with it a considerable load of tasks and values that the state should follow. One of the aspects of material dimension of the idea of the rule of law in von Mohl will be the concepts related to the broadly understood position of the individual in this species of state.

In order to make the above-mentioned analysis, it is first necessary to examine the meaning of the two terms in von Mohl, namely 'subject' (*Unterthan*) and 'citizen' (*Bürger, Staatsbürger*). According to the Württemberger, the subjects were all inhabitants of the state, insofar they were obliged to obey the authorities and to provide benefits for the community. In von Mohl, the notion of the subject is associated primarily with such species of state as theocracy or despotism, in which the inhabitant is mostly burdened with obligations towards the broadly understood community. Nevertheless we should also note that von Mohl did not link negative connotations to the notion of the subject in the state. Moreover, he also noticed that in the rule of law the individual often acts in this position, with the difference that in this species of state its duties are determined by generally applicable law (which is also a protective instrument for the individual).[950]

What is characteristic for the species of rule of law in von Mohl, is the presence of individuals in the role of citizens, which is illustrated by the statement: "Every state has subjects, but only the rule of law has citizens."[951] Just as being a subject comes with obligations to the state, so citizenship corresponds to the rights on a reciprocal basis, i.e. the right of the individual (citizen) corresponds to the duty of the state and vice versa.[952] According to von Mohl these rights take the three basic dimensions. First of all, therefore, it is the right to demand that the state perform certain tasks (above all, support the achievement of life goals). Secondly, they are so-called "negative civic liberties of the individual" (*die negativen Freiheitsrechte des Einzelnen*), defined as all the principles on the basis of which the individual in the state derives either the right to specific actions or to free itself from certain actions in that state. For von Mohl, the third dimension of citizenship is the right to participate in state governance (although it is not present in all types of

950 R. v. Mohl, *Encyklopädie der Staatswissenschaften*, Zweite Auflage..., pp. 122–123.

951 Idem, Staatsr.Württem.1.1840, p. 316.

952 R. Suppé, *Die Grund- und Menschenrechte in der deutschen Staatslehre des 19. Jahrhunderts*, Berlin 2004, p. 117.

rule of law).[953] They will later be further specified as civil or "fundamental rights" (*staatsbürgerliche Rechte, Grundrechte*) and "political rights."

We should therefore note the duality of perception of individuals in Mohl's rule of law. On the one hand, the scholar was not able to tear himself away from the old, absolute understanding of the individual as a subject, having first and foremost responsibilities towards the state (monarch). On the other hand, however, he noticed that in the modern *Rechtsstaat* idea, corresponding to the development of humanity, the individual must also have broadly understood rights relating to the state. In addition, the above-presented understanding of the subject-citizen by von Mohl will result in the conviction that an individual in a state cannot have only rights but must also have some obligations.

However, one cannot forget that von Mohl was not consistent in using the terms 'subject' and 'citizen.' These concepts were generally not the same for this thinker. However, despite the fact that he made the aforementioned distinction, he often used them interchangeably in his writings (e.g. speaking of "subjects' rights"). He also used other terms such as "individual" (*Einzelne*), "*Staatsgenosse*," which could be translated as "state comrade," "participant" (*Theilnehmer, Theilhaber*), or "participant in the state" (*Staatsteilnehmer*).[954] However, it must be acknowledged that although this is a side issue, it indicates a specific terminological uncertainty of von Mohl. Its sources should be sought in the functioning of the scholar in the era of absolutism. For the purposes of the present subsection, the word citizen will be used to indicate an individual that has both rights and obligations. This is dictated not only by today's understanding of this concept, but also by the fact that the whole of this chapter concerns the rule of law, whose special feature in von Mohl was the presence of citizens.

Robert von Mohl's concepts related to fundamental rights in a state consistent with the idea of *Rechtsstaat* belonged to the positivist trend described in chapter one. The German liberal should be considered a supporter of codification and positivization of fundamental rights in the state. According to him the rule of law will provide the framework that these rights need in order to exist and develop. They will not be abstract norms, external to the state and existing somewhere outside it, but will result from its purpose, and the tasks that von Mohl set for the rule of law.[955]

953 R. v. Mohl, *Encyklopädie der Staatswissenschaften*, Zweite Auflage…, pp. 123–125.
954 Z. A. Maciąg, op. cit., p. 88.
955 R. Suppé, op. cit., pp. 121–122.

The scholar's first contact with the issue of civil rights took place on the basis of an analysis of this type of regulations functioning in the Württemberg system.[956] Analyzing the system reigning in his homeland, von Mohl did not talk about the abstract rights of individuals in the natural law approach, but focused on civil rights (*Rechte der Staatsbürger*).[957] During his initial attempt to analyze the subject of individual rights, von Mohl applied a method in which theory and practice were combined. By analyzing and commenting on the legal norms in Württemberg, von Mohl synthesized his ideas for the first time.[958] It should be noted that the civil rights that appear in the Württemberg constitution are identical to the concepts relating to the rule of law at the time. The citizen should therefore enjoy equality before the law, freedom of thought and conscience, protection of property, freedom of movement and economic freedom. In the early period, von Mohl did not add the right to assemble, although the scholar did not exclude it. At a later stage of his work, von Mohl expanded his understanding of *Rechtsstaat* and the rights of its citizens by passive and active right to participate in political processes or the right of association.[959]

The idea of the fundamental rights of individuals was developed by von Mohl in the later period of his work. Finally, the scholar was able to introduce the division of fundamental rights that was compatible with the then trends, to his idea of the *Rechtsstaat*. First of all, he distinguished "civil rights" (*staatsbürgerliche Rechte, staatsbürgerlichen Rechte im engeren Sinne*), relating to citizens' freedom in relation to the state, and political rights (*politischen Rechte*), seemingly less important, and relating to participation in government (which shall, very importantly, be limited to a set number of citizens[960]). These two components make up the concept of constitutional or fundamental rights (*Grundrechte*) in von Mohl.[961] Thus, the division into political rights and civil liberties (characteristic of early German liberalism) is clearly visible.[962]

956 Ibid, p. 113.

957 G. Gozzi, op. cit., p. 242. It's worth noting that von Mohl praised England for developing the rights of it's citizens: S. Kirste, *Philosophical Foundations of the Principle of the Legal State (Rechtsstaat) and the Rule of Law*, [in:] J. R. Silkenat, J. E. Hickey Jr., P. D. Barenboim (eds.), op. cit.

958 R. Suppé, op. cit., pp. 114–115.

959 G. Gozzi, op. cit., p. 242.

960 R. v. Mohl, *Encyklopädie der Staatswissenschaften*, Zweite Auflage..., p. 233.

961 Ibid, pp. 222–223.

962 R.-J. Grahe, op. cit., p. 89.

For the first time von Mohl wrote about civil rights in the *Constitutional law of the Kingdom of Württemberg*. He defined these norms as "(...) all the rights of citizens of the state in relation to it, which belong to them as such, without any special acquisition."[963] Civil rights are therefore rights that are strongly associated with the concept of citizenship. Every citizen has them without the need for their special acquisition or granting, they set the rules according to which relations between the legal state and individual should function.[964] In other words, von Mohl's concept of civil rights can be defined as a set of principles that the state should follow in its relations with the individual (e.g., such that say, which areas of life cannot be violated). In von Mohl, there is a separation of these civil rights from the political rights that were associated with belonging to a specific state or from obtaining a certain privilege of a political nature.[965] It should be remembered that since the notion of citizen is characteristic only of legal state, then civil rights will also exist only in the idea of *Rechtsstaat*. We cannot speak of their presence in theocracy, patrimonial or despotic state.[966]

On the margins of considerations on civil rights in the Mohl's idea of the *Rechtsstaat*, we should emphasize the position of the scholar that differed from the trend prevailing at the time, according to which scientific papers, but also legal provisions focused exclusively on the rights of individuals in the state, omitting their obligations. According to von Mohl, this was to prove not only the focus on the atomistic and egoistic understanding of the lives of individuals in the state, but also on the deep distrust towards the rulers.[967] In addition, another argument demonstrating that von Mohl belongs to the supporters of the positivization of civil and political rights will be his negative assessment of the regulations of the then French and US constitutions regarding individual rights. According to von Mohl, these were "questionable" and "of unspecified scope." Therefore, the current list of civil and political rights in short statements, both in the US and French systems, on the basis of various types of general declarations, was not recognized by the scholar as proper. Von Mohl was afraid that such a broad and general definition of rights could be difficult to make decisions relating

963 R. v. Mohl, Staatsr.Württem.1.1840, p. 312.

964 R.-J. Grahe, op. cit., p. 87.

965 R. v. Mohl, Staatsr.Württem.1.1840, p. 313.

966 Ibid, p. 316. R. Suppé, op. cit., p. 119.

967 R. v. Mohl, *Encyklopädie der Staatswissenschaften*, Zweite Auflage..., p. 127. An example for von Mohl was the fact that in the *Staatslexkion* of Welcker and von Rotteck, there was not even a separate article regarding the issue of the "subject": Idem, *Encyklopedia umiejętności politycznych*..., p. 111.

to individual facts and lead to uncertainty and misunderstanding. According to von Mohl, the introduction of such general statements was only recommended, when it meant a significant change in the country and constituted only a starting point for new, more detailed legislation.[968]

We should begin our description and analysis of the catalogue of civil rights in von Mohl's legal state by stating that the concepts of the scholar regarding this subject are found in numerous of his works. These will be, first of all, the aforementioned *Constitutional Law of the Kingdom of Württemberg*, the *opus magnum* of the liberal, i.e. the *Encyclopaedia of state sciences, Constitutional Law, International law, and Politics*. The analysis of the above works allows us to reconstruct the catalogue of civil liberties (or "civil rights in a narrow sense" - as the scholar said to distinguish them from political rights), which are present in the concept of *Rechtsstaat* by Robert von Mohl.

The initial right, primary in relation to others, is for von Mohl the citizen's right to "permanent participation in the state" (*bleibende Theilnahme am Staat*). Therefore, every citizen has the right to "be a citizen," to live in the state and to benefit from this fact. The sole situation, where the expulsion of a citizen from the state is allowed is the case where it proved that its life goals are irreconcilable with the idea of the state and the universal good. In this case the state can apply expulsion as a punishment and as a measure serving the interest of general security.[969]

Equality before the law, which von Mohl understood primarily as equality of all citizens in the process of taking into account their permitted life goals and aspirations, will connect with this principle. The citizens are equal in legal sense therefore they do not only have the freedom to pursue these goals, but also the right to demand support from the state in justified cases. Citizens must have freedom. Personal freedom of citizens as a rule of law is a guarantee of the free pursuit of individuals to achieve their life goals.[970] What is related to the freedom of citizens and the principle of the protection of the individual (*Schutz der Person*) is "the right to relativity and justice on the part of the authorities regarding arrest, house search and seizure of letters."[971] Von Mohl argued that in the rule of law all necessary cases of violations of civil liberties should be,

968 R. v. Mohl, *Encyklopädie der Staatswissenschaften*, Zweite Auflage…, pp. 231–232. R. Suppé, op. cit., pp. 117–118.

969 R. v. Mohl, *Encyklopädie der Staatswissenschaften*, Zweite Auflage…, pp. 223–224. R.-J. Grahe, op. cit., p. 90.

970 Idem, *Encyklopädie der Staatswissenschaften*, Zweite Auflage…, pp. 225–226, 328–329.

971 Ibid, p. 227.

first of all, absolutely necessary, and secondly, as mild as possible (in proportion to achieving the intended purpose). All interference must be justified by provisions of generally applicable law. Also, any rights acquired by citizens in a proper manner must be secured against unauthorized interference by the state.[972]

The principle of "equality of citizens' rights and burdens (obligations)" (*Gleichheit der bürgerlichen Rechte und Lasten*) will be linked with such principle of equality of citizens. A situation in which civil rights and obligations would be unevenly distributed would be contrary to the idea of *Rechtsstaat* postulated by von Mohl. According to the scholar, this state of affairs characterizes the less developed species of states, such as the patrimonial state or theocracy.[973] It was unacceptable for von Mohl that one citizen (or their group) would only benefit and the other would only suffer losses. In von Mohl, everyone has equal or the same right to expect support from the rule of law.[974]

The postulate related to the idea of the rule of law (especially with its legal aspect) is the citizen's right "only to obey within limits of constitution" (*blos verfassungsmässiger Gehorsam*").[975] A citizen in a state organized according to the *Rechtsstaat* idea is obliged to act in accordance with the principles of reason and law. Norms resulting from hierarchically ordered sources of law, to which a citizen is subject, must comply with the highest legal act in the state, i.e. a constitutional act. The ordinances should be in accordance with the acts of law, and they cannot contradict the constitution. If the legal claim of the state against a citizen does not comply with this rule, then the citizen is not obliged to obey.[976]

What proved extremely liberal and also very popular during the German Spring of Nations, was the demand of von Mohl that the rule of law should be governed by the broadly understood principle of "freedom of thought" (*Denk-Freiheit, Meinungsfreiheit*), associated with the postulate of the comprehensive, also spiritual, development of the individual.[977] In von Mohl, the right to freedom of thought takes two dimensions. First of all, it is the right of a citizen of the rule of law to scientifically deal with all dimensions of human knowledge, i.e. the freedom of scientific research. This activity may not be prohibited nor

972 Ibid. Idem, Staatsr.Württem.1.1840, p. 392.
973 Idem, Staatsr.Württem.1.1829, p. 286. Similarly: Idem, Staatsr.Württem.1.1840, p. 335.
974 Ibid, p. 335.
975 Ibid, p. 323.
976 Ibid, p. 324.
977 R.-J. Grahe, op. cit., p. 118. R. v. Mohl, *Encyklopädie der Staatswissenschaften*, Erste Auflage..., p. 330.

penalized in any way.[978] Secondly, it is the right to express your thoughts on any subject, to anyone who voluntarily wants to hear it. It should be remembered, however, that in Württemberger this is not an absolute right, because such action of a citizen cannot violate rights of others, i.e. not only the rights of other citizens, but also, very importantly, of other countries, and cannot incite to violate these rights.[979] It is worth noting, therefore, that in von Mohl the right to express one's opinion is limited not only by the rights of other individuals, but also by rights of other states. The right to express opinions is also connected with the postulate of freedom of the press, widely discussed in the German areas in the mid-nineteenth century.[980] Von Mohl was among those who postulated free expression of thought with use of print, images, etc. Freedom should also include book trading. However, it should be remembered that, as in the case of "freedom of thought," freedom of press cannot violate applicable law.[981]

Undoubtedly, the demand for freedom of thought in von Mohl is related to the demand for religious freedom (*freie Religionsuebung*). As was the case with freedom of thought, according to the German liberal the religious liberty should be subjected to clear, yet very similar restrictions. To put it concisely, it can be stated that the beliefs and religious activities of a citizen in a rule of law cannot threaten the rights of other citizens, the general public and the state. An individual following a particular religion also has no right to demand a change in the rules that are prevailing in the state and good for the general public. In other words, community has priority over the individual. According to von Mohl, the only solution in this situation was emigration. He represented a similar view in relation to various religious associations and organizations. An attempt to carry out legal changes was the sole possible way of influencing the broadly understood life of the state. However, if an organization is unable to make these changes, it must comply with applicable laws, even if they would be contrary to its principles. It is worth noting that von Mohl was in favor of separation of church and state institutions.[982]

---

978 R.-J. Grahe, op. cit., p. 119.

979 R. v. Mohl, *Encyklopädie der Staatswissenschaften*, Zweite Auflage…, p. 329. Similarly: Idem, Staatsr.Württem.1.1840, pp. 352–353.

980 R.-J. Grahe, op. cit., pp. 40, 121

981 R. v. Mohl, Staatsr.Württem.1.1840, p. 363.

982 Idem, *Encyklopädie der Staatswissenschaften*, Zweite Auflage…, pp. 329–330. It is worth noting that the only state that, according to von Mohl, successfully introduced the broadly understood separation of church from state (or the religious and state

From the point of view of the subsidiary role of the state in rule of law, the right to associate (*Associations-Recht*) proves very important for von Mohl. As previously indicated, the task of Mohl's rule of law (above all its administration) is to support citizens in achieving their life objectives when their individual strength is not enough to achieve the said goals on their own. However, between the individual level and the state level, the German liberal also distinguished the level of associations. This postulate, undoubtedly connected with the concept of society discussed in the second chapter, states that before an individual is supported by the state, it should seek help in voluntary associations and communities. Therefore, the individuals in the Mohl's *Rechtsstaat* have the right to establish associations in which participation is voluntary. However, the purposes of these associations must be allowed, that is, they cannot oppose both the law and the goals of individuals and the general public. Of course, measures taken by citizens' organizations must comply with the law. In addition, they cannot paralyze the activities of state organs or pose any threat to them (what stems from the above is the belief of von Mohl that state should control and supervise the associations). The state must have legal instruments to maintain its unity and order (including legal order) and use them with all its decisiveness against those citizens and their organizations, that threaten them. It should be remembered, however, that the Württemberger did not rule out the existence of political associations. He did not find it necessary to prohibit the existence of this type of associations.[983] Moreover, according to von Mohl, associations will also play an active role in exercising the political rights of citizens.[984]

Speaking of the right of citizens to associate, it should be noted that many representatives of German doctrine at that time thought that any possibility of association of citizens should be dependent on the consent of the state, and political associations should be banned. Von Mohl, with his views, also voting in the Frankfurt Parliament for citizens' right to freedom of assembly and association, undoubtedly belonged to the liberal wing of the then German doctrine.[985]

---

matters) was the USA.: Ch. A. Lerg, *Amerika als Argument: Die deutsche Amerika-Forschung im Vormärz und ihre politische Deutung in der Revolution von 1848/49*, Bielefeld 2011, p. 322.

983 R. v. Mohl, Staatsr.Württem.1.1840, pp. 378–379.

984 Idem, *Encyklopädie der Staatswissenschaften*, Zweite Auflage. . ., p. 330.

985 J. Hähnle, op. cit., p. 115. More about the right to associate in von Mohl: R. v. Mohl, *System der Präventiv-Justiz oder Rechts-Polizei*, Tübingen 1834, pp. 131–142. On the then understanding of the right to associate also: K. Welcker, *Association*, [in:] *Das Staats-Lexikon, Encyklopädie der sämmtlichen Staatswissenschaften für alle Stände*, K. Welcker (ed.), Dritte Auflage, Erster Band, pp. 758–787.

According to von Mohl, the protection of citizens' rights and strengthening their position in the state to be guaranteed by "the right to lodge a complaint and petition" ("*Recht der Beschwerdeführung und der Petition*"). The existence of this right is based on the belief that the nature of every authority is rooted in the desire to constantly expand its influence and transgress the law.[986] Even the most accurate statutory definition of citizens' rights will not protect against abuse and violations by the authorities. The concept of the rule of law in von Mohl, therefore, includes the right of citizens to lodge a complaint against these actions of the state (e.g. through officials) that in their opinion are unfair (unlawful). He called this right the *Beschwerde* i.e. complaint. Von Mohl also distinguished conditions in a state where applicable law may not be able to keep up with the development of the population, which is why there is a need, for example, to regulate new facts. In view of the above, von Mohl granted the citizens of *Rechtsstaat* the right to petition (*Petition*), by means of which they could demand the improvement of certain institutions, or the removal of their shortcomings. However, this right should not be confused with legislative initiative in today's sense of the word.[987]

It should be noted that von Mohl introduced a strict distinction between the right to complaint (*Beschwerde Recht*) and the right to petition (*Petitions Recht*). Under the term "complaint" he understood a "claim" against the actions of a particular official. The right to complain appears whenever there is a violation of law, and its purpose is to restore compliance. A citizen is therefore not entitled to lodge a complaint against an official's action only because, for example, he or she is dissatisfied with the decision. On the other hand, von Mohl called "petition" or the right to petition the process of directing written applications by one or more people, in which they ask a specific authority for something. Therefore, the right to petition in von Mohl should be combined with the notion of citizens' application to the state (its representatives or officials). It should also be noted that the petition does not generate an obligation for the state to comply with the request. The scope of the petition was outlined broadly by the thinker, stating that it may relate to all matters that fall within the scope of the state's activity and life.[988] What is also very important is that in von Mohl every citizen has the right to petition. So neither age, gender, nor status matter. Everyone capable of this has the right to express their views and needs also by petitioning the authorities. They can also demand actions for third parties, even without their knowledge

---

986 R. v. Mohl, *Encyklopädie der Staatswissenschaften*, Zweite Auflage. . ., p. 640.
987 Ibid, p. 639. Idem, Staatsr.Württem.1.1840, p. 414.
988 Idem, SVuP.1, pp. 224, 229–230.

and will.[989] The state, on the other hand, is required not only to respect the above rights, but also to establish institutions that would properly consider complaints and petitions.[990]

One of the most important civic rights, which similarly to the freedom of thought was widely discussed in the German *Vormärz* period, was the freedom of movement, and freedom of choice of residence, and the right to move and emigrate (*Freizügigkeit, Recht der Ortsveränderung, Auswanderungsfreiheit*). Thus citizens of the rule of law have not only the right to move freely, but also to emigrate. According to von Mohl, in a situation where a citizen of a given country is not able to achieve life goals in it, he or she not only has the right, but even the moral obligation to leave it. It does not matter that the state may suffer a loss due to the said migration. So if a citizen fulfills all legal and factual obligations towards the state, it may be left, as that state is a creation existing for people, and not vice versa.[991] In the above understanding of the right to move and freedom of movement, von Mohl relied on a completely individualistic paradigm. He put the interests of the individual above the interests of the state. Furthermore, he also believed that leaving a state where an individual was unable to secure its development was its moral duty.[992]

In the first edition of the *Encyclopaedia...*, von Mohl included, in the scope of civil rights, the protection of property (*Schutz des Eigenthumes*) against unauthorized state interference. The scholar argued that any concessions from citizens' property in the direction of the state should be determined by law in order to avoid any arbitrariness.[993] We find evidence of changes in his concept in the fact that this right was not included in the second edition of the *Encyclopaedia...*, and the scholar did not explain it in any way. However, one should not think that liberal von Mohl withdrew his demand for property protection. He continued to regard property as the basis for "the life of the state," also stating that the state should support various types of business ventures. A feature of the *Rechtsstaat*

989 Ibid. Other German liberals also spoke about the right to petition (*Petitionsrecht*); for example Johann Christoph von Aretin or Karl Theodor Welcker. More on this topic: J. Ch. v. Aretin, *Staatsrecht der Konstitutionellen Monarchie*, Erster Band, Altenburg 1824, p. 160, K. Welcker, *Petition*, [in:] *Das Staats-Lexikon, Encyklopädie der sämmtlichen Staatswissenschaften für alle Stände*, K. Welcker (ed.), Elfter Band, Leipzig 1864, pp. 459–472.

990 R. v. Mohl, *Encyklopädie der Staatswissenschaften*, Zweite Auflage. . ., pp. 227–228.

991 Ibidem, p. 224. R. Suppé, op. cit., p. 116.

992 R.-J. Grahe, op. cit., p. 144.

993 R. v. Mohl, *Encyklopädie der Staatswissenschaften*, Erste Auflage. . ., p. 228.

that is found in both editions of *the Encyclopaedia...* was also the right of citizens to hold private property and economic freedom.[994]

In addition to the above-mentioned civil rights (which von Mohl called "civil rights in the narrow sense"), individuals in the state also enjoy the so-called "Political rights." One should note the scholar's criticism of the trend that prevailed in science, but also in the legislation, of overlapping of scopes of civil and political rights. Thus, von Mohl clearly separates political rights from civil rights.[995] In contrast to the latter, which in the most brief way can be described as regulations on the extent of state interference in the lives of residents, political rights relate to the participation of citizens in the state governance.

This kind of entitlement comes in second place, because the scholar devoted less attention to its analysis compared to civil rights. The most important thing, however, is to say that political rights, unlike civil rights, are not acquired simply by being a citizen. Von Mohl stated that the right to participate in public affairs is vested equally, but only in those of the citizens, who possess the appropriate characteristics. In other words, for the Württemberger, the condition for eligibility to hold offices, vote, have passive electoral rights, or representation rights, was prior demonstration of having certain attributes. As the scholar stated: "proof of eligibility [to participate in political life – author's note] consists in holding certain personal attributes, or meeting certain legal and general conditions."[996] This approach to political rights signals that it will be impossible to talk about equality of citizens, when it comes to issues of state policy. This inequality will also be seen in the scholar's opposition to universal suffrage.

Given the earlier disagreement of von Mohl with the trend of German doctrine consisting in focusing only on the rights of individuals in the state, perhaps one should also point out an equally important issue, which are the obligations of citizens in the rule of law. The scope of these obligations is determined by the scope of the rights of political sovereignty in the state, i.e. the authority responsible for achieving the objectives of the rule of law. Every right of state authority, which is very important - based on law, results in the citizen's obligation to obey. Furthermore, if a citizen does not comply with a specific prohibition or order, the state authority may use force against such.[997]

---

994 Idem, *Encyklopädie der Staatswissenschaften*, Zweite Auflage. . ., pp. 226, 585.

995 Ibid, p. 233.

996 Ibid, p. 329. A more detailed reference to these "abilities" is found in the section devoted to democracy and electoral rights in von Mohl's thought.

997 Ibid, p. 222. On the rights and obligations of citizens in von Mohl also: H. Schmitz, op. cit., pp. 66–67.

One should point to evolution in the views of the Professor from Tübingen. In the early *Constitutional law of the Kingdom of Württemberg*, the issue of citizens' obligations (as opposed to their rights) is described in a very limited way only. The scholar created a chapter entitled "on the rights of citizens of the state," but it is impossible to find a chapter in this work that would deal with the duties of citizens.[998] Decades later, as part of the *Encyclopaedia of Sciences of State*, duties already play an important role in von Mohl's concept. Also during his work in the Frankfurt Parliament, von Mohl clearly stated that not only rights, but also responsibilities were associated with civil rights (*Staatsbürgerrechte*).[999] It seems legitimate to state that by placing emphasis on the obligations of citizens in the state, and without fundamentally changing his views on their rights, von Mohl adopted a more conservative position in this respect, directed at the objective of the state and its fulfilment.[1000] As noted above, later in his work, von Mohl accused other German liberals (above all, centred around the *Staatslexikon* of von Rotteck and Welcker) of focusing too much on the rights of individuals in the state, and omitting their duties.[1001] In the *Encyclopaedia...* he spoke in a demonstrative way about "Rights and obligations of the subjects" and also about "moral obligations of citizens towards the state."[1002]

Therefore, the general duties of a citizen of the state, which also correspond to the citizen of the *Rechtsstaat*, include in von Mohl, above all, the respect for the state and its law, and if necessary, to support and defend it. What is very important, it is the duty of every citizen to subordinate its life goals to the goals of the general public. In the event of a collision between the achievement of an individual and universal goal, the latter shall prevail.[1003] Due to the fact that the legal order is a prerequisite for the functioning of the rule of law, the duty of a citizen in von Mohl is to comply with all legal obligations and to respect the legal order. Where the state power is entitled to act and order, the citizen must surrender to it. This obedience, however, is limited by law. This means that where a specific order of authority has no legal basis, the citizen is not required to obey. As noted

998 O. Luchterhandt, *Grundpflichten als Verfassungsproblem in Deutschland. Geschichtliche Entwicklung und Grundpflichten unter dem Grundgesetz*, Berlin 1988, pp. 189–190.

999 J. Hähnle, op. cit., p. 112.

1000 O. Luchterhandt, op. cit., p. 193.

1001 According to von Mohl, the proof of this was the lack, in the *Staatslexikon* of an article referring to "*Unterthan*," i.e. a subject (in the meaning of von Mohl, a citizen bearing obligations and burdens towards the state): Ibid, p. 194.

1002 Ibid.

1003 R. v. Mohl, *Encyklopädie der Staatswissenschaften*, Zweite Auflage. . ., pp. 513–514.

earlier, von Mohl only allowed a violation of the legal order if the implementation of a legal norm is sacrificed for a higher good or purpose. However, then the infringer was obliged to bear all the consequences of its act, i.e. legal and factual ailments.[1004]

Referring to the "burdens" that citizens should bear as duties to the state, the scholar advocated for full equality in so-called "personal burdens," that is, relating to all kinds of intangible benefits of a citizen to the state (e.g. the same obligation for everyone to comply with the law). On the other hand, relative equality appears in the case of "material burdens," i.e. those relating to property and material relations. Here, the burden should be distributed in a proportionate manner in relation to the size of the property of a particular citizen (much like today's tax progression).[1005]

In von Mohl the susbtantiation of citizen obligations in the state occurs as part of their analysis in terms of morality (ethics). Speaking of the moral obligations of citizens towards the state, the scholar distinguished three factual conditions.[1006] The first, in which the state, its institutions and activities correspond to the degree of development of the nation and its life goals. In this case, it is the citizens' responsibility to "fuse with the state." A citizen should not only respect and defend it, but also voluntarily provide services not required by law, and demonstrate opposition to activities that violate it. A citizen should fulfill every obligation imposed, even when the authorities are unable to enforce this obligation. It is also the duty of the citizen to provide authorities with all and true explanations whenever they have reasonable grounds to requests such.[1007]

The second factual condition distinguished by von Mohl is the situation in which there are no significant discrepancies between the species of the state and the level of development of the nation, but there are already noticeable differences and the resulting need for organizational changes. In such a situation, every citizen has moral obligation to demand changes in the state. However, this can only be done in accordance with the legal order and proportionality principles, so that the request for change does not result in greater damage than the expected profits.[1008]

1004 Ibid, p. 514. B. Stöcker, op. cit., p. 41.
1005 Idem, Staatsr.Württem.1.1829, p. 287. O. Luchterhandt, op. cit., p. 192.
1006 O. Luchterhandt, op. cit., p. 194.
1007 R. v. Mohl, *Encyklopädie der Staatswissenschaften. . .*, pp. 528–529.
1008 Ibid, pp. 529–530.

The third and most drastic situation occurs when the idea and goals of the state are in conflict with the life goals of the nation inhabiting it. This state of affairs makes a citizen, according to von Mohl, not only entitled, but also obliged to demand changes in the state. If the state seeks to cause harm to a citizen, it is his or her duty to apply all legal means to prevent it. If these measures are ineffective, the citizen has the right to refuse to obey and to passively resist.[1009]

"Strengthening and extending the freedom of the nation" (*Befestigung und Erweiterung der Volksfreiheit*) was both the main scientific and political postulate of von Mohl, which was manifested not only in his works, but also in his public activities.[1010] And indeed, it cannot be denied that the Württemberger, in many of his views, presented a liberal attitude, which was further confirmed by his votes in the Frankfurt Parliament. The catalog of civil liberties, understood as the highest political principles attributable to every citizen, is extensive. It includes the right to unhindered development of personality of an individual and its social relations, personal and economic freedom (freedom of property) as well as freedom of religion, opinion and association. It is also worth pointing out the right to complain as an important element of the Mohl's *Rechtsstaat*. As already noted, the *Rechtsstaat* was a state based on principles of reason. The fundamental rights functioning in this species of state appear as a logical necessity resulting from the rationality, on which this species is based.[1011] Thus, von Mohl clearly links rights and fundamental freedoms with the purpose of the state (rule of law). The classic liberal triad postulating freedom, equality and ownership undergoes a modification here. There are more requirements for state as well as requirements of the state. In addition, the exercise of fundamental rights may be limited by the purpose of the state (the general good has priority over the good of the individual). Freedoms will also be limited when it comes to the idea of separation of powers, which will be discussed in the next chapter.[1012] One can agree with the view that von Mohl, in his unique way, took over the concept of freedom derived from natural law, in which (of course after taking into account the goals of the state and other individuals) a space of individual freedom distant from the community organism emerges. Therefore, despite the fact that the rule of law state in von Mohl often intervenes in the lives of its citizens, they

1009 Ibid, p. 529.

1010 Idem, *Lebenserinnerungen von Robert von Mohl 1799–1875*, Bd. 1. . ., p. 139. R.-J. Grahe, op. cit., p. 86.

1011 R.-J. Grahe, op. cit., pp. 90–93. R. Suppé, op. cit., p. 119.

1012 B. Stöcker, op. cit., p. 42.

are allowed to perform any activities that are not incompatible with the rights of third parties, or do not hinder or prevent the state from fulfilling its general objectives.[1013]

However, civil rights are only one element of fundamental rights in the Mohl's concept of *Rechtsstaat*. As the scholar drew a dividing line of political rights, he should be considered a supporter of the concept of the so-called "apolitical freedoms," not associated with the concept of political rights and their exercise in the state.[1014] The scholar's understanding of political rights, emphasizing their selectivity, the need for the citizen to prove the "eligibility" to participate in governance, exposes the scientist's inconsistency. On the one hand, he postulated equality before the law, but on the other he excluded all political activity from this sphere.[1015] He also rejects the idea of equal and universal suffrage, which is decisive from the viewpoint of political participation of citizens.[1016] On the other hand, in the matter of obligations, unlike many other liberals of the mid-nineteenth century Germany, von Mohl adopted the concept of citizens' obligations as "obvious mutual benefits," which they must provide to the state in order for it to perform its tasks. The rights and obligations of individuals therefore correspond to the rights and obligations of the authorities in the state.[1017]

In the science concerning the duties of citizens towards the state, von Mohl preferred such a situation, in which citizens could, in the most uninterrupted manner possible, without state paternalism, take care of their own interests. In essence, therefore, the state should not impede this process through forced obligations, but rather remove obstacles in a subsidiary manner. Such a relationship between the state and its citizens required cooperation between them so that the state does not disintegrate. As stated by von Mohl, this required a "covenant" of the monarch and the inhabitants, a combination of "monarchical and parliamentary principles," so that citizens would fulfil their moral obligations to the state with "joy," supporting it whenever necessary. However, Otto Luchterhandt is right in stating that von Mohl, in some way idealizing the actual conditions, overestimated both the rationality and the ability of citizens to moral behaviour towards the state organization.[1018]

1013 R. Suppé, op. cit., pp. 120–121.
1014 Ibid, p. 121.
1015 B. Stöcker, op. cit., p. 40.
1016 R. Suppé, op. cit., pp. 120–121.
1017 B. Stöcker, op. cit., p. 41.
1018 O. Luchterhandt, op. cit., pp. 196–197.

4.3. Sources of law

A rule of law cannot function without legal norms. As already mentioned, "the sanctity of all laws" is the supreme principle of the rule of law state in Robert von Mohl, and maintaining legal order covers at least half the scope of its activity. This subsection will attempt to answer the question of what this order should look like, and on what principles it should be based on.[1019]

As we will demonstrate the main source of law for von Mohl is the written (positive) law. In addition to this type, according to the scholar, the source of law will also include customary law and court activities. There is no doubt, however, that in "representative forms of the rule of law" the main role will be played by legal norms arranged in three large groups.[1020] Throughout the entire period of his scientific activity, the German liberal was attached to his three-level classification of normative acts in the state. This classification was based on the division into laws that can be called state or constitutional (*Verfassungsgesetze*), "ordinary acts (laws, statutes)" (*einfache Gesetze*), which are issued by the political authority in the state (primarily a monarch in von Mohl) in consultation with a representative body, and ordinances (*Verordnungen*), issued by the authorities unilaterally and autonomously.[1021] In this subsection we will demonstrate that the aforesaid division is based on the prominence that each type of source of law has in the state. In von Mohl the highest-level statutes, all kinds of constitutional acts, will contain the basis for all further legal institutions. "Ordinary" acts will regulate individual legal issues in a manner consistent with higher-order norms. Ordinances, which are the third type of legal act, will not contain new laws, but only provisions leading to the enforcement of norms contained in higher-order acts.[1022]

1019 see also the article, P. Lesiński, *«Rechtsstaat» and it's legal order according to Robert von Mohl*, "Zeszyty Naukowe Uniwersytetu Rzeszowskiego. Seria Prawnicza. Prawo." 31/2020.

1020 Despite the fact that the aforementioned nomenclature (constitutional act, act, ordinance) is appropriate for the species of the state of law in von Mohl, he still believes that the distinguished types of laws or rights in the state may also appear in other species. Therefore, regulations corresponding to constitutional and ordinary statutes or ordinances will be found not only in the rule of law. For example a holy scripture may play the role of constitutional act in theocracy. So von Mohl was writing about naming, and the nature of the pertinent norms remains the same. R. v. Mohl, *Encyklopädie der Staatswissenschaften*, Zweite Auflage..., p. 155. Ch. H. Schmidt, *Vorrang der Verfassung und konstituionelle Monarchie: eine dogmengeschichtliche Untersuchung zum Problem der Normenhierarchie in den deutschen Staatsordnungen im frühen und mittleren 19. Jahrhundert (1818–1866)*, Berlin 2000, p. 160.

1021 R. v. Mohl, *Encyklopädie der Staatswissenschaften*, Zweite Auflage..., pp. 145–146.

1022 Idem, SVuP.2.1, pp. 404, 405, 417.

As already indicated at the beginning of this section, according to von Mohl there may be also other sources of legal norm, extending the sources of law based on the above-mentioned triad. Therefore, before analyzing the above-mentioned triad, which is undoubtedly of paramount importance, it is worth devoting a moment to Mohl's perception of the role of customary law. This is important because it will prove that the Württemberger was not an implacable supporter of exclusively written law. As an empiricist above all, he recognized customary law and, moreover, he also accepted its existence.

For von Mohl, there was no doubt that written law is not the sole source of law in the state. There was also the customary, "people's" law (*Volksrecht*).[1023] For the German liberal, customary law manifested itself as a system that grew out of all sorts of historical, political, but also religious experience, of a given community, and what was of utmost importance, it also related to the most common problems of everyday life. The impulse for the creation of a norm of customary law is the need to regulate a given state or actual relationship in a given community. On the other hand, its validity is sanctioned by "community of beliefs" (*Vereinigung der Ueberzeugungen*) concerning the validity of the norm of customary law thus created. Von Mohl does not appear to be an opponent of such norms. Moreover, in his teaching we find a statement about a kind of "eternity" of customary law. He is characterized by the belief that as long as there are specific communities of people (including nations), they will produce custom-based norms (despite the fact that as written law develops, customary law will lose its significance).[1024]

Speaking of customary law as a source of rights and obligations in a state, one cannot fail to address the issue of the relationship between this source of law and written law. Von Mohl described this relationship in an unclear manner. As a supporter and promoter of the idea of *Rechtsstaat* he, at the same time, also stated: "There is no relationship that would not be able to obtain its right both by statute and by the consciousness of the nation."[1025] Therefore, it should be stated that he holds written law and customary law as two equivalent and, what is more, also legal orders in the state. One cannot resist the impression that von Mohl, based on empirical analysis of reality (in which customary law functioned), was not able to ignore customary norms as a source of law, but on the other hand was well aware of the enormity of problems that the existence of the two, parallel

1023 Idem, *Encyklopädie der Staatswissenschaften*, Zweite Auflage…, p. 144.
1024 Idem, SVuP.2.1, p. 385.
1025 Ibid, p. 394.

legal orders can introduce in the functioning of the state. Seeking a way out of a possible collision of customary and written norms, von Mohl did not seem to give priority to the latter. He stated that in the event that in the interpretation process it is not possible to resolve the collision between these two types of laws, it is the time of their creation that should decide, with priority given to this norm that appeared later.[1026] Unfortunately, von Mohl did not exhaustively develop his ideas regarding the relationship between customary law and statutory law. It can be assumed, however, that the concept presented above resulted from the scholar's overarching belief that the state and all its institutions should correspond to the level of civilization (*Gesittigung*) of the nation. The scientist was convinced that the law, and especially the constitution of a state, should always reflect the level of development of the nation, as well as its customs.

The aforedescribed approach of von Mohl to customary law gains a kind of explanation, when we analyze the scholar's views on the concepts of the so-called German Historical School.[1027] It should be noted that von Mohl's views coincide with those of the historical school, saying that customary laws, the ways of life of individual nations, their characteristics and legal awareness should be taken into account in the creation of law. The content of law cannot depend solely on the preferences and approval of the legislative authority.[1028] It cannot be said, however, that von Mohl made a full reception of historical school's views on law. First of all, one should note his opposition to the view of comprehending the law as a phenomenon arising spontaneously in a given nation (similarly as e.g. language). Von Mohl regarded this understanding of law as superfluous "mysticism."[1029]

Therefore, also the historical school's understanding of the legislative activity of the state, understood as describing and conferring the statutory form to standards independently created in the nation, did not find support of the Württemberger.[1030] One may conclude that he considered this understanding of

1026 Ibid, pp. 395–397.

1027 The creator of this trend was Friedrich Carl von Savigny. The main assumptions of this thought was treating the law as a historical phenomenon, reflecting the history and spirit of a particular nation. The historical school opposed codification and the concepts of the law of nature. More about the views of the German historical school: R. Gmür, *Savigny und die Entwicklung der Rechtswissenschaft*, Münster 1962, K. Opałek, J. Wróblewski, *Niemiecka szkoła historyczna w teorii prawa*, "Przegląd Nauk Historycznych i Społecznych," t. 5 1954, pp.237–317.

1028 R. v. Mohl, SVuP.2.1, p. 381.

1029 Ibid.

1030 Ibid, p. 382.

the legislative activity of the state incomplete, and at least partly disagreed with such view.[1031] On the one hand, because von Mohl did not completely dissociate himself from the so-called "spiritual factor" in relation to legislation, he argued that its task is to observe and give legal (statutory) dimension and the possibility of execution of customary laws functioning in a given nation (this may also indicate a desire to avoid collision between customary and written law). On the other hand, however, he was strongly convinced that the state cannot limit itself to merely reading legal norms encoded in the consciousness of the nation. Therefore, the state must also make laws independently, autonomously.[1032] This approach is due to the belief that the faster and stronger development of states and societies (it is worth remembering that von Mohl wrote during the industrial revolution in Germany at that time) causes that the legal awareness and customary norms functioning in them are no longer sufficient to regulate their relations in comprehensive way. This situation means that the state must create and introduce certain laws independently. Observing the trends prevailing in society and nation, and anticipating their development, the state through the law has the task of influencing the life of the community, so as to at least support its development or resolve conflicts. Von Mohl even granted the state the right to act against established beliefs in the nation, if a more important interest of the community would speak for that.[1033]

To sum up the above remarks, it should be stated that von Mohl (as in many cases, in fact) opted for the golden middle way. He not only allowed the existence of customary law in the state, but also was of the opinion that it should be taken into account in the legislative process, and that to the largest possible extent. Nevertheless it should not form the basic reference point. On the other hand, such a reference point should be the maintenance of "unity and organic order" ("*Einheit und organischen Ordnung*"). In addition, according to von Mohl, the task of the state was to organize and change the unjust and improper customary laws functioning in the nation.[1034]

The less important sources of law, yet marked in the Mohl's legal state, include the court activities. It should be noted that the German liberal presented the so-called continental approach to law and he is convinced that the courts are

1031 On discrepancies between a conservative and a liberal approach to law: H, Uhlenbrock, *Der Staat als juristische Person: Dogmengeschichtliche Untersuchung zu einem Grundbegriff der deutschen Staatsrechtslehre*, Berlin 2000, p. 60.

1032 R. v. Mohl, SVuP.2.1, p. 382.

1033 Ibid, pp. 382–384.

1034 Ibid, p. 383.

appointed primarily to apply the law to specific conditions, and not to settle disputes according to their own views. However, just like in many other areas of Mohl's understanding of the state, there are specific exceptions to the rule. The most important, rational situation, where the court is able to create a legal norm that should be mentioned here, is a gap in applicable law. Von Mohl was convinced that every court is obliged to issue a judgment in the case submitted and it cannot justify its inactivity, e.g. by the lack of provisions relating to a specific case. Thus, the scholar came to the conclusion that, in a situation of a gap in law, the courts not only can, but are actually obliged to issue a ruling based on the legal norm they have created. What's more, von Mohl formulated something similar to a precedent, stating that a judgment issued in this way under the so-called "court habit" (*Gerichtsgebrauch*) becomes the norm for other courts of relevant jurisdiction.[1035]

There is no doubt that the main axis of the analysis of sources of law in von Mohl's science will be the constitution-act-ordinance triad. Issues of applicability of customary law or lawmaking, although noteworthy, are side problems. Whereas the aforementioned triad appears in most of works by von Mohl, and what is also important - throughout the entire period of his work.

Before we discuss von Mohl's perception of the constitution or, more specifically, the "basic law," we should look briefly at the history of the meaning of the concept of *Verfassung* in German legal science. While today the term *Verfassung* means the constitution of the state in the strict sense, it was not always the case. Explanation of the history of this concept will thus allow us to avoid terminological ambiguities and will modernize the von Mohl concept.[1036]

Initially, the concept of *Verfassung* in the German lands was broadly understood as a specific shape or condition of the state, which was composed of and influenced by various factors of historical development, as well as natural,

---

1035 Ibid, pp. 387–388. Also Leon Petrażycki distinguished the so called "Law of court practice." More: L. Petrażycki, *Teoria prawa i państwa w związku z teorią moralności*, T. II, Warszawa 1960, pp. 387–398. S. Tkacz, *O "Pozytywności" i "Oficjalności" Prawa w Teorii Leona Petrażyckiego*, "Ruch Prawniczy, Ekonomiczny i Socjologiczny," ROK LXVII - zeszyt 1 - 2005, p. 83.

1036 Translator of the Polish edition of the *Encyclopaedia...* translated the Mohl's *Verfassung* as "organization." Aware of the ambiguity of this term (also meaning the then written constitutional act), Białecki decided to use the word "constitution" only when von Mohl spoke about the written act or group of constitutional acts. This view should be considered right and should be adopted: R. v. Mohl, *Encyclopaedia umiejętności politycznych...*, p. 120.

nation-specific circumstances and laws. In this sense, therefore, the concept of *Verfassung* did not describe a specific, superior legal act of the state, but rather the overall system and conditions in which it operates. This understanding of the concept of *Verfassung* was in line with the old so-called "pre-constitutional" German science, for which it was not a normative term, but rather empirical, denoting a specific factual condition of a given state.[1037] The term "constitution," in the end of the 17th century, was understood as an act issued by the emperor, regardless of its meaning and content. This historical understanding of the word constitution as the superior law was supplanted in the German area in the process of reception of modern constitutional concepts. At the turn of the seventeenth and eighteenth centuries, the word constitution began to approach its present understanding of the word *Verfassung*, meaning primarily a constitutional act, but also the form of the government of a given state. In this sense, therefore, each state had its own *Verfassung*, also understood as the state system, form or organization.[1038] With the development and spread of postulates of the democratic Enlightenment movements, the notion of *Verfassung* - a constitution as a legal act has been consolidated. This legal act will make the power in the state no longer be based on largely unclear laws of nature or divine order, but instead will be limited on the basis of set and clear constitutional norms. As mentioned earlier, the so-called the constitutionalization of the rules of functioning of the states of the German area falls in the 19th century. It was particularly in the first half of that century, when establishment of state constitutions (especially in the south of Germany) was perceived as a bourgeoisie's way to introduce rules that would limit the absolute power of kings and princes.[1039]

It is not surprising, therefore, that the concept of *Verfassung* is often present in the doctrine of von Mohl and it is given significant importance. It should be noted that the Württemberger belongs to these of the German authors, who (by looking at American and Western European models) not only postulated the hierarchical order of sources of law, but also were the precursors of understanding the term *Verfassung* (the constitution) as a source of law standing above others.[1040] The concept of *Verfassung* that Antoni Białecki translated using the word "organization," appears in von Mohl already in the early *Constitutional Law*

1037 Ch. H. Schmidt, op. cit., p. 94.
1038 Ibid, pp. 94, 95.
1039 A. Benz, op. cit., pp. 135–136.
1040 Ch. H. Schmidt, op. cit., p. 122.

of the Kingdom of Württemberg of 1829 and 1831.[1041] However, we find its most elaborate definition on the pages of the *Encyclopaedia...*:

> "The organization is the sum of institutions and provisions defining a certain specific objective of the state, organizing and maintaining the main body intended for this purpose, describing in terms of form, boundaries and holders the state authority required for it, and finally regulating, in a fundamental way, the relations between participants of the state (both individuals and social circles) and the public."[1042]

The analysis of the above definition allows us to conclude, that von Mohl perfectly fits the German trend of understanding the concept of *Verfassung* described above. *Verfassung* is not the today's written constitution, but a much broader concept, concisely speaking, meaning the fundamental nature of a given state. Under this concept, the scholar will understand the species and form to which the states will belong, and what their purpose will be.[1043] Organization by von Mohl was in principle something general as well as permanent, defining the directions, which the state should follow.[1044] Importantly, the above understanding of the concept of the Organization will not change throughout the entire period of Württemberger's work.[1045] May it be in the *Constitutional Law, International law, and Politics* or the last edition of the *Encyclopaedia...*, the Organization was always understood by von Mohl as the general principles and "content" of the state, determining its purpose, power relations and the position of citizens.[1046] It is also worth noting that the Organization as a concept defining the essence and general principles of the system of a given state was, according

---

1041 As Georg Jellinek later states, the *Constitutional law of the Kingdom of Württemberg* was a groundbreaking work, with extreme importance for the progress of the study of constitutional law in Germany: G. Jellinek, *Gesetz und Verordnung, Staatsrechtliche Untersuchungen auf Rechtsgeschichtlicher und Rechtsvergleichender Grundlage*, Freiburg I. B. 1887, p. 115. In this work, Erich Angermann noticed a turn to positive law in von Mohl: E. Angermann, op. cit., p. 35.

1042 R. v. Mohl, *Encyklopädie der Staatswissenschaften*, Zweite Auflage. . ., p. 136. B. Granzow, *Robert von Mohls Gedanken zu einem parlamentarischen Regime auf berufsständischer Grundlage*, Heidelberg 1959, p. 88.

1043 Idem, Staatsr.Württem.2.1846, p. 3. The concept of "Organization" was used in the work to distinguish between its meaning and what von Mohl understood as a written constitution of the state.

1044 Idem, *Encyklopädie der Staatswissenschaften*, Zweite Auflage. . ., p. 137.

1045 For the purposes of this work, the concept of "Organization" highlighted by von Mohl will always be capitalized to distinguish the usual understanding of the word.

1046 Idem, SVuP.2.1, p. 408.

to von Mohl, not reserved exclusively for the legal state species of state. In fact, according to von Mohl, each state has an Organization, although it is expressed in various forms. According to the scholar, it was not necessary for the constitutional provisions to be included in one document (constitution) or even to be written down at all. Therefore, political principles can be found in various, larger numbers of legal acts or even in customary law.[1047]

When studying works of von Mohl we should be careful not to identify the above concept of the Organization, which is nonetheless considered to be something immaterial, one can say transcendent and more difficult to grasp, with a written constitutional act having a legal dimension. It is worth noting that differences also occur in terminology. Von Mohl never used the word Organization (*Verfassung*) to denote a constitutional act, always using the terms "constitutional act" ("*Verfassungs-Urkunde*") or "written basic law" ("*geschriebene Grundgesetz*") instead. Moreover, not all norms contained in the written constitutional act must belong to the Organization of the state and vice versa: "Not everything that is contained in a specific constitutional law belongs to the organization of the state, just as not the whole organization of the state is reflected in the constitutional act."[1048]

The above view is reflected in von Mohl's belief that it is not a *sine qua non* condition for the written constitution to be contained in only one legal act. It can be said that the scholar presented a peculiar, approach, close to the Anglo-Saxon one, stating that there could be many constitutional acts "scattered throughout the entire legal order."[1049] Von Mohl concludes that the essence of rule of law includes the statement, that its institutions may only be established by common agreement. Von Mohl was in favour of establishing a constitution on the basis of a contract between the ruler and the people, but he also allowed a situation in which the constitution would be put in force (promulgated) without participation of representation. In both cases, however, it must define and protect the rights and obligations of both parties.[1050]

According to von Mohl, the objective of constitutional provisions contained in one or many acts of law was to resolve the most important political issues, i.e. a specific concretization of the ideas contained in the Organization of the state (and in no case may they contain legal norms reserved for its administration).[1051]

1047 Idem, *Encyklopädie der Staatswissenschaften*, Zweite Auflage. . ., p. 137.
1048 Idem, Staatsr.Württem.2.1831, pp. 6, 9.
1049 Idem, *Encyklopädie der Staatswissenschaften*, Zweite Auflage. . ., p. 145.
1050 Idem, Staatsr.Württem.1.1829, s. 86, J. Hähnle, op. cit., pp. 23–24.
1051 R. v. Mohl, Staatsr.Württem.2.1831, pp. 6–7.

The provisions of constitutional acts refer, in von Mohl, to the objectives of the state, the form of its rule, the general obligations and rights of state power, as well as the civil and political rights of the state's residents, and their protection.[1052] It may happen, however, that due to their great importance for the state, particular norms are introduced into such acts (e.g. relating to more specific issues, such as the judiciary).[1053] The most important assertion concerning the constitutional norms is that, in von Mohl, they gain the supreme position and the priority over all the remaining norms. The provisions of governmental (constitutional) acts are thus, in works of the Württemberger, characterized in that they include "higher order norms."[1054] The "constitutional act" is therefore the "first act of the state" ("*das erste Gesetz des Staates*") and no "ordinary" act can contradict it.[1055]

It should not come as a surprise that von Mohl, as a representative of the liberal-constitutional wing of German science of the state, saw many advantages in adopting constitutional acts in states. First of all, it was about establishing higher, somewhat inviolable norms to protect citizens against the omnipotence of authorities. It is symptomatic, therefore, that it is the concept of constitution that connects, in von Mohl, as well as in all German liberalism, with the issues of fundamental and civil rights.[1056] The adoption of a constitution in a state has many advantages, above all relating to the legal and political awareness of its citizens. Simple and general norms are easier to comprehend and assimilate than complicated and casuistic regulations (the postulate of generality and "simplicity" of law will be manifested in von Mohl with all power, when discussing the so-called "ordinary laws"). Nevertheless it should not be forgotten, that the Württemberger, rational as always, also noticed the disadvantages and dangers potentially linked with the functioning of constitutional acts in a rule of law. This is, first and foremost, the abuse of general principles of systemic rank. Von Mohl was afraid that, by their nature the capacious and general constitutional norms could be abused and misinterpreted in accordance with a particular immediate interest (e.g. political). The conviction that the Organization of the state must correspond to the degree of development of the nation resulted in von Mohl's view that constitutional norms must also do so. According to von Mohl, imposing a constitution on certain nations that would not stand in the

1052 Idem, SVuP.2.1, p. 410.

1053 Idem, *Encyklopädie der Staatswissenschaften*, Zweite Auflage..., p. 142.

1054 Ch. H. Schmidt, op. cit., pp. 158–161.

1055 R. v. Mohl, Staatsr.Württem.1.1829, p. 81.

1056 Idem, *Encyklopädie der Staatswissenschaften*, Zweite Auflage..., p. 142.

relationship or not even result from their internal aspirations and conditions, would be unacceptable and would lead to detrimental results.[1057]

In view of the above, von Mohl's view is that the constitutional provisions must be altered in a situation, where they no longer meet the objectives of the state. The scholar is characterized by the belief that what seems intentional at a given moment may not always be appropriate after a given time interval and under different conditions. So he reserved the right to amend the basic norms, although of course he was not in favour of frequent and rapid changes, which would prevent citizens from establishing strong ties with constitutional norms.[1058] It is also worth mentioning that von Mohl foresaw the existence of a "constitutional court" (*Staatsgerichtshof*) in the state. Due to the fact that it is not possible to avoid constitutional disputes, collisions between the government and the representative body, there must be an institution in the state that will resolve these disputes.[1059] Von Mohl saw the existence of such an institution as a "triumph of political education" and a harmonious embodiment of the idea of *Rechtsstaat*.[1060] On the other hand the Württemberger believed that the best guarantee of observing and maintaining the constitutional order seemed to rest in the appropriately high character and level of political development of the nation, which should identify with its supreme constitutional act.[1061]

Ordinary acts of law (*einfache Gesetze, Gesetze*) are the second most important source of law in the country. When analyzing the issue of the role of an act of law in a legal state, one should first refer to determining the difference between the act and constitutional norms in von Mohl's thought. As already stated, the goal of organizational norms is to lay "general foundations," rules for the legal order. As part of these principles, the goals and limits of the state's operation are defined. The act, on the other hand, has the objective of developing and "filling in legal content" in those areas defined by the constitution. In addition, if something does not find a place in it, then the act may regulate it, but even then it must comply with the "spirit" of higher-order norms.[1062] From the above, the von Mohl's postulate appears, stating that the laws must correspond to the "spirit and positive content of constitutional and fundamental laws," and their amendment

1057 Ibid, pp. 142–143.

1058 Idem, Staatsr.Württem.1.1829, p. 87. J. Hähnle, op. cit., p. 25.

1059 R. v. Mohl, Staatsr.Württem.2.1840, pp. 761–764.

1060 Idem, *Die Verantwortlichkeit der Minister in Einherrschaften mit Volksvertretung*, Tübingen 1837, p. 25. J. Hähnle, op. cit., p. 26.

1061 Ibid.

1062 R. v. Mohl, SVuP.2.1, p. 413.

may only take place in accordance with higher-order norms.[1063] Thus, the first requirement regarding the act appears, i.e. its compliance with higher-order norms (systemic, constitutional). Therefore, in order to be legally binding act must comply with them, if it is not so, it is not binding.[1064]

Referring to the very definition of the term "Act" (*Gesetz*), it should be stated that despite the fact that it appears in many of von Mohl's works, its material dimension is always essentially similar. The act was understood by him first as a permanent, "imperative norm" (*eine befehlende Norm*), referring to specific issues of the life of the state and its citizens, issued by the relevant authority, and being its formally expressed will.[1065] By means of acts, the rule of law state regulates those relations between residents that either do not create specific rights or obligations between them (for example, of a civil law nature) or when certain relations or factual conditions require legal clarification. In addition, the state uses acts to introduce and safeguard its own interests and aspirations.[1066] Nevertheless the act in von Mohl does not assume solely a formal nature, i.e. it is not merely a "formally expressed will of state authority."[1067] The scholar stated that the most important subject of the regulations of state legislation are all the orders and prohibitions of power, which refer to the rights of citizens, either by extending, or by limiting them. For this reason, he also demands that the act should be adopted in consultation with the representation of the nation (which, as will be demonstrated later, will distinguish an act from a regulation).[1068]

Turning to the discussion of the features that should characterize an act in the Mohl's rule of law, we should remind the reader about the rational view of the scholar, referring to the very reason why the new act can be issued. The sole reason for that is the so called "real necessity."[1069] According to von Mohl, there is no place for any whims, anxiety or conceit in the legislation, also of those in power. Any law introduced without real necessity will not only be superfluous, but also harmful to the state.[1070] Therefore, the law cannot be an abstract

---

1063 Ibid, pp. 145–146. Ch. H. Schmidt, op. cit., p. 161. On the issues of legislation in von Mohl: L. Łustacz, *Ustawa i rozporządzenie w klasycznej doktrynie francuskiej i niemieckiej*, Warszawa 1968, pp. 171–173.

1064 R. v. Mohl, SVuP.2.1, p. 386. Ch. H. Schmidt, op. cit., p. 123..

1065 R. v. Mohl, *Encyklopädie der Staatswissenschaften*, Zweite Auflage. . ., p. 144.

1066 Ibid, pp. 144–145.

1067 I. Maus, op. cit., p. 21.

1068 R. v. Mohl, Staatsr.Württem.2.1840, pp. 67–68.

1069 Idem, SVuP.2.1, pp. 419–420.

1070 Ibid.

phenomenon created to satisfy unjustified aspirations, or to regulate factual conditions that do not require it. Von Mohl is characterized by a logical and liberal view that if the state is to support the life goals of a particular nation, then its law (as an instrument for this) is to serve it. Therefore, certain rights must result from the main task of the state, which is to support the life goals of a particular nation.[1071] Therefore, it should be stated that since for von Mohl the state is not a creation for itself, its law does not exist for itself either.

It is worth noting that in terms of determining the rules for introducing new laws, von Mohl did not stop at the inexplicable statement about the need for the so-called "real necessity." On the contrary, he made a fairly detailed analysis of when it appears in the state. The obvious postulate is that the new law should be introduced when applicable regulations are not sufficient, contain gaps, or other formal and material errors. It seems that much more important, also from the point of view of the already analyzed goals of the rule of law, is von Mohl's conviction that the generally understood development of society (or the economy, etc.) requires the introduction of a new law. Once again, one can see the scholar's conviction about the servant role of the state, which should follow the development of the nation, also by adopting appropriate regulations.[1072]

Referring to the features which, according to von Mohl, should characterize "good laws" we should note that it seems that the most important one (also from the point of view of historical context) is the feature of generality. According to him, the act must be a general rule. Both the subjective and the objective scope of the act should include as many as possible specific relations regulated by its respective provisions.[1073] The conviction about the generality of the act is also revealed in the postulate that its content should be limited to "basic principles" (*Grundsätze*) while avoiding unnecessary casuistry. In other words, legislation should be as abstract as possible.[1074] Thus von Mohl should be considered an opponent of all casuistic approaches to law. He is characterized, above all, by the belief that it is not possible to regulate all possible factual conditions with law. In addition, he also states that the need for the most general provisions is also an improvement in the process of applying the law (especially on the side

1071 R. v. Mohl, *Encyklopädie der Staatswissenschaften*, Zweite Auflage..., p. 151.

1072 Idem, SVuP.2.1, p. 421.

1073 Ibid, p. 428.

1074 Idem, *Encyklopädie der Staatswissenschaften*, Zweite Auflage..., p. 153. Similarly: Idem, SVuP.2.1, p. 429.

of the judge).[1075] It is the general nature that will distinguish von Mohl's act from decisions made in individual cases, be it by courts or by administrative bodies.[1076]

Further features of "good acts" distinguished by von Mohl include the postulate of appropriate time during which the new law will be introduced.[1077] The postulate that the law should not contain orders or bans that the addressee of the norm will find impossible to meet (*Ad impossibilia non datur obligatio*) also appears in many passages of his works.[1078] Importantly, these provisions cannot oblige to impossible things in a legal sense (incompatibility with higher-order norms), but also in factual one (according to von Mohl this constitutes the incompatibility of the provision with human nature).[1079] Therefore, an act may also contain only such norms that are enforceable (also by coercion).[1080] In addition, it is very important for the legislator to take into account customary law and customs, as well as the level of civilization of a given nation, in the lawmaking process.[1081]

The demand for equality of all residents of the state before the law, which has been highlighted earlier, is connected with the demand that the act should be equally binding for all residents of the state. It should be remembered that equality before the law forms one of the basic features of "modern rule of law" in von Mohl.[1082] However, what is very important for the scholar, i.e. the postulate of equality before the law does not mean that one cannot create (when the need arises) particular provisions, referring, for example, to specific branches of the state economy. The principle of equality says that all who are under the rule of a given law are to be treated equally.[1083]

Extremely important, this time from the point of view of the state, is von Mohl's belief that all legislation should be consistent, and comply with the

1075 Ibid, p. 430.
1076 Idem, *Encyklopädie der Staatswissenschaften*, Zweite Auflage. . ., p. 146.
1077 Idem, SVuP.2.1, p. 425. On the desirable characteristics of acts in von Mohl: Z. A. Maciąg, op. cit., pp. 95–97.
1078 R. v. Mohl, *Encyklopädie der Staatswissenschaften*, Zweite Auflage. . ., pp.155, 148. Similarly: Idem, SVuP.2.1, p. 431.
1079 Ibid, p. 433.
1080 Idem, *Encyklopädie der Staatswissenschaften*, Zweite Auflage. . ., p. 145.
1081 Idem, SVuP.2.1, p. 386. Idem, *Encyklopädie der Staatswissenschaften*, Zweite Auflage. . ., p. 153.
1082 Idem, SVuP.2.1, p. 434.
1083 Ibid, p. 435. Karl Salomo Zachariae believed similarly. More: K. S. Zachariae, *Vierzig Bücher vom Staate*, Bd. IV, Heidelberg 1840, pp. 23–25.

principles arising from the general idea on which it is based. Therefore, acts must "go in the same direction," that is, not only they must not introduce contradictory regulations, but they are also to reflect the most important goals and the idea of a given state.[1084] The scholar believed that when individual parts of the legislation in the state "move in other directions" (they are not consistent), it will result in disputes regarding its role and responsibilities.[1085] Therefore, the above also implies the postulate that all laws should be in line with the spirit of the system, which will also ensure the homogeneity of all state activities.[1086]

The law should be stable and function as long as possible. This does not mean, however, that von Mohl was an opponent of introducing changes in legislation. He accepted them, but argued for the widest possible impediment to their introduction, which would protect the state against recklessness, "ad hoc" and carelessness in the introduction of a new law.[1087] Von Mohl's objection to the simple process of reception of foreign law should also be raised here (even if certain regulations proved successful in another state). The law must comply with the factual conditions in the state, where it is to operate. Due to the fact that it rarely happens that identical factual conditions occur, a simple reception may be, according to von Mohl, a mistake.[1088]

A liberal, but also rational view is the requirement that acts should not violate the rightly and justly acquired private rights (e.g. property). Otherwise, the certainty and reliability of the entire legal order would be destroyed. On the other hand, the scholar allowed certain exceptions in which, in the name of a higher interest (e.g. that of a community or entire state), individual rights could be limited. The violation of private law by the state can therefore only occur if there is a legitimate and important social interest, which not implemented, would cause great harm to the community, and secondly, if the violation of private law is covered by compensation. Acts of law should also be characterized by "appropriateness of measures." Under this concept von Mohl understood the desire to ensure that in every single case the actions of the state, and the means applied, corresponded to the benefits that can be achieved. He therefore advocated that acts should not regulate subordinate issues by multiplying the costs of

---

1084 R. v. Mohl, SVuP.2.1, p. 436.
1085 Ibid, p. 437.
1086 Idem, *Encyklopädie der Staatswissenschaften*, Zweite Auflage. . ., p. 151.
1087 Ibid, p. 148.
1088 Ibid, p. 151.

introducing the institutions they set up. Therefore, the implementation of an act may not generate costs exceeding the expected benefits thereof.[1089]

Many interesting postulates that demonstrate the liberalism of von Mohl relate to the formal dimension of acts. He listed five conditions for the formal correctness of an act, stating that it should be understandable and not giving raise to any doubt. The act should reflect the actual will of the legislator and be concise, and its content should be specified and divided in a way that facilitates its use. It should also utilize an appropriate language.[1090]

Referring to the first postulate, it should be pointed out that, according to von Mohl, it would be unfair to demand that citizens obey an act that is incomprehensible to them and raises doubts (although of course we are talking about citizens with general education enabling them to read specific legal norms).[1091] Undoubtedness of the act means that its provisions must be explicit and devoid of double meaning. One word should always mean one thing, and sentences should be simple, also in grammatical terms.[1092] The above postulate is connected with von Mohl's liberal belief relating to the language of the act. The scholar is strongly convinced that the act is not only intended for judges, but also for "ordinary" citizens. Therefore its language must be as understandable as possible for them, and not for just those, who have relevant education in this field. Hence the acts should use, to the greatest possible extent, utilize commonly used vocabulary, and all specialist terms should be explained.[1093]

As already noted, the act should, according to the Württemberger, determine the actual will of the legislator. It is primarily about avoiding situations in which, through the messy or unprofessional coining of law, norms establishing goals other than its intentions are introduced into the legal order. Therefore, both the subjective and objective scope of the act must be appropriate. This means that it cannot regulate too much or too little, and it cannot contain provisions relating to other factual conditions, functioning within different subjective and objective

1089 Ibid, pp. 149, 153.

1090 Idem, SVuP.2.1, p. 438.

1091 Ibid.

1092 Idem, *Encyklopädie der Staatswissenschaften*, Zweite Auflage…, p. 153. Idem, SVuP.2.1, pp. 441–442.

1093 Von Mohl put it briefly, stating that a code cannot speak the language of philosophers. Ibid, pp. 440, 449, Idem, *Encyklopädie der Staatswissenschaften*, Zweite Auflage…, p. 154.

scopes.[1094] Therefore, an act may not express less than the legislator wanted to regulate. On the other hand, its scope cannot be too wide.

The act should also be as concise as possible. Of course, the volume of the act is a relative value, because - according to von Mohl - its scope determines the scope of the subject to be regulated. What the scientist meant was not the unjustified shortening of content of acts, but rather the avoidance of excess repetitions. The act should properly regulate specific issues using as few concise sentences as possible.[1095] The act formulated in this way is to be absorbed faster in the legal awareness of citizens and will be more readily understandable.[1096] What is revealed again, is von Mohl's belief that a broad knowledge of law is indispensable.

The appropriate scope of the act is of great importance to von Mohl both for its proper understanding and in order to facilitate its application. Therefore, an act should relate only to facts of a given type.[1097] It should regulate them comprehensively so that there is no need to search for relevant provisions in other acts of law. On the other hand, if there are different subjective regulations in the act, they should be clearly separated in it. The act should be edited in such a way that the most general issues appear in its beginning, to provide the basis for more specific issues, which are included in further parts of the legal act.[1098]

As already mentioned, the so-called "common ordinances and provisions" formed the lowest rank of Mohl's hierarchy of law. The essence of the ordinances is their content of orders implementing specific provisions of acts of higher order. Therefore, they perform *strictly* executive function in relation to the acts with which they obviously cannot contradict. It should be emphasized that in von Mohl regulations differ from acts in that they do not require the cooperation of citizens (as was the case with acts of law).[1099] This is primarily due to the subordinate function of the regulations, which can not introduce new norms, but only regulate their implementation. Therefore their issue was, according to von Mohl, vested solely in the state authorities, and also - in certain cases - in their authorized bodies. Interestingly, the right to issue them can be both provided for in an act, and then it will have a specific scope, or it may arise as a logical necessity to comply with the provisions of an ordinary act.[1100]

1094 Idem, SVuP.2.1, p. 443.
1095 Idem, *Encyklopädie der Staatswissenschaften*, Zweite Auflage. . ., p. 154.
1096 Idem, SVuP.2.1, p. 444.
1097 Idem, *Encyklopädie der Staatswissenschaften*, Zweite Auflage. . ., p. 154.
1098 Idem, SVuP.2.1, pp. 446–448.
1099 R.-J. Grahe, op. cit., p. 84.
1100 R. v. Mohl, *Encyklopädie der Staatswissenschaften*, Zweite Auflage. . ., p. 146.

It should be noted that the understanding of acts and regulations of von Mohl is symptomatic for the entire so-called "early constitutional doctrine" of the rule of law in Germany. One of the main aspirations at the time was limiting executive (royal) power, connected with a relatively large margin of actions being reserved for the legislative branch. The above described trend is reflected in the analysis of differences between the act and the ordinance. While the scope of the former is virtually unlimited, a ordinance needs to be justified to be introduced. However, its task is only to comply with acts, while prohibiting the introduction of new legal norms (which shall be reserved for the act).[1101] The Mohl's belief that the regulation should only execute acts corresponds to the contemporary dominant trend in the liberal doctrine in form of the belief that government activity should be based only on compliance with acts.[1102] It is worth noting, however, that von Mohl was not consistent in his views. While the above understanding of the regulation is appropriate for him during the *Vormärz* period, it begins to change later. This is evidenced by the conviction, explained in the pages of the third edition of the *Police science...* of the need for the existence, within the legal system, of "statements" of state authorities that are unrelated to the legislative branch and the acts of law, relating to the police activities of the state (so-called "police ordinances," *Polizeiverordnungen*.[1103] In special cases (and von Mohl did not mean periods, when the legislative body is not able to assemble here), the government is entitled to issue regulations that have the force of law, where the activities of legislative bodies in the field of police activity are not appropriate.[1104]

An analysis of the formal aspect of the rule of law presented above necessitates that we state that Robert von Mohl represented many of the typical features of the era. Not only within the meaning of the constitution, but above all in the understanding of the concept of law by this scholar, we can observe the most important features of German liberalism, as well as the effects of tensions between the broadly understood state and society during the *Vormärz* period.[1105]

Organization ("*Verfassung*") is located at the very top in hierarchy of sources of law, which, according to von Mohl, usually adopts the form of a written constitution or group of constitutional acts. The "modern rule of law" must be based on constitutional norms, which are higher-order norms, that are difficult

1101 Idem, Staatsr.Württem.2.1840, p. 199.
1102 E. Angermann, op. cit., p. 147.
1103 R. v. Mohl, Polizeiwiss.1.1866, pp. 45–47.
1104 E. Angermann, op. cit., pp. 149–150. L. Łustacz, op. cit., p. 173.
1105 R.-J. Grahe, op. cit., p. 81.

to change, permanent and guaranteeing, above all, civil rights, and at the same time shape citizens' relations with the authorities. So one can clearly see the liberal postulate to protect citizens (bourgeois) against the arbitrariness of German princes or kings. However, it should be noted that von Mohl did not explicitly postulate institutionalized protection against situations of violation of the constitution, but only an option for a citizen to refuse to obey such laws. Moreover, in a situation where acts violate legal principles not included in the constitution, the citizen has, according to von Mohl, either to comply with such laws or to break the law, having to bear of all possible consequences thereof.[1106]

We should agree with the view that the early liberal German understanding of the act (as presented by von Mohl) forms the apex of the understanding of this concept in accordance with the principles of the *Rechtsstaat*. An act established in cooperation with the people, was to be a general and universal norm (which according to von Mohl was particularly important in the rule of law).[1107] The complicity of the national representation was to protect the principle of freedom of the citizen, while the principle of generality and universality was to protect against particular state attacks on the sphere of civil and social liberties. The act in accordance with the *Rechtsstaat* principle is the result of the general will expressed in the state, and the rule of such act means the rule of civil liberties.[1108]

It is worth noting that Mohl's postulate of the generality and universality of the act is also connected with the previously expressed equality before the law principle forming part of the rule of law. An act may contain only norms equal for everyone, i.e. general and abstract norms, because equality before the law is only possible with acts of general and universal content.[1109] As von Mohl stated: "These general norms gain great importance precisely in the rule of law, because it is in it that the participants of the state experience changes and determination of their legal relationship not through arbitrary orders of human or supernatural authority, but solely through general laws that bind everyone on an equal basis."[1110]

The act is the basis for the further operation of the state administration. It is also worth remembering that, in von Mohl, the differences between an act and a regulation reflect the then functioning conflict between the authority (monarch)

1106 R. v. Mohl, Staatsr.Württem.2.1840, pp. 392–393. I. Maus, op. cit., p. 23.

1107 U. Karpen, op. cit., pp. 66–67, E.-W. Böckenförde, *Staat. Gesellschaft, Freiheit, Studien zur Staatstheorie und zum Verfassungsrecht*. . ., pp. 69, 86.

1108 Ibid., p. 70.

1109 U. Karpen, op. cit., p. 68.

1110 R. v. Mohl, Staatsr.Württem.1.1840, p. 193.

and the people (representative body). "Important" legal norms such as acts (as opposed to regulations) should only be established in consultation with the people, which was also to be the way to secure individual civil liberties.[1111]

It would seem that based on the study of the triad of sources of law in the state, it is the state that, for von Mohl, is the source of all law, so that apart from positive law there cannot be other norms. However, in addition to positive laws, von Mohl also lists the customary law as source of law.[1112] One should also remember about the so-called "philosophical constitutional law" and its regulations, coexisting with positive law. However, we cannot resist the impression that the scholar's explanation of the relationship between these two legal orders and their possible collisions remains blurred and unclear, which only confirms von Mohl's statement that, in the end, "a rational reader is able to find the truth."[1113] However, agreeing with Eric Angermann, we cannot deny von Mohl that in his understanding of the sources of law, and their hierarchy, he was basing on the analysis of real conditions in a respective state, and not on abstract concepts.[1114]

4.4. Administration and its operation in a legal state

The most elaborate ideas regarding the operation of the rule of law can be found in von Mohl's views concerning the functioning of administration and police.[1115] Wishing to bring the reader a bit closer to the historical context of the functioning of these concepts in Germany, we should trace them back to the beginning of the second half of the 18th century. It was back then that the first symptoms of development of a police state appeared, connected with specific rulers acquiring the right to establish taxes. This led to the creation of a strong administrative apparatus and a class of officials serving it. Along with the development of the above phenomena, not only the ethos of the public service was shaped, but also the ethos of the so-called "police state" (*Polizeistaat*). If we elaborate further the issues raised in the introduction, we should note that the police state was understood as a state characterized by wide range of its activities

1111 R.-J. Grahe, op. cit., pp. 84–85.

1112 H. Schmitz, op. cit., pp. 97–98.

1113 R. v. Mohl, *Encyklopädie der Staatswissenschaften*, Zweite Auflage…, p. 192. P. v. Oertzen, op. cit., pp. 104–105.

1114 E. Angermann, op. cit., p. 116.

1115 More on the history of the term *Verwaltung* (administration): H. Strunz, *Der Verwaltungsbegriff*, [in:] *Gestaltung öffentlicher Verwaltungen*, M. Hofmann, K. Zapotoczky, H. Strunz (eds.), Berlin-Heidelberg 1993, pp. 7–9.

that permeated the absolute majority of the life spheres of its inhabitants. What characterized it in these activities was an efficient, and well-disciplined administrative apparatus. Along with the development of the idea of a police state, the science of administration (called *Kameral - und Polizeiwissenschaft* back then) also developed (primarily in the 18th century).[1116]

The administration (clerical apparatus) in the police states was not bound in its proceedings by any norms, except for directives (orders) issued each time by the ruler or his senior officials. There was no legal protection, in the current understanding of the word, in state-individual relations. These relations were based on the specific concept of the ruler's care and protection over his subjects.[1117] The emergence of liberal ideas in the German states in the early 19th century initiated the erosion of the method of administration and police states described above. The adoption of modern constitutions, allowing citizens (and no longer subjects) to exercise power, reforming the governance structure or, finally, the emergence of local government are just some of the symptoms of administrative liberalization in the early nineteenth century in Germany.[1118] Wilhelm Josef Behr is considered the first author who, in line with the stream of modernization described above, replaced the previously used police concept (*Polizei*) with the concept of administration (*Verwaltung*). The whole second volume of his work entitled *The system of applied general science of state or state art (politics)*[1119] is devoted to administrative issues. This thinker stressed the need for organic activity of administration, based on lasting and clear principles, and securing and safeguarding of citizens' rights.[1120]

The notion of administration also appears in Robert von Mohl, and the whole science referring to it and its operation occupies one of the most prominent places in the scholar's thought. The considerable importance of administration in the Mohl's concept of the rule of law is revealed in our analysis of its concept, when we compare it with the aforediscussed concept of the Organization. According to definition by von Mohl administration is:

1116 B. Dennewitz, *Die Systeme des Verwaltungsrechts*, Hamburg 1948, p. 16. W. Thieme, *Verwaltungslehre*, Köln 1977, p. 31.

1117 B. Dennewitz, op. cit., p. 17.

1118 Ibid, p. 30.

1119 *System der angewandten allgemeinen Staatslehre oder der Staatskunst (Politik).*

1120 W. J. Behr, *System der Staatslehre oder der Staatskunst (Politik)*, Bd. 2, Frankfurt am Main 1810, pp. 3–10.

> "(...) All the laws and activities of the state, intended to realize the essence of the organization, and thus the realization, by the state, the life objective of the nation, in all relevant relations, and through general instructions and specific actions."[1121]

So it is a concept opposite to the Organization, yet after joining with it, it constructs a comprehensive image of the state. While the Organization (but also acts) is to define permanent and unchanging rules, the administration is to implement them in the context of individual facts. Therefore, von Mohl associated the administration with the constant operation and actual activity of the state.[1122] The scholar himself best expressed the relationship and difference between these two terms, saying that the administration refers to the Organization as "Execution to intent, as a means to an end."[1123]

From the above-mentioned relation of administration to higher, timeless and basic norms arising from the Organization of a given state, follows von Mohl's conviction that the entire administration, its conduct and the norms that it is guided by cannot, under any circumstances, be incompatible with the Organization. Therefore, the administration is understood as a "set of tools" playing in relation to the Organization (but also a constitutional act) a role that may not necessarily be subordinate, but most certainly is ancillary. In von Mohl this conviction finds its fruition in the statement that the administration cannot set its own goals. Its goals must be directly derived from the general objectives of the state.[1124] Consequently, the administration cannot grant itself any right. The basis of its powers are the norms contained in the Organization of the state and not only in the written constitution, but also in the principles arising from the very essence of the state (its species and form). According to von Mohl, only if the administration's activities are in line with the basic principles of the state "does it build a truly harmonious, well-grounded and satisfactory whole for everyone."[1125]

The concept of police (*Polizei*) is connected with the concept of administration. *Police science...* is one of the scholar's most widespread and recognized achievements. Among other things, it was thanks to his attempt to combine the old *Polizei* from the times of absolutism with the principles of modern legal state

1121 R. v. Mohl, *Encyklopädie der Staatswissenschaften*, Zweite Auflage..., pp. 136–137.
1122 Idem, Staatsr.Württem.2.1846, p. 4.
1123 Idem, Staatsr.Württem.2.1831, p. 4.
1124 R. v. Mohl, *Encyklopädie der Staatswissenschaften*, Zweite Auflage..., pp. 138–139. Idem, Polizeiwiss.1.1866, p. 3.
1125 Idem, Staatsr.Württem.2.1831, p. 5.

that von Mohl permanently entered the canon of theoreticians of state and law. It should be emphasized that German science agrees that Mohl's *Police Science according to the principles of legal state* became the most widespread German work on police in the nineteenth century.[1126]

As noted in an earlier part of the present work, according to von Mohl, an individual during his existence in a state may encounter two types of obstacles on the path to achieving its life goals.[1127] To support citizens in overcoming these obstacles, the state needs and creates two types of institutions: justice system (*Rechtspflege, Justiz*) dealing with the unlawful and hostile activities of other people, and a second type of activity of the state authority, whose task is to support overcoming the so-called *force majeure* or external obstacles, which von Mohl called the police activity.[1128]

The police forming part of the state administration (*Staatsverwaltung*) was defined as:

> "(...) all those state institutions and activities that, through the use of state authority, seek to remove external obstacles, not consisting in breaking the law, that may stand in the way of comprehensive and rational development of human forces, and which both the individuals and the permitted associations of individuals do not, nor are able, to overcome themselves."[1129]

1126 H. Maier, *Die ältere Deutsche Staats- und Verwaltungslehre*, München 1980, p. 219.

1127 R. v. Mohl, Polizeiwiss. 1.1844, pp. 9–10.

1128 Ibid. The cameralist Johann Heinrich Gottlob von Justi (1717–1771) was one of the first among many German theoreticians of the science of the eighteenth century police, who understood *Policey* as primarily a state policy limited to the goal of the so-called internal security. Despite the fact that Justi did not understand the concept of *Policey* as a specific institution intended for protection against dangers, but also the metaphysical concepts of the so-called certainty and order were central to the police in the state: P. Nitschke, *Von der Politeia zur Polizei: Ein Beitrag zur Entwicklungsgeschichte des Polizei-Begriffs und seiner herrschaftspolitischen Dimensionen von der Antike bis ins 19 Jahrhundert*, "Zeitschrift für Historische Forschung" Vol. 19, No. 1 (1992), p. 18.

1129 R. v. Mohl, Polizeiwiss. 1.1866, pp. 6–7. More about the concepts of the Police at the time: G. Zimmermann, *Die Deutsche Polizei im neunzehnten Jahrhundert*, Bd.1, Hannover 1845. W. Szwarc, *Zarys ewolucji pojęcia "policji" w monarchii pruskiej w XVIII i XIX w.*, [in:] *Wybrane problemy teorii i praktyki państwa i prawa*, H. Groszyk, L. Dubel (eds.), Lublin 1986, pp. 117–133. On the notion of police also: K. Dąbrowski, *Ewolucja pojęcia policji w kontekście genezy żandarmerii w Niemczech*, "Annales Universitatis Mariae Curie-Sklodowska, Sectio G (IUS)," Vol. XXV, 3, pp. 205–208.

It should be noted that the task of the police understood as the sum of these state institutions and their activities to help the citizen, in the Mohl's rule of law is to remove obstacles standing in the way of life tasks of individuals, using the state authority, in those cases where these individuals are not able to cope with them on their own, or cooperating jointly.[1130] Just as the task of justice is, for von Mohl, to protect against injustice, the task of police to provide broadly understood support in the implementation of the interests of citizens.[1131] Von Mohl defined the police as the other half of the internal institutions of the rule of law, serving its purpose, with its significance often outweighing other types of state administration.[1132] In this case, the concept of police includes "all state art" (*ganze Staatskunst*) referring to the 18th-century tendencies. It is worth noting that the Mohl's concept of police differs slightly from the one that was widely accepted at that time. Under the term "police" the scholar understood all the so called "activities for prosperity" (*Wohlfahrtsmassnahmen*), excluding legal protection.[1133] It can be said that it encompasses most areas of human life, but in this respect it is based on the principle of subsidiarity. Therefore, the most important principle of the state's police activity is to intervene only where the forces of the individual or social communities are not able to achieve the goals of human life alone. In the opinion of the German liberal, if the state police acted in a different way, it would not only limit the freedom of citizens, but also threatened the state with forfeiting its forces required in other, necessary cases.[1134]

Von Mohl saw the police as a "helping authority" (*Hülfsgewalt*), which was thus not only something required but even adopting a dimension of a kind of blessing. It can be concluded that the police was far more important to him than the justice system. This is due to the fact that its existence is undeniably more often felt by an ordinary citizen than the functioning of the judiciary. In addition, the police also has a much broader material scope of activity. The prominence of police administration is demonstrated by the scholar's belief that while ordinary citizens have a chance to live their life without the support and assistance of the judiciary, it is not possible to do so without the support of the police.[1135]

Taking the abovementioned understanding of the concept of police by von Mohl into account we must state that he strongly opposed the contradistinction

1130 R. v. Mohl, Staatsr.Württem.2.1840, p. 276.
1131 Idem, Polizeiwiss. 1.1866, p. 6.
1132 Idem, Polizeiwiss. 1.1844, pp. 12–14.
1133 K. Sobota, op. cit., p. 308.
1134 R. v. Mohl, Staatsr.Württem.2.1840, p. 276.
1135 Idem, Polizeiwiss.1.1844, p. 14.

of the rule of law (*Rechtsstaat*) and the idea of the police state (*Polizeistaat*), which was clearly noticeable in German science at the time. According to von Mohl: "The state must take care of both law and the police."[1136] In addition, in von Mohl's definition thereof, police activity is not just about preventing negative things, as Friedrich von Bülau or Karl Salomo Zachariae thought, for example. In von Mohl's rule of law the police, in addition to removing various types of negative phenomena, must also provide the citizens with support of a positive nature.[1137] Therefore, von Mohl did not treat police as a factor hostile to civil liberties and a frequently used measure that was applied to cover the arbitrariness of officials, as did Zachariae or Johann Christoph von Aretin.[1138] The concept of police is not narrowly understood in von Mohl, as it was Prussian *Landrecht* or the concepts of Aretin, Zachariae and Bülau. So this is not an understanding of police solely as a state activity aimed at ensuring public order. Similarly to Stahl, police activity is seen much more broadly, it is not only to postpone and eliminate dangers, but also to act in a positive way and support citizens.[1139]

The above analysis demonstrates that von Mohl's police and its activities constitute the most important aspect of his science of administration in a rule of law. Therefore, before discussing the principles of police operation, it is worth to briefly analyze the general principles that the scholar formulated for the entire state administration (the more so, as by complementing the principles of police, they will complete the picture of the functioning of the rule of law in general).

The basic postulate that von Mohl formulated towards the entire state administration is that it accomplishes its goals in the most appropriate, reliable and simplest way possible.[1140] The entire administration should be uniform, that is, it is to create a coherent union with the entire state. Each department of administration must therefore be regulated by the same rights and served by the same types of officials. Von Mohl hence appears as an opponent of all kinds of particularisms

1136 Idem, Polizeiwiss.1.1866, p. 10. Referring to the relationship between the judiciary and the police, von Mohl pointed out that in the concept of justice, all actions and institutions of the state that deal with all illegal activities of citizens overlap. He distinguished here not only the civil (*Civil-Justiz*) and criminal (*Criminal-Justiz*) courts, but also the so-called "preemptive justice" (*Praeventiv-Justiz*), whose task, in von Mohl, is to prevent a violation of law. In all these matters, as von Mohl said, it was about the law and the law was not the subject of the Police's activity: Ibid, p. 65.

1137 Ibid, p. 8.

1138 Idem, Polizeiwiss. 1.1844, p. 14.

1139 E. Angermann, op. cit., p. 130.

1140 R. v. Mohl, Staatsr.Württem.2.1846, p. 4.

and unnecessary differences in the operation of state administration. He also broke with resorting to customs, which were still present in his sources of law. Nevertheless he did not find a place for various types of customary or regional conditions in organization of administration. This view was based on the belief that the administration must implement the state's principles set out in the Organization (the idea on which it is based) in the best (fastest, most secure) way. To be able to do this, it must be uniform, which also means functioning within uniform forms.[1141] The organization of administration should meet both the purpose of the rule of law, the actual relations prevailing in the state, and the needs of the nation. The organization and operation of the administration must therefore take into account the level of education of the nation, the independence of citizens and their willingness to associate voluntarily. "Independence of citizens" is in this respect forms an extremely important factor, setting the boundaries of the state's activity, because the rule of law by definition cannot, according to von Mohl, assist the inhabitants in fulfilling the tasks they can perform on their own.[1142]

Appropriate substantive division of its individual institutions is important for von Mohl from the point of view of efficiency and properties of state administration. It should be organized on the basis of joining common scopes and separating those that are strange to each other. Officials should only be assigned to one type of cases. The territorial division and hierarchy within which the state administration functions must also be appropriate.[1143] In von Mohl's thought the official should be as independent as possible within his clearly defined field of activity. The matters should be dealt with at the lowest possible level of administration, so that the higher instances are not overloaded with large number of appeals, which, as a consequence, may lead to issuing erroneous decisions.[1144] Therefore, the administration's operation should be as complex and extensive as possible, also in relation to the forms in which it is to operate.

The number of offices and officials will also depend on the scope of administration. According to von Mohl, administration should be large enough to effectively fulfill its functions. The number of offices and officials should be as small as possible, although this does not mean a non-reflective elimination of required

1141 Idem, Staatsr.Württem.2.1831, p. 10.

1142 Idem, *Encyklopädie der Staatswissenschaften*, Zweite Auflage. . ., pp. 247–248.

1143 Idem, Staatsr.Württem.2.1831, p. 11. Idem, Staatsr.Württem.2.1831, p. 12. At that time von Mohl distinguished the following divisions of the state administration: internal affairs, justice, state police activity, foreign affairs, war and tax administration.

1144 Ibid, p. 13.

institutions. It is more about efficiency and rationality in creating administrative bodies. This does not change the fact that von Mohl advocated the simplest forms possible and avoided all "pedantism." If there is such a possibility (also from the point of view of legal certainty), cases should be considered by individuals, and not collective bodies.[1145]

It is worth noting that von Mohl had a very rational approach to the costs of state administration. Its "Cheapness" (*Wohlfeilheit*) is not a significant requirement because the most important postulate for von Mohl was the proper fulfillment of its objective. The scholar argued that in order to achieve this in an effective manner the lowest possible cost should be employed, nevertheless, whenever there was justification for significant expenses, the state should bear them. Therefore, von Mohl did not support the forced reduction of the state administration budget. He was aware that extensive administrative institutions, typical for his idea of the rule of law would involve high costs. It is only important that these costs are rationally justified and that as many tasks as possible are passed on to private forces (citizens).[1146]

As previously noted, the concept of the rule of law is most profoundly reflected in von Mohl on the pages of "police science." Therefore, the principles of police operation, illustrating the ideology of the functioning of the entire state in the concept of a Württemberg scholar, are of great importance for the entire *Rechtsstaat* idea. At the outset, it should be noted that the merits of von Mohl in the field of police science can be considered on three different levels. First of all, he was able to present, in a systematic way, all the activities of the then state in the field of broadly understood security and welfare policies. Secondly, (and this seems to be the most important thing for his entire doctrine), he reconciled his police teaching with the contemporary liberal ideas, referring, among others, to the individual. This resulted in, among others, in the subsidiary understanding of the role of state intervention, which (unlike the eighteenth-century *Polizeistaat*) could not support prosperity in a forced manner. Thirdly, Mohl's police studies laid the foundations for a modern understanding of administrative law, the aim of which was to implement acts of law.[1147] "*Polizei*" (as in the eighteenth century) means the majority of the scope of the internal administration of the state, although excluding the aforementioned "pre-emptive justice."

1145 Idem, *Encyklopädie der Staatswissenschaften*, Zweite Auflage…, p. 248.
1146 Ibid, pp. 250–251.
1147 H. Maier, op. cit., p. 220.

All of the branches of the state's police activity are still based on the 18th century division, although they sometimes adopt new shapes and dimensions.[1148]

Considering the scope of police activity of the state, it can be stated that it is very wide in von Mohl, extending to virtually most areas of human life. The police is therefore to deal with both the "physical personality of the citizens" (*die physische Persönlichkeit der Bürger*), their "spiritual personality" (*geistige Persönlichkeit der Bürger*), as well as their "relationship to the material world" (*Verhältniss zur Güterwelt*). According to von Mohl there are no other possible areas.[1149]

Although it is not the purpose of the present work to describe Mohl's concepts in a comprehensive manner, referring to individual branches of the state's police activity, however, we should nevertheless indicate briefly, what each of the fields of activity was to be based on. According to von Mohl the care for "physical personality" encompasses active population policy of the state, caring for the right number of its citizens, including migration activities or even birth control.[1150] This scope also includes "health policy" (*Gesundheitspolitik*) providing health care institutions, or the "*Armenpolizei*," which goal was to fight poverty not only by preventing e.g. unemployment, but also by creating shelters. According to von Mohl, the rule of law must ensure that all citizens do not lack basic resources to support their life.[1151]

In addition to physical qualities, von Mohl's rule of law is also characterized by its concern for spiritual qualities, above all, the "education of reason" (*Ausbildung des Verstandes*), understood as supporting mental development and rationality, both among young people, and adults. The rule of law should promote moral attitudes, combat drunkenness, gambling, and indifference towards the others. The ambiguity of von Mohl's views regarding the role of churches in the rule of law indicates scholar's withdrawal from his initial view excluding religious matters from the scope of the rule of law. Von Mohl did not preclude the rule of law state from supporting religious institutions. One should not forget about the state's concern to educate citizens' "good taste" (*Bildung des Geschmacks*), i.e. aesthetics in the broad sense.[1152]

1148 R.-J. Grahe, op. cit., p. 108.

1149 B. Stöcker, op. cit., p. 54.

1150 More about the so-called "population police," the *Bevölkerungspolizei* in von Mohl: M. Fuhrmann, *Volksvermehrung als Staatsaufgabe? Bevölkerungs- und Ehepolitik in der deutschen politischen und ökonomischen Theorie des 18. und 19. Jahrhunderts*, Paderborn, München, Wien, Zürich, 2002, pp. 217–223.

1151 R. v. Mohl, Polizeiwiss. 1.1866, pp. 73–74. B. Stöcker, op. cit., p. 52.

1152 R. v. Mohl, Polizeiwiss. 1.1866, pp. 73–74.

The last, third area of state police activity is concern for the material sphere of citizens' lives. According to the scholar, the role of the state is to enable everyone to acquire and protect already acquired property, to abolish all forms of slavery and serfdom. It is not only legal form of protection but also the actual protection against, for example, fire, flood or damage caused by wild animals. The state should also widely facilitate and support business operations, ensure access to raw materials and facilitate commerce. The Württemberger was not afraid of protectionist activities on the part of the state, for example in the form of sales support for domestic products.[1153]

Thus, it is clear that the concept of state police activity covers all of its activities that are aimed at supporting the interests of citizens, which von Mohl referred to in his definitions, be it of a state or a rule of law. The conditions for police support of the abovementioned spheres of life of citizens in the Mohl's state of law can be summarized as follows; the goal must be legally acceptable and rational, it must not be immoral, there must be means available to achieve it, the need for the goal must be universal, and it could not be possible to attain it with private forces only.[1154]

Analysis of the principles of state police activity in the mind of Robert von Mohl should begin with recalling the most important principle of the rule of law, which was freedom of its citizens. A citizen has the right to do everything that allows him or her to achieve rational goals, as long as they do not infringe the rights of third parties or, which is of utmost importance, do not adversely affect the community.[1155] Based on this overriding assumption, it is necessary to analyze the principles of state police activity, which in von Mohl's science were not only elaborated in depth (he devoted a whole work to them), but best reflect Mohl's vision of the role of the rule of law in the lives of citizens.

While elaborating the above principles, we should state that the task of the police is not to take care for the legal order in the state. On the other hand, would it support interests of citizens contrary to the law, it would contradict the idea of the rule of law and oppose its task, i.e. maintaining the legal order, which in von Mohl is, after all, a condition for all further state activity. Therefore, the objective pursued by a citizen cannot be unlawful.[1156] The same applies to "morality of the

---

1153 Ibid, pp. 73–74. B. Stöcker, op. cit., p. 53.

1154 R. v. Mohl, Polizeiwiss. 1.1866, pp. 36–37. H. Schmitz, op. cit., p. 70.

1155 R. v. Mohl, Polizeiwiss. 1.1866, pp. 19, 28.

1156 Ibid, p. 29. Idem, *Encyklopädie der Staatswissenschaften*, Zweite Auflage…, pp. 281–282.

goal." The rule of law cannot support immoral objectives. Although it is not the most important task of the rule of law to safeguard morality, it should also support the education and strengthening of moral principles in the nation.[1157]

On the other hand, due to the scholar's belief that the state will always lack sufficient resources to meet all requirements, it should focus on legitimate and as general (universal) objectives as possible.[1158] Von Mohl did not take away the importance of particular, isolated goals of individuals, but due to the scarcity of state funds, he argued for the priority of those goals that are able to satisfy the needs of the greatest possible number of citizens.[1159] So he wished rather not that the fulfillment of every goal was of use for all citizens, but that the state did not support particular objectives. Von Mohl includes the following examples of "generally needed" police activities of the state: road construction or establishment of universities, while unacceptable actions include supporting individual entrepreneurs. Thus, the activity of the state consists of, figuratively speaking: not the transport of goods of one merchant from place to place, but on the construction of roads so that all merchants can do it.[1160]

One of the most important, if not the most important condition for police support of the state, resulting directly from the idea of the rule of law presented above, is to help citizens where an individual or group of individuals cannot defeat the so-called "external obstacle" (*äußeres Hinderniß*).[1161] Von Mohl described these enterprises as exceeding the forces of an individual, which were in disproportion with the economic, intellectual, physical or spiritual forces of individuals and theirs associations. What appears here, again, is the principle of subsidiarity of state activities. In von Mohl it is dictated by two beliefs. The first of them states that supportive actions of the state in a situation, where the citizen is able to overcome a specific obstacle, saying it in the language of von Mohl, would in essence be a denial of its freedom. Instead of supporting it, the state would limit it.[1162]

Secondly, according to von Mohl, the state cannot get involved in police projects that could successfully have been carried out without it. Engaging in such ventures (due to financial constraints) may result in a lack of funds for activities

1157 Ibid, p. 282. Idem, Polizeiwiss.1.1866, pp. 38–39.

1158 Ibid, p. 24.

1159 Idem, *Encyklopädie der Staatswissenschaften*, Zweite Auflage. . ., pp. 282–283.

1160 Idem, Polizeiwiss.1.1866, pp. 13, 30–31.

1161 Ibid, p. 20.

1162 Ibid, pp. 20, 31. Similarly: Idem, *Encyklopädie der Staatswissenschaften*, Zweite Auflage. . ., p. 283.

that only the state is able to implement. In addition, the scholar presented the view that, as a rule, ventures carried out by the state involve higher expenses.[1163] The state implements them not only more expensively, but also slower than private forces. This happens, if only because of various types of turmoil, such as e.g. changes in governments, which may cause delays in their implementation. Equally important for von Mohl was the fact that the state (public institutions) often has a tendency to exaggerate, overscale investments, putting too much pressure on magnificence. Private forces, on the other hand, only do what is "useful and necessary."[1164]

At this point, it is necessary to emphasize the role of not only individuals, but also private associations for the satisfaction of interests and life goals. What, for von Mohl, was most significant in police support, was to enable, within the rule of law, the widest possible freedom of association. Citizens' association are not only a precondition for not wasting state forces, but also for overcoming social atomism, as known from the 18th century police states.[1165] Speaking about the role of private associations, von Mohl once again turned his attention to the West of Europe and the Atlantic circle that fascinated him. He appears as a supporter of leaving a wide space for associations and private ventures, legislating to facilitate their activities, and the state granting them a special credit of trust. Great Britain was, for the scholar, a positive example of the private activity of individuals, where at the time, for example, many railway lines were in private hands. Thus, von Mohl's view on this issue can be summarized as follows: wherever it is rational and in accordance with the principle of subsidiarity, certain areas of activity should be vested in private hands. The state and its police activities must be limited to those moments, when citizens are unable to overcome specific obstacles to their life goals.[1166] There is no doubt that the state, with the help of its police, is obliged to support only the rational aspirations of its citizens. Speaking of examples of supporting irrational intentions, von Mohl referred to the creation of "Kabbalah and astrology chairs at universities." He was also convinced that there is no need to build roads, bridges or canals, where there was little traffic.[1167] In his teaching about the police, von Mohl revealed himself as an

1163 Idem, Polizeiwiss.1.1866, p. 24.
1164 Ibid, p. 25.
1165 Idem, *Encyklopädie der Staatswissenschaften*, Zweite Auflage. . ., p. 283.
1166 Idem, Polizeiwiss.1.1866, p. 24. Ibid, p. 22.
1167 Ibid, p. 29.

opponent of all luxury in the state's activity, but also as an advocate of its activity wherever it proved necessary.

In the activities of the state police, von Mohl also referred to the principle of the common good (*Gemeinwohl*), stating that in case of doubt the community was always more important. Therefore, police activity must be in accordance with the common good, and priority cannot be given to individuals or small groups of them. In the mind of Württemberger, the common good is becoming a very important factor in the state, determining its unity and essence. This common good is to coin the life of a nation into an organic unity, therefore it is not allowed to take actions that would harm the common good. Monopolies, where the interest of the monopolist (individual-entrepreneur) usually contradicts the interest of the community, were one of such examples for the scholar. It should be emphasized that in this case von Mohl reserved the state the right to take over the monopoly or at least to introduce protection against its abuses.[1168]

As mentioned in the introduction to this work, von Mohl's solution of the issue of the admissibility of the use of coercion by the state well illustrates his embedding between the eras of: declining absolutism and initial liberalism. One of the most important views on the use of coercion by the state police, which is worth quoting in this place, is the scholar's statement that the state has no right to interfere or punish if the citizen willingly harms himself or herself. On the other hand, the analysis of von Mohl's concepts relating to the use of force by the police allows us to conclude that priority will always be given to the good of the community over the good of individuals. When we analyze the principles according to which the rule of law may resort to coercion, we notice that it was the last resort for von Mohl. Wherever a citizen's specific behaviour can be attained without coercion, the state should abstain from applying it.[1169]

The admissibility of state resorting to coercion can, in von Mohl's teaching, be illustrated by the following statements. First, a specific objective of the state must be universally recognized as legitimate and it can only be achieved through coercion. Secondly, coercion is justified when the activity of an individual threatens the rights of third parties. While the individual at von Mohl has the right to harm itself without the interference of the state, it is nevertheless its duty to protect other citizens against improper behaviour of their "comrades" in the state. Similarly, the reason for a state to use coercion is when a minority poses a threat to achievement of set goals of the majority.[1170] And thus, for the scholar, the

1168 Ibid, p. 35.
1169 Ibid, pp. 50, 53.
1170 Ibid, pp. 51–52.

following were examples of justified coercion: protection against plague or fire protection (in construction) - due to the general requirements of this objective, as well as control of the operation of pharmacies or pawnshops - to maintain order.[1171]

Von Mohl's discussion of the issue of coercion demonstrates how he tried to find the golden mean between the liberal, "modern" understanding of *Rechtsstaat* and the old, absolutist concept of the police. The police (*Polizei*) was not seen by him as an opposite to the *Rechtsstaat*.[1172] Therefore, he didn't agree, first of all, with all radical, liberal views saying that the use of coercion is allowed only in legal matters, and not the police-administrative ones. He affirmed the right to use coercion, whenever the interest of the common good was threatened by the interest of an individual.[1173] Nevertheless, von Mohl was certainly not in favour of the state's unlimited right to coerce in matters of police-administration as it was the case in an absolutist state. He made the intervention in the private sphere of the individual dependent on the general good and advocated full compensation for it.[1174]

The last problem that we will raise in this subsection, connected with the issue of the functioning of the administration, which was also very popular at that time, will be von Mohl's perception of the problem of bureaucracy. It currently seems that the term bureaucracy was first used in 1745 by the French philosopher Vincent de Gournay. Under this concept he understood the form of government exercised by an independent elite of professionals, who had direct access to the instruments of power (the scope of power was increasing, which caused absolute rulers to feel threatened by the increasingly independent bureaucratic elite).[1175]

1171 Idem, *Encyklopädie der Staatswissenschaften*, Zweite Auflage. . ., pp. 283–285.

1172 W. Jann, *Staatslehre- Regierungslehre – Verwaltungslehre,* [in:] S. v. Bandemer, G. Wewer (eds.), *Regierungssystem und Regierungslehre*, Opladen 1989, p. 54.

1173 About the use of coercion in von Mohl also: V. Müller, *Staatstätigkeit in den Staatstheorien des 19. Jahrhunderts*, Wiesbaden 1991, pp. 150–151.

1174 E. Angermann, op. cit., pp. 154–155.

1175 A. Benz, op. cit., p. 156. This specific term was adapted to German language from French. B. Wunder, *Bürokratie: Die Geschichte eines politischen Schlagwortes*, [in:] A. Windhoff-Héritier (ed.) *Verwaltung und ihre Umwelt. Festschrift für Thomas Ellwein*, Opladen 1987, pp. 277–278. Concerning the problematics of bureaucracy one cannot ignore the literary output of Max Weber. On bureaucracy in Weber more: M. Weber, *Gospodarka i społeczeństwo. Zarys socjologii rozumiejącej*, Warszawa 2002, s. 164. R.A. Hilbert, *Bureaucracy as Belief, Rationalization as Repair: Max Weber in a Post-Functionalist Age*, "Sociological Theory" 1987, Vol. 5(1), s. 70–86. L. Dubel, *Problem biurokracji w tradycji myśli socjalistycznej*, Lublin 1988, s. 8–20.

Referring to von Mohl's analysis of bureaucracy, it should be emphasized that, in addition to the work by Friedrich Rohmer entitled *The Old and New German Bureaucracy*,[1176] the Württemberger's article *On Bureaucracy* of 1846 formed one of the earliest attempts to discuss the phenomenon of bureaucracy in a separate work.[1177] It is worth noting that the term itself became then one of the favourite negative slogans for both the conservatives and liberals. The former used it especially to demonstrate the tendency, which they perceived as negative, of late-absolutist states fighting against former privileges of estates. The liberals used it to describe all kinds of expansion of the state's activity to subsequent areas of social or economic life.[1178]

So when it comes to the meaning of the concept of "Bureaucracy" (*Bueraukratie*), the German liberal defined it as follows: "(...) The bureaucracy (...) is nothing more than a false understanding of the task of the state, (...)," which is expressed, among others, in the functioning of officials who focus too much on the formal dimension of their work.[1179] The scholar did not, therefore, connect the concept of bureaucracy neither with a system in which administrative decisions are taken not by collegiate bodies, but by individual officials, nor with the concept of government or governance.[1180]

According to von Mohl, bureaucracy as a phenomenon can occur when the state falsely interprets and executes its tasks (this dimension, however, is less common). Most often, bureaucracy manifests itself when the state, in its activities, goes beyond the limits of "rational and useful activity," perceiving the functioning of the nation as its "sole property." This is manifested in that the state wishes to deal with matters that do not fall within the scope of its activities, but instead, from the legal viewpoint, to the scope of activities of individuals and their social associations. According to von Mohl, another dimension of the bureaucracy was the situation in which the state entrusts administrative matters to officials who "make governing their own profession," which, among other things, results in the creation of a state organization based on a community of officials.[1181]

1176 F. Rohmer, *Deutschlands alte und neue Bureaukratie*, München 1848.

1177 More: R. v. Mohl, *Ueber Bueraukratie*, "Zeitschrift für die gesammte Staatswissenschaft," Heft 2, 1846, pp. 330–364.

1178 K. v. Beyme, *Politische Theorien im Zeitalter der Ideologien 1789–1945*. . ., p. 191.

1179 R. v. Mohl, SVuP.2.1, pp. 108–109.

1180 Ibid, pp. 100–101.

1181 Ibid, p. 108.

Bureaucracy was understood by von Mohl as a phenomenon that was a type of perversion of the correct understanding of the concept of state. It manifested itself, above all, as he called it "the absorption of all public life by the state." There is no doubt that the occurrence of the phenomenon of such bureaucracy in the state contradicted the postulates of the liberal movements in Germany at that time. For von Mohl, it was important to create various types of voluntary associations, that were to educate the citizens to develop the reaction of opposition to the omnipotence of bureaucracy.[1182]

Robert von Mohl appeared as an opponent of all negative manifestations of bureaucracy, such as "unnecessary empty writing" (*unnützte Schreiberei*) or the "gruff tone towards the citizen" (*barsche Ton gegen die Bürger*).[1183] According to von Mohl use of the common sense would help to avoid "unnecessary writing." Von Mohl was, above all, in favour of the most rational and realistic approach of officials to each and every case. They perceive it not only as the "file number" but above all a specific case, a specific person, as well as focus on the fastest and simplest achievement of the required goal. One of the basic rules regarding the functioning of officials is the scholar's statement that just as the state exists for the people and not the other way round, the officials also exist for the state and not the state for the officials.[1184]

At state level, according to von Mohl, measures against bureaucracy included, among others, improving the competences of officials.[1185] One of the most important remedies was the introduction of parliamentary governments (the influence of parliament and political parties on the government) to overcome the dualism between the monarch (government) and the parliament. However, it seems that von Mohl overestimated the possibilities of the parliamentary government's influence on bureaucratizing the state. He could not yet know that in some countries, such as France and Italy, the existence of a parliamentary government further cemented the bureaucracy, which had to compensate for the lack of homogeneity and continuity in ministries that were largely susceptible

---

1182 R. Vierhaus, *Liberalismus, Beamtenstand und konstitutionelles System*, [in:] *Liberalismus in der Gesellschaft des deutschen Vormärz*, W. Schieder (ed.), Göttingen 1983, p. 41.

1183 R. v. Mohl, SVuP.2.1, p. 115.

1184 Ibid, pp. 118, 121.

1185 More on the approach of the German doctrine to the issue of the clerical corps: G. Smyk, *Początki ewolucji podstawowych pojęć i definicji w europejskiej nauce administracji*, "Studia z Dziejów Państwa i Prawa," 17, 2014, pp. 119–120.

to parliamentary influence.[1186] According to von Mohl, another remedy against the development of bureaucracy should be "development of communal life" (*die Ausbildung der Gemeindelebens*). He believed that "a strong and extensive self-government of municipalities" is one of the important measures to reduce bureaucracy. The scholar also considered the general political and civic education of the inhabitants as one of the main factors preventing bureaucracy.[1187]

In his understanding of the state activity von Mohl proved his strong independence. He distanced himself not only from contemporary conservatives, but also from liberals. He did not perceive state's administration (*Polizei* in particular) as a kind of degeneration that should be eliminated, but rather as a peculiar phenomenon of a modern state, what is more, he tried to rationalize it. As Klaus von Beyme notes, no German before von Mohl analyzed the phenomenon of "*Polizei*-activity" in such a dispassionate and objective manner.[1188] First of all, he did not share the position of earlier liberals that every extension of the state's activity was a mistake. For von Mohl, this was an inevitable process. This does not mean, however, that the scholar did not notice the dark sides like bureaucracy. He criticized the so-called "ruling from behind the desk" (*Schreibtischherrschaft*) with the so-called "glaciers of files" (*Aktengletschern*). What we see in von Mohl is thus the criticism of excessive formalism, impersonality and pettiness of administrative proceedings. Both the state and the society should act to overcome the shortcomings of bureaucracy and administration. According to von Mohl, the means for that were both the complaints and the establishment of private associations, as well as the slow development of attitudes, and a sense of citizenship among the residents.[1189]

In order to summarize this argument, it should be stated that the idea of police by von Mohl is undoubtedly the most important attempt to modernize the scope of knowledge that was derived from the absolutism era. In his concepts relating to the police activities of the state von Mohl used two sources. On the one hand, he referred to the police state. He referred to an actively ruling and regulating state, dealing with everything, but unfortunately devoid of a specific objective. On the other hand, the scholar referred to the then modern idea of the *Rechtsstaat*, which was expressed in the conviction that the state administration

---

1186 K. v. Beyme, *Politische Theorien im Zeitalter der Ideologien 1789–1945*. . ., pp. 192–193.
1187 R. v. Mohl, SVuP.2.1, p. 128.
1188 K. v. Beyme, *Geschichte der politischen Theorien in Deutschland 1300–2000*. . ., p. 321.
1189 Idem, *Politische Theorien im Zeitalter der Ideologien 1789–1945*. . ., pp. 191–192.

(of which police activities were part) should operate on new principles, have tasks different than those from earlier periods.[1190]

Therefore, the most important principle of Mohl's *Polizeiwissenschaft* is the belief that it can only act if the citizens alone are not able to achieve the commonly accepted, required and permitted goal.[1191] Referring to the principle of subsidiarity of the state (rule of law), von Mohl created the antithesis to the state of police absolutism, omnipotent and overwhelming. Police, despite the fact that it exists and has broad functions, is, as Josef Isensee rightly pointed out, individually and liberally oriented.[1192] However, referring to the liberal concept of self-aid did not mean that all state aid was rejected completely. The idea was that the state should simply refrain from imposing its help on the citizens, because the impulses for action should come from them and not from the institution of the state. Therefore, there is no area of public, cultural, economic or social life in von Mohl that would be excluded from the administration of the state. Nevertheless the rule remains that in these areas, the state is to act only as much as it is actually required to.[1193] It should be remembered, however, that von Mohl did not rule out the use of coercion by the state, especially where the interest of a larger group of people prevails over individual interest.[1194]

The police thus does not only have a negative character, based only on removing obstacles or protecting against dangers.[1195] In von Mohl, the police (and thus the state) also has a second dimension manifested in a focus on promoting good and prosperity.[1196] The police is not, therefore, a concept contrary to the rule of law, but rather a mean to implement its idea. Without the police, the rule of law state would be just a "judicial state" focused only on safeguarding the rights of individuals, which would be incompatible with its nature.[1197] It should be noted that the concept of police presented by von Mohl, among others in the *Staatslexikon* of Rotteck and Welcker differed from the concept presented by other liberals. The von Aretin concept will serve us as an example here.[1198]

1190 H. Maier, op. cit., pp. 232–233.

1191 K. Wolzendorff, *Die Entwicklung des Polizeibegriffs im 19. Jahrhundert*, Marburg 1906, p. 51.

1192 J. Isensee, op. cit., pp. 59–60.

1193 E. Angermann, op. cit., pp. 127, 129. W. Hilz, *Subsidiaritätsprinzip und EU-Gemeinschaftsordnung*, Opladen 1998, pp. 30–31.

1194 H. Maier, op. cit., p. 221.

1195 Ibid, pp. 227–228.

1196 K. Wolzendorff, op. cit., pp. 50–51.

1197 H. Maier, op. cit., p. 228.

1198 K. Wolzendorff, op. cit., p. 52.

The latter stated that according to its proper understanding, the police could only care about maintaining security and order. Any interference of the police in the broadly understood well-being of citizens constitutes an unacceptable violation of their freedom.[1199] Zachariae reasoned likewise, stating that the purpose of the police was not to promote the welfare of the nation. The police should only avert dangers, so its objective is only negative.[1200] As Hans Maier aptly states, von Mohl, standing between epochs, trusting realism and rationality, with his social liberalism, reveals himself as an opponent of the Kant's school of law of nature. So he fights for a combination of the idea of the police and the rule of law, which matches the spirit of his times.[1201]

1199 J. Ch. v. Aretin, *Staatsrecht der konstitutionellen Monarchie*, Bd. 2, Abt. 1, Altenburg 1827, pp. 177–178.

1200 C. S. Zachariae, *Vierzig Bücher vom Staate*, Bd. 4, Heidelberg 1840, p. 288. K. Wolzendorff, op. cit., p. 60.

1201 H. Maier, op. cit., pp. 232–233.

Chapter V The power and representation in state

5.1. The concept of power

The final research task undertaken in the present monograph is an attempt to analyze Mohl's perception of various aspects of the phenomenon of power in the state. In order to achieve this goal, we should first focus on the very concept of power, then it will be worth to proceed to analyzing the issue of parliamentary representation in the state (which was an issue that was widely discussed at that time) to conclude by discussing the perception of the problem of democracy by von Mohl, with the main axis in form of analysis of the idea of universal suffrage.

The concept of power proposed by the German liberal does not seem to be groundbreaking. The appearance of this phenomenon in the state was a logical necessity stemming from its existence, in other words; the existence of power forms an immanent part of the concept of state. Thus, its presence is, in von Mohl's mind, the effect of the very purpose for which the state exists (i.e. supporting the implementation of various life tasks of the inhabitants and their associations). For if the state is to be an ordered creation, it is to function and perform the functions imposed on it, it must contain a force capable of issuing binding orders and execution of their performance. Importantly, von Mohl introduced a distinction between the origins of power, depending on the species to which the state belonged. In a rule of law, the scholar found the authority of state power in the "common, free will of the participants."[1202] This view proves once again that von Mohl revolved around the idea of contractualism, as the source of legitimization for the state to act as such.[1203]

As already noted, the scope and political position of power in Robert von Mohl's thoughts is a reflection of the scholar's view of the role of the state in people's lives. In earlier parts of the work we were able to conclude that he was in favor of a strong and active state, supporting its citizens. Thus is not surprising then that when speaking about the features of state power, von Mohl puts its might, uniformity and ability to undertake a wide range of activities in the foreground.[1204] Therefore, the power of the state is evidenced by its ability

---

1202 R. v. Mohl, *Encyklopädie der Staatswissenschaften*, Zweite Auflage…, p. 116.

1203 Ibid, pp. 115–116. H. Schmitz, op. cit., p. 103. More on the subject of power in the doctrine of Robert von Mohl: W. Pauly, op. cit., p. 73.

1204 R. v. Mohl, *Encyklopädie der Staatswissenschaften*, Zweite Auflage…, p. 606.

to fend off obstacles (which stand in the way of achieving the life goals of its inhabitants) swiftly and effectively. The scope of its activity, similarly to the goals of the state, results, in von Mohl, from the degree of civilization development of the inhabitants of the respective state (and thus the state power will be the most extensive in rule of law).[1205] Importantly, the German liberal, speaking of the power of authorities, did not only speak about the rights it should have, but also about an adequate "physical strength" capable of enforcing these rights. This also concerns a well-developed administration and executive apparatus. This postulate should be combined with the extensive administrative (police) functions in the doctrine of von Mohl, which we described in the previous chapter. It is also worth noting that the Württemberger believed that a sufficiently strong power of authorities has one more goal: the awareness of a consistent and strong response against actions against the state, which should discourage anyone who would like to do so, already at the stage of preparation.[1206]

Important in the context of highlighting the general image of state power in the doctrine of Robert von Mohl is the scholar's requirement of its uniformity.[1207] The division of state power into a legislative, executive and judicial element in accordance with the teachings of Montesquieu, has been one of the distinguishing features of the liberal concept of the state since the 18th century.[1208] Also, many representatives of early German liberalism (most of whom were looking at France) saw, in the idea of the separation of powers, a protective measure against abuses by the state (implying an absolute monarch here).[1209]

The German scholar was of the opinion that the introduction of the separation of powers into three equal and mutually inhibitory centres would pose a threat of an existential nature to the state.[1210] Von Mohl ordered to treat the

---

1205 Ibid, p. 116.

1206 Ibid, pp. 606–607.

1207 On this topic: Z. A. Maciąg, op. cit., p. 99.

1208 Liberal demands also include democratic legislation and guaranteeing citizens their parliamentary representation.

1209 U. Karpen, op. cit., pp. 40, 60.

1210 It is also worth noting that many representatives of German doctrine were of the opinion that the concept of people's sovereignty and the concept of separation of powers were incompatible. It was believed that since power would come from the people as a whole, it should also form a single whole. Heinrich Ahrens was among those, who spoke in this way. More: L. Gall, *Benjamin Constant, Seine politische Ideenwelt und der deutsche Vormärz*, Wiesbaden 1963, p. 177. On the separation of powers also: K. Welcker, *Gleichgewicht der Gewalten*, [in:] *Das Staats-Lexikon*,

state as a unified creation, the division of which, in any respect, would lead to anarchy.[1211] Therefore, power should not only be strong and eternal, but also, and perhaps above all, uniform. It is worth remembering, however, that von Mohl does not categorically demand that this uniform power shall be vested in the hands of a monarch. Of course he will be a supporter of the monarchy as a state system, but he will never rule out that in a given state all power could be concentrated, e.g. in the hands of a people's assembly. He just wanted the whole scope of management of state affairs to be vested in the hands of a single entity.[1212]

Von Mohl criticized, in particular, the ideas of Montesquieu. He regarded his theories of separation of powers to be explicitly illogical, emphasizing their fallacy.[1213] In the opinion of the German liberal, the separation of power into smaller and independent centres did not guarantee the implementation of systemic protection against its abuse (which was one of the main goals of this idea). What's more, the emergence of several equal and independent centres in the state may, in Württemberger's opinion, result in rivalry and conflicts between them. Therefore the idea of Montesquieu would lead to an artificial breaking of the unity of state power.[1214] In addition, von Mohl believed that the situation, in which the citizens would be equally subjected to three different centres of power, was unacceptable. It would lead to chaos, for example connected with the risk that these three powers could issue contradictory orders.[1215] Continuing his criticism of the concept of Montesquieu, he stated that it is inconsistent with logic to recognize the judiciary as a separate entity. Due to the scope of its activity, which

Encyklopädie der sämmtlichen Staatswissenschaften für alle Stände, K. v. Rotteck, K. Welcker (eds.), 6 Bd., Leipzig 1862, pp. 651–655.

1211 R. v. Mohl, Geschicht.u.Lit.1, p. 274. Idem, *Encyklopädie der Staatswissenschaften*, Zweite Auflage. . ., p. 121. M. Racky, op. cit., pp. 79, 115.

1212 Ibid, p. 143. Michael Racky rightly notes that in this aspect von Mohl's concept resembles the program of "monarchical principle," as proposed by Friedrich Julius Stahl. Also on this subject: W. Boldt, *Verfassungsgeschichtlie Betrachtungen*, Münster 2004, p. 173.

1213 R. v. Mohl, Geschicht.u.Lit.1, pp. 272–273.

1214 Ibid, pp. 274–275.

1215 Idem, *Encyklopädie der Staatswissenschaften*, Zweite Auflage..., pp. 118–119. What's interesting is von Mohl's view allowing a kind of exception, that is the religious (church) power. Von Mohl reserved for the religious association a wide autonomy from the influence of state power, the condition of which was that in exercising their power they did not fall within the scope of state action.

is the application of legal provisions, he considered the judicial power to form part of the executive power.[1216]

Power in the state of Robert von Mohl is also eternal and "all-encompassing" (*allumfassend*). The feature of eternity should, in this case, be understood more in terms of continuity. This means that the state authority lasts as long as the state lasts, it does not cease, for example, in the event of the death of the entity exercising it. The fact that the state power is all-encompassing means that there are no exclusions from its rule, it extends to the entire territory of the state, and all the individuals staying within it.[1217]

An important feature of state power, especially from the point of view of later considerations regarding the concept of "head of state," is its irresponsibility. For von Mohl, the fact that state power cannot be subject to any liability is above all a logical necessity, arising from its very essence. According to the German scholar, responsibility can only be borne to entity that stands higher in the hierarchy of the state. Power is highest in the hierarchy of the state, so it has no one to respond to. On the basis of the above statements, however, it cannot be accepted that the power in the Mohl's concept of the state is unlimited. Von Mohl attributed to it primarily the restrictions of a moral nature, resulting from the essence and tasks of the state (which will be discussed later in this section).[1218]

As already stated, the duties of state power derive from von Mohl's general goals of the state, so they are primarily based on supporting residents in achieving their life goals or ensuring order and respect for the law. The duties of the authority are also correlated with its rights, and first and foremost the rights it has in relation to its citizens.[1219] Therefore, the authorities have the right to demand that all citizens comply with and act in accordance with the principles of the system and the law. It is worth noting that in this case von Mohl emphasizes, once again, the equality of all citizens before the law, which certainly should be written on the side of evidences for his liberalism. Secondly, the state authority has the right to take all actions in line with the constitutional, systemic and legal principles aimed at achieving the state's goals. At this point it should be emphasized that von Mohl allowed the state authorities to depart from compliance with these principles, but only at the time of extraordinary circumstances.[1220]

1216 Ibid, pp. 121–122. John Locke, for example, presented a similar view.
1217 Ibid, *Encyklopädie der Staatswissenschaften,* Zweite Auflage…, p. 119.
1218 Ibid, pp. 117, 119–120.
1219 B. Stöcker, op. cit., p. 41.
1220 R. v. Mohl, *Encyklopädie der Staatswissenschaften*, Zweite Auflage…, pp. 327–328.

The concept of state power in Robert von Mohl also includes the concept of the so-called "Head of state" (*Staatsoberhaupt*), acting as a guarantor of the coherence of the entire state organism, its representative and the personification of all state power.[1221] Much like the very existence of state power, also the existence of the head of state appears in the doctrine of von Mohl as a logical requirement. Since the concept of the highest, uniform and all-encompassing power exists, there must be an entity that will implement it (exercise it) in relation to the citizens. In short, according to von Mohl, the task of the head of state is to govern.[1222] In von Mohl there is no clearly determined postulate regarding the shape of this institution. The professor from Tübingen tended to the view that it will always depend on the conditions prevailing in the state. We are talking here first of all about the level of civilization of the respective nation (as already known for having an impact on the species of the state in general). What is of note here is von Mohl's opposition to the exclusive sovereignty of the nation. The scholar did not agree with the concept that the entire nation is always the sovereign, but also an individual (monarch) needn't have to be. So, as with the methods of acquiring state power, so also with the entities exercising it, von Mohl observes the admissibility of many solutions (which does not mean that he will not support just some of them).[1223] His views will include both the exercise of power by the monarch, a group of aristocrats, but also by the people in a democratic state.

An analysis of the rights and obligations of the head of state in the doctrine of a German scholar allows us to conclude that they are coherent and constitute an elaboration of the general rights and obligations of the state and state authority. Speaking in a highly generalized manner, von Mohl listed the rights and obligations that the head of state has. One of its most important duties is caring for maintaining legal order, as well as acting on the basis and within the limits of the law, i.e. in accordance with the rule of law.[1224] Von Mohl returns here to the rule of law principle, as the prerequisite for the functioning of each state. The head of state is to help its subjects, residents, citizens, but also their associations, wherever their own forces are not sufficient to achieve life goals. It

---

1221 Idem, Staatsr.Württem.1.1829, pp. 182–183. A. Bosiacki, *Robert von Mohl i początki koncepcji państwa prawnego*, [in:] *Idee jako źródło instytucji politycznych i prawnych*, L. Dubel (ed.), Lublin 2003, pp. 325–326. R. v. Mohl, *Encyklopädie der Staatswissenschaften*, Zweite Auflage…, p. 200. H. Schmitz, op. cit., p. 64.

1222 R. v. Mohl, *Encyklopädie der Staatswissenschaften*, Zweite Auflage…, p. 209.

1223 Ibid, pp. 116–117, 615–616. However, it should be remembered that von Mohl will be in favor of the monarchical system here.

1224 Ibid, p. 520.

is morally obliged to know the actual state of affairs in the state and should be devoted to it honestly performing its duties. It is worth paying attention to von Mohl's great idealism in this aspect. He required the head of state not only to stick to the provisions of laws, when performing its duties, but also wanted its activities to be guided by the principles of morality. In exercising its function, the head of state also has the right to demand that the state covers the costs of its own activities. However, von Mohl emphasized that these must always be justified costs. Therefore, there is no place, in public activity, for not only waste, but also all kinds of luxury. He saw the sources of the real dignity of the office in simplicity, and not in trumpery.[1225] The exclusive rights of the head of state in the concept of Robert von Mohl also include organizing the representation of the state on the international arena (appointing ambassadors), appointing officials or managing armed forces.[1226]

It seems that the most important view of von Mohl concerning the concept of the head of state remains its irresponsibility. This is the result of the scholar's acceptance of the paradigm of irresponsibility of state power. Since it is the highest, it cannot respond to anyone. The same applies to its personification or the head of state. Therefore, the head of state is not held responsible. For von Mohl, there was no doubt that the head of state would not always act morally, and that he or she could break the law. However, this is not a sufficient justification for him to introduce, for example, its criminal responsibility for these acts. What is also worth noting here, is the source of this view. The irresponsibility of the head of state in the Württemberger's doctrine can be described as a minor evil. According to von Mohl, the introduction of the principle of criminal liability of head of state could lead to conflicts in the state and even to civil war.[1227] Therefore, in accordance with the principle of irresponsibility, the issuing of a specific decision by a head of state, for example within the limits of legal norms and competences, cannot be the basis for its liability, even if that the decision was harmful or immoral.[1228] Therefore, von Mohl also excludes any kind of political responsibility of the head of state. What we see here, once again, are unvoiced references to the parliamentary monarchy system. The head of state - the monarch was not to be held responsible for his or her actions. However,

---

1225 Ibid, pp. 521–524.

1226 Ibid, pp. 212–215.

1227 Ibid, p. 218. In addition, the scholar will also look for ways to soften his thesis on the lack of responsibility of the head of state, e.g. through ministerial responsibility.: M. Racky, op. cit., p. 152.

1228 R. v. Mohl, *Encyklopädie der Staatswissenschaften*, Zweite Auflage. . ., p. 219.

it should be remembered that, according to von Mohl, irresponsibility covered only the head of state. The rule did not even apply to its closest associates.[1229] The scholar's reference to the concept of the so-called "ministerial responsibility" (*Ministerverantwortlichkeit*), which was subject to a vivid discussion in German science in the first half of the 19th century. This idea was an attempt to find entities that would be responsible for decisions in the state, in place of non-responding monarchs.[1230]

Speaking about the Mohl's concept of irresponsibility of the head of state, one cannot forget about the special and dangerous powers that he granted it in urgent and extraordinary circumstances. The scholar thus stated:

> "When it comes to maintaining and saving the state in the face of an unexpected danger, and there is no time or opportunity to base it on the normal, legal path, the head of state

1229 Ibid, pp. 219–220.

1230 According to von Mohl, the head of state should also be subject to stronger legal protection, manifesting itself, e.g. in more severe penalties for crimes committed against it.: Ibid, pp. 220–221. As for the institution of the responsibility of ministers before a representative body (the so-called *Ministerverantwortlichkeit*) this is one of the main effects of the development of the constitutional-liberal movement in Germany. Developed in the United Kingdom at first, it later gained popularity in other European countries. While adopting a somewhat different shape everywhere, it always relied on the possibility of dismissing the minister by means of a parliamentary vote. In Germany, during *Vormärz*, the adoption of the principle of ministerial responsibility before parliament was an indirect effect of the so-called "monarchical rule" (according to art. 57 of the *Wiener Schlussakte*). The ministers became those who, in response to the aspirations of the bourgeoisie, had to take responsibility for the government's actions in the place of "untouchable" monarchs. It is worth noting that it was the constitution of Württemberg that was the first to introduce comprehensive provisions resolving the issues of ministerial responsibility. Similar provisions were also included in the constitution of Baden.: D. Willoweit, op. cit., pp. 281–282, M. Racky, op. cit., pp. 151–152. Von Mohl, on the other hand, earned the distinction of the first German writer, who, during *Vormärz*, created the most thorough work regarding ministerial responsibility. In addition to presenting a deep historical outline, he also elaborated very detailed suggestions for conducting proceedings following a complaint against a minister. It certainly forms an attempt to present possibilities for limiting royal power (in this case of the ministers appointed by the monarch) by a representative body. So as far as the ruler was "untouchable" the minister who, for example, violated the constitution, should be held accountable.: R. v. Mohl, *Die Verantwortlichkeit der Minister in Einherrschaften mit Volksvertretung, rechtlich, politisch und geschichtlich entwickelt*..., pp. 3–28, M. Racky, op. cit., p.157, L. Gall, op. cit., ps. 272, H. Schmitz, op. cit., pp. 81–82.

has the right to take the necessary interim measures, even such that are compromising the existing institutions and rights."[1231]

He was therefore in favor of the head of state having special prerogatives, enabling it to remove immediate danger threatening the state. It is noteworthy that von Mohl was, in fact, in favor of legitimizing situations in which one should resort to *de facto* extra-law measures, in the name of higher necessity. Analyzing the above issue we should also note the scholar's view that it is inappropriate to impose a constitutional or statutory limitation of the powers of the head of state to act only in situations provided for by law. On the contrary, only the situation in which the head of state will have the legitimacy of being able to act in emergency conditions can protect the state against great damages, which could arise, was the head of state unable to act.[1232] The conclusion is obvious: the state was so valuable to the German scholar that he allowed it to act outside the law and even against it.

On the other hand, however, he noticed the risk that acting under a "state of emergency" might tempt the head of state to violate the rights of citizens. Therefore, he was in favor of defining cases and exceptional situations entitling the head of state to resort to non-legal means or to issue normative acts outside the applicable procedure.[1233] It should also not be forgotten that von Mohl formulated the requirement for the body of parliamentary representation to approve normative acts issued in emergency situations.[1234] The problem of assessing the admissibility of the head of state's actions in emergency situations has two dimensions, which are clearly seen in von Mohl. On one hand we cannot object the rightness of view saying that there may be situations not provided for by law and threatening, for example, the very raison d'état of the state, understood as its overriding interest.[1235] In such situations, the highest representatives of the state authority must have the right to act in an extraordinary manner. The problem arises whenever there is abuse of this institution, for example to achieve short-term political goals. That is why it is extremely important, and the scholar seemed to notice this too, to introduce institutions to prevent the abuse of the institution of emergency operations.

1231 R. v. Mohl, *Encyklopädie der Staatswissenschaften,* Zweite Auflage. . ., p. 209.

1232 Ibid, pp. 216, 606–607.

1233 Idem, SVuP.2.1. pp. 624–625.

1234 H. Hamacher, *Carl Schmitts Theorie der Diktatur und der intermediären Gewalten,* Neuried 2001, p. 70.

1235 More: M. Żmigrodzki, *Racja stanu* [in:] *Encyklopedia politologii,* t.1. . ., pp. 590–591.

As was the case with citizens, in the concept by von Mohtl the head of state also has a whole set of moral obligations. It seems that in quite detailed scope of the so-called "moral obligations in the state" the scholar attempted to balance the principle of irresponsibility, in some sense guided by the naive faith that the head of state will comply with these obligations. Therefore, for von Mohl, the greater the influence on the affairs of the state, the greater the moral obligations of certain entities. It makes no difference, whether the head of state was elected by the people or it inherited its function, it will always have the moral obligation to do everything that can contribute to the well-being and prosperity of the nation.[1236]

There is also no doubt that within his concept of the head of state von Mohl did not explicitly form a thesis stating who that should be. On the other hand, the analysis of his texts demonstrates that, when speaking of the head of state, he referred primarily to the monarchical ruler. Before we examine Mohl's concept of the monarchy, we should first investigate the general historical, political and legal background of this systemic institution.

It is noteworthy that in all constitutions of the four great states of the German south of the first half of the nineteenth century, the monarch was the entity to which the vast majority of power in the state belonged. Even the legislative initiative was vested in the hands of monarch, as was making the most important political decisions or the entire executive and administrative apparatus.[1237] So even in the most liberal states of southern Germany, the monarch held sovereign and indivisible power.[1238] Despite the ever stronger, often rebelling, aspirations of the bourgeoisie, which was gaining power, aiming at political emancipation, most of the power remained in the hands of the monarchs. Although they agreed to limit it with provisions of the constitution, they also reserved the sovereignty of decision-making, for example in extraordinary matters.[1239] In

1236 R. v. Mohl, *Encyklopädie der Staatswissenschaften,* Zweite Auflage…, p. 520.

1237 H. Boldt, op. cit., s. 240, D. Willoweit, op. cit., pp. 281–282. For example, the 1818 constitution of the Kingdom of Bavaria, in its first article stated: "The king is the head of state, an in his essence unites all the rights of state power, and executes them in accordance with the provisions of this constitution that was granted by him. His person is holy and untouchable." Source: https://www.bavarikon.de/object/GDA-OBJ-00000BAV80000807 [accessed 20/02/2019].

1238 M. Kriele, *Einführung in die Staatslehre. Die geschichtlichen Legitimitätsgrundlagen des demokratischen Verfassungsstaates*, Stuttgart, Berlin, Köln 2003, p. 280.

1239 Ibid, p. 279. More on this subject: D. Grimm, *Deutsche Verfassungsgeschichte 1776–1866 Vom Beginn des modernen Verfassungsstaats bis zur Auflösung des Deutschen Bundes*, Frankfurt am Main 1988, p. 113.

the result of the aforesaid, the concept of constitutional monarchy appeared in Germany.[1240]

Von Mohl himself, speaking of the "constitutional state" (*Das constitutionelle Staat*) distinguished four of its main features: first, exercise of power in accordance with the principles and objectives of the idea of the rule of law (of course, in the meaning of this concept by von Mohl), secondly, the exact definition of the laws relating to the exercise power by constitutional act or acts, thirdly, the exact specification of the residents' demands in relation to the state authority, and finally, the introduction of institutions in the state that will protect citizens against violation of their rights by the state authority (establishment of a representative body). Furthermore, a constitutional state cannot be characterized by exceptional legal favouritism, e.g. of certain social groups.[1241]

Von Mohl's perception of the monarch's position in such a state coincides with the issue of the so-called "duality" between the monarch and parliament (this problem will be discussed in more detail in the subsequent subsection). It was particularly in the states of the liberal south that during the *Vormärz* the conflict, with monarch on one side and the representation of nation (e.g. a parliamentary assembly) intensified. Monarchs usually depended on retaining as much state power as possible in their possession, while the parliament (typically dominated by the bourgeoisie, which was growing in strength), on seizing as much of that power, as possible. Thus, one of the opponents was a parliament consisting mostly of the rapidly emancipating German bourgeoisie, and the other a monarch, remembering the times of absolutism and finding it hard to imagine giving away most of his power and assuming a neutral position and role in the state, understood as "guardian of the constitution."[1242] In addition to the notion of representation (as discussed in the next subsection), the answer to

1240 H. Boldt, op. cit., p. 55. The concept of constitutional monarchy was already popular in Germany at that time, and applied, e.g. by Karl von Rotteck in his work *Staatsrecht der konstitutionellen Monarchie*.

1241 R. v. Mohl, Geschicht.u.Lit.1, p. 268.

1242 M. Racky, op. cit., p. 76. A similar role was envisaged for the monarch by Benjamin Constant, who defined the royal authority as "neutral power" (*une pouvoir neutre*), while the power of government and ministers as "acting power" (*une pouvoir actif*).: L. Jaume, *La théorie de l'autorité chez Benjamin Constant*, "Historical Reflections / Réflexions Historiques," Vol. 28, No. 3, p. 468. P. Królak, *"Dziewięćdziesiąt dziewięć cudzych pomysłów, i jeden autora." Porównanie myśli konstytucyjnej Wincentego Niemojowskiego i Benjamina Constanta*, "Czasopismo Prawno-Historyczne," T. LXIV, z.2, 2012, p. 469.

tensions of this kind was the appearance of the so-called "monarchical principle" (*das monarchische Prinzip*) within German doctrine. This conservative response to the liberal aspirations of the German bourgeoisie stated that it was solely the monarch, who was the sole holder of sovereign power in the state. According to the monarchical principle, the constitution was only a limitation, or rather a self-limitation of royal power, but most certainly it was not its source.[1243] Pursuant to this principle, admittedly, cooperation of parliamentary bodies in governing the state was allowed (e.g. as part of approving the budget or taxes, the so-called *Steuerbewilligung*), but they were denied the right of legislative initiative.[1244] The monarchical principle quickly gained significant popularity among the rulers of German states, that were still functioning on the principle of a more or less omnipotent political position, reflecting their negative attitude towards the idea of sovereignty of the people.[1245]

As far as the views of Robert von Mohl are concerned, at least at the beginning he seemed to be in favor of the monarchical principle.[1246] Already in the *Constitutional law of the Kingdom of Württemberg* he was writing that state power belongs exclusively to the monarch. Whenever he was speaking about the bodies of authority, they were merely officials of the ruler, acting on his behalf.[1247] A state ruled by monarchical principle means primacy and the highest value of the ruler's will, possessing all the state power. No action may be taken in it without the consent of the ruler or its officials.[1248] Von Mohl did not, however, directly support an absolute monarchy or even a despotic state. In his view monarchical

---

1243 E.-W. Böckenförde, *Recht, Staat, Freiheit, Studien zur Rechtsphilosophie, Staatstheorie und Verfassungsgeschichte*, Frankfurt am Main 1992, p. 278.

1244 A. Biefang, A. Schulz, *From Monarchical Constitutionalism to a Parliamentary Republic; Concepts of Parliamentarism in Germany since 1818*, [in:] *Parliament and Parliamentarism A Comparative History of a European Concept*, P. Ihalainen, C. Ilie, K. Palonen (eds.), New York Oxford 2016, p. 64.

1245 D. Willoweit, op. cit., pp. 283–284. It is worth remembering the already mentioned Friedrich Julius Stahl, who was one of the main theorists of the monarchical principle. About the so called monarchical principle: M. Bożek, *Władza ustrojodawcza w niemieckim konstytucjonalizmie monarchicznym*, [in:] *Tendencje rozwojowe myśli politycznej i prawnej*, M. Maciejewski, M. Marszał, M. Sadowski (eds.), Wrocław 2014, pp. 291–295.

1246 Later, of course, it evolves towards a parliamentary monarchy.

1247 W. Pauly, op. cit., p. 73.

1248 R. v. Mohl, Staatsr.Württem.1.1829, p. 175. Similarly: Idem, Staatsr.Württem.1.1840, p. 185. Interestingly, in the second edition of this work, von Mohl allowed the monarch to be a woman, albeit in exceptional cases only.

power is subjected to limitations, most of which are the consequence of the very idea of rule of law. In other words, its powers are broad, but they are exercised within the framework of an act or acts of constitutional nature.[1249]

Advocating a monarchical system (with representation of the nation) is one of the scholar's most solid and well-grounded views. Despite the fact that he distinguished and even analyzed various other political forms (above all democracy), he will always see the most advantages in the monarchy. Von Mohl argued that the highest value of the monarchical system was a consequence of historical experience. So, despite the seeming irrationality in form of entrusting the conduct of all affairs in the state to one person, he also noticed that the most developed peoples of the world live under this form of government (although he did not mention Americans, for example).[1250] Still the fact, that he opted for a monarchical system should not bewilder us, after we analyze the very concept of state power in von Mohl. The undoubted advantages of the monarchy were the strong concentration of power, its uniformity and efficiency of operation. In scholar's opinion, an individual will always rule faster and more effectively than a collegial body. Nevertheless, he was not an uncritical supporter of the monarchy, because he saw the potential risks arising from entrusting the controls of the governance in the state, and the fate of the nation to one person. Importantly, these risks did not lead the scholar to reject the idea, but to try to find institutions protecting the monarchy against abuse by the ruler.[1251]

It should also be concluded that the advocacy of a monarchical system resulted from the scholar's general aversion to democracy. He saw specific and significant drawbacks of entrusting the rule of state to a number of individuals. According to von Mohl, collegiate bodies are, to a much greater degree, characterized by jealousy and personal conflicts, which destabilize them. The view associated with disagreement with universal suffrage is also the belief that few people in the state have the required knowledge to manage their affairs in a fair way. Moreover, differences of opinions, which may even be so deep that they will render the solution of an issue impossible, are also an indispensable element of collegiate bodies. In addition, one should not forget that collegiate bodies stay in sessions for a long time and the scholar finally concluded: "no collegiate body

---

1249 Idem, Staatsr.Württem.1.1829, pp. 175–176.

1250 Idem, *Encyklopädie der Staatswissenschaften*, Zweite Auflage…, p. 351.

1251 Ibid, p. 352. It is also worth remembering that von Mohl was in favor of hereditary monarchy comparing it to the electoral monarchy, as a form that has historically proved its uselessness: Ibid, p. 621.

will ever approve of great and new thoughts, because their majority is usually occupied by mediocrity."[1252]

When we analyze the position of the head of state in the concept of Robert von Mohl, we will see the belief of its superior position. On the other hand, however, the scholar was in favour of creating such institutions in the state that would protect citizens against abuse of power on its part; bad will, lack of legal knowledge, etc.[1253] Therefore the representative monarchy is the form of political system which, according to von Mohl, could ensure, on the one hand, the efficiency of exercise of power by its strong centre, and, on the other, the protection of citizens against abuse, e.g. through the right of veto in certain situations, or the monarch's duty to consult his decisions with the representation of the nation.[1254]

The summary of the analysis of the concept of state power in Robert von Mohl's thought should start with the statement that it forms an example of variations within German liberalism. There is no doubt that the division of state power, but also its responsibility, are considered to be one of the crucial postulates of classical liberal thought. For von Mohl, the concept of state power is a reflection of the very understanding of state. The scholar was in favour of a strong state, with broad competences to interfere in the affairs of its citizens. The concept of both uniformity and irresponsibility of state authority is just a consequence of this mental attitude.

As already mentioned, power in the state was indivisible for von Mohl. The scientist, convinced of the need for a strong, uniform state, feared that the division of power would weaken it, and perhaps even trigger anarchy in the state. It also seems that the fear of losing the homogeneity of the state resulted from his fear of returning to feudal relations, when the unity of decision-making centres was barely achieved.[1255]

The concept of the irresponsibility of state power requires special emphasis. Mohl's postulate that the head of state should not only be irresponsible for its actions, but also that it should be able to take extraordinary actions in the event of special circumstances, clearly shows similarity to the concept of a "state of exception" by the 20th-century scholar, Carl Schmitt.[1256] His concept of a state

---

1252 Ibid, pp. 616–618.

1253 Idem, Staatsr.Württem.1.1829, p. 183.

1254 Ibid, pp. 183–184, 194–195.

1255 H. Schmitz, op. cit., pp. 105–106, E.-W. Böckenförde, *Die Theorie der Gewaltenteilung*, [in:] E. Mass, P.-L. Weinacht, *Montesquieu-Traditionen in Deutschland*, Berlin 2005, p. 157.

1256 M. Rysiewicz, *"Gdy prawo ustaje i wkracza siła..." Stan wyjątkowy w myśli prawnopaństwowej Carla Schmitta*, "Dialogi Polityczne" 13/2010, pp. 82–87.

of exception also provided for the possibility for the sovereign to suspend the provisions of applicable law, in the event there was need to defend higher-order interests (including stability of the state).[1257] There is no doubt Mohl's justification for this institution can be considered rational. The idea is for the state authorities to be able to take appropriate measures to avoid greater damage that could occur if it were inactive. It should be remembered that von Mohl required the exceptional actions of the head of state to be accepted by the representative body as soon as possible, which was to form a safeguard.[1258]

The concept of irresponsibility of the head of state should be considered to be unfair and not meeting the standards of 21st century power. This idea is against the principle of equality of all citizens before the law. According to it, the head of state should also be responsible (before the same law). The head of state should be understood more as a body, not being an authority in itself, but only its executor. This position requires that it is held responsible on the same terms as the rest of the citizens.[1259] One should agree with the view that von Mohl confused the state authorities, as such, with its representatives. Representatives of state authority (head of state) must be responsible for their actions. On the other hand, the very essence of power must rely on its possession of means enabling effective achievement of the goals, for which it was established.[1260]

Referring now to the concept of the head of state, we must admit that Adam Bosiacki was right, when he defines it as a modern concept, with connections with the concept of royal power in Benjamin Constant, but also the concept of the so-called "Guardian of the constitution" in Carl Schmitt.[1261] There is no doubt

1257 T. Buksiński, *Trzy teologie polityczne Carla Schmitta*, "Filozofia Publiczna i Edukacja Demokratyczna," T. III, Nr. 1, 2014, p. 27.

1258 R. v. Mohl, SVuP.2.1. pp. 624–625. H. Hamacher, op. cit., p. 69.

1259 H. Schmitz, op. cit., p. 119.

1260 Ibid, pp. 104–105.

1261 A. Bosiacki, *Robert von Mohl i początki koncepcji państwa prawnego...*, pp. 325–326. More on this subject: Idem, *Polski klasyczny liberalizm. O recepcji liberalizmu w polskiej myśli politycznej pierwszej połowy XIX w.*, "Studia Iuridica Lublinensia," vol. XXV, 3, 2016, pp. 114–115. A. Sylwestrzak, *Władza Trzecia "Neutralna,"* "Zeszyty Prawnicze UKSW," vol. 11, nr 4 (2011), p. 38. Creating his concept of decisionism Carl Schmitt stated that "Souvereign is he who decides on the exception." For Schmitt, like for von Mohl, the state was a primary factor neutralizing chaos and social conflicts. It takes a central place in his political ideas. However the idea of decisionism is often viewed as a negation of the *Rechtsstaat*. C. Schmitt, *Politische Theologie: Vier Kapitel von der Lehre von der Souveränität*, München und Leipzig 1934, p. 11. K. J. Kaleta, K. Koźmiński, *Charakter władzy suwerennej w koncepcjach*

that in von Mohl the notion of the head of state has a wide meaning range. It can consist of one or more people. However, a comprehensive analysis of his views makes it necessary to state that when he is talking about the head of state, he was primarily thinking of monarchs. He was in favor of a rule of law in form of a monarchy, in which the ruler remains the owner and disposer of all state power. In addition, an analysis of the beginnings of von Mohl's work allows us to qualify him to the group of scholars supporting the then version of German constitutionalism. He accepted both the divisions, which often gave rise to conflicts, between the government and the representative body, advocating uniformity of power and rejecting parliamentary rule.[1262] As will be demonstrated, von Mohl later advocated monarchy, albeit with a parliamentary system.[1263]

5.2. Parliamentary representation and its role

To complete the picture of the concept of power in Robert von Mohl, as described in the previous subsection, we should pay attention to one more issue that is present in the work of this thinker. We are talking about the problem of introducing parliamentary governments in accordance with the so-called "representation" (*Repräsentation*) principle. The analyzes made by von Mohl, and the solutions proposed by him, perfectly match the political and social climate of the German area of mid-nineteenth century, which was marked by, inter alia, the struggle of the emerging middle class for political subjectivity. Therefore, before we discuss the postulates put forward in this regard by the German thinker, it is worth to attempt a brief description of the ideological climate accompanying him in the formulation of his proprietary proposals.

The beginnings of the nineteenth century in German states were characterized by the lack of specific actual conditions that would facilitate the development of parliamentary-representative form of government. Above all, there was a lack of a uniform state organism, and a strong sense of national unity, which, as demonstrated earlier on the example of France or, above all, England, were factors that stimulated the development of the abovementioned system of government.[1264] When we compare these to its western neighbors, the middle class

---

ładu konstytucyjnego Hansa Kelsena i Carla Schmitta, "Filozofia Publiczna i Edukacja Demokratyczna," T.II, 2013, N. 2, pp. 82, 155–156.

1262 U. Bermbach, op. cit., p. 355.

1263 H. Schmitz, op. cit., p. 84.

1264 H. Brandt, *Landständische Repräsentation im deutschen Vormärz*, Berlin 1968, ps. 33. It should be mentioned that in the 19th century in German-speaking area, it became increasingly popular not to draw example from France but to refer to England in the

and the bourgeoisie were underdeveloped, and were just beginning their political emancipation (which was to result, inter alia, in the introduction of parliamentary governments). On the other hand, the nobility and the aristocracy were stagnant, and lacked the ambition to introduce political changes.[1265]

According to the monarchical rule mentioned above, the vast majority of power in German states belonged to kings and princes. So neither the revolutionary patterns flowing from France (which, as noted earlier, evoked fear rather than admiration), nor the period of so-called "Sturm und Drang" permeating the entire German cultural circle, were able to threaten the actual monopoly of monarchic rulers.[1266] Situations in which German kings or princes had to pact with the people were scarce, although their existence cannot be denied. In some of the state-related affairs they thus had to cooperate, consult or even obtain permission of representative bodies. This was due to the idea of representation that had been spreading since the late 18th century, whose popularity and development depended on the strength of the bourgeois strata in the respective state in relation to the absolute monarchy. For example, depending on the state, the monarch had to accept the influence of representative bodies on tax legislation.

In the first half of the nineteenth century the idea of representing the people in the German area was accomplished by the establishment of assemblies called *Landsstände*. These representative bodies adopted a bicameral system, where the upper house consisted of aristocrats, representatives of elites, churches, universities as well as persons appointed by the monarch. The lower house included representatives of the city bourgeoisie and landowners. The tasks of *Landsstände* was by no means legislation (the legislative initiative was in the hands of the government, while they could only advise or propose appropriate regulations). However, they had an impact on tax matters in the form of so-called

---

search for suitable models for parliamentary governments. This resulted in the appearance of analyzes of the English parliamentary system (for example by Friedrich Christoph Dahlmann). Robert von Mohl also contributed to German thought in the field of analysis of parliamentary systems. It is worth remembering that von Mohl criticized German thinkers for their exaggerated admiration for French thought.: HHF Eulau, *Early Theories of Parliamentarism*, "The Canadian Journal of Economics and Political Science / Revue canadienne d'Economique et de Science politique," Vol. 8, No. 1 (Feb., 1942), pp. 46–47. F.C. Dahlmann, *Die Politik auf den Grund und das Muss der gegebenen Zustände zurueckgeführt*, Bd. 1, Leipzig 1847, pp. 53–79.

1265 H. Brandt, *Landständische Repräsentation im deutschen Vormärz...*, p. 35.

1266 Ibid, p. 36.

Steuerbewilligung - approval of fiscal burdens. Pursuant to the liberal demands of the time, most German regimes envisaged the requirement to obtain the consent of a representative body in the event that the new law would interfere with property or civil liberties.[1267] It is also worth mentioning that the elections to such bodies were of a two-stage nature. That is, those entitled to vote in a constituency elected people (they can be called electors) and only those people elected the actual deputies. Dietmar Willoweit rightly notes that this picture of German early parliamentarism still captured its aristocratic character. Land ownership, not the urban bourgeoisie, still dominated, and the significance of the representative body itself was limited.[1268] In view of the above, it must be stated that in the German states of the first half of the nineteenth century, dualism was growing, slowly transforming into a conflict between the monarch and the representative body. The government did not have parliamentary legitimacy, it was dependent and appointed by the monarch all the time, and the principles of ministerial responsibility were also introduced. Therefore we can state that most certainly parliamentarism functioned as a political postulate, but it was not a reality.[1269]

Over time this dualism intensified, to become one of the most important political issues of most German states at the time. It must be remembered that in their constitutions from the first half of the nineteenth century, the government and representative bodies were strictly separated. As already mentioned, all power remained in the hands of the monarch, which was manifested, for example, by the lack of influence of representative bodies on appointing of ministers. Representative bodies, whose role in the understanding of the German doctrine was only to defend the rights of citizens against violations by the monarch and the government, naturally became opposition bodies in relation to them. The constitutional practice assumed rather constant rivalry, a struggle between the governmental factor (omnipotent monarch) and the parliamentary

1267 D. Willoweit, op. cit., pp. 282–283.

1268 Ibid, p. 282. It is also worth remembering that in early German liberalism the parliament was understood as an assembly of the nation's elite. A typical representative, therefore, was usually a man of intelligence, education and material status. The assembly was to be a body composed of the best and the wisest, it was certainly aristocratic in its character. This were also features of the Frankfurt Parliament, where there were, for example, many representatives of universities present.: U. Karpen, op. cit., p. 69.

1269 Ibid., p. 70.

one (the people). The abovementioned conflict-raising dualism is one of the main characteristics of early German parliamentarism.[1270]

There is no doubt that the views of Robert von Mohl on issues of the parliamentary system and representation not only evolved, but also reflected the historical context and spirit of those times.[1271] An analysis of the concept of a German scholar leads to the conclusion that at the beginning of his scientific and journalistic path he was inclined towards the abovementioned monarchical principle. This is further evidenced by his views expressed in the *Constitutional Law of the Kingdom of Württemberg* and the *Responsibility of ministers in monarchies...* At the beginning of his activity, von Mohl was a supporter of the monarch's political domination and saw the role of the representative body solely in the protection of civil liberties.[1272] In von Mohl's opinion, legislation and jurisdiction were not enough to protect the people from abuse by the ruler. They were also too weak, when confronted with the majesty and position of the head of state (monarch).[1273] Therefore, it was the role of an assembly of elected deputies, at least on the early stages of von Mohl's work, to prevent the monarch from violating citizens' rights. It was the exclusive function of this body. Therefore, the monarch should not be significantly constrained in exercising all power in the state. Thus, according to the monarchical principle, all power was to be in the hands of the ruler, and the representatives of the people were only to have the ability to protect the population against unconstitutional initiatives of the governing.[1274] The aforesaid view finds its perfect illustration in the following quote:

> "There is no question of any co-governance of the people, of their participation in state power, or of the separation of any part of it from the state. This is not altered by the fact that in individual cases, namely in legislation and tax matters, people's representatives are to be asked for their consent first."[1275]

1270 H. H. F. Eulau, op. cit., pp. 44–45. H. Boldt, op. cit., p. 88. U. Karpen, op. cit., pp. 70–71.

1271 About von Mohl views on parliamentary issues also: E. Angermann, op. cit., pp. 388–448.

1272 U. Scheuner, op. cit., p. 26. E. Angermann, op. cit., p. 394.

1273 R. v. Mohl, Staatsr.Württem.1.1829, pp. 451–452. Similarly: Idem, Staatsr. Württem.1.1840, p. 532.

1274 Ibid, p. 535. Von Mohl will often refer to parliamentary bodies as "Security Measures" (*Sicherungsmittel*) for citizens' claims against the state.: B. Granzow, op. cit., p. 96.

1275 R. v. Mohl, Staatsr.Württem.1.1829, pp. 453–454. Similarly: Idem, Staatsr. Württem.1.1840, pp. 532–533.

At an early stage of work, von Mohl can even be considered a supporter of the dominant dualism, preserving of the *status quo*. The monarch is to hold all power, and parliamentary representation can only limit it, where it would violate the rights of citizens. It is clear that he wanted to preserve the unity of state power, and thus also its great strength and speed of action. Therefore, the position of Württemberger was at first fundamentally opposed to the then liberal trends, which were calling for the widest possible assurance of parliamentary representation participation in state governance.[1276] He was rather part of the dominant view in Germany at the time, stating that the role of the representative body was to protect the rights of citizens without transferring the power to govern the country to it. Advocating the *status quo* at the time does not mean that von Mohl did not see the issue of dualism on the monarch-parliament line. This is also the source for his support for the concept of the responsibility of royal ministers before parliament as a kind of security valve for resolving legal and political conflicts.[1277]

These initial beliefs began to lose strength and evolve over time. This is evidenced by the views of von Mohl expressed in the book *Responsibility of ministers in monarchies*.... Despite the fact that von Mohl was always in favor of the aforementioned traditional dualism on the line between the monarch and the representative body, he began to doubt whether this state of affairs could be maintained for any longer. Although he did not explicitly postulate the parliamentary system yet, he was right to see the disadvantages of the dualistic system, manifesting itself primarily in the increase of social tensions. At this stage, however, he could not find a solution to this problem.[1278] Robert von Mohl noticed that the representative monarchy seemed to be a "middle class" system. In view of the apathy of the aristocracy and the working masses, who did not yet have a common goal, he appeared as a representative of the so-called "middle class" ("*Mittelstand*"). It is also important that von Mohl draws attention to the

---

1276 H. Boldt, pp. 235–236.

1277 Ibid, p. 239.

1278 R. v. Mohl, *Die Verantwortlichkeit der Minister in Einherrschaften mit Volksvertretung, rechtlich, politisch und geschichtlich entwickelt*..., pp. 4–5. K. v. Beyme, *Einleitung*. . ., p. XXX. Years later, referring to this work, von Mohl finds that it was imperfect due to the novelty and incomplete understanding of the subject matter it concerned.: R. v. Mohl, *Lebenserinnerungen von Robert von Mohl 1799–1875*, Bd. 1..., pp. 269–270. U. Scheuner, op. cit., p. 26. K. v. Beyme, *Geschichte der politischen Theorien in Deutschland 1300–2000*. . ., p. 325. Idem, *Einleitung*. . ., p. XXIX. H. Brandt, *Landständische Repräsentation im deutschen Vormärz*. . ., pp. 243–244.

shortcomings of the parliamentary system, which, in his opinion, are manifested by clashes between parties and frequent changes of government. It is clear, how the great a proponent of uniformity, stability and strength of the state was the German scholar. Every time, and also in the case of the parliamentary system, he attempted to emphasize all its features that may result in instability of the state organism.[1279]

Another, very important step in the process of evolution of von Mohl's views on issues of representation and parliamentarism was brought by the publication of the article *On different compisition of the representative system in England, France and Germany*,[1280] in which we witness a clear fascination with the system of British parliamentarism. In the 1840s the thinker will initiate a slow process of moving away from the previously presented views, towards a clear admiration for the British system, and advocating a parliamentary system.[1281] However, before we go on to present von Mohl's perception of the model prevailing in England, it is first worth getting to know his views regarding the systemic relations prevailing in German area at the time.[1282] This is important because it will provide us with a contrasting background for the positive assessment of the English system.

As far as parliamentarism in Germany is concerned, we will find nothing but criticism from von Mohl. It will not be an exaggeration to state that he perceived the contemporary condition of German parliamentarism as tragic, and significantly different from its English, but also the French counterpart. The features of the German system included not only the strong conflict between the government and the representative body (which did not unite for the purposes of the state, but rather appeared as natural opponents), but also inappropriate staffing policy in ministries or pettiness of parliamentary debates. The excessive

---

1279 R. v. Mohl, Staatsr.Württem.1.1840, pp. 534–535.

1280 Idem, *Ueber verschiedene Auffassung des repräsentativen Systems in England, Frankreich und Deutschland*, "Zeitschrift für die gesamte Staatswissenschaft," Bd. 3, H. 3, 1846, pp. 451–495.

1281 H. Boldt, op. cit., p. 246.

1282 As far as France is concerned, for von Mohl it formed and intermediate example, located between the extreme dualism of parliament and government functioning in Germany and their total fusion in England. Despite the fact that he generally assessed the French system positively, he criticized the excessive influence of the government on elections or too little restriction of electoral rights.: K. v. Beyme, *Geschichte der politischen Theorien in Deutschland 1300–2000...*, p. 326. R. v. Mohl, SVuP.1, pp. 48–49.

influence of the government (monarch) on the organs of representation, weakness and insufficient education of the public, or uncertainty of citizens' views were, for von Mohl, the typical features of parliamentarism in German states. It is worth noting, however, that in the scholar's opinion this state of affairs was not the fault of the "lesser ability" of the Germans as a nation to introduce a parliamentary system. He was inclined to see the causes for that in the state fragmentation of the German area, and the resulting feudalization of actual conditions, to a greater or lesser extent.[1283] Already after the Spring of Nations, the scholar will further strengthen his view, considering the Germans as a nation of educated people, having respect and a sense of law, as well as a calm and patient disposition, which resulted in the belief that it was not in the German mentality that the reasons for the failure of the parliamentary system lay.[1284]

Against the background of a very critical analysis of relations prevailing in Germany, the thinker's delight over the contemporary parliamentary system of England will become even clearer. Analyzing the British parliamentary representation system, the scientist distinguished its most important features, which, as it turns out later, he will later advocate. The basic characteristic and advantage of the English system was the fact that it did not feature dualism, and therefore hostility and competition between the government and parliamentary centre.[1285] For von Mohl, the advantage was that the government always enjoyed parliamentary support or originated from it. The scholar stated:

> "The Ministry [government - author's note] is nothing more than a collective commission of both chambers, formed of the most outstanding and influential members of majority, but it is never an opposing force or one acting against the parliament, hatched from the individual will, and views of the ruler. With the decisive change in the majority, the ministry also changes, so there is always agreement between the decisive factors of power, although naturally, the struggles between the majority and the minority can be forceful."[1286]

The fact that the "ministerium" [government- author's note] was nothing more than the "executive committee" of the two chambers, seems to be the most important advantage of the British system in the view of von Mohl. It is now clear how much the German scholar has become an opponent of dualism. Only

1283 Ibid, pp. 50–64.
1284 Ibid, pp. 382–383.
1285 U. Bermbach, op. cit., p. 355.
1286 R. v. Mohl, SVuP.1, p. 35.

the appointment of a government from a parliamentary majority, as is the case in England, seemed to be a solution to this problem for him.

On the basis of an article written in the mid-nineteenth century, it can be stated that another extremely important feature of the British system was for von Mohl the fact that the parliament did not play a "negative" role, i.e. that of protecting citizens' rights against violations by the government, only. The scholar drew attention and seemed to accept that the position of monarch in the English system was no longer dominant, and that it often had to accept ministers, who did not match its personal views.[1287] What formed another important feature of British parliamentarism was, for the German liberal, that the parliament (and thus the government) found support in the major groups of English society, which was dominated by the numerous and, what is also important, politically aware, so called middle class.[1288] Therefore, one should agree with Peter Pulzer that, in his characteristic of the parliamentary system of United Kingdom, von Mohl managed to capture its most important features. The thinker recognized the dusk of the rule of kings, the merger of the legislature and the executive (a strong combination of government and parliament), reliance on the prevailing middle class or strong public opinion as the crucial elements of English parliamentarism.[1289] In his positive valuation and admiration for the British system of governance we see a clear departure from his beliefs voiced a decade earlier.

It is worth adding that the Mohl's assessment of the British system is part of the trend in German science, which at that time was looking at England in search of reform patterns. It should be remembered, however, that while von Mohl, speaking of England, noticed the advantages of its system and advocated (albeit in a later period only) their introduction in Germany to overcome systemic dualism, there were thinkers, for example Friedrich Julius Stahl, who literally did the opposite. In 1845, in his work *The Monarchical Principle* (*Das monarchische Prinzip)*, Stahl made a similar analysis of the British system, but found that it was essentially useless and not applicable to German conditions.[1290]

1287 Ibid.

1288 Ibid, p. 36. The concept of the "middle estate" (German *Mittelstand*) can now be compared to the concept of middle class.

1289 P. Pulzer, *Responsible Party Government in the German Political System*, [in:] *Party Government and Political Culture in Western Germany*, H. Döring, G. Smith (eds.), London and Basingstoke 1982, p. 10. On the evaluation of the English system by von Mohl: Ibid, p. 10, U. Bermbach, op. cit., pp. 355–356.

1290 K. v. Beyme, *Einleitung...*, p. XXXI. H. Brandt, *Landständische Repräsentation im deutschen Vormärz...*, p. 245, D. Jörke, M. Llanque, *Parliamentarism and Democracy in german Political Theory since 1848*, [in:] *Parliament and Parliamentarism*

To sum up this part of the discussion, it should be stated that von Mohl's support for the British system was in fact support for a the state adopting such a system, which would meet social needs.[1291] The scholar noticed that the systemic dualism between the government, monarch and representative organs could not remain unresolved for long periods, as it would threaten modernization and development.[1292]

Von Mohl will reach the apex of his parliamentary concepts after the Spring of Nations (in 1852), with the publication of article entitled *The representation system, its shortcomings and remedies. The political letters of an old liberal.*[1293] Despite the fundamental failure of the idea of parliamentarism in Germany (the failure of the Frankfurt Parliament, as indicated in chapter one), von Mohl did not turn his back on supporting this form of government. What's more, in his 1852 article he argued more strongly for the introduction of this system and outlined how it should look.

The scholar's criticism of dualism prevailing between the government and parliament is constant throughout all periods. According to the German scholar, this unsatisfactory condition was the consequence of two causes, firstly the rejection of the parliamentary system of government (in favor of the monarchical principle) and the "false shape of representative bodies." False that is, such that failed to reflect the actual image of society.[1294] First of all, von Mohl meant that MPs were not elected on the basis of the interests they were supposed to represent, but on the simple principle of population. As we will demonstrate, von Mohl was in favor of introducing representation on the basis of social groups, i.e. the election of deputies, who were to represent, for example, the interests of landowners, craftsmen and burghers.[1295] There is also no doubt that Mohl's assessment of the system prevailing in German states was sharper than six years earlier. He assessed the persistent and even deepening dualism between the monarchical government and parliament as a negative, or even threatening.[1296] In order to

---

A Comparative History of a European Concept..., s. 263–264, W. Boldt, op. cit., p. 175. More differences between the Stahl and von Mohl concepts: E. Angermann, op. cit., pp. 402–303.

1291 H. Brandt, *Landständische Repräsentation im deutschen Vormärz...*, p. 246.

1292 U. Bermbach, op. cit., pp. 355–356.

1293 R. v. Mohl, *Das Repräsentativsystem seine Mängel und die Heilmittel. Politische Briefe eines Altliberalen* "Deutsche Vierteljahrs Schrift" Drittes Heft 1852, pp. 145–235.

1294 Idem, SVuP.1, p. 405. K. v. Beyme, *Einleitung...*, p. XXXIII.

1295 Ibid, p. XXXIV.

1296 R. v. Mohl, SVuP.1, pp. 29, 386.

describe options for the development of the systemic situation (evolution of dualism), he used the metaphor in the form of an antithesis: "Corruption or parliamentary government" ("*Corruption oder parlamentarische Regierung*").[1297]

Von Mohl noticed that the aforementioned dualism lead to a situation, in which the government (monarchs and individual ministers) wish the representatives that support them (are pro-government) to sit on the representative body. This resulted in frequent interference by the government in elections to representative bodies, so that in effect they would be favorable to it. Von Mohl called this situation "corruption."[1298] According to the Württemberger the "system of corruption" was a situation in which the government attempted, by all means, to win the support of the majority in parliament. The desire to maintain unity of power (government and parliament) led to an increase in social discontent. As a result, the Parliament represented not the interests of citizens but that of a narrow group of rulers. This socio-political situation, in von Mohl's views, meant that only the voluntary limitation of power on the part of the ruler (on a parliamentary-constitutional basis) was able to save the monarchy as a system, which he was a supporter of.[1299]

What we notice in this period, is also the pessimism in the scholar's attitude. The thinker mentioned false, even utopian hopes that a cordial agreement between the prince and the people would ever be reached. Despite the existence of the constitutional norms, which were to guarantee peaceful coexistence of these factors, the dispute was not to be resolved.[1300] According to von Mohl, it was difficult to talk about safeguarding citizens' rights. Toxic conflicts have emerged in the states, with frequent hatred of the government and monarch, and injustice against individuals. He considered a rule consistent with the monarchical principle as dangerous, especially for the institution of the monarchy itself. Its unlawful, and often immoral actions to gain influence on parliamentary bodies were to cause ever greater hatred of citizens towards the government. According

---

1297 K. v. Beyme, *Einleitung...*, p. XXXIII. Idem, *Repräsentatives und Parlamentarisches Regierungssystem: eine begriffsgeschichtliche Analyse*, "Politische Vierteljahresschrift," Vol. 6, No. 2 (Juni 1965), p. 156.

1298 R. v. Mohl, SVuP.1, p. 395. H. Boldt, op. cit., pp. 249–250. By "the system of corruption" von Mohl understood a situation in the state, in which the unity and omnipotence of state power is maintained by its representatives at all costs, even at the price of direct and indirect bribery of parliamentarians and the increase in public dissatisfaction: R. v. Mohl, SVuP.1, p. 398.

1299 B. Granzow, op. cit., p. 95.

1300 R. v. Mohl, SVuP.1, pp. 385–386.

to the scholar, this state of affairs could not continue in a longer run, ending up with a downfall.[1301]

Thus, von Mohl had a clear statement that once the injustice of the "corruption system" was proven, the only remedy was to introduce a parliamentary system. The parliamentary system understood the German liberal as such a system, in which the government would each time be elected among the parliamentary majority and commanded by its leaders.[1302] The government would rule according to the line of a dominant majority, which would ensure agreement between it and the parliament.[1303]

It should be remembered, however, that von Mohl's support for the introduction of a parliamentary system did not mean his departure from the monarchy. The scholar was still a supporter of hereditary monarchy, the prince, in his thoughts, was the holder of state power all the time, and his consent was required for many government activities, e.g. legislation. The monarchical ruler personified the state in von Mohl's conception, and represented it in external relations. However, it still had to act in harmony with the parliamentary majority in its rule, and its interests or personal view could not be dominating.[1304]

The views of von Mohl from the mid-nineteenth century allow us to classify him as a resolute opponent of the monarchical rule proposed by Stahl, which was not to meet the spirit and needs of time.[1305] The Württemberger was in favour of limiting the role of the monarch by the parliamentary body. He consciously agreed to a large limitation of the monarch's systemic position in the state, saying: "This limitation is large. What's more: it should be large (...)."[1306] According to von Mohl, the state could no longer be governed by the monarch's personal views, but instead, by the program of the parliamentary majority.[1307] The monarch must therefore agree to limit its will.[1308]

Before discussing the parliamentary system proposed by Robert von Mohl, it is worth taking a moment to understand the very meaning of the concept of representation in the state, especially since it was parliamentary representation that was to form the mean to overcome the aforementioned dualism.

1301 Ibid, p. 399.
1302 Ibid, pp. 395, 400–401.
1303 H. Boldt, op. cit., p. 250. More: D. Jörke, M. Llanque, op. cit., p. 264.
1304 R. v. Mohl, SVuP.1, pp. 381, 401.
1305 Ibid, p. 403. D. Jörke, M. Llanque, op. cit., p. 264.
1306 R. v. Mohl, SVuP.1, pp. 403–404.
1307 Ibid, pp. 403–404.
1308 Ibid, p. 404. H. H. F. Eulau, op. cit., pp. 48–49.

In the definition of the scholar, representation is:

> "(...) Representation or substitution within the meaning of the state is such an institution, through which some or all of the subjects secure their impact on the affairs of the state, with the agency of smaller number of representatives appearing in their name.."[1309]

The task of representation is to protect both the state and citizens from bad governance that could arise in the event of direct participation of all those entitled to make decisions. Therefore this time the postulate of the stability of the state is implemented through a system of representation, which in the scholar's view is to protect against barratry and chaos.[1310] In addition, the task of representation is to exert influence, so as to protect the rights and interests of citizens in the state.[1311] The representative system enables the state to gain an organ allowing it to obtain knowledge about the interests and life goals of the nation, which means that its institutions can also support them.[1312] For the scholar the two of the most important tasks of representation were first of all governance, and second, protection of the rights of subjects against violations by the government.[1313] It should be concluded that von Mohl departed from his earlier views on the role of the representative body in the state. Now its tasks include not only the protection of rights, but also participation in governance. Nevertheless we should remember, and read it as a non-liberal postulate, that von Mohl saw no need for the parliamentary representation to be elected by all members of the nation.[1314] Therefore, for von Mohl the concepts of representation and sovereignty of the people and universal suffrage were not inseparable. What's more, he found limitation of electoral rights to be more practical (as discussed further in the next subsection).[1315]

According to the German liberal, professional knowledge and commitment of the members of the assembly were one of the most important determinants of proper performance of its function by the representative body. Whether members of the parliamentary assembly will represent such traits cannot be entrusted to chance, and their abilities must be taken into account in the process

---

1309 R. v. Mohl, SVuP.1, pp. 8–9.

1310 Idem, *Encyklopädie der Staatswissenschaften*, Zweite Auflage..., p. 237. B. Granzow, op. cit., p. 99.

1311 R. v. Mohl, SVuP.1, pp. 12–13.

1312 Ibid, pp. 21–23. B. Granzow, op. cit., p. 100.

1313 R. v. Mohl, SVuP.1, p. 26.

1314 Ibid, p. 10.

1315 K. v. Beyme, *Geschichte der politischen Theorien in Deutschland 1300–2000...*, p. 325. Idem, *Politische Theorien im Zeitalter der Ideologien 1789–1945...*, p. 195. B. Granzow, op. cit., pp. 99–100.

of regulating the electoral system. According to von Mohl, the most likely occurrence of these features will be come to fruition whenever the personal interests of deputies will be linked to the very rights and interests they are to represent. Then they will not only hold adequate knowledge of specific problems, but also enthusiasm to solve them, or to defend specific solutions. It should be noted that, what von Mohl presents here is the criticism of the then political practice of Germany, in which he distinguished two types of deputies: opponents of the government or its supporters (usually officials dependent on it or those who wished to become them).[1316]

According to the scholar there are three types of interests and rights the defense of which should be vested in representative bodies. These were the rights that concerned the organized unity of the entire nation, the rights that concerned specific, larger or smaller groups of citizens, and those that concerned only individuals. The shape of the parliamentary assembly must take into account the existence of these interest groups in modern society, of course in a proportionate manner.[1317] The task of deputies is to represent and defend these interests.[1318] It should also be remembered that von Mohl opposed the geographical division of constituencies. He believed that the geographical criterion would not correspond to the real structure of interests in society.[1319] His criticism of the geographical criterion for the division of constituencies was also based on the belief that there was no way to find the right number of people representing a sufficiently high level of knowledge (enabling reliable exercise of a mandate). According to von Mohl, this meant that representatives from geographically divided constituencies were divided according to a single criterion only. As already noted, they were either supporters or opponents of the government.[1320] The scholar was thus in favor of the criterion of representing a particular interest as appropriate for the electoral system.[1321]

On the other hand, in order to operate satisfactorily (help in achieving life goals), the state should have knowledge about the demands and needs of specific social circles. The social circle in the state should therefore be given the opportunity to have its own representative body, and the number of these representations should be determined by the actual conditions in the state. However, the existence

1316 H. Brandt, *Landständische Repräsentation im deutschen Vormärz…*, pp. 250–251.
1317 R. v. Mohl, SVuP.1, pp. 408–409.
1318 U. Bermbach, op. cit., p. 357.
1319 R. v. Mohl, SVuP.1, pp. 411–412.
1320 Ibid, p. 409.
1321 Ibid, p. 412

of such a circle is determined by the existence of a specific, permanent common interest connecting specific individuals.[1322]

In the von Mohl concept, the representative system should consist of three types of representative assemblies.[1323] First, "special assemblies" ("*Sondernvertretungen*"); whose task would be to protect and represent the rights of individual, significant social circles. These bodies would only consist of members of that particular social circle and be convoked on a regular basis. In these assemblies of a corporate nature, positions were to be determined within specific groups of interest. Von Mohl also provided for their cooperation in the legislative process and possible protective measures to prevent unlawful initiatives of the general assembly.[1324] Secondly, "collective assemblies" ("*die zusammengesetzten Vertretungen*"). In von Mohl the scope of their activities was similar to that of "special assemblies." The only difference was that they were only to be convened when a case affecting more than one social circle occurred. Only representatives from the respective "special assemblies" would participate in these assemblies. These bodies would only be convoked when required. And thirdly, the "general assembly" ("*Gesammtvertretung*"), consisting of representatives elected from all the "special assemblies." In this general assembly members would no longer appear as representatives of their particular social circle, but as representatives of the entire nation, subject to a free mandate.[1325] The exclusive competences of the general assembly were foreign affairs (including deciding on war and peace), political affairs, organization of state administration, matters of budget, or army. They were also the protection of civil rights, justice system and legislation.[1326] The general assembly also had the right of veto over the legislative proposals of the remaining assemblies.[1327]

1322 Ibid, pp. 413, 416.

1323 Ibid, p. 417.

1324 Ibid, p. 418.

1325 Ibid. p. 417. G. Leibholz, *Die Repräsentation in der Demokratie*, Berlin, New York 1973, pp. 189–190. It should also be noted that von Mohl was in favor of the concept of "free mandate." He believed that this type of representation is more appropriate for practical reasons, as it facilitates reaching a consensus in parliament. If the actions of elected representative do not gain the support of voters, these should not elect such a representative again, after he served his term.: R. v. Mohl, *Encyklopädie der Staatswissenschaften*, Zweite Auflage…, pp. 241–242, K. v. Beyme, *Einleitung*…, pp. XXXIV-XXXV.

1326 R. v. Mohl, SVuP.1, p. 418.

1327 H. Brandt, *Landständische Repräsentation im deutschen Vormärz*…, p. 252.

As already mentioned, the basis for election of "special assemblies" would be communities of interests, primarily of a material nature. The Württemberger distinguished three large basic circles of these. The first, centred around material interests, consisting of representatives of landowners, entrepreneurs, merchants, but also hired employees. The second should gather representatives of "spiritual interests" ("*geistigen Interessen*"), church people, artists, scholars, and government officials. The third and last circle of interests was based on "territorial coexistence." The interests of municipalities and other territorial units were to be represented here by their representatives.[1328]

Another evidence of von Mohl's inclination towards the British system is the special role he attributed to the opposition in the parliamentary system. According to the thinker the very existence of opposition was natural, and also important for the state. Its activities should help to manage the affairs of the state in a rational way. For von Mohl, due to the constant possibility of changes in the parliamentary majority, the opposition will have to be constantly ready to take responsibility for the affairs of the state, which will lead to its professionalization. One can see here a clear reference of the scholar to the institution of "his/her Majesty's Most Loyal Opposition" from United Kingdom, and thus another confirmation of the influence of Anglo-Saxon thought.[1329]

Despite the fact that von Mohl never opposed the parliamentary system of government, over the years he began to notice, more and more - as the time went by, of its shortcomings and actual conditions that inhibited its introduction in Germany.[1330] The ideas of von Mohl, despite being appreciated in the field of German science, were never taken into the political practice of any of the states. Prussia's strong position in the unification process led to the strengthening of the monarchy's position towards its independence. The German theory moved rather towards the domination of the monarch over the representative body, in order to prevent dualism which von Mohl also opposed.

Therefore von Mohl's scepticism concerning the possibility of introducing parliamentary governments in Germany along the lines of the English model, becomes more visible over time. The 1860s and the end of the scholar's life demonstrate his growing acceptance and adaptation to the existing political

1328 U. Bermbach, op. cit., p. 357. H. Brandt, *Landständische Repräsentation im deutschen Vormärz…*, p. 251.

1329 R. v. Mohl, SVuP.1, pp. 400–402. B. Granzow, op. cit., p. 94, H. H. F. Eulau, op. cit., p. 49.

1330 Ibid.

conditions. At that time, the scholar could be counted among those of the moderate liberals, who accepted the status quo. As Bismarck's former opponent von Mohl seemed to accept the policy of the Iron Chancellor.[1331] Looking at the functioning of the Reich, and earlier Prussia, and revising his views, von Mohl noticed that a monarchical system could also function together with a government that was not elected by the parliament. So he no longer clung to the view of the necessity of introducing a parliamentary system of government for the survival of the monarchy.[1332]

Few of von Mohl's views have undergone such a large and complex evolution as the problem of parliamentary representation in the state. From his acceptance of the *status quo*, and thus the insignificant role of the parliament, through its gradually increasing position, to the final resignation accepting a state of affairs, which was different from that proposed by him. There is no doubt that the proposal of the parliamentary representation system created by the thinker in the mid-nineteenth century must be considered both original and a complicated one. It can be accused of excessive fragmentation (up to three levels) or questioned whether representatives of particular interest groups will be able to act as representatives of the entire nation in the general assembly. On the other side von Mohl can be undoubtedly credited with searching for an exit path from the impasse and the negative situation of the German states of the mid-nineteenth century. Von Mohl, who after all remained in favor of maintaining the monarchy, tried to find a way to save it by introducing reforms just in time to prevent radicalization. He wanted to halt democratic aspirations, avoid the republican system, and reconcile the monarchy and the middle class again.[1333] It should be remembered that in 1848/49, as a minister, von Mohl had the opportunity to observe the imperfections arising from democracy and that Germany, as a whole, was not ready for it yet. Despite the failure of the parliamentary system in the fight against the monarchy, he still remained in favour of the representation system and propagated it in many of his writings, creating his own concept of what it should look like.[1334]

This made von Mohl to turn to the system of the then United Kingdom, advocating parliamentarism in its English version. He argued for the election of a

1331 H. Boldt, op. cit., pp. 234, 260–261. E. Angermann, op. cit., p. 91.

1332 H. Boldt, op. cit., p. 261.

1333 H. Brandt, *Landständische Repräsentation im deutschen Vormärz...*, pp. 252–253. U. Bermbach, op. cit., p. 358.

1334 R. Piloty, *Das Parlamentarische System. Eine Untersuchung seines Wesens und Wertes*, "Archiv für Rechts- und Wirtschaftsphilosophie" Vol. 11, No. 1 (1917/1918), p. 66.

government from a parliamentary majority, which was to result in the end of the systemic dualism. The monarch in von Mohl's concept was to symbolize the unity of the state, and represent it outside. Of course, it still had to accept the policy pursued by the parliamentary majority. For von Mohl, the most important advantage of the parliamentary system was undoubtedly the agreement that prevailed not only between the government and parliament, but also between the government and the people (whose representatives were sitting in the parliament).[1335] It seems legitimate to conclude that such an understanding of the monarch's position composes well with the concept of the head of state presented earlier. It was supposed to be the highest standing entity in the systemic hierarchy, but it had to agree its policy with the parliamentary majority. Therefore, the position of the monarch in the Mohl's approach to parliamentarism also resembles the present-day systemic position of the British monarch.

It is also worth noting that in the concept of the parliamentary system by von Mohl it is not difficult to find many of its main and previously presented ideas. First of all, the focusing on individual social groups and their interests, which should implement them in the field of representative bodies.[1336] That is why it was so important to present the concept of society as a series of communities based on common interests. Getting to know the cited concepts of society makes it easier to understand the views on representation.

Therefore we should emphasize the pragmatic concentration of the thinker on community of interest, as the factor that plays the main role in the parliamentary representation system. The scholar stayed away from metaphysical statements referring to the representation of the "entire, invisible" nation, in favor of a pragmatic, realistic reconciliation of the concept of representation with the reality prevailing in the state.[1337] What was most important, according to him, was to identify the groups of interest within the society and secure them their parliamentary representation. This made von Mohl an opponent of geographical or quantitative criteria for determining the panel of the representative body. What was to be represented in it, were - first of all - the circles of interest functioning in the society.[1338] However, as we already mentioned, in the modern Germany that was united for the first time in history, the parliamentary system proposed by von Mohl, although commonly known, was not introduced. Once again,

1335 U. Bermbach, op. cit., pp. 356–357.
1336 U. Scheuner, op. cit., pp. 27–28.
1337 K. v. Beyme, *Einleitung...*, p. XXXI.
1338 H. Brandt, *Landständische Repräsentation im deutschen Vormärz...*, p. 250.

accepting the *status quo* at the end of his days, von Mohl abandoned his earlier ideas, never to return to them.[1339]

5.3. Assessment of the phenomenon of democracy and issues of electoral rights

Democracy was perceived by Robert von Mohl as one of the possible forms of rule in the legal state. An analysis of the scholar's views in this regard demonstrates that he was, if not an opponent, certainly a sceptic, when speaking of democracy. We will find confirmation of von Mohl's scepticism regarding the democratic system (people's rule) in his disagreement with the idea of universal suffrage.

In the Württemberger's doctrine, representative democracy was the youngest kind of rule of law in the historical sense.[1340] We should take note of his opposition to those views, which treated democracy as the sole system possible for the rule of law. The political form was secondary for him, the most important was choosing it so that the state could adequately satisfy the needs and allow for implementation of life goals by individuals. He also objected the view that democracy was the only human "worthy" system, stating: "For a reasonable person it is worthy to always select the best means to achieve its goals, and if necessary give up part of its freedom if this is a condition of achieving a more important benefit."[1341] The above quote confirms the scholar's pragmatic approach. What was important were not the abstract rights, but for the state to support the citizen in an efficient manner, even at the price of limitation of its freedoms. According to the scholar, democracy was an extremely imperfect form of government, in which the undoubted advantages are outweighed by the irreparable drawbacks. Von Mohl considered democracy to be a system based on "mediocrity" (*Mittelmässigkeit*). In the context of our further considerations on the issue of electoral law, it should be stated that the scholar referred primarily to the intellectual mediocrity of citizens. The additional drawback of democracy was to be its excessive dependence of the government (and thus the state) on elections, which formed the characteristic of the system, after all.[1342] In von Mohl's views

1339 U. Scheuner, op. cit., p. 28. Interestingly, this system was only introduced in Germany 58 years later, and as part of a republican system.: W. Kaltefleiter, *Die Funktionen des Staatsoberhauptes in der parlamentarischen Demokratie*, Köln und Opladen 1970, p. 190.

1340 H. Schmitz, op. cit., p. 82.

1341 R. v. Mohl, *Encyklopädie der Staatswissenschaften*, Zweite Auflage…, pp. 342–343.

1342 Idem, SVuP.1, p. 387.

on the democratic system, we can again see the fear of demagoguery, the exploitation of various social issues to achieve short-term electoral benefits, and thus the fear of destabilization of the state.[1343]

Democracy was something very uncertain for the German liberal, a kind of Pandora's box that should better remained closed. It thus prevented the functioning of permanent and stable governance in the state. Referring to the relations in Germany at the time, he argued that the introduction of a democratic system would, in his view, lead to "communism," which he identified with unlimited and disorderly rule of the masses. Remembering that the phrase about "communism" appeared in von Mohl after the Spring of Nations experience, we should also stress his fear of the working masses exploiting a democratic system. A specific opposition to democracy was only reinforced by von Mohl's conviction that the introduction of this system would not automatically solve social problems, and therefore the underlying causes of people's dissatisfaction.[1344]

Thus, one can see his opposition to the perception of democracy as a system, the introduction of which would eliminate the disadvantages of the monarchical system.[1345] The scholar is further characterized by his perception of the dangers arising from democracy, as characteristic of the then German liberal trend, as more dangerous than the vices that the monarchy undoubtedly possessed. Especially in the second half of the nineteenth century, critics of democracy and gender equality among German liberals will intensify, as clearly manifested in their dislike of universal suffrage.[1346] On the other hand, it should be remembered that von Mohl did not fundamentally reject democracy. Despite all the flaws, he accepted this system as one of the possible forms acceptable for the rule of law. He even stated that the representative democracy faced "great future," at the same time attempting to find ways to corrects its flaws.[1347]

In the doctrine of von Mohl, one of the measures to overcome the disadvantages of democracy, which for him was the instability of government caused by electoral struggles, was to create a stable party system, based on British standards. The concept of political parties appeared relatively late in his thought, i.e. in the second half of the 19th century and it seems to be a creative development of the

1343 As an example, the scholar gave was the contemporary issue of slavery in the USA.: Ibid, p. 388.

1344 Ibid.

1345 Ibid, p. 389.

1346 U. Rosenbusch, *Der Werg zum Frauenwahlrecht in Deutschland*, Baden-Baden 1998, p. 242.

1347 H. Schmitz, op. cit., pp. 84–85.

already described idea of social circles. Von Mohl could not be counted to the opponents of the existence of political parties in the state, because he believed that their functioning was conditioned by the facts and the form of government.[1348] In the scientist's definition, a "state party" means:

> "(...) all those who want to give the state authority a certain direction, introduce appropriate conditions and institutions, but finally, depending on the specific system, either take over the rule in a lawful manner, or at least exert a certain pressure on it."[1349]

The formation of the parties was, for von Mohl, conditioned by the ability of citizens to participate in the management of the state.[1350] In the context of the revolutionary movements of the time, one should raise the scholar's postulate that parties cannot oppose the foundations of the state system. Therefore, the principle of (political) parties is to accept the constitutional foundations, on which the state is based.[1351] In von Mohl, therefore, one can see the formation of political parties in society, and secondly, an attempt to construct their position in the state and the party system in such a way, that they do not threaten the stability of the government. Hence the demand for compliance of party programs with the constitutional principles of the state system. Referring to the situation in Germany at the time, according to the scholar, political parties should accept both monarchy and the civil liberties acquired.[1352] In our analysis of the Mohl's concept of "state party" we must conclude that, in many places, it meets its contemporary definitions. "Giving authority a certain direction" can be equated with the possession of a specific program by a political party in today's understanding. Also, the goal of taking over governments or exerting certain pressure on them

1348 R. v. Mohl, *Encyklopädie der Staatswissenschaften*, Zweite Auflage. . ., p. 652.

1349 Ibid, pp. 649–650.

1350 Ibid, p. 650. One should not forget about von Mohl's liberal view regarding the representation of minorities in a state. For the scholar it was unwise to ignore, whether in parliament or in general in the state, the attitudes and views represented by minorities. He was in favour of securing their rights. Such action was primarily aimed at reflecting the actual socio-political relations in the state, and refers to the structure of parliament. Ibid, pp. 242–243.

1351 Ibid, p. 651.

1352 At the same time it is worth noting that the party situation in Germany at that time did not gain the scholar's approval. He criticized both reactionary, democratic and liberal currents. He opposed both the democrats attacking the monarchy, as well as the reactionaries wishing to destroy the systemic foundations of the state. He was also not found of his contemporary liberals, who became so-called negation party, criticizing only the government's strong position.: B. Granzow, op. cit., pp. 95–96.

is consistent with the element of "gaining power and maximizing position in the political system" raised today.[1353] On the other hand, what von Mohl did not raise strongly, were the factors constituting the political party today, such as its organized structures and social support.[1354] We should also emphasize the postulate of von Mohl that a party should implement goals in a manner consistent with the law in place of its operation.

In von Mohl's opinion, for a party system to have a positive impact on the state and its system, it must be stable. Hence the two-party system postulate, based on the British example. The party system in the state should therefore operate on the basis of the existence of two strong parties with established positions. One of them would rule, while the other would remain ready to take over the ruling at all times.[1355] There is no doubt that in this aspect one can again see the concern and postulate to order democracy, that is to say that it should not have a destabilizing effect on the state.[1356] Unfortunately, the political reality of Germany at that time, as described in the first chapter, provided von Mohl with abundant evidence that the introduction of a two-party system, patterned on the British one, would be simply impossible there.[1357] In addition, Prussian imperialism, in which there was no room for party pluralism, influenced the process of creating the party system of Germany.

One of his most explicit views, demonstrating the eclecticism and somehow selective character of Robert von Mohl's liberalism, was his opposition to universal suffrage. The issue of universal suffrage was not widely discussed in Germany until the Spring of Nations revolution. Prior to it the introduction of modern constitutions and the limitation of monarchical absolutism were all considered more significant issues.[1358] In most German states, the indirect electoral system dominated, and the electoral law strengthened the privileged position of the possessing classes.[1359] With the rise of revolutionary sentiment, the issue of universal suffrage was increasingly discussed. Various positions

---

1353 W. Sokół, *Partia polityczna*, [in:] *Encyklopedia politologii*, t.1. . ., p. 453.

1354 Ibid, p. 453

1355 B. Granzow, op. cit., p. 95. More on today's understanding of the concept of a party system: W. Sokół, *System partyjny* [in:] *Encyklopedia politologii*, t.1. . ., p. 653.

1356 K. v. Beyme, *Einleitung...*, pp. XXXVIII–XXXIX.

1357 Ibid, p. XXXIX.

1358 W. Gagel, *Die Wahlrechtsfrage in der Geschichte der deutschen liberalen Parteien 1848–1918*, Düsseldorf 1958, p. 7.

1359 The most liberal electoral law functioned in Württemberg and Bavaria, where over 2/3 of men over 25 holding citizenship could vote: A. Biefang, A. Schulz, op. cit., p. 63.

were represented, from conservative views supporting the feudal electoral law, through electoral law limited by status, to the postulate of universal suffrage.[1360]

Representatives of German liberalism, coming to a great extent from the middle class, faced the following dilemma: either the threat of putting an end to the dominance of the so-called "middle classes" (*Mittelstände*) in parliament by allowing the masses to participate, or speaking in favour of limitation of electoral rights. There is no doubt that German liberalism has a lot of merit in the struggle for citizens' rights, but it certainly cannot be credited with fighting for full equality of all members of the nation. As Walter Gagel notes, that there was equality before the law did not determine equality of political rights at all. Therefore, universal suffrage was not seen as the natural right of citizens, but as a political, state right and as such limited by status.[1361] Moderate German liberalism was in favour of limiting electoral law. The main fear of German liberals was that they believed that the lower classes of society were too susceptible to influence and therefore threatened by populism and demagogy. Therefore, postulates of limiting political rights, in particular electoral law, appeared in the doctrines of German liberal thought. What became the main concept thereof was the so-called "independence" (*Selbstständigkeit*) of a citizen, who was to make political choices. The concept of independence, social independence (primarily in terms of property), was the key word of the bourgeoisie, applied not to allow the masses to rule. In the liberals' opinion, only the upper classes were able to make political decisions independently.[1362] As already signaled, the lower classes, whose vulnerability to influence was the main argument of the liberals against granting them electoral rights, were most certainly not independent. In the eyes of many of them (including Karl Theodor Welcker) universal suffrage could pose a threat to the freedoms guaranteed under the new German constitutions.[1363]

1360 W. Gagel, op. cit., p. 7. The events of the February 1848 revolution in France also resulted in a new wave of popularity of the idea of universal suffrage: Ibid p. 8. More about the issue of electoral law in German areas in the 19th century: A. S. Kahan, *Liberalism in Nineteenth-Century Europe. The Political Culture of Limited Suffrage*, New York 2003, pp. 50–65, 67–77, 93–101, 141–152.

1361 W. Gagel, op. cit., pp. 10–11.

1362 Ibid, pp 9, 11. K. Klotzbach, *Das Eliteproblem im politischen Liberalismus*, Wiesbaden 1966, pp.96–97.

1363 W. Gagel, op. cit., pp. 9–10. Negative effects, of "plebiscite caesarism" from the times of Napoleon I, were also feared, in form of a system largely based on a special kind of relationship between the monarch and the people, bypassing parliamentary bodies.

Robert von Mohl's views on universal suffrage should be considered as in line with the mainstream of moderate German liberalism. Throughout his life the scholar remained an opponent of universal suffrage. What is also characteristic is the scholar's identification of universal suffrage with a democratic system.[1364]

The most important concepts related to universal suffrage appear in von Mohl already after the Spring of Nations. His views clearly demonstrate the then liberal conviction of the aristocratic nature of electoral law, democracy and parliamentarism. Regulations regarding electoral law were one of the most important in representative democracy for von Mohl.[1365] First of all, the scholar argued for the participation of only those citizens, who have an appropriate level of knowledge about the activities they undertake. Thus, he excluded from the universal electoral law not only the persons, who did not have an adequate level of knowledge, but also who did not lead their lives in accordance with generally accepted principles of morality (for example, prodigals).[1366] According to von Mohl, citizens who (according to the canon of German liberalism at the time) were unable to make independent decisions, could not hold the right to vote. Von Mohl included, *ex definitio*, also women, mentally ill, and those unfit, prodigal, "private servants," minors, and what is very important, also those receiving social support from state budged, to such persons.[1367]

Von Mohl, like Alexis de Tocqueville, treated participation in elections (and thus in the management, administration of the state), not only as a right but also as a duty. He even accepted coercing the citizens to execute this right.[1368] So he did not understand the right to vote as inherent, resulting from the nature of human rights, but rather as an obligation that everyone capable of doing so should exercise.[1369] The scholar believed that experience, good will and independence of

1364 K. v. Beyme, *Politische Theorien im Zeitalter der Ideologien 1789–1945...*, p. 197.

1365 R. v. Mohl, *Encyklopädie der Staatswissenschaften*, Zweite Auflage..., p. 344.

1366 Ibid, pp. 237–240, 344. It is worth noting the critical assessment formulated by von Mohl and concerning the then prevailing electoral system in the Kingdom of Württemberg, which he himself considered too liberal, allowing too many citizens to make political decisions, many of whom did not hold the required qualities to make them. Idem, SVuP.1, pp. 334–335. B. Granzow, op. cit., p. 103.

1367 R. v. Mohl, *Das deutsche Reichsstaatsrecht. Rechtliche und politische Eröterungen...*, p. 342.

1368 Idem, *Encyklopädie der Staatswissenschaften*, Zweite Auflage..., p. 335. More about the views of Alexis de Tocqueville: M. Tracz-Tryniecki, *Myśl polityczna i prawna Alexisa de Tocqueville*, Kraków 2009.

1369 R. v. Mohl, SVuP.1, p. 43. Idem, *Das deutsche Reichsstaatsrecht. Rechtliche und politische Eröterungen...*, pp. 353–354.

views were all required to exercise this right, also understood as duty, in a proper manner. The electoral law should be structured so that these features dominate public decision-making.[1370]

It was clear to von Mohl that human nature means that one cannot expect rational choices from all the citizens. Not everyone had the necessary insight and skills to make decisions that would have a positive impact on the state.[1371] What we see in von Mohl at the end of his life is his increasing pessimism, further confirmed by his believe that only a relatively low number of citizens was capable of making "good choices." So he opposed the views he expressed earlier that there was "as much education" in the German nation as anywhere else. On the contrary, he saw that there were undoubtedly many gaps in political consciousness.[1372] We should also pay particular attention to another significant view of Robert von Mohl. He stated that the "barbaric" system of the state is the one in which "(...) the vote of the very first man in the state counts exactly as that of a common beggar, the vote of the most famous scholar does not mean more than that of an ordinary peasant, and that of a great industrialist does not count more than that of his hired hand."[1373] Based on the above statement, it can be concluded that the Württemberger advocated the domination and crucial influence of an educated middle class, in terms of exercising public functions and taking part in elections.[1374] In other words, the thinker turned towards a kind of electoral census. The criterion here was primarily to prove the citizen's maturity, "independence" and wisdom in life, for example by holding the appropriate education or property.

Another manifestation of fear of universal suffrage is his belief (not scarce in German liberalism) that this idea is incompatible with the parliamentary system. One can see the fear of the party fragmentation in parliament, resulting from universal elections, which would in turn destabilize the state.[1375] We should also notice the von Mohl's restrictions imposed on passive suffrage. The requirement that only people with appropriate qualifications can be allowed to be elected was for von Mohl the sole barrier against the catastrophic consequences of universal

1370 Idem, SVuP.1, pp. 334–335. Idem, *Encyklopädie der Staatswissenschaften*, Zweite Auflage. . ., p. 360. Idem, SVuP.2.1, pp. 21–22.
1371 Idem, SVuP.3.2, p. 719.
1372 Idem, *Das deutsche Reichsstaatsrecht. Rechtliche und politische Eröterungen. . .*, pp. 356–357.
1373 Ibid, p. 358.
1374 Idem, SVuP.3.2., p. 720.
1375 Ibid, p. 721.

suffrage. In other words, if everyone can elect, they should only elect from among those who guarantee the proper conduct of the affairs of the state[1376]

Speaking about universal suffrage we should also notice that he also distinguished the institution of the so called "universal plebiscite" ("*Allgemeine Abstimmung*") in form of a simple answer to a "yes" or "no" question concerning the most important issues in the state. In this case, contrary to his views concerning universal suffrage, von Mohl allowed for the widest possible participation of citizens, provided only that they had legal capacity (*Rechtsfähigkeit*) to do so. However, he continued to exclude women, criminals or the mentally ill from that institution. The difference from the idea of universal suffrage was the lack of the requirement of independence described earlier, which results in the admission of, for example, proletarians.[1377]

The conclusions resulting from the above considerations can only be the following: von Mohl didn't support democracy, and as such he fits perfectly into the mainstream of German moderate liberalism. He saw rather a threat, than any benefits, in the institutions of universal suffrage, and the democracy itself. He identified this idea with socialists, and gave it a negative overtone. He feared the demagogization of politics, resulting from the economic issues of that time, and of granting political rights to the masses and the poor, which was inevitably to lead to anarchy and the collapse of the state.[1378] Limiting the electoral law, especially in relation to the proletariat (so that it does not win the majority) makes von Mohl a typical representative of German liberalism of that time. The ability to vote, the electoral law were treated by the scholar as not a right vested in every human being, but a specific "public function" that required appropriate qualifications from its holder. The possibility of voting is therefore a kind of "mission" that the citizen must fulfil, while taking care of the common good.[1379]

1376 Idem, SVuP.1, p. 28. Idem, *Encyklopädie der Staatswissenschaften*, Zweite Auflage…, pp. 240–241.

1377 Idem, SVuP.2.1., pp. 295–296, 302.

1378 K. v. Beyme, *Einleitung...*, p. XXXVI. U. Bermbach, op. cit., p. 356. M. G. Schmidt, *Demokratietheorien*, Wiesbaden 2006, p. 176.

1379 D. Jörke, M. Llanque, op. cit., p. 264. U. Rosenbusch, op. cit., p. 245.

Conclusion

Work Summary

Summary and evaluation of the content thereof, as appropriate for an ending of a scientific work, in this case on the vision of state by Robert von Mohl, should begin with the statement that he was a thinker of the times of breakthrough. Throughout his life there were processes of great changes in the mentality, politics and economy of German society and states. Undoubtedly, therefore, the life of Robert von Mohl falls on one of the most interesting times in German history, lasting from the fall of the First Reich to the creation of the Wilhelminian Germany.[1380] The decline of absolutist rule, the search for a new understanding of the role of the state in people's lives, and finally the industrial revolution meant that the old order was passing away, paving the way for more or less liberal aspirations. So, like Saint Augustine or Dante Alighieri, von Mohl stands in his perception of the state between epochs in thought related to it.

This is demonstrated by the ideological attitude of the scholar himself, as highlighted in the monograph. Being open to new thought currents and proclaiming the idea of *Rechtsstaat* emerging from the "liberal trunk," von Mohl did not reject, in an a priori manner, the achievements of the past. He tried to select what was right from the absolutist concept of the police state. So he attempted to combine his positive values with the liberal, then modern postulates of the rule of law.

As we proved, Robert von Mohl can certainly not be included in the group of scholars who only worked in the sphere of theory. In parallel with his activities at the university, he developed public activity, whether as a deputy (including the Frankfurt Parliament) or as a diplomat. The abovementioned contact with political reality and actual problems related to the state should also be considered crucial for von Mohl's creation of his own visions. This is readily evident in relation to the issues he researched. It covers most of the then vividly discussed issues. We are talking here not only about the role of the state, and the idea of the rule of law, but also about the formation of societies, the emergence of nations, and issues of organization of public administration or parliamentary representation. All these issues were studied by von Mohl, drawing on theoretical achievements and practical experience, which often led him to evolution or

1380 K-P Schroeder, op. cit., p. 135.

change of his views. One cannot ignore the fact that in his work von Mohl always relied on thorough research. As proven, on the example of the concept of society, the scholar based his conclusions on a prior, in-depth examination of the views functioning in relation to the respective issue.

The purpose of this work was to demonstrate Mohl's perception of the state in a comprehensive manner. Also, the scholar himself tried to make every of his views constituting the idea of the state coherent with others and building a complete and logical picture. The starting point here seems to be a reflection on the question: how should modern state (as for the conditions at the time) look like, corresponding to a sufficiently high level of population development?

We find the confirmation of the thesis stating that von Mohl applied in-depth analyses in his scientific work, in his basing of idea of the state on the conclusions drawn from research on the human individual. As part of this work, we proved the thesis that von Mohl's state was an entity created to help people achieve their life goals. That is why it was very important, from the viewpoint of accomplishment of goals of the present monograph, to analyze the beliefs of the scholar concerning the individual and the social circles. Von Mohl, particularly at the early stage of his life, understood the lives of human individuals through the lens of individualism and diversity. Initially, it even led him to the conclusion that it is impossible to classify people's life goals. It wasn't until later that, when expanding his definition of the state based on empirical observation, von Mohl was able to separate the group of the most common goals of individuals' lives. It should be concluded that this was related to the extension of the definition of the state by the scholar. Over the years, it has been receiving increasingly complex tasks, including the task of supporting the goals of human life. The introduction of their classification proves, once again, von Mohl's attempt to build a consequent and consistent perception of the state. If the state was to support the goals of human life, they had to be defined. It should be remembered, however, that the scholar never imposed on the individual his scheme of importance of achieving life goals, although he considered it to be the closest to the ideal. Von Mohl also presented the idea of individual spheres of human life. Their image proves that the thinker believed that the state was not an all-encompassing entity. On the contrary, the human individual had many other "spheres" outside of which it led its life.

Von Mohl was a precursor in many respects. Precursor activities also include his achievements in the field of the beginnings of German sociology. The Württemberger was one of the first scholars who noticed the so-called "social issue" (*Soziale Frage*) and initiated its analysis. He noticed changes in the social structure occurring in Germany in the 19th century, the formation of the proletariat, and the urban bourgeoisie. Activity in this area led him to create his original concept of society that is a collection of so-called "social circles." The example of the fact that he initially referred to the concept of estates of the realm in his analysis of social circles, and later changed them into the concept of "social circles" proves the evolution of his views and the adaptation of the conceptual apparatus to the changing reality.

Von Mohl also created a catalogue of principles that guided the process of social community formation. The most important of these was the occurrence, between individual members, of common interest (this factor also gained significance in the Mohl's vision of the idea of representation). Importantly, it did not have to be only an economic interest. The scholar noticed the influence of economic factors on people's lives, but was not limiting his thoughts to them. As indicated earlier, there is firm belief in German science, that von Mohl was the author of original discovery, and the precursor of the concept of society in German areas. An unquestionable contribution of von Mohl is the proclamation of the concept of society as a phenomenon standing outside the state, one can say between the sphere of the individual and the sphere of the state. It is worth noting, however, that von Mohl devoted little space to the issue of society in the early days of his work. The subsequent development of research in this area and the study of the independence of the state from society proves the development in von Mohl's thought.

Nevertheless, we cannot forget that the Mohl's idea of society and the vision of sciences of society, were marked by numerous ambiguities. From the scholar's terminological uncertainty about how to properly call society, to mechanical copying of the sciences of state scheme to the scheme of sciences of society (and finally admitting their imperfections, and abandoning them at a later stage of his activity). Thus, the idea of society is present in von Mohl, furthermore - it is something that is independent of the state, but it does not gain its final shape yet. Comparing his vision of society with the one presented by Heinrich von Treitschke is an action leading to the proper positioning of von Mohl on the ideological map of Germany. In contrast to von Mohl, Treitschke stood for the identity of the concepts of state and society, which was not present in von Mohl. Treitschke understood society through the prism of the state, and the spirit of the nation, which of course is missing in von Mohl. One can say that the Prussian understanding of the state and society collided here with the South German, liberal one. Both in terms of the concept of society and the system of sciences of society, von Mohl set new paths, broke old thinking patterns, but did not avoid errors and ambiguities. It seems that these are the direct consequence of the scholar's pioneering role in this field.

We find another confirmation that von Mohl's idea of the state was a comprehensive one in that the scholar built a complete, separate system of state sciences. His statement that it should contain "all state sciences and only state sciences" forces us to position him as a writer guided by their narrow and literal meaning. This approach is characteristic for the mid-nineteenth century authors of Germany. In addition to the theoretical assumption about the clarity of the argument and the proper presentation of the matter (i.e. the state in this case), von Mohl wanted to alter the system of state sciences in a way that they would be perceptible for the widest possible population - citizens (hence he turned his attention to encyclopaedic approaches, which he valued).

Württemberger's intention was to present the state from all possible points of view, so that his argument was complete. Therefore, when speaking about the state, in addition to dogmatic knowledge, he also presented historical knowledge (referring to facts). And in addition to the law, he also analyzed the state in terms of morality and politics. He was not afraid of references to the concepts of natural law. They gain concretization in the form of so-called "philosophical law," which was to supplement constitutional law (which, however, had the precedence over the former).

But not only law was important for von Mohl in the functioning of the state and its citizens. His observation of reality and empirical approach forced von Mohl to conclude that legal coercion could not enforce all actions required for the common good from the citizens. That is why von Mohl appealed to morality. He believed that every citizen should contribute to the implementation of the common good in a voluntary manner, resulting precisely from these needs and convictions of a higher nature. It seems that von Mohl replaced the factor of influence of religious norms (occurring, for example, in Stahl) with an abstractly understood morality. On the one hand, he opposed the influence of religion on the state, but on the other he was aware that statute law would not be able to regulate all possible facts. What we should note here is the similarity of postulates by von Mohl with the views of Leon Petrażycki. The latter has the idea of mutually complementary legal (imperative-distributive) and moral (unilaterally imperative) norms. What Petrażycki called morality concerned only the internal experiences (emotions) of the individual, and it did not give rise to absolute obligations towards another individual (as was the case with legal norms).[1381] Petrażycki said: "The appropriate debts (obligations) that form

1381 L. Petrażycki, *O nauce, prawie i moralności. Pisma wybrane*, Warszawa 1985, pp. 249–253. M. Kik, *Leona Petrażyckiego Filozofia Prawa*, "Czasopismo Filozoficzne," nr

bilateral relationships will be called legal relations. (. . .) Obligations which are free to others, obligations without a claim will be called moral obligations."[1382] Like von Mohl, Petrażycki believed that compliance with legal norms formed the necessary minimum. However, moral norms and the voluntary (by assumption) compliance with them were something right, yet additional for Petrażycki. He thus compared legal and moral norms to water and wine. So a man can function without wine, but not without water: "(...) ordinary water, from the standpoint of the universal economy of organic life is thus more important and valuable than even the best wine, even champagne >>."[1383]

Also, the distinction of politics (*Staatskunst*) as one of the first German scholars should be credited as an achievement of von Mohl. For him, politics was a field of state science dealing with rational ways of achieving the objectives of the state. The system of state sciences by von Mohl proves not only the scholar's strong tendency to systematize the scope of knowledge. It was also aimed at the thorough exploration of the state. It further demonstrates how strong were the theoretical foundations that von Mohl wished to base upon. It also proves that the centre of his reflection was the state, as evidenced by the expansion of this system to the realm of sciences of society.

In von Mohl one of the most extensive, if not the most extensive of them all, is the concept of state. The very analysis of its understanding within the so-called *Allgemeine Staatslehre* provides us a lot of valuable information. Unlike for Adam Müller, the state did not have a metaphysical dimension for von Mohl it was just one of the spheres of life among which the individual revolves during its existence. So he was alien to thinking about the state in a total sense, as an entity embracing the whole life of the individual. According to von Mohl, its

---

1, 2006, p. 56. B. Brożek, *Emocje jako fundament prawa. Uwagi o teorii Leona Petrażyckiego*, [in:] B. Brożek, J. Stelmach, Ł. Kurek, K. Eliasz (eds.), *Naturalizm prawniczy: stanowiska*, Warszawa 2015, p. 261.

1382 L. Petrażycki, *O Pobudkach Postępowania i o Istocie Moralności i Prawa*, Warszawa 2002, p. 44.

1383 Ibidem, p. 72. The separation of law and morality is characteristic of American realism, represented by Olivier Wendell Holmes Jr. E. Hunter Taylor, *H. L. A. Hart's Concept of Law in the Perspective of American Legal Realism*, "The Modern Law Review," vol. 35, No. 6 (Nov. 1972), p. 606. One of the fathers of American legal realism stated: "When I emphasize the difference between law and morals I do so with reference to a single end, that of learning and understanding the law. For that purpose you must definitely master its specifics marks, and it is for that I ask you for the moment to imagine yourselves indifferent to other greater things." O. W. Holmes, *The Path of the Law*, "Harvard Law Review," Vol. X. March 25, 1897, no. 8, p. 459.

genesis was the lack of power in the more primary spheres. Therefore, the sole entity possessing the power to provide people with an ordered life under the law was the state. The state appears here as one of the ultimate consequences of the development of human life circles. It is therefore a necessary complement to such spheres as family, tribe, etc.

The science of the genesis of the state in von Mohl's thought is based on empiricism, draws on historical experience, but also on slightly more abstract concepts. In von Mohl the state appears as a factor regulating and ordering people's lives. Von Mohl was far from considering only a single way for formation of a state as right and proper. He saw the possibility of creating it on the basis of a religious idea, although he did not consider it right. His liberalism is further evidenced by a reference to the concept of a social contract, which he associated with what he considered a modern rule of law. The view that the state is not supposed to replace other spheres of human life, but only supplement them and, if required, aid the individuals, should be considered liberal.

The very definition of state in von Mohl underwent evolution, which is noticeable when analyzing its individual dimensions from the earliest to the latest one. Initially, he perceived the state in a general way, did not give it special functions, primarily in the scope of guaranteeing assistance to individuals. The most elaborate concept of the state appears in the *Encyclopaedia...* it was there that von Mohl gave it the function of supporting individuals in their life aspirations. In many places, Mohl's perception of the state refers to the views of both earlier and contemporary thinkers. Making the goals of the state dependent on the level of development of its inhabitants, one can find the influence of Montesquieu, and we also see the concept of "collective will," the vision of "universal will" found in Jean Jacques Rousseau (the concept of collective will also appears in Karl von Rotteck). With Johann Caspar Bluntschli he shared the belief that guarding the legal order cannot be the sole objective of the state, and that there is need for inseparability of its territory and the influence of the national character on its shape. The proof of von Mohl's rooting in the Western European and liberal tradition is the comparison of his vision of the state with the one presented by Heinrich von Treitschke.[1384] While Treitschke perceived the state as the embodiment of the ethnic, national element, von Mohl saw in it rather as a tool for achieving community goals.

Willingness to strike a balance and find the golden mean is visible in von Mohl when we go on to analyze population and territorial relations in the state.

1384 Also on this subject: Duk-Yung Kim, op. cit., pp. 45–47.

The population should be relatively large, so as not to burden the state. Therefore, it should correspond to the territory of the state. All these factors were interrelated, but there was a single goal: to provide the state with the possibility of optimal development. The population factor was so important to von Mohl that he reserved the state administration the possibility of influencing population relations, so that they would not pose a threat to the state.

Von Mohl's pragmatism is undoubtedly demonstrated in his analysis of the issue of nationality. Remembering the times in which the scholar came to create, that is the period of the formation of the German national consciousness, the impact of language as recognized by von Mohl as one of the most important national factors, should be emphasized. Closely observing the reality von Mohl noticed the processes of national emancipation in German states. His lack of precise separation of the German concepts of *Nation* and *Volk* and the reference to the notion of a tribe, well reflect the terminological uncertainty and specific trembling that were characteristic for that period. The scholar was of the opinion that the state should respect the so-called "national facts" but it should certainly not respect them at all costs. This pragmatism of von Mohl is evidenced by the development of his perception of nationality issues. In the mid-nineteenth century, at the height of the German Spring of Nations, von Mohl devoted much attention to the "nationality factor" in the state, and even formulated a kind of catalogue of natural rights arising from the creation of nationalities. However, during the emergence of the Second Reich, he did not hesitate to say that the national rights of Poles and French simply cannot be respected and that the land occupied by the Empire cannot be lost to them.

The concept of state species, which constitutes the introduction to discussing the idea of the rule of law, is based, like most ideas in von Mohl, on thorough and thoughtful observation of historical reality. By pointing to individual species of states, such as the classical state in antiquity, theocracy, despotism or the patriarchal and patrimonial state, he created the foundations for his original concept of *Rechtsstaat*. All these species were less developed than the rule of law, and the people creating them were at a lower level of civilizational development.

For von Mohl the rule of law was therefore the species of state that occurred among peoples at the highest level of development. Like in Welcker, the *Rechtsstaat* was considered by the Württemberger a peculiar invention that responded to the demand and level of development of the nineteenth century, when it was already known that the feudal, absolutist organization of the state proved inefficient. The key assumption underlying the Mohl's *Rechtsstaat* idea was the belief in the servant role of the state in relation to the nation (understood as the general population of the respective state). For von Mohl, the objective of the rule of law was to ensure legal security and to support the population in achieving its life goals and the fullest possible development.

The Mohl idea of the rule of law finds its roots both in early liberal thinking of the state in Germany, and in the aspirations of the emerging German bourgeoisie. The basis here is the freedom of the individual, its free choice of life goals and their implementation. However, the task of the rule of law is to enable and support the individual in these activities. This happens firstly by ensuring legal order, and secondly by providing the individual with subsidiary assistance. The above comes down to von Mohl's understanding of the rule of law both through its formal and material aspects. The idea of subsidiary support for the individual by the rule of law deserves special emphasis here. Thus, the rule of law is to support the individual only when it is unable to cope alone, and it does not provide *a priori* suport, nor does it assume the responsibility of the individual for itself. Without any doubt, this idea is von Mohl's strongest link with the present, with the principle of a social market economy that also functions in Germany. In addition to individual freedom, there is also the postulate of the common good. Thus, individual freedom is not unlimited. Within it, there must be respect for the aspirations of not only other individuals but also for the abstract common good. It is also worth noting that the scholar's understanding of the rule of law coincides (especially in relation to its tasks) with his general understanding of the state. This makes it clear that von Mohl, when speaking of a state in general, actually referred to his vision of *Rechtsstaat*.[1385]

The rule of law of von Mohl is also based on a number of liberal principles. Civil liberties characteristic of this species are personal, economic and property freedom. The scholar also spoke about the freedom of religion, freedom of thinking, association and the citizen's right to lodge a complaint against the actions of authorities. We should emphasize the guarantee of freedom of association here. This idea is highly complementary to the vision of the role of the subsidiary legal state presented above. Therefore, the individual should firs seek help among various types of communities, before turning to the state for

1385 It should be mentioned that kind of similar to the *Rechtsstaat* was the specific concept of the "rule of law" developed in XIX-th century England by Albert Venn Dicey. English "rule of law" and *Rechtsstaat* were objects of many comparisons. There are many similarities between these two ideas, but the most important of them is the desire to secure the liberty of people and legal limitation of authorities. More: J. v. Orth, *Exporting the Rule of Law*, "North Carolina Journal of International Law and Commercial Regulation," Vol. 24, N. 1, p. 72. A. V. Dicey, *Introduction to the study of the law of the constitution*, Indianapolis 1982, p. 107–115.

support. The concept of fundamental rights vested in all citizens was characteristic of the then liberal German currents. On the other hand, the suspension between epochs and the specific selectivity of von Mohl's liberalism is evidenced by his concept of political rights. In contrast to civil rights, one had to prove their specific abilities to exercise them, manifested primarily in proving independence, and having a sufficiently high level of knowledge.

We find further evidence of von Mohl's reliance on experience and empiricism in his belief that, in addition to written law, also the custom and activity of courts can be the source of law in the state. One should also remember about the philosophical constitutional law and about the fact that von Mohl has not quite clearly defined the relationship between the written order and the whole of the aforementioned rest. There is no doubt, however, that the basis of the rule of law's activity should be the written law, which is subject to extensive analysis of von Mohl. The rooting of the scholar in liberal doctrine is further proved by his conviction that constitutional norms should be at the top of the hierarchy of sources of law. Higher-order norms, difficult to change and guaranteeing civil liberties, should protect citizens against arbitrary decisions of authorities. The "ordinary" act of law, standing lower in the hierarchy, should be an overall and general norm, and also a norm created in cooperation with the people. The postulate of the generality and universality of the act was also to fulfill the principle of equality before the law prevailing in the rule of law. In contrast, the relationship between an act and a regulation well illustrates the conflict between the monarch and the people at that time. The act of law, comprehensively regulating certain obligations of citizens, had to be created in consultation with the representation of the people. The regulation, being only an implementing act, could be issued by the monarch autonomously.

In the context of the features that should characterize "good" laws in the thought of Robert von Mohl, it is worth pointing out to the similarity of his views with what Luvois Fuller was saying about the so-called "procedural law of nature." According to this thinker, "good" and morality-based law should meet eight requirements. It should be based on general principles and avoid ad hoc settlements. It must be transparent and should be promulgated. Good law is also a non-retroactive law. The law should also be clear and avoid excessive detail. It must have internal coherence and consistency. What is similar to von Mohl is the prohibition of imposing impossible norms, hence the law must "be compliable with." It should also be characterized by the greatest possible stability and invariability. Finally, all public bodies should act in accordance with the law.[1386]

1386 L. L. Fuller, *Moralność prawa*, trans. S. Amsterdamski, Warszawa 1978, pp. 68–140.

Von Mohl also stated that the law should "follow" the level of nation's civilization. Therefore, the task of the state was to introduce such legal regulations that would enable its citizens to develop as freely as possible, and at the same time correspond to the level of development at which they were located. In this aspect, there is a similarity with the statements of Olivier Wendell Holmes, who said:

> "The law embodies the history of the development of a given nation over the centuries, and cannot be treated as if it consisted only of axioms and theorem sourced directly from a mathematics textbook. To understand it we need to know its past and take into account the direction, in which it seems to develop. In the process of interpretation, we must alternately take into account history and modern legal theories. (. . .) The essence of the law in every age is the adoption of solutions that are most helpful and useful, but its form and individual mechanisms, as well as the extent to which it is able to achieve the assumed results, depends, to a large extent, on its past."[1387]

As Marcin Kusaj rightly notes, in Holmes the law is to be a tool for accomplishing specific social goals. The law must therefore change along with the changing goals of the society.[1388] Holmes stated "A system of a law at any time is the resultant of present notions of what is wise and right on the one hand, and, on the other, of rules handed down from earlier states of society and embodying needs and notions which more or less have passed away."[1389]

Mohl's idea of the *Rechtsstaat* does not end with the statement that the rule of law should support its citizens. Von Mohl formulated the entire extended concept of the administrative apparatus and the principles of its operation for achieving this goal. He also tried to incorporate the idea of police, as known

---

More on Fuller's procedural law of nature: R. Tokarczyk, *Historia Filozofii Prawa w Retrospektywie Prawa Natury*, Białystok 1999, pp. 312–315. For more on the relationship between law and morality in Fuller: R. Tokarczyk, *Relacje moralności i prawa w doktrynie Lona L. Fullera*, Etyka 15, 1977, pp. 77–112. C. Murphy, *Lon Fuller and the Moral Value of The Rule of Law*, "Law and Philosophy" 2005, 24, p. 243. D. Luban, *The Rule of Law and Human Dignity: Re-examining Fuller's Canons*, "Hague Journal on the Rule of Law" 2, 2010, p. 31

1387 O.W. Holmes, *The Common Law*, London 1963, p. 1. After: M. Kusaj, *Narodziny amerykańskiego realizmu – Common Law Olivera Wendella Holmesa*, [in:] M. Sadowski (ed.), *Ze studiów nad prawem, administracją i ekonomią, Acta Erasmiana VI*, Wrocław 2014, p. 91.

1388 Ibidem, p. 92. E. Hunter Taylor, H. L. A. *Hart's Concept of Law in the Perspective of American Legal Realism*, "The Modern Law Review," vol. 35, No. 6 (Nov. 1972), p. 611.

1389 O. W. Holmes, *The collected legal papers*, Mineola, New York 2007, p. 156. M. R. Cohen, *Justice Holmes and the Nature of Law*, "Columbia Law Review," vol. 31, no. 3 (Mar. 1931), p. 360.

from the absolutist times, into the rule of law. That is why, in von Mohl, the police is supposed to act as subsidiary, within the framework of the law, and respect individual freedoms. Von Mohl also allowed departure from individual freedoms, and the use of coercion by the police, where the public interest would outweigh the particular interest.

We find the denial of classical principles of liberalism also when we analyze the idea of separation of powers in von Mohl. Unlike Karl von Rotteck, von Mohl opposed the separation of powers. He perceived it as a threat to the power of the state, and was in favor of a strong state. Hence the support and conviction of the need for a unified power, protecting the state against the possibility of falling into anarchy. By speaking so firmly and continuously against the concept of any separation of powers in the spirit of classical liberalism, von Mohl proved once again not only the uniqueness of his ideas, but also the "weakness" of whole German liberalism. The concept of irresponsibility of the head of state also constitutes a departure from liberal demands. Here, once again, we can see of what great value was the state itself for von Mohl. He allowed the authorities to act against the law in the event of a threat to vital state interests. The concept of uniformity of power and irresponsibility of the head of state is associated with von Mohl's inclination to support the monarchy. Later, this concept was supplemented with a parliamentary system with the role of a monarch similar to the British one.

The concept of the parliamentary system can be described as a constant search, by von Mohl, for the right way to heal the situation in Germany. To this end, he analyzed the British system, for which he spared no praise. In the process of evolution of views, von Mohl created an original system, but it was also a complicated one. It corresponded with the idea of social groups based on a community of interests that were to be represented at various levels of the parliamentary system. He sought ways to reconcile the monarch with the society. Did he present suggestions? Definitely. Were they right? It is not known because Germany has taken a completely different path. Von Mohl was certainly not a supporter of democracy, as he was afraid of it. He was afraid of demagogy and lack of education of participants in political processes. Therefore, he opposed universal suffrage. According to him one should prove sufficient knowledge to be allowed to participate in political decisions. These views, once again, classify von Mohl as a representative of German liberalism, referring to the so-called *Juste milieu,*[1390] the golden mean looking for a path between the demagogic rule of the crowd and the absolute power of the monarch.

1390 G. Dietze, op. cit., p. 548.

To sum up not only the conclusions contained in the ending, but also the entire work, it should be stated that the idea of the state of von Mohl can be considered characteristic of German liberalism. It undoubtedly refers to lofty ideas, such as freedom of individuals and limitation of power, but at the same time it is ready for far-reaching compromises. Fearing that the state would lose stability and the ability to fulfill its roles, it would even allow rejection of the idea of separation of powers. The idea of a rule of law is a good example of the aforesaid mode of thinking of von Mohl. It is based on the maxim that the state exists for man and not man for the state. It also aims to provide citizens with prosperity and freedom. On the other hand, it must be stable and strong, which means that it apply coercion to citizens. We should ask the question, whether von Mohl was a liberal? He was certainly a representative of German liberalism. As already mentioned, despite the general orientation on currents flowing from Western Europe, this trend was characterized by a great readiness to give up the most radical, liberal demands, which can clearly be seen on the example of the Württemberger Robert von Mohl.

The current value of the von Mohl views in the context of today's legal institutions in Poland and Germany.

We decided to divide the analysis of the relationship between the idea of the state in the thought of Robert von Mohl and contemporaneity into two areas. The first is to compare the rule of law and democratic rule of law adopted in the constitutions of Germany and Poland, respectively, with the understanding of the *Rechtsstaat* by von Mohl. We will be talking here first of all about the "axiological foundation" on which these states are based, shaping the state-citizen relationship and the fundamental rights of citizens in Germany and Poland relating to them. The second area of our comparison will take the form of an analysis of the social state clause and the state implementing the principles of social justice, as adopted in the basic laws of Germany and Poland, respectively. Their understanding will be compared with the concept of subsidiary support of citizens by the state in achieving their life goals, as present in Robert von Mohl.

Von Mohl developed his ideas regarding the state in times of revolutionary unrest in Germany. He witnessed the collapse of the order, which was exemplified by the notion of a police state and the emergence of a new order in which the individual (citizen) obtained a subjective position in relation to the state. As concluded earlier the characteristic feature of von Mohl's rule of law is that the individual held a whole set of rights that defined its position in the state, e.g. the right to associate or the freedom of expression.

There is no doubt that today the "Basic Rights" (*Grundrechte*) adopted in the German Constitution of 1949 have a similar dimension. Their importance for the entire constitutional order of Germany is demonstrated by their listin at the very beginning of the German basic law in the first chapter thereof. Undoubtedly, the reference to fundamental rights intended to protect citizens against abuse by the state was caused by the tragic experiences of the Third Reich.[1391] In the process of creating a constitution for West Germany at that time, reference was made to the liberal concept of *Rechtsstaat*. It was one of the ways of "authenticating" Germany at the time in the eyes of the Western Allies in the process of the so-called *Westbindung*. Therefore, two understandings of the *Rechtsstaat* concept were quoted. Firstly, in the formal sense as the implementation of the rule of law. Secondly (which seems to be more important) in the material sense, in which the *Rechtsstaat* was defined as an idea assuming the division of power in the state, the responsibility of the government before a representative body or the safeguarding of fundamental rights in the constitution.[1392]

Therefore, it should be assumed that the principle of the rule of law in Germany has both a formal and material dimension, resulting from the sum of regulations adopted in its constitution. We are talking primarily about articles 1–19, art. 103 section 2 or art. 97.[1393] It should be remembered, however, that the fundamental rights adopted in articles 1–19 do not form a closed catalogue. They must also be treated as a set of specific signposts setting out the principles of relations between the state and the citizen.[1394] The material dimension of the *Rechtsstaat* concept also results from the axiology on which the German constitution is based. It refers to the principles of human dignity, freedom and justice.[1395]

1391 J. W. Tkaczyński, *Prawo Ustrojowe Niemiec*, Kraków 2015, pp. 52–53. The Basic Law for the Federal Republic of Germany of 23 May 1949, source: *Basic Law for the Federal Republic of Germany*, transl. Ch. Tomuschat, Berlin 2019. All further direct references to the provisions of the German constitution are based on this source. More about the concept of "basic rights": M. Borowski, *Grundrechte als Prinzipien*, Baden-Baden 2007, pp. 499.

1392 B. Stöcker, op. cit., pp. 179, 258. D. Janicka, *Ustawa zasadnicza w praktyce Republiki Federalnej Niemiec (1949–1989)*, Toruń 2009, p. 132.

1393 Ibid, p. 97.

1394 J. W. Tkaczyński, op. cit., p. 85. There are also other rights indicated, not included in the first chapter, the so-called "Rights similar to fundamental rights, governed by art. 93 item 1 point 4a of the German constitution. We are talking, among others, about articles 101, 103 and 104. In addition, these are also the rights listed in art. 20, section 4, art. 33, art. 38. More on this topic: M. Bożek, *System konstytucyjny Republiki Federalnej Niemiec*, Warszawa 2017, p.39. One should also remember about fundamental rights on the basis of individual constitutions of the federal states. More on this topic: J. W. Tkaczyński, op. cit., pp. 53–57.

1395 M. Bożek, *System konstytucyjny Republiki Federalnej Niemiec*. . ., p. 27.

What is important from the point of view of the analysis of the rule of law, and the democratic rule of law, respectively, in the German and Polish constitutions are the provisions that introduce them. In Germany it will be art. art. 20 section 3, and in Poland art. 2 (we should also indicate art. 7 of the Constitution of the Republic of Poland, saying that "The organs of public authority shall function on the basis of, and within the limits of, the law," introducing the rule of law in formal terms).[1396]

With regard to the rule of law rule in the German basic law, it can be stated that it is a kind of "superior norm" from the applicability of which all other rules arise. We are talking about binding authorities with the provisions of constitution, the principle of separation of powers, the principle of democracy and the principle of the republican form of government. It is also expressed in the prohibition of excessive state intervention, but also in the principle of the social state.[1397] The above, contemporary characterization of the rule of law (*Rechtsstaat*) demonstrates what path underwent the understanding of this idea in Germany from the constitution of the Weimar Republic to the current constitution. It is often described as a "path from formal to material" understanding of the *Rechtsstaat* idea. To sum up, it should be emphasized that today's understanding of rule of law in Germany has a formal-material dimension. On the one hand, we are talking about the rule of law in the literal sense, on the other hand, there is axiological load carried by this idea.[1398]

Moving to Poland, we have to refer to the principle of a democratic rule of law. It is considered a very roomy general clause setting the "axiological minimum" in relation to the position of the individual in the state. Marek Safjan also rightly notices its similarity to the principle of protecting human dignity, as adopted in the constitution of Germany. Therefore, we are talking about specific superior determinants of the position of the individual in the state.[1399] The Constitution of the Republic of Poland does not clarify the principle of a democratic rule of

---

1396 Constitution of the Republic of Poland of 2 April 1997, source: https://www.sejm.gov.pl/prawo/konst/angielski/kon1.htm [access: 7/01/2020]. All further direct references to the provisions of the constitution of the Republic of Poland [RP] are based on this source.

1397 M. Bożek, *System konstytucyjny Republiki Federalnej Niemiec...*, p. 28.

1398 B. Stöcker, op. cit., p. 204. G. Dietze, op. cit., p. 547.

1399 M. Safjan, *Wyzwania dla państwa prawa*, Warszawa 2007, p. 124. About the "democratic state based on the rule of law" in polish constitution more: A. Łuszczyński, M. Łuszczyńska, *What ought to be a person's relationship to society?*, Rzeszów 2011, pp.154–161.

law. Its concretization was effected both through the jurisprudence of the Polish Constitutional Tribunal and the statements of doctrine representatives. Their analysis shows that the principle of a democratic rule of law (like its German counterpart) is the sum of the principles arising from the axiology, on which the constitution is based.[1400] Therefrom stem the principles of the rule of law, supremacy of the constitution, separation of powers, safeguarding the citizens the right to an impartial, independent and fair court, and protecting civil rights and liberties.[1401] We must also point to equality before law, national sovereignty and the principle of proportionality.[1402] The features of modern democratic rule of law also include granting individuals the possibility of making free choices.[1403]

In the context of Robert von Mohl's views on the operation of administration in the state, it should be emphasized that the prohibition of excessive formalism in the activities of state authorities is derived from the principle of democratic rule of law. This limitation was taken over in Poland from German law. In one of its rulings, the Polish Supreme Administrative Court stated: "the position that excessive judicial formalism is preferred over respect for justice and the rule of law, as well as other rights directly arising from the Constitution is incorrect."[1404] Already here we see similarities of the aforesaid general principles of rule of law in Germany, and the democratic rule of law in Poland to Mohl's understanding of the *Rechtsstaat*. Giving the idea of the rule of law a material dimension should be considered the main similarity. Both von Mohl and German and Polish doctrine do not perceive *Rechtsstaat* only in formal terms. The idea of the rule of law does, in all cases, contain a specific load of axiological values, on which the state is to be based.

It would be a mistake, however, not to point out the differences between von Mohl's concepts and the modern understanding of the analyzed overarching systemic principles. What comes to the fore here is the difference in perception of the principle of separation of powers. The separation of powers in Poland is safeguarded by art. 10 of the constitution, and in Germany by art. 20, section 2

1400 R. A. Tokarczyk, *Paradygmatyczne ujęcie koncepcyjnych i ustrojowych aspektów demokratycznego państwa prawa*, [in:] M. Aleksandrowicz, A. Jamróz, L. Jamróz (eds.), *Demokratyczne państwo prawa. Zagadnienia wybrane*, Białystok 2014, p. 138.

1401 Ibidem, pp. 139–140.

1402 B. Banaszak, *Konstytucja Rzeczypospolitej Polskiej. Komentarz*, Warszawa 2012, pp. 18–19.

1403 R. A. Tokarczyk, *Paradygmatyczne ujęcie koncepcyjnych i ustrojowych aspektów demokratycznego państwa prawa*. . ., p. 147.

1404 B. Banaszak, op. cit., p. 45.

and art. 92 of the basic law.[1405] Von Mohl presented the view of indivisibility of power in the state. He opposed the idea of separation of powers by Montesquieu, considering it to be weakening and dangerous for the state. One should also remember the similarities and differences in the principle of nation sovereignty and the principle of democracy. Art. 20, section 2 of the German constitution and art. 4 of the Polish constitution introduce the principle of sovereignty of nation into the German and Polish regimes.[1406] It is true that von Mohl did not rule out the existence of a democratic state, but the analysis of his views demonstrates clearly that he was in favour of monarchy (of course limited by applicable constitution).[1407]

As demonstrated earlier, von Mohl was also an opponent of universal suffrage. This view is in clear contradiction with the regulations of both the Polish and German constitution. In article art. 38 section 1 of the German constitution we find reference to the representation of the nation from universal, direct, free, equal and secret elections. In Poland the art. 96 section 2 of the constitution speaks of universal, equal, direct and proportional elections to the Sejm in a secret ballot. Pursuant to article 97 section 2 of the Polish constitution, elections to the Senate are universal, direct and held in a secret ballot. The President of Poland, pursuant to art. 127 section 1, however, is elected in universal, equal, direct and secret ballot. Speaking of democracy and the representation system, there is a similarity in the performance of mandates by representatives. Von Mohl advocated the so-called "free mandate." The representative in the parliamentary assembly was therefore guided by the interest of the whole nation, and could not be bound by any instructions. The principle of a "free mandate" in Poland is safeguarded by art. 104 item 1, and in Germany by art. 38 section 1 of the basic law.

Referring to more detailed constitutional regulations, one should first point to the already mentioned catalogue of fundamental rights of the German constitution. The inclusion of a chapter on fundamental rights at the very beginning, as Wolfgang Rudzio aptly put it, requires that the German state be described as "anthropocentric."[1408] The articles 1–19 listing the fundamental rights resemble the norms appearing in the constitutions of German states before the Spring of

1405 More: J. W. Tkaczyński, op. cit., pp. 157, 228.

1406 More: Ibid, p. 155.

1407 B. Stöcker, op. cit., p. 183.

1408 W. Rudzio, *Das politische System der Bundesrepublik Deutschland*, Opladen 1991, p. 46.

Nations (*Vormärz*).[1409] So they are primarily liberal in nature. It can be said that they formulate the basic principles of the state-citizen relationships and give the individual a number of freedoms from state interference. What is important in determining the civic rights in Poland, is the art. 5 of the constitution introducing the order for "securing" by the Polish State freedoms and human and citizen rights. The specification of these rights and freedoms is contained in chapter II of the Constitution of the Republic of Poland entitled "Freedoms, rights and obligations of man and citizen."

The starting point for the fundamental rights enshrined in the German constitution are the norms contained in its three initial articles. We are talking about the obligation to protect the inviolable human dignity (this value is the most important and forms the basis of the constitutional order of Germany), the right to free development of personality and the principle of equality of all before the law.[1410] Jan Wikor Tkaczyński, talking about art. 1 section 1 of the German constitution rightly states: "(...) the guarantee of human dignity demonstrates, by its very positioning at the head of the constitution, that it is not man that is to be for the state, but the state for man."[1411] Based on earlier considerations, one can say that von Mohl expressed a very similar view in relation to the state. As for the issue of human dignity under the Polish constitution, it is introduced by art. 30. Pursuant to it, it is "inherent and inalienable," inviolable, protected and, what is important, also the source of human and citizen freedom and rights.

Equality before the law, equality between men and women and a prohibition of discrimination are introduced in the German system by art. 3 of the basic law, and in the Polish constitution by art. 32 and art. 33 thereof. In the context of the von Mohl idea, it must be stated that he understood equality before the law, above all, as equality of all citizens in the process of state taking their permitted life goals and aspirations into account. This equality was to guarantee them not only freedom in achieving these goals but also the right to demand support from the state in achieving them.

1409 For example, one can point to art. 19–42 of the Constitution of the Kingdom of Württemberg of 25 September 1819, source: http://www.verfassungen.de/bw/wuerttemberg/verf1819-i.htm [access: 08/01/2020], or paragraphs 7–25 of the Constitution of the Grand Duchy of Baden of 22 August 1818, source: http://www.documentarchiv.de/nzjh/verfbaden.html [access: 08/01/2020]. More about the issue of fundamental rights in the German Constitution: D. Janicka, op. cit., pp. 127–154.

1410 D. Janicka, op. cit., p. 133. M. Bożek, *System konstytucyjny Republiki Federalnej Niemiec…*, pp. 35–36.

1411 J. W. Tkaczyński, op. cit., p. 86.

The German constitution implies the right of every German citizen to develop freely, with the sole restrictions in form of the rights of third parties, the constitutional order or, importantly, moral orders (art. 2 section 1). This norm corresponds to art. 31 of the Polish constitution introducing legal protection for human freedom, but also the obligation to respect the freedoms and rights of other individuals. The exercise of constitutional freedoms and rights may be limited under the Polish constitution only by statute and only because of a necessity resulting from the need to ensure public safety or order, environmental protection, public health and morality, or the freedoms and rights of others. In this aspect, there are clear similarities between the abovementioned rights and what von Mohl said about the free development of the human individual. He granted every individual the right to freely select and achieve its life goals. On the other hand, in this process the individual had to respect the aspirations of other individuals and the norms resulting from law and morality.[1412]

Further similarities to von Mohl's views can be found when analyzing art. 4, of the German constitution and art. 53 of the constitution of the Republic of Poland. They introduce freedom of conscience, religion and freedom of belief. They also provide for a prohibition of discrimination on grounds of religion. The freedom of religious practices as a principle of the *Rechtsstaat* is also present in von Mohl's views. This freedom, however, could not violate the laws in force in the state. As a rule, the *Rechtsstaat* of von Mohl also foresaw "freedom of thought," which was understood as the possibility of conducting scientific research freely and the freedom to express beliefs. On the basis of the German constitution, freedom of speech, the prohibition of censorship and freedom of science are guaranteed in art. 5. What is important, however, is its section 3 statement that says: "Freedom of teaching shall not release any person allegiance to the constitution." One should also remember about the possibility, as introduced by this article, to limit the freedom of speech by the provisions of general acts.[1413]

1412 The Constitution of the Republic of Poland also refers to the freedoms and rights of national and ethnic minorities. In article 35 section 1 it provides national minorities with the right to preserve and develop their own language, culture, customs and education. It is worth remembering von Mohl's ambivalent and pragmatic approach to the issue of respect for national identity differences within the state. More on the rights of national minorities under the Polish constitution: M. Chmaj (ed.), *Wolności i prawa człowieka w Konstytucji Rzeczypospolitej Polskiej*, Warszawa 2008, pp. 58–59. In German constitution the protection of ethnic and religious minorities is provided by art. 3 item 3.

1413 More about fundamental rights of freedom of thought and freedom of religion in German constitution: M. Borowski, *Die Glaubens- und Gewissensfreiheit des Grundgesetzes*, Tübingen 2006, pp. 821.

In Poland, we should point to art. 14 and art. 54 of the constitution, introducing freedom of press and media as well as freedom of expression and prohibition of preventive censorship.

Important from the point of view of the relationship between the von Mohl concept and the present are the norms arising from art. 9 section 1 of German basic law and art. 12 and art. 58 section 1 of the Polish constitution. We speak here about guarantee of freedom of association.[1414] *Associations-Recht* - the right of citizens to associate freely was one of the main designations of the rule of law in the thought of Robert von Mohl. Like in von Mohl, in Germany and Poland, the objectives of associations must be in accordance with applicable law, and the state has the right to ensure their compliance with this requirement. The right of association also corresponds to the freedom of assembly provided for in article 8 of German constitution and art. 57 of the Polish constitution, and the freedom to establish political parties as provided for in art. 11 section 1 of the Polish constitution and, albeit indirectly, in art. 21 section 1 of the German basic law.

An analysis of the subsequent provisions of the constitutions of the Federal Republic of Germany and the Republic of Poland reveals the similarity between art. 10 (Germany) and art. 49 (Poland) introducing the secret of correspondence and the freedom and protection of the secret of communication. A similar demand came from von Mohl, speaking about the need for "relativity and justice on the part of the authorities as regards arrest, house search and seizure of letters." It is not difficult to guess that this "seizure of letters" is a historical protection of the secret of communication. Von Mohl argued that its restrictions should be applied only in absolutely necessary cases, and would be based on an act. Similar restrictions on confidentiality of communication exist in Poland and Germany. When it comes to the postulate regarding "home search" it corresponds to the articles 13 and 50 of the constitutions of Germany and Poland, respectively, introducing the inviolability of the apartment. Von Mohl also argued that a state according to idea of the *Rechsstaat* should fulfill the so called postulate of *Freizügigkeit,* i.e. right to change residence or move out of the state. Similar principle is safeguarded by art 52 of the Polish constitution. In Germany functions art. 11 granting the freedom of movement within the territory of Federation.

One of the basic postulates of nineteenth-century liberals was the protection of private property. As noted earlier, in von Mohl property was one of the "foundations of the state" (along with the population and territory). He advocated the citizens' right to private property and economic freedom. On the other hand, he provided for a restriction of property rights in case of legitimate interest

1414 More on this law in the Polish constitution: M. Chmaj (ed.), op. cit., pp. 120–123.

of the community. The abovementioned von Mohl postulates correspond to art. 14 of the German constitution and art. 21 and art. 64 of the Polish constitution. They introduce a guarantee for the right of inheritance and property and provide that expropriation is permitted only for public purposes and for just compensation. We should also emphasize the section 2, of art. 14 of the German constitution, which reads: "Property entails obligations. Its use shall also serve the public good."[1415] Also here we see common points between the ideas of von Mohl, and the modern regulations. Von Mohl respected private property, but argued that in the event of a collision, the public interest was more important than the interest of the individual. What seems significant in this context, is the judgment of the Federal Constitutional Court, in which the absolute priority of individual interests over general interest was questioned.[1416] Of course, as in Poland also in Germany, expropriation is possible for the good of the general public, and on the basis of an act, and should be carried out in accordance with the principle of proportionality. However, one can see the connection of this understanding with what von Mohl said. In fact, it follows from the principles of rational reasoning. It is therefore wrong when an individual, using its proprietary right, blocks the possible development of the community. A great example are situations of expropriation for road construction.

According to von Mohl, every citizen of *Rechtsstaat* had the right to "permanently participate in the state" and thus, in fact, be a citizen. A similar principle is introduced by art. 16 section 1 of the German constitution and art. 34 section 2 of the Polish constitution. What is important, however, von Mohl predicted the possibility of expelling a citizen from the state at the time of stating that his life goals were not in line with the idea on which it was based and the principles of the common good. This is certainly a difference, when compared with modern regulations adopted in the legal orders of Germany and Poland. They do not provide for penalties of expelling a citizen from the state and prohibit deprivation of citizenship. The catalogue of similarities in terms of civil rights ends with the issue of the right of citizens to submit complaints and petitions. This right is guaranteed by art. 17 of the German constitution stating that everyone "has the right individually or jointly with others to address written requests or complaints to competent authorities and the legislature." Legal norm of a similar content

1415 On this topic: W. Rudzio, op. cit., p. 47.

1416 Judgment of the Federal Constitutional Court of 12 January 1967, I BvR 169/63, thesis 24, source: http://www.servat.unibe.ch/dfr/bv021073.html#Rn014 [access: 07/01/2020]. D. Janicka, op. cit., p. 145.

is introduced by the provision of art. 63 of the Polish constitution.[1417] These regulations correspond to the right, present in von Mohl's *Rechtsstaat*, to "lodge a complaint and petition" ("*Recht der Beschwerdeführung und der Petition*").

With regard to the obligations of citizens, it should be noted that the constitution of the Federal Republic of Germany does not explicitly provide for universal obligations of citizens. One can only point to art. 12 section 2, and art. 12a providing for civil and military service obligations.[1418] We should also refer to art. 33 section 1 of the German constitution, speaking of "equal rights and civic obligations" of every German in every federal state.[1419] Polish constitution grounds more obligations of citizens. We should start with the preamble saying about Polish citizens "equal in rights and obligations towards common good - Poland."[1420] The duty of "loyalty to the Republic of Poland and concern for the common good," the obligation to comply with the law of the Republic of Poland and to bear public burdens and services is also important. However, what connects the abovementioned regulations with von Mohl's views will be equality (of course, excluding political rights, as distinguished by von Mohl, and regarding participation in state administration). Von Mohl argued for "equality of citizens' rights and burdens (obligations)" - (*Gleichheit der bürgerlichen Rechte und Lasten*). In a state consistent with the *Rechtsstaat* idea, there can be no question of uneven privileging of one citizen at the expense of others in terms of their civic rights and obligations.

As noted above, another scope of similarities between von Mohl's views on the state and the present day will be demonstrated by the analysis of the principle of the social state (Germany) and the state implementing the principles of social justice (Poland).

In German constitution, the principle of the social state is introduced by articles 20 and 28. In art. 20, section 1 we find the statement that "The Federal Republic of Germany is a democratic and social federal state." Whereas the article 28 section 1 says: "The constitutional order in the *Länder* must conform to the principles of a republican, democratic and social state governed by the rule of

---

1417 More about this right in the Polish constitution: M. Chmaj (ed.), op. cit., pp. 147–150.

1418 M. Bożek, *System konstytucyjny Republiki Federalnej Niemiec...*, p. 39.

1419 Interestingly, during the work on the German constitution, its draft assumed the presence of art. 19 of the following wording: "Everyone has a duty of loyalty to the constitution and should respect and observe the constitution and the law." More on that subject: Z. A. Maciąg, op. cit., p. 417.

1420 M. Chmaj (ed.), op. cit., p. 53.

law within the meaning of this Basic Law."[1421] By means of the abovementioned regulations, the most synthetic character of the German system is defined, which is defined by the principles of a democratic, social, federal, republican state and the rule of law.[1422]

The concept of a social market economy (*Soziale Marktwirtschaft*) is linked with the idea of social state. The idea of a social market economy is considered to be a response to the disadvantages of both unrestrained capitalism (proper for the 19th century) and the centrally planned economy.[1423] The creators of this concept, above all Alfred Müller-Armack and Ludwig Erhard, recognized the freedom of the individual as the basis of the state system.[1424] On the other hand, they did not negate the need for the state to provide social security for its citizens.[1425] Therefore, the assumptions of the social market economy, which form the basis of the system on which Germany's economic and social life is based, include both recognition of the free market, as the most important element of the economic life of the state, and counteracting monopolies. Economic processes should occur spontaneously. The state, on the other hand, guarantees citizens freedom of competition and introduces their social security, by protecting weaker participants of the "market game."[1426] It emphasizes the freedom and

1421 Ibid, p. 50.

1422 J. W. Tkaczyński, op. cit., p. 152.

1423 H. Lampert, *Porządek gospodarczy i społeczny w RFN*, Warszawa 1993, p. 63. Regarding the disadvantages of XIXth century capitalism we shouldn't forget about the Catholic Social Teaching, and the role of Pope Leo XIII in it's creation. More: M. Sadowski, *Państwo w doktrynie papieża Leona XIII*, Wrocław 2002.

1424 M. Kubiak, M. Kubiak, *Ordoliberalizm a koncepcja i praktyka społecznej gospodarki rynkowej*, "Studia Gdańskie" XXXI, p. 379.

1425 K. Zaradkiewicz, *Art. 20 [Społeczna gospodarka rynkowa jako podstawa ustroju gospodarczego]*, [in:] M. Safian, L. Bosek (eds.), *Konstytucja RP. Tom I. Komentarz do art. 1–86*, Warszawa 2016, thesis 24, [Legalis Legal Information System – access 02/08/2019]. T. T. Kaczmarek, P. Pysz, *Ludwig Erhard i Społeczna Gospodarka Rynkowa*, Warszawa 2004, pp. 106–109. The main the work of Ludwig Erhard, in which he presented his views is his *Prosperity for All*. More: L. Erhard, *Dobrobyt dla wszystkich*, Warszawa 2012.

1426 U. Zagóra-Jonszta, *System gospodarczy ordoliberalizmu a ekonomia klasyczna i keynesizm. Próba porównania*, [in:] E. Okoń-Horodyńska (ed.), *Społeczna Gospodarka Rynkowa, Materiały z ogólnopolskiej konferencji naukowej w Jaworze 27–29 Maja 1991*, Katowice 1991, p. 27. J. Bokajło, *Alfreda Müllera-Armacka styl: Społeczna Gospodarka Rynkowa*, [in:] E. Mączyńska, P. Pysz (eds.), *Ordoliberalizm i Społeczna Gospodarka Rynkowa Wobec Wyzwań Współczesności*, Warszawa 2013, p. 121.

responsibility of individuals for themselves, but also the need for even enrichment and creation of wealth.[1427]

As far as the constitution of the Republic of Poland is concerned, there are two articles relating to the social activity of the state. In the aforementioned art. 2 it refers to the Republic of Poland as a "democratic state ruled by law and implementing the principles of social justice." Unlike the German constitution, the Polish constitution directly refers to the idea of social market economy. Pursuant to art. 20 of the Constitution of the Republic of Poland "A social market economy, based on freedom of economic activity, private ownership, and solidarity, dialogue and cooperation between social partners, shall be the basis of the economic system of the Republic of Poland."[1428] The view dominating in Polish doctrine is that art. 2 and art. 20 of the constitution introduce the principle of the social state, as known from Germany, on the Polish soil.[1429] It is therefore reasonable to consider them together, the more so (as it will be shown) they are understood by both the doctrine, and case law, in a very similar way.

Both on German and Polish grounds, the principle of the social state and the principle of the state implementing social justice were the subject of judicial analyzes performed by FCC and CT, respectively. Judges from Karlsruhe emphasized that the social state clause is a kind of postulate addressed to the legislator, which should constitute a legal order based on justice, freedom, equality and fairness.[1430] The Polish Constitutional Tribunal also recognized the order

---

1427 L. Erhard *Gedanken aus fünf Jahrzehnten*, K. Hohmann (ed.), Düsseldorf, Wien, New-York 1988, p. 461, After: S. Behrends, *Rozwój realnych systemów ekonomicznych w społecznej gospodarce rynkowej*, [in:] E. Mączyńska, P. Pysz (eds.), op. cit., p. 134.

1428 Ibid, p. 14.

1429 K. Zaradkiewicz, *Art. 20 [Społeczna gospodarka rynkowa jako podstawa ustroju gospodarczego]…*, thesis 62, [Legalis Legal Information System – access 02/08/2019]. K. Strzyczkowski, *Zasada państwa sprawiedliwości społecznej jako zasada publicznego prawa gospodarczego*, "Ruch Prawniczy, Ekonomiczny i Socjologiczny," LXIX, z. 4, 2007, p. 11. P. Winczorek, *Komentarz do Konstytucji Rzeczypospolitej Polskiej z dnia 2 kwietnia 1997 r.*, Warszawa 2000, p. 15. In Poland, the articles that concretize the principles of social justice are 19 (care for veterans), 67 (right to social security), 68 (right to healthcare) and 69 (provision of assistance to the disabled by the state).

1430 D. Janicka, op. cit., pp. 100–101. P. Badura, op. cit., p. 492. FCC ruling of 13 January 1982, ref. Akt 1 BvR 848, 1047/77, 916, 1307/78, 350/79 und 475, 902, 965, 1177, 1238, 1461/80, thesis 68, source: http://www.servat.unibe.ch/dfr/bv059231.html [access: 07/01/2020]. In the ruling of 19 December 1951, ref. Akt 1 BvR 220/51, thesis 30, source https://opinioiuris.de/entscheidung/766 [access: 07/01/2020], FCC ruled: "The most important scope of activities relating to the implementation of the social state belongs to the legislator."

expressed in art. 2 to realize social justice as a general clause addressed to the legislator.[1431] This is a specific metanorm that defines one of the state's overarching goals.[1432] This goal is to be achieved by the legislator, creating an order based on justice in the state.[1433] The Polish constitution combines a democratic state ruled by law and social justice. In other words: a state that does not implement social justice cannot be considered a democratic legal state. The idea of justice, in its minimal dimension, is understood here as striving to maintain balance in social relations. It manifests itself, for example, in the state avoiding the creation of a situation of unjustified privilege of certain groups.[1434]

In both Germany and Poland, the social state is defined as an active state. It is a state capable of providing its citizens with multidimensional care.[1435] This care is also expressed by the state's concern for an even increase in prosperity and leveling of social differences.[1436] The social state as well as the state that implements social justice is designed to provide the individual with a minimum existence within a balanced socio-economic system.[1437] Therefore, an individual has the right to receive aid from the community in a situation where "not being

---

1431 More about the meaning of the term "general clause": L. Leszczyński, *Stosowanie generalnych klauzul odsyłających*, Zakamycze 2001, p. 27. Idem, *Generalne klauzule odsyłające – ujęcie teoretycznoprawne*, "Annales Universitatis Mariae Curie-Sklodowska" Sectio G "IUS," vol. LXIII 2, 2016, p. 11–26. The "social noxiousness of the act" is an example of general clause in polish criminal law. More: M. Budyn-Kulik, M. Kulik, *Społeczna szkodliwość czynu jako klauzula generalna w prawie karnym*, "Annales Universitatis Mariae Curie-Sklodowska" Sectio G "IUS," vol. LXIII 2, 2016, p.261–277.

1432 K. Strzyczkowski, op. cit., p. 14.

1433 B. Banaszak, op. cit., p. 53

1434 M. Domagała, J. Podkowik, M. Zubik (eds.), *Konstytucja RP w orzecznictwie Trybunału Konstytucyjnego oraz SN i NSA*, Warszawa 2018, p. 197.

1435 P. Badura, op. cit., p. 494.

1436 D. Janicka, op. cit., p. 101. R. Hoffmann, *Beamtenstreik und Verfassungsverständnis vom Sozialstaat*, "Kritische Justiz," Vol. 4, No. 1 (1971), p. 49. H. F. Zacher, *Der Sozialstaat als Prozeß*, "Zeitschrift für gesamte Staatswissenschaft / Journal of Institutional and Theoretical Economics," Bd. 134, H. 1. (1978), p. 15. J. W. Tkaczyński, op. cit., p. 190.

1437 Ibid. J. Oniszczuk, *Konstytucja Rzeczypospolitej Polskiej w orzecznictwie Trybunału Konstytucyjnego*, Zakamycze 2000, p. 156. P. Tuleja, *Normatywna treść praw jednostki w ustawach konstytucyjnych RP*, Warszawa 1997, p. 92. After: K. Strzyczkowski, op. cit., p. 17. J. Oniszczuk, *Konstytucja Rzeczypospolitej Polskiej w orzecznictwie Trybunału Konstytucyjnego na początku XXI w.*, Zakamycze 2004, pp. 271–272.

at fault, it is not able to meet the life needs necessary for a dignified survival of this individual and its family, in the current social and economic reality."[1438]

Unlike Germany, the Polish constitution explicitly refers to the idea of a social market economy, although it does not define it. A number of judicial and doctrinal statements filled this gap. A state based on a social market economy is a state that is active in the economic sphere. There is no doubt that it safeguards free market, freedom of contract, security of private property, and free competition. On the other hand, however, it may affect the economy in order to avoid the negative effects associated with the functioning of the free market and the capitalist system.[1439]

The principle of the social state in the German system, as well as the principle of the state implementing social justice in Poland, and the principle of the social market economy associated with them show great similarity. They both draw on two sources. The first is of a liberal nature, emphasizing the need for a free market, private property and freedom in the exchange of goods and services. The other is social in nature, so state interventionism is allowed, and social solidarity and cooperation between social groups are introduced. However, state intervention must always be proportionate and rational. There must be a balance between market and the social factor.[1440]

Turning to the links between the concept of the state in Robert von Mohl and the principle of the social state in Germany and the principle of the state that implements the principle of social justice in Poland, it is necessary to emphasize and focus on the idea of subsidiarity.[1441] As already indicated, the task of the state in von Mohl is to support citizens in "overcoming life obstacles" and achieving "life goals," in a situation when they are unable to do so, either on their own, or with the help of various types of communities functioning in the

---

1438 Judgment of the Constitutional Tribunal of 25 February 2014, ref. no. SK 18/13, J. Oniszczuk, *Konstytucja Rzeczypospolitej Polskiej w orzecznictwie Trybunału Konstytucyjnego na początku XXI w. . ..*, p. 18. See the judgment of the Constitutional Tribunal of 4 November 2015, ref. no. K 1/14, J. Oniszczuk, *Konstytucja Rzeczypospolitej Polskiej w orzecznictwie Trybunału Konstytucyjnego na początku XXI w. . .*, p. 16.

1439 M. Nasiłowski, *Próba zdefiniowania społecznej gospodarki rynkowej*, [in:] E. Okoń-Horodyńska (red.), op. cit., p. 165. B. Banaszak, op. cit., pp. 155–166.

1440 P. Winczorek, op. cit., p. 33. Judgment of the Constitutional Tribunal of 31 July 2015, ref. no. K 41/12. After: J. Oniszczuk, *Konstytucja Rzeczypospolitej Polskiej w orzecznictwie Trybunału Konstytucyjnego na początku XXI w...*, p. 61.

1441 B. Stöcker, op. cit., p. 274.

society. In view of the above, the state should provide assistance to citizens, but it must be provided in a subsidiary way, taking into account the conditions and the effectiveness of meeting the needs. In this context, it should be remembered that Walter Eucken, one of the prominent representatives of ordoliberalism (the source idea for the social state and social market economy) did not postulate an extensive system of social benefits. The key was to be the individual's responsibility for itself, the state was only to intervene, when the individual was unable to take care of itself.[1442]

German science also defines the social state through the prism of subsidiarity. The social state is opposed here to the welfare state. The first one respects the freedom of individuals, the second one is interventionist and prevents instilling a sense of self-responsibility in citizens.[1443] A social state is a state that seeks to sense and respond to the needs of society.[1444] Certainly, it is not a state that imposes its help on its citizens, determining its scope in advance. As Josef Isensee observes, a social state provides assistance to an individual when it is not able to achieve a specific goal, and when there is an objective need to provide it.[1445] This stance of the state is related to the one expressed in art. 1 of the German constitution, i.e. the duty to protect the dignity of the human individual and its free development.[1446] Also the art. 6 of the German constitution that guarantees state protection and care for marriages, families, mothers and children born out of wedlock has a subsidiary dimension. Section 2 states: "The care and upbringing of children is the natural right of parents and a duty primarily incumbent upon them. The state shall watch over them in the performance of this duty." The right to receive aid from the state and to take into account their good also belongs to the family and mother under art. 71 of the Polish constitution. Also art. 18 of the Polish

---

1442 J. Czech-Rogosz, op. cit., p. 113. Eucken laid out his ideas in his work entitled *Die Grundlagen der National ökonomie*: W. Eucken, *Podstawy Polityki Gospodarczej*, Poznań 2005.

1443 H. F. Zacher, *Vierzig Jahre Sozialstaat – Schwerpunkte der rechtlichen Ordnung*, [in:] N. Blüm, H. F. Zacher (eds.), *40 Jahre Sozialstaat Bundesrepublik Deutschland*, Baden-Baden 1989, pp. 25–26. We shouldn't forget that one of the precursors of subsidiarity principle was German Catholic bishop Wilhelm von Ketteler. More M. O'Malley, *Currents in Nineteenth-Century German Law, and Subsidiarity's Emergence as a Social Principle in the Writings of Wilhelm Ketteler*, "Journal of Law, Philosophy and Culture," Vol. II, No. 1 (2008), pp.23–53.

1444 P. Badura, op. cit., p. 493.

1445 J. Isensee, *Verfassung ohne Soziale Grundrechte: ein Wesenzug des Grundgesetzes*, "Der Staat," Vol. 19, No. 3 (1980), pp. 367–368.

1446 P. Badura, op. cit., p. 493.

constitution introduces the concept of state protection over family, marriage and parenthood. In Poland, the requirement for the state to act in accordance with the principle of subsidiarity is also underlined. Therefore, the state cannot act in a top-down manner, arbitrarily steering market mechanisms.[1447] According to the Polish Constitutional Tribunal, the influence of the state on economic processes can only be indirect (e.g. by exemption from tax burdens).[1448] The determinant of all social activities of the state must be the preservation of the widest possible freedom of individuals.[1449]

It should also be noted that von Mohl's idea of state subsidiarity is linked with John Finnis's concept of subsidiarity. Finnis took the position that state activities should never take over and dominate initiatives undertaken at lower levels of social relations.[1450] Therefore, for the individuals and their communities, the state should assume the role of a supporting and coordinating factor only. The state is to "help the individuals help themselves," based on their own ingenuity and initiative.[1451] On the other hand, Finnis, like von Mohl, found that taking over individual goals by the state was not only ineffective, but also unfair.[1452]

The requirement of rationality and adequacy of state intervention also corresponds to the principle of subsidiarity. As with von Mohl, it should be focused on the widest possible preservation of individual freedoms. In addition, any state action must be rational, justified and feasible. Von Mohl spoke about the need to support the most general and widespread needs in the nation. This was dictated by insufficient public funds. What is of great importance in this context, are the constitutional norms, whose role is to secure the state budget against

---

1447 K. Zaradkiewicz, *Art. 20 [Społeczna gospodarka rynkowa jako podstawa ustroju gospodarczego]...*, theses 55, 59, [Legalis Legal Information System – access 02/08/2019].

1448 Judgment of the Constitutional Tribunal of 17 January 2001, ref. no. K. 5/00.

1449 M. Biliński, A. Żurawik, *§ 15. Społeczna gospodarka rynkowa jako konstytucyjna zasada ustroju gospodarczego...*, thesis 5, [Legalis Legal Information System - access 02/08/2019]. Cf. S. Behrends, op. cit., pp. 135–136.

1450 D. Schwartz, *Perfectionism and Subsidiarity: Comments on John Finnis' Human Rights and the Common Good*, "Jerusalem Review of Legal Studies," Vol. 8, No. 1 (2013), p. 125.

1451 J. Finnis, *Prawo naturalne i uprawnienia naturalne*, translated by K. Lossman, Warszawa 2001, p. 164.

1452 D. Schwartz, *Perfectionism and Subsidiarity: Comments on John Finnis' Human Rights and the Common Good*, "Jerusalem Review of Legal Studies," Vol. 8, No. 1 (2013), p. 127. M. Jarvard, *Subsidiarity and Autonomy*, "History of European Ideas," Vol. 19, no. 4–6, p. 797.

excessive expenditure on social purposes. In article 109 section 2 of the German constitution, the federation and the federal states are obliged to maintain a general economic balance. The requirement to maintain the state budget balance is implemented in Poland by constitutional prohibitions on covering the deficit by incurring liabilities in the central bank of the state and exceeding the level of public debt of 3/5 of GDP. Therefore, both in Poland and Germany, the implementation of the social tasks of the state must comply with the principles of proportionality and rationality.[1453]

The above analysis requires us to conclude that there are many similarities between von Mohl's views on the state and contemporary systemic principles expressed in the constitutions of Germany and Poland. Certainly, these include giving the idea of the rule of law a material dimension in the form of linking it with the catalogue of civil rights to guarantee the freedom of the individual in the state. These similarities must also include von Mohl's conviction of the need for social activity of the state. One of the ambitions of the German thinker was to secure the state against the negative effects of the industrial revolution. The state should therefore counteract the impoverishment of the working masses and provide citizens with a minimum of existence.[1454] That is why, besides the guarantee of economic freedom and criticism of communism, von Mohl gives the state the opportunity to influence economic and social processes.[1455] The most important similarity here is based on the idea of subsidiarity. Both von Mohl, as well as German and Polish doctrine are convinced that state aid must be provided to an individual whenever it is unable to accomplish its specific objective. Regarding the differences between Mohl's understanding of *Rechtsstaat* and contemporaneity, it is necessary to point out the unequal political rights of citizens. Von Mohl was an oponent of equal electoral rights. He predicted that the possibility of influencing political processes in the state should be granted to a small number of citizens, who meet certain requirements. This view, as well as opposition to the division of powers, is in conflict with the principles expressed in the constitutions of the Republic of Poland and the Federal Republic of Germany.

1453 J. W. Tkaczyński, op. cit., pp. 191–192. More: FCC decision of 12 October 1976, ref. no. 1 BvL 9/74 and FCC ruling of 10 November 1998, ref. no. 2 BvR 1057, 1226, 980/91. K. Strzyczkowski, op. cit., pp. 16, 24.

1454 B. Stöcker, op. cit., pp. 213, 265.

1455 Ibid, p. 266.

References

Robert von Mohl's works

1. Mohl R. v., *Bevölkerung,* [in:] *Das Staats-Lexikon, Encyklopädie der sämmtlichen Staatswissenschaften für alle Stände*, Bd. 2, C. v. Rotteck, C. Welcker (eds.), Altona 1846
2. Mohl R. v., *Das Bundes-Staatsrecht der Vereinigten Staaten von Nord-Amerika. Erste Abtheilung: Verfassungs-Recht.* Stuttgart und Tübingen 1824
3. Mohl R. v., *Das deutsche Reichsstaatsrecht, Rechtliche und politische Eröterungen*, Tübingen 1873
4. Mohl R. v., *Das Reprästativsystem, seine Mängel und die Heilmittel. Politische Briefe eines Altliberalen,* "Deutscher Vierteljahrs Schrift," H. 3, 1852
5. Mohl R. v., *Das Staatsrecht des Königreiches Württemberg*, Erster Theil, Tübingen 1829
6. Mohl R. v., *Das Staatsrecht des Königreiches Württemberg*, Zweite Auflage, Erster Band *das Verfassungsrecht,* Tübingen 1840
7. Mohl R. v., *Das Staatsrecht des Königreichs Württemberg*, Zweiter Band, Tübingen 1831
8. Mohl R. v., *Die deutschen Universitäten, ihre gegenwärtigen Missstände und deren Heilung,* "Deutscher Vierteljahrs Schrift," H. 2, 1839
9. Mohl R. v., *Die Geschichte und Literatur der Staatswissenschaften in Monographieen dargestellt*, Erster Band, Erlangen 1855
10. Mohl R. v., *Die Geschichte und Literatur der Staatswissenschaften in Monographieen dargestellt*, Zweiter Band, Erlangen 1856
11. Mohl R. v., *Die Geschichte und Literatur der Staatswissenschaften in Monographien dargestellt*, Dritter Band, Erlangen 1858
12. Mohl R. v., *Die Literatur des gesammten württembergischen Rechtes aus dem letzten Jahrzehnd, historisch kritisch dargestellt*, Stuttgart 1830
13. Mohl R. v., *Die Nichtigkeit der Ansprüche des Obersten Air Augustus d'Este auf Thronfähigkeit in Grossbritannien und Hannover. Gegen die Gutachten von Dillon, Klüber und Zachariä nachgewiesen*, Tübingen 1835
14. Mohl R. v., *Die Öffentliche Rechtspflege des Deutschen Bundes. Ein publicistischer Versuch.* Stuttgart und Tübingen 1822
15. Mohl R. v., *Die Polizeiwissenschaft nach den Grundsätzen des Rechtsstaates, 2Bde,* Tübingen 1832,

16. Mohl R. v., *Die Polizeiwissenschaft nach den Grundsätzen des Rechtsstaates, 2Bde,* Tübingen 1844
17. Mohl R. v., *Die Polizeiwissenschaft nach den Grundsätzen des Rechtsstaates, 2Bde,* Tübingen 1866
18. Mohl R. v., *Die Staatsromane*, "Zeitschrift für die gesamte Staatswissenschaft," Bd. 2, 1845
19. Mohl R. v., *Die Verantwortlichkeit der Minister in Einherrschaften mit Volksvertretung, rechtlich, politisch und geschichtlich entwickelt,* Tübingen 1837
20. Mohl R. v., *Die Vergangenheit, Gegenwart und Zukunft der politischen Ökonomie*, "Deutscher Vierteljahrschrift," H. 3, 1840
21. Mohl R. v., *Dissertatio inauguralis sistens discrimen ordinum provincialium et constitutionis repraesentativae,* Tubingae 1821
22. Mohl R. v., *Encyklopädie der Staatswissenschaften,* Erste Auflage, Tübingen 1859
23. Mohl R. v., *Encyklopädie der Staatswissenschaften*, Zweite Auflage, Tübingen 1872
24. Mohl R. v., *Encyklopedia Umiejętności Politycznych*, t. 1 i 2, Warszawa 2003
25. Mohl R. v., *Gesellschafts-Wissenschaften und Staats-wissenschaften*, "Zeitschrift für die gesamte Staatswissenschaft," Bd. 7, 1851
26. Mohl R. v., *Gesetz, Gesetzgebende Gewalt, Gesetzgebung,* [in:] J. C. Bluntschli, K. Brater (eds.), *Deutsches Staats-Wörterbuch,* Vierter Band, Stuttgart und Leipzig 1859
27. Mohl R. v., *Kritische Bemerkungen über die Wahlen zum deutschen Reichstage*, Tübingen 1874
28. Mohl R. v., *Lebenserinnerungen von Robert von Mohl 1799–1875*, Bd. 1, Stuttgat und Leipzig 1902
29. Mohl R. v., *Lebenserinnerungen von Robert von Mohl 1799–1875*, Bd. 2, Stuttgart und Leipzig 1902
30. Mohl R. v., *Literarhistorische Uebersicht über die Enzyklopädien der Staatswissenschaften*, "Zeitschrift für die gesamte Staatswissenschaft," Bd. 2, 1845
31. Mohl R. v., *Mohl, Benjamin Ferdinand von,* [in:] "Allgemeine Deutsche Biographie 22" (1885), pp. 54–55, [Online-Version]; URL: https://www.deutsche-biographie.de/pnd117090158.html#adbcontent,
32. Mohl R. v., *Nordamerikanisches Staatsrecht*, "Kritische Zeitschrift für Rechtswissenschaft und Gesetzgebung des Auslandes," Bd. 27, 1855

33. Mohl R. v., *Prospectus*, "Zeitscrhfit für die gesammte Staatswissenschaft," Tübingen 5. Febr. 1843
34. Mohl R. v., *Rechtliche und politische Eröterungen über die Bundesreformakte. Von einem Süddeutschen*, Erlangen 1863
35. Mohl R. v., *Repräsentatives und Parlamentarisches Regierungssystem: eine begriffsgeschichtliche Analyse*, "Politische Vierteljahresschrift," Vol. 6, No. 2 (Juni 1965)
36. Mohl R. v., *Revision der völkerrechtlichen Lehre vom Asyle*, "Zeitschrift für die gesamte Staatswissenschaft," Bd. 9, 1853
37. Mohl R. v., Sarwey O. v., *Geschichte der Rechtsgesetzgebung und Rechtsordnung unter König Wilhelm*, Stuttgart 1841
38. Mohl R. v., *Staatsrecht, Völkerrecht und Politik*, Bd. 1. *Staatsrecht und Völkerrecht*, Tübingen 1860
39. Mohl R. v., *Staatsrecht, Völkerrecht und Politik*, Bd. 3, *Politik*, Bd. 2, Tübingen 1869
40. Mohl R. v., *Staatsrecht, Völkerrecht, Politik*, Bd.2, *Politik*, Bd.1, Tübingen 1862
41. Mohl R. v., *System der Präventiv-Justiz oder Rechts-Polizei*, Tübingen 1834
42. Mohl R. v., *System der Präventiv-Justiz oder Rechtspolizei*, Tübingen 1834. Second edition, 1845. Third edition 1866
43. Mohl R. v., *Über die verschiedene Auffassung des represäntativen Systemes in England, Frankreich und Deutschland*, "Zeitschrift für die gesamte Staatswissenschaft," Bd. 3, 1846
44. Mohl R. v., *Übersicht der neueren völkerrechtlichen Literatur*, "Zeitschrift für die gesamte Staatswissenschaft," Bd. 3, 1846
45. Mohl R. v., *Ueber Bueraukratie*, "Zeitschrift für die gesammte Staatswissenschaft," Heft 2, 1846
46. Mohl R. v., *Ueber die Errichtung staatswissenschaftlicher Fakultäten auf den deutschen Universitäten*, "Deutscher Vierteljahrs Schrift," H. 4, 1849
47. Mohl R. v., *Ueber die Nachteile, welche sowohl den Arbeitern selbst als dem Wohlstande und der Sicherheit der gesammten bürgerlichen Gesellschaft von dem fabrikmässigen Betriebe der Industrie zugehen*, "Archiv der politischen Ökonomie und Polizeiwissenschaften," Bd. II
48. Mohl R. v., *Ueber verschiedene Auffassung des repräsentativen Systems in England, Frankreich und Deutschland*, "Zeitschrift für die gesamte Staatswissenschaft," Bd. 3, H. 3, 1846,

49. Mohl R. v., *Vorschläge zu einer Geschäftsordnung des verfassungsgebenden Reichstages*, Heidelberg 1848
50. Mohl R. v.,, [in:] *Das Staats-Lexikon, Encyklopädie der sämmtlichen Staatswissenschaften für alle Stände*, Bd. 10, C. v. Rotteck, C. Welcker (eds.), Altona 1848, pp. 692–721

Another reference literature

1. Ahrens H., *Das Naturrecht oder die Rechtsphilosophie nach dem gegenwärtigen Zustande dieser Wissenschaft in Deutschland*, Braunschweig 1846
2. Ahrens H., *Naturrecht oder Philosphie des Rechts und des Staates*, Zweiter Band, Wien 1871
3. Aretin J. Ch. v., *Staatsrecht der constitutionellen Monarchie*, Leipzig 1838
4. Aretin J. Ch. v., *Staatsrecht der konstitutionellen Monarchie*, Bd. 2, Abt. 1, Altenburg 1827
5. Aretin J. Ch. v., *Staatsrecht der Konstitutionellen Monarchie*, Erster Band, Altenburg 1824
6. Aristotle, *Etyka Nikomachejska*, trans. D. Gromska, Warszawa 1982
7. Behr W. J., *System der Staatslehre oder der Staatskunst (Politik)*, Bd. 2, Frankfurt am Main 1810
8. Bluntschli J. C., *Allgemeine Staatslehre*, Stuttgart 1886
9. Bluntschli J. C., *Despotie*, [w:] *Bluntschli's Staatswörterbuch in drei Bänden*, E. Löning (ed.) Erster Band, Zürich 1869
10. Bluntschli J. C., *Patrimonialstaat und patrimoniale Staatsidee* [in:] *Bluntschli's Staatswörterbuch in drei Bänden*, E. Löning (ed.), Dritter Band, Zürich 1872
11. Bluntschli J. C., *Psychologische Studien über Staat und Kirche*, Neumünster bei Zürich 1844
12. Bluntschli J. C., *Staatswissenschaft*, [in:] *Deutsches Staats- Wörterbuch*, J. C. Bluntschli, K. Brater (eds.), Bd.10, Stuttgart/Leipzig 1867
13. Bluntschli J. C., *Über den Unterschied der mittelalterlichen und der modernen Staatsidee*, München 1855
14. Bülau F., *Encyklopädie der Staatswissenschaften*, Leipzig 1856
15. Dahlmann F. C., *Die Politik auf den Grund und das Muss der gegebenen Zustände zurueckgeführt*, Bd. 1, Leipzig 1847
16. Dicey A. V., *Introduction to the study of the law of the constitution*, Indianapolis 1982

17. Erhard L., *Dobrobyt dla wszystkich*, Warszawa 2012
18. Eucken W., *Podstawy Polityki Gospodarczej*, Poznań 2005
19. Fichte J. G., *Reden an die deutsche Nation*, Hamburg 1978
20. Filmer R., *Patriarcha or the Natural Power of Kings*, London 1680
21. Finnis J., *Prawo naturalne i uprawnienia naturalne*, translated by K. Lossman, Warszawa 2001
22. Fuller L. L., *Moralność Prawa*, trans. S. Amsterdamski, Warszawa 1978
23. Godwin W., *An Inquiry Concerning Political Justice*, Vol. 1–2, London 1793
24. Haller K. L. v., *Handbuch der allgemeinen Staaten-Kunde*, Winterthur 1808,
25. Haller K. L. v., *Politische Religion oder biblische Lehre über die Staaten*, Winterthur 1811
26. Haller K. L. v., *Restauration der Staatswissenschaften oder Theorie des natürlich-geselligen zustands, der Chimäre des künstlich-bürgerlichen entgegengesetzt*, Winterthur 1816,
27. Haller K. L. v., *Restauration der Staatswissenschaften oder Theorie des natürlich-geselligen Zustands, der Chimäre des künstlich-bürgerlichen entgegengesetzt*, 1 Bd., Winterthur 1820
28. Haller K. L. v., *Restauration der Staatswissenschaften oder Theorie des natürlich-geselligen Zustands, der Chimäre des künstlich-bürgerlichen entgegengesetzt*, Bd. 2, Winterthur 1820
29. Haller K. L. v., *Satan und die Revolution*, Luzern 1834
30. Hegel G. W. F., *Grundlinien der Philosophie des Rechts, Naturrecht und Staatswissenschaft im Grundrisse*, Berlin 2017
31. Hegel G. W. F., *Grundlinien der Philosophie des Rechts, oder Naturrecht und Staatswissenschaft im Grundrisse*, Berlin 1820
32. Hegel G., *Zasady filozofii prawa*, trans. A. Landman, Warszawa 1969
33. Held J., *Staat und Gesellschaft vom Standpunkte der Geschichte der Menschheit und des Staats*, Erster Theil, Leipzig 1861
34. Held J., *Territorium*, [in:] *Das Staats-Lexikon*, Dritte Auflage, Vierzehnter Band, K. Welcker (eds.), Leipzig 1866
35. Herbart J. F., *Allgemeine Practische Philosophie*, Göttingen 1808
36. Hobbes T., *Lewiatan czyli materia, forma i władza państwa kościelnego i świeckiego*, trans. Cz. Znamierowski, Warszawa 2005
37. Holmes O. W., *The collected legal papers*, Mineola, New York 2007

38. Humboldt W. v., *Ideen zu einem Versuch, die Gränzen der Wirksamkeit des Staats zu bestimmen*, Breslau 1851
39. Jarra E., *Ogólna Teorja Prawa*, Warszawa 1922
40. Jellinek G., *Gesetz und Verordnung, Staatsrechtliche Untersuchungen auf Rechtsgeschichtlicher und Rechtsvergleichender Grundlage*, Freiburg I. B. 1887
41. Knies K. G. A., *Die Statistik als selbständige Wissenschaft*, Kassel 1850
42. Locke J., *Dwa traktaty o rządzie*, trans. Z. Rau, Warszawa 2015
43. Locke J., *List o tolerancji*, Warszawa 1963
44. Luden H., *Handbuch der Staatsweisheit oder der Politik*, Jena 1811
45. Martens G. F., *Versuch über die Existenz eines positiven Europäischen Völkerrechts und den Nutzen dieser Wissenschaft*, Göttingen 1787
46. Mayer O., *Deutsches Verwaltungsrecht*, Bd. I, Leipzig 1895
47. Mayr G. v., *Begriff und Gliederung der Staatswissenschaften Zur Einführung in deren Studium*, Tübingen 1910
48. Mayr G. v.,*Statistik und Gesellschaftslehre*, Freiburg 1895
49. Mill J. S., *Considerations on Representative Government*, London 1861
50. Montesquieu, *O duchu praw*, trans. T. Boy-Żeleński, Kraków 2003
51. Müller A. H., *Die Elemente des Staatskunst*, Berlin 1809
52. Neumann Fr. J., *Volk und Nation*, Leipzig 1888
53. Nott J. C., Gliddon R., *Types of mankind*, Philadelphia 1854
54. Petrażycki L., *O nauce, prawie i moralności. Pisma wybrane*, Warszawa 1985
55. Petrażycki L., *O Pobudkach Postępowania i o Istocie Moralności i Prawa*, Warszawa 2002
56. Petrażycki L., *Teoria prawa i państwa w związku z teorią moralności*, T. II, Warszawa 1960
57. Puchta G. F., *Das Gewohnheitsrecht*, Erlangen 1828
58. Ricci G., *Del Municipio considerato come unità elementare della città e della nazione italiana*, Livorno 1847
59. Rohmer F., *Deutschlands alte und neue Bureaukratie*, München 1848
60. Rössler C., *System der Staatslehre, A. Allgemeine Staatslehre*, Leipzig 1857
61. Rotteck C. v., *Allgemeine Geschichte vom Anfang der historischen Kenntniss bis auf unsere Zeiten*, Freiburg 1812–1827
62. Rotteck C. v., *Lehrbuch des Vernunftrechts und der Staatswissenschaften*, Bd. 2, Stuttgart 1840

63. Rotteck C. v., *Lehrbuch des Vernunftrechts und der Staatswissenschaften*, 4. Bde, Stuttgart 1829–1835
64. Rotteck C. v., Welcker C., *Staats-Lexikon oder Encyklopädie der Staatswissenschaften*, 1 Bd., Altona 1834
65. Rousseau J. j., *Umowa społeczna*, trans. A. Peretiatkowicz, Kęty 2002
66. Schlözer A. L. v., *Allgemeines Staatsrecht und Staatsverfassungslehre*, Göttingen 1793
67. Schlözer A. L. v., *Theorie der Statistik*, Göttingen 1804
68. Schmitt C., *Politische Theologie: Vier Kapitel von der Lehre von der Souveränität*, München und Leipzig 1934
69. Schmitthenner F., *Zwölf Bücher vom Staate, oder systematische Encyklopädie der Staatswissenschaften*, Dritter Band, Giessen 1843
70. Stahl F. J., *Das Monarchische Prinzip, eine staatsrechtlich-politische Abhandlung*, Berlin 1845
71. Stahl F. J., *Die Philosophie des Rechts nach geschichtlicher Ansicht*, Heidelberg 1833
72. Stahl F. J., *Die Philosophie des Rechts*, Bd. 2, *Rechts- und Staatslehre auf der Grundlage christlicher Weltanschauung*, Heidelberg 1854
73. Stahl F. J., *Die Philosophie des Rechts*, Bd. 2, *Rechts- und Staatslehre auf der Grundlage christlicher Weltanschauung*, Heidelberg 1845
74. Stahl F. J., *Die Revolution und die konstitutionelle Monarchie*, Berlin 1848
75. Stahl F. J., *The Philosophy of Law, The Doctrine of Law and State on the basis of the Christian world-view*, Book IV: *The doctrine of State and the Principles of State Law*, translated by Ruben Alvarado, Wordbridge Publishing 2009
76. Stahl F. J., *The Philosophy of Law, The Doctrine of Law and State on the basis of the Christian world-view*, Book II: *Principles of Law*, translated by Ruben Alvarado, Wordbridge Publishing 2007
77. Stein L. v., *Der Socialismus und Kommunismus des heutigen Frankreichs*, Leipzig 1848
78. Stein L. v., *Geschichte der Sozialen Bewegung in Frankreich von 1789 bis auf unsere Tage*, 1 Bd., Leipzig 1850
79. Stein L. v., *System der Staatswissenschaft*, 1 Bd., Stuttgart und Tübingen, 1852
80. Treitschke H. v., *Die Gesellschaftswissenschaft ein kritischer Versuch*, Leipzig 1859

81. Tuthill F., *The History of California*, San Francisco 1866
82. Welcker K., *Association*, [in:] *Das Staats-Lexikon, Encyklopädie der sämmtlichen Staatswissenschaften für alle Stände*, K. Welcker (ed.), Dritte Auflage, Erster Band
83. Welcker K., *Gleichgewicht der Gewalten*, [in:] *Das Staats-Lexikon, Encyklopädie der sämmtlichen Staatswissenschaften für alle Stände*, K. v. Rotteck, K. Welcker (eds.), 6 Bd., Leipzig 1862
84. Welcker K., *Petition*, [in:] *Das Staats-Lexikon, Encyklopädie der sämmtlichen Staatswissenschaften für alle Stände*, K. Welcker (ed.), Elfter Band, Leipzig 1864
85. Zachariae C. S., *Vierzig Bücher vom Staate*, Bd. 4, Heidelberg 1840
86. Zachariae K. S., *Vierzig Bücher vom Staate*, Bd. 2, Stuttgatt und Tübingen 1820
87. Zachariae K. S., *Vierzig Bücher vom Staate*, Bd. IV, Heidelberg 1840

Monographs

1. Angermann E., *Robert von Mohl 1799–1875 Leben und Werk eines altliberalen Staatsgelehrten*, Neuwied 1962
2. Balicki Z., *Metody Nauk Społecznych i ich rozwój w XIX stuleciu*, Warszawa 1903
3. Bartosiak J., *Rzeczpospolita między morzem a lądem. O wojnie i pokoju*, Warszawa 2018
4. Benz A., *Der moderne Staat: Grundlagen der politologischen Analyse*, München 2008
5. Berber F., *Das Staatsideal im Wandel der Weltgeschichte*, München 1973
6. Beyme K. v., *Geschichte der politischen Theorien in Deutschland 1300–2000*, Wiesbaden 2009
7. Beyme K. v., *Politische Theorien im Zeitalter der Ideologien 1789–1945*, Wiesbaden 2002
8. Bleek W., *Geschichte der Politikwissenschaft in Deutschland*, München 2001
9. Böckenförde E.-W., *Recht, Staat, Freiheit, Studien zur Rechtsphilosophie, Staatstheorie und Verfassungsgeschichte*, Frankfurt am Main 1992
10. Böckenförde E.-W., *Staat, Gesellschaft, Freiheit, Studien zur Staatstheorie und zum Verfassungsrecht*, Frankfurt am Main, 1976
11. Boldt H., *Deutsche Staatslehre im Vormärz*, Düsseldorf 1975
12. Boldt W., *Verfassungsgeschichtlie Betrachtungen*, Münster 2004
13. Borowski M., *Die Glaubens- und Gewissensfreiheit des Grundgesetzes*, Tübingen 2006

14. Borowski M., *Grundrechte als Prinzipien*, Baden-Baden 2007
15. Bożek M., *System konstytucyjny Republiki Federalnej Niemiec*, Warszawa 2017
16. Brandt H., *Landständische Repräsentation im deutschen Vormärz*, Berlin 1968
17. Buchner W., *Kant - Państwo i Prawo*, Kraków 1996
18. Chmieliński M., *Atomizm a indywidualizm. Rozważania nad myślą polityczną i prawną Wilhelma von Humboldta*, Łódź 2004
19. Citkowska-Kimla A., *Romantyzm polityczny w Niemczech. Reprezentanci, idee, model*, Kraków 2010
20. Czapliński W., Galos A., Korta W., *Historia Niemiec*, Wrocław, Warszawa, Kraków 1990
21. Czubiński A., *Węzłowe problemy rozwoju socjaldemokracji niemieckiej (1847–1993)*, Poznań 1994
22. Dann O., *Nation und Nationalismus in Deutschland 1770–1990*, München 1996
23. Dennewitz B., *Die Systeme des Verwaltungsrechts*, Hamburg 1948, p. 16. W. Thieme, *Verwaltungslehre*, Köln 1977
24. Dilthey W., *Gesammelte Schriften I. Band, Einleitung in die Gesiteswissenschaften*, Göttingen, 1990
25. Doehring K., *Allgemeine Staatslehre, Eine systematische Darstellung*, Heidelberg 2004
26. Dubel L., *Historia doktryn politycznych i prawnych do schyłku XX wieku*, Warszawa 2009
27. Dubel L., *Problem biurokracji w tradycji myśli socjalistycznej*, Lublin 1988
28. Duk-Yung Kim, *Georg Simmel und Max Weber*, Wiesbaden 2002
29. Ebel F., Thielmann G., *Rechtsgeschichte. Von der Römischen Antike bis zur Neuzeit*, Heidelberg 2003
30. Ehrle P. M., *Robert von Mohl als Leiter der Tübinger Universitätsbibliothek (1836–1844)*, Tübingen 1875
31. Forsthoff E., *Deutsche Verfassungsgeschichte der Neuzeit*, Stuttgart, Berlin, Köln, Mainz 1972
32. Forsthoff E., *Deutsche Verfassungsgeschichte der Neuzeit. Ein Abriß*, Stuttgart 1961

33. Fuhrmann M., *Volksvermehrung als Staatsaufgabe? Bevölkerungs- und Ehepolitik in der deutschen politischen und ökonomischen Theorie des 18. und 19. Jahrhunderts*, Paderborn, München, Wien, Zürich, 2002
34. Fukuoka A., *The Sovereign and the Prophets, Spinoza on Grotian and Hobbesian Biblical Argumentation*, Leiden 2018
35. Füßl W., *Professor in der Politik: Friedrich Julius Stahl (1802–1861)*, Göttingen 1988
36. Gablentz O. H. v. d., *Der Kampf um die rechte Ordnung*, Köln und Opladen 1964
37. Gablentz O. H. v. d., *Einführung in die Politische Wissenschaft*, Köln und Opladen 1965
38. Gagel W., *Die Wahlrechtsfrage in der Geschichte der deutschen liberalen Parteien 1848–1918*, Düsseldorf 1958
39. Gall L., *Benjamin Constant, Seine politische Ideenwelt und der deutsche Vormärz*, Wiesbaden 1963
40. Garner J. W., *Introduction to Political Science a treatise on the origin, nature, functions, and organization of the state*, New York, Cincinnati, Chicago 1910
41. Gmür R., *Savigny und die Entwicklung der Rechtswissenschaft*, Münster 1962
42. Görtemaker M., *Deutschland im 19. Jahrhundert Entwicklungslinien*, Bonn 1989
43. Grahe R.-J., *Meinungsfreicheit und Freizügigkeit. Eine Untersuchung zum Grundrechtsdenken bei Robert von Mohl*, Münster 1981
44. Granzow B., *Robert von Mohls Gedanken zu einem parlamentarischen Regime auf berufsständischer Grundlage*, Heidelberg 1959
45. Grimm D., *Deutsche Verfassungsgeschichte 1776–1866 Vom Beginn des modernen Verfassungsstaats bis zur Auflösung des Deutschen Bundes*, Frankfurt am Main 1988
46. Grosser D., *Grundlagen und Struktur der Staatslehre Friedrich Julius Stahls (Staat und Politik 3)*, Köln, Opladen 1963
47. Grünfeld E., *Lorenz von Stein und die Gesellschaftslehre*, Jena 1910
48. Grygieńć J., *Wola powszechna w filozofii politycznej*, Toruń 2012
49. Hähnle J., *Die politischen Ideen Robert von Mohls. Ein Beitrag zur Geschichte des älteren süddeutschen Liberalismus*, Tübingen 1921
50. Hamacher H., *Carl Schmitts Theorie der Diktatur und der intermediären Gewalten*, Neuried 2001

51. Haratsch A., *Die Geschichte der Menschenrechte*, Potsdam 2010
52. Hartung F., *Deutsche Verfassungsgeschichte vom. 15. Jahrhundert bis zur Gegenwart*, Stuttgart 1950
53. Heywood A., *Ideologie polityczne. Wprowadzenie*, Warszawa 2008
54. Hilz W., *Subsidiaritätsprinzip und EU-Gemeinschaftsordnung*, Opladen 1998
55. Hirst M.E., *Life of Friedrich List and selections from his writings*, London 1909.
56. Isensee J., *Subsidiaritätsprinzip und Verfassungsrecht, Eine Studie über das Regulativ des Verhältnisses von Staats und Gesellschaft*, Berlin 2001
57. Janicka D., *Ustawa zasadnicza w praktyce Republiki Federalnej Niemiec (1949–1989)*, Toruń 2009
58. Jaskólski M., *13 różnych esejów o historii myśli politycznej i nie tylko*, Warszawa 2013
59. Jayme E., *Internationales Privatrecht, Ideengeschichte von Mancini und Ehrenzweig zum Europäischen Kollisionsrecht*, Heidelberg 2009
60. Jonas F., *Geschichte der Soziologie*, T. 2, Reinbek bei Hamburg 1968
61. Kaczmarek T. T., Pysz P., *Ludwig Erhard i Społeczna Gospodarka Rynkowa*, Warszawa 2004
62. Kahan A. S., *Liberalism in Nineteenth-Century Europe. The Political Culture of Limited Suffrage*, New York 2003
63. Kalisz A., Leszczyński L., Liżewski B., *Wykładnia Prawa, Model Ogólny a Perspektywa Europejskiej Konwencji Praw Człowieka i Prawa Unii Europejskiej*, Lublin 2011
64. Kaltefleiter W., *Die Funktionen des Staatsoberhauptes in der parlamentarischen Demokratie*, Köln und Opladen 1970
65. Kamiński S., *Nauka i Metoda. Pojęcie nauki i klasyfikacja nauk*, Lublin 1992
66. Kimminich O., *Deutsche Verfassungsgeschichte*, Frankfurt am Main 1970
67. Klemperer K. v., *Germany's New Conservatism Its History and Dilemma in the Twentieth Century*, Princeton New Jersey 1968
68. Klotzbach K., *Das Eliteproblem im politischen Liberalismus*, Wiesbaden 1966
69. Korab-Karpowicz W. J., *Historia Filozofii Politycznej od Tukidydesa do Locke'a*, Kęty 2010
70. Koslowski P., *Staat und Gesellschaft bei Kant*, Tübingen 1985
71. Kostrubiec J., *Nauka o państwie w myśli Georga Jellinka*, Lublin 2015

72. Kotarbiński T., *Elementy teorii poznania, logiki formalnej i metodologii nauk*, Warszawa 2003

73. Kotarbiński T., *Sprawność i błąd: (z myślą o dobrej robocie nauczyciela)*, Warszawa 1960

74. Kriele M., *Einführung in die Staatslehre. Die geschichtlichen Legitimitätsgrundlagen des demokratischen Verfassungsstaates*, Stuttgart, Berlin, Köln 2003

75. Lampert H., *Porządek gospodarczy i społeczny w RFN*, Warszawa 1993

76. Leibholz G., *Die Repräsentation in der Demokratie*, Berlin, New York 1973

77. Lerg Ch. A., *Amerika als Argument: Die deutsche Amerika-Forschung im Vormärz und ihre politische Deutung in der Revolution von 1848/49*, Bielefeld 2011

78. Leszczyński L., *Stosowanie generalnych klauzul odsyłających*, Zakamycze 2001

79. Lichtblau K., *Zwischen Klassik und Moderne Die Modernität der klassischen deutschen Soziologie*, Wiesbaden 2017

80. Lindenfeld D. F., *The Practical Imagination The German Sciences of State in the Nineteenth Century*, Chicago 1997

81. Luchterhandt O., *Grundpflichten als Verfassungsproblem in Deutschland. Geschichtliche Entwicklung und Grundpflichten unter dem Grundgesetz*, Berlin 1988

82. Łustacz L., *Ustawa i rozporządzenie w klasycznej doktrynie francuskiej i niemieckiej*, Warszawa 1968

83. Łuszczyński A., Łuszczyńska M., *What ought to be a person's relationship to society?*, Rzeszów 2011

84. Łuszczyński A., *Podstawy Metodologiczne Badań Politologicznych*, Rzeszów 2005

85. Maciąg Z. A., *Kształtowanie zasad państwa demokratycznego, prawnego i socjalnego w Niemczech (do 1949 r.)*, Białystok 1998

86. Maier H., *Die ältere Deutsche Staats- und Verwaltungslehre*, München 1980

87. Malarczyk J., *U źródeł włoskiego realizmu politycznego: Macchiavelli i Guicciardini*, Lublin 1963

88. Meierhenrich J., *The Remanants of the Rechtsstaat, An Ethnography of Nazi Law*, Oxford 2018

89. Müller V., *Staatstätigkeit in den Staatstheorien des 19. Jahrhunderts*, Wiesbaden 1991
90. Nipperdey T., *Deutsche Geschichte 1800–1866 Bürgerwelt und starker Staat*, München 1991
91. Oertzen P. v., *Die soziale Funktion des staatsrechtlichen Positivismus*, Frankfurt am Main 1974
92. Oniszczuk J., *Konstytucja Rzeczypospolitej Polskiej w orzecznictwie Trybunału Konstytucyjnego*, Zakamycze 2000
93. Oniszczuk J., *Konstytucja Rzeczypospolitej Polskiej w orzecznictwie Trybunału Konstytucyjnego na początku XXI w.*, Zakamycze 2004
94. Ottoman H., *Geschichte des politischen Denkens*, Bd.3: *Neuzeit*, Stuttgart 2008
95. Paluszyński T., *Historia Niemiec i państw niemieckich zarys dziejów politycznych*, Poznań 2006,
96. Pankoke E., *Sociale Bewegung - Sociale Frage - Sociale Politik Grundfragen der deutschen "Socialwissenschaft" im 19. Jahrhundert*, Stuttgart 1970
97. Pauly W., *Der Methodenwandel im deutschen Spätkonstitutionalismus, Ein Beitrag zu Entwicklung und Gestalt der Wissenschaft vom öffentlichen Recht im 19. Jahrhundert*, Tübingen 1993
98. Peukert H., *Das Tradierte Konzept Der Staatswissenschaft*, Berlin 2005
99. Pöggeler W., *Die deutsche Wissenschaft vom englischen Staatsrecht. Ein Beitrag zur Rezeptions- und Wissenschaftsgeschichte 1748–1914*, Berlin 1995
100. Racky M., *Die Diskussion über Gewaltenteilung und Gewaltentrennung im Vormärz*, Frankfurt am Main 2005
101. Reinhard F. E., *Karl Ludwig von Haller. Ein Lebensbild aus der Zeit der Restauration*, Bachem 1915
102. Roggen R., *<Restauration> - Kampfruf und Schimpfwort Eine Kommunikationsanalyse zum Hauptwerk des Staatstheoretikers Karl Ludwig von Haller (1768–1854)*, Freiburg 1999
103. Rosenbusch U., *Der Werg zum Frauenwahlrecht in Deutschland*, Baden-Baden 1998
104. Rüdiger A., *Die Staatswissenschaft an der Universität Halle im 18. Jahrhundert*, Tübingen 2005
105. Rudzio W., *Das politische System der Bundesrepublik Deutschland*, Opladen 1991
106. Sadowski M., *Islam religia i prawo*, Warszawa 2017

107. Sadowski M., *Państwo w doktrynie papieża Leona XIII*, Wrocław 2002

108. Safjan M., *Wyzwania dla państwa prawa*, Warszawa 2007

109. Schmidt Ch. H., *Vorrang der Verfassung und konstituionelle Monarchie: eine dogmengeschichtliche Untersuchung zum Problem der Normenhierarchie in den deutschen Staatsordnungen im frühen und mittleren 19. Jahrhundert (1818–1866)*, Berlin 2000

110. Schmidt M. G., *Demokratietheorien*, Wiesbaden 2006

111. Schmitz H., *Die Staatsauffassung Robert von Mohls unter Berücksichtigung der verfassungs-geschichtlichen Entwicklung und des positivistischen Staatsdenkens*, Köln 1965,

112. Schroeder K-P., *Vom Sachsenspiegel zum Grundgesetz. Eine deutsche Rechtsgeschichte in Lebensbildern*, München 2001

113. Sławski S., *Dostęp Polski do morza a interesy Prus Wschodnich*, Gdańsk 1925

114. Stagl J., *A History of Curiosity The Theory of travel 1550–1800*, Abingdon 1995

115. Stöcker B., *Die Gemeinwohltheorie Robert von Mohls ale ein früher Ansatz des sozialen Rechtsstaatsprinzips*, München 1992

116. Stolleis M., *Geschichte des öffentlichen Rechts in Deutschland*, München 1992

117. Suppé R., *Die Grund- und Menschenrechte in der deutschen Staatslehre des 19. Jahrhunderts*, Berlin 2004

118. Szacki J., *Historia myśli socjologicznej*, Warszawa 2002

119. Tkaczyński J. W., *Prawo Ustrojowe Niemiec*, Kraków 2015

120. Tokarczyk R., *Historia Filozofii Prawa w Retrospektywie Prawa Natury*, Białystok 1999

121. Tracz-Tryniecki M., *Myśl polityczna i prawna Alexisa de Tocqueville*, Kraków 2009

122. Uhlenbrock H., *Der Staat als juristische Person: Dogmengeschichtliche Untersuchung zu einem Grundbegriff der deutschen Staatsrechtslehre*, Berlin 2000

123. Vinx L., *The Guardian of the Constitution. Hans Kelsen and Carl Schmitt on the limits of constitutional law*, Cambridge 2015

124. Wąsicki J., *Związek Niemiecki i Druga Rzesza Niemiecka 1848–1914*, Poznań 1989

125. Wawrykowa M., *Dzieje Niemiec 1789–1871*, Warsaw 1980

126. Weber M., *Gospodarka i społeczeństwo. Zarys socjologii rozumiejącej*, Warszawa 2002
127. Weller K., Weller A., *Württembergische Geschichte im südwestdeutschen Raum*, Stuttgart und Aalen 1972
128. Willoweit D., *Deutsche Verfassungsgeschichte Vom Frankreich bis zur Wiedervereinigung Deutschlands*, München 2005
129. Winczorek P., *Komentarz do Konstytucji Rzeczypospolitej Polskiej z dnia 2 kwietnia 1997 r.*, Warszawa 2000
130. Wolff-Powęska A., *Niemiecka myśl polityczna wieku oświecenia*, Poznań 1988
131. Wolzendorff K., *Die Entwicklung des Polizeibegriffs im 19. Jahrhundert*, Marburg 1906
132. Wronkowska S., Ziembiński Z., *Zarys Teorii Prawa*, Poznań 2001
133. Załęski P. S., *Neoliberalizm i społeczeństwo obywatelskie*, Toruń 2012
134. Zieliński Z., *Niemcy Zarys Dziejów*, Katowice 2003
135. Zimmermann G., *Die Deutsche Polizei im neunzehnten Jahrhundert*, Bd.1, Hannover 1845
136. Zippelius R., *Geschichte der Staatsideen*, München 1994

Parts in the collective works

1. Baranowska M., *Jana Jakuba Rousseau refleksa o naturze* człowieka, [in:] P. Fiktus, H. Malewski, M. Marszał (eds.), *"Rodzinna Europa": europejska myśl polityczno-prawna u progu XXI wieku*, Wrocław 2015
2. Behrends S., *Rozwój realnych systemów ekonomicznych w społecznej gospodarce rynkowej*, [in:] E. Mączyńska, P. Pysz (eds.), *Ordoliberalizm i Społeczna Gospodarka Rynkowa Wobec Wyzwań Współczesności*, Warszawa 2013.
3. Bermbach U., *Liberalismus*, [in:] *Pipers Handbuch der Politischen Ideen*,I. Fetscher, H. Muenkler (eds.), Bd. 3, München 1986
4. Biefang A., A. Schulz, *From Monarchical Constitutionalism to a Parliamentary Republic; Concepts of Parliamentarism in Germany since 1818*, [in:] *Parliament and Parliamentarism A Comparative History of a European Concept*, P. Ihalainen, C. Ilie, K. Palonen (eds.), New York Oxford 2016
5. Bleek W., *Die Tübinger Schule der gesamten Staatswissenschaft*, [in:] *Schulen der deutschen Politikwissenschaft*, W. Bleek, H. J. Lietzmann (eds.), Opladen 1999
6. Blöch E., *Haller, Karl Ludwig von*, [in:] *Allgemeine Deutsche Biographie*, Bd. 10, Leipzig 1879

7. Böckenförde E.-W., *Die Einheit von nationaler und konstitutioneller politischer Bewegung im deutschen Frühliberalismus*, [in:] *Moderne deutsche Verfassungsgeschcichte (1815–1918)*, E-W. Böckenförde (ed.), Köln 1972
8. Böckenförde E.-W., *Die Theorie der Gewaltenteilung*, [in:] E. Mass, P.-L. Weinacht, *Montesquieu-Traditionen in Deutschland*, Berlin 2005
9. Bokajło J., *Alfreda Müllera-Armacka styl: Społeczna Gospodarka Rynkowa*, [in:] E. Mączyńska, P. Pysz (eds.), *Ordoliberalizm i Społeczna Gospodarka Rynkowa Wobec Wyzwań Współczesności*, Warszawa 2013
10. Bosiacki A., *Egalitaryzm a elitaryzm w klasycznej koncepcji państwa prawnego w Niemczech XIX wieku*, [in:] *Księga pamiątkowa dedykowana Profesorowi Romanowi A. Tokarczykowi*, t. V, Z. Władek, A. Bereza (eds.), Lublin 2014
11. Bosiacki A., *Robert von Mohl i początki koncepcji państwa prawnego*, [in:] *Idee jako źródło instytucji politycznych i prawnych*, L. Dubel (ed.), Lublin 2003
12. Bosiacki A., *Z zagadnień koncepcji państwa prawnego w myśli niemieckiej XIX w.*, [in:] *Pro bono Reipublicae, Księga jubileuszowa Profesora Michała Pietrzaka*, P. Borecki, A. Czohara, T. J. Zieliński, (eds.), Warszawa 2009
13. Bożek M., *Władza ustrojodawcza w niemieckim konstytucjonalizmie monarchicznym*, [in:] *Tendencje rozwojowe myśli politycznej i prawnej*, M. Maciejewski, M. Marszał, M. Sadowski (eds.), Wrocław 2014
14. Brandt H., *Karl von Rotteck (1775–1840)*, [in:] *Politische Theorien des 19. Jahhunderts Konservatismus, Liberalismus, Sozialismus*, B. Heidenreich (ed.), Berlin 2002
15. Brożek B., *Emocje jako fundament prawa. Uwagi o teorii Leona Petrażyckiego*, [in:] B. Brożek, J. Stelmach, Ł. Kurek, K. Eliasz (eds.), *Naturalizm prawniczy: stanowiska*, Warszawa 2015
16. Bryl A., *Między historią a teorią – kilka uwag na temat statusu doktryn politycznych i prawnych jako specjalizacji naukowej* [in:] *Myślenie o Polityce i Prawie, przedmiot, metoda, praktyka*, I. Barwicka-Tylek, A. Czarnecka, M. Jaskólski, J. Malczewski (eds.), Warszawa 2015
17. Burska- Cieślak J., *Geneza pojęcia socjalnego państwa prawnego w doktrynie niemieckiej*, [in:] *Państwo ustrój konstytucja studia*, L. Antonowicz et al. (ed.), Lublin 1991
18. Chmieliński M., *Moralność a prawo w doktrynie polityczno-prawnej Immanuela Kanta*, [in:] *Moralność i władza jako kategorie myśli politycznej*, J. Justyński, A. Madeja (eds.), Warszawa 2011

19. Chmieliński M., *Polityczna wizja społeczeństwa w poglądach Wilhelma Humboldta*, [in:] *Przez tysiąclecia: państwo-prawo-jednostka*, t. III, A. Lityński, M. Mikołajczyk (eds.), Katowice 2001
20. Conze W., *Staat und Gesellschaft in der frührevolutionären Epoche Deutschlands*, [in:] *Entstehung des modernen souveränen Staates*, H.-H. Hofmann (eds.), Köln, Berlin 1967
21. Czubiński A., *Rozwój poczucia narodowego i dążeń do zjednoczenia narodowego w krajach niemieckich w dobie kapitalizmu (1776–1945)*, [in:] *Pojęcia "Volk" i "Nation" w historii Niemiec*, A. Czubiński (ed.), Poznań 1980
22. Dietze G., *Staatsrecht und Rechtsstaat*, [in:] Beyme K. v. (ed.) *Theory and Politics, Theorie und Politik, Festschrift zum 70. Geburtstag für Carl Joachim Friedrich*, Haag 1871
23. Ekeløve-Slydal G. M., *Jeremy Bentham's Legacy: A Vision of an international Law for the Greatest Happiness of All Nations*, [in:] *Philosophical Foundations of International Criminal Law: Correlating Thinkers*, M. Bergsmo, E. J. Buis (eds.), Brussels 2018
24. Füßl W., *Friedrich Julius Stahl (1802–1861)*, [in:] *Politische Theorien des 19. Jahhunderts Konservatismus, Liberalismus, Sozialismus*, B. Heidenreich (ed.), Berlin 2002
25. Górecki O. A., *Metodologia głównych orientacji badawczych teorii polityki w analizie doktryn polityczno-prawnych* [in:] *Myślenie o Polityce i Prawie, przedmiot, metoda, praktyka*, I. Barwicka-Tylek, A. Czarnecka, M. Jaskólski, J. Malczewski (eds.), Warszawa 2015
26. Gozzi G., *Rechtsstaat and individual rights in German constitutional theory*, [in:] *The Rule of Law History, Theory and Criticism*, P. Costa, D. Zolo (eds.), Dordrecht 2007
27. Hamerow T. S., *Die Wahlen zum Frankfurter Parlament*, [in:] *Moderne deutsche Verfassungsgeschcichte (1815–1918)*, E-W. Böckenförde (ed.), Köln 1972
28. Hortsmann R.-P., *Hegels Theorie der bürgerlichen Gesellschaft*, [in:] *G. W. F. Hegel: Grundlinien der Philosophie des Rechts*, L. Siep (ed.), Berlin/ Boston 2017
29. Kirste S., *Philosophical Foundations of the Principle of the Legal State (Rechtsstaat) and the Rule of Law*, [in:] Silkenat J. R., Hickey Jr. J. E., Barenboim P. D. (eds.), *The Legal Doctrines of the Rule of Law and the Legal State (Rechtsstaat)*, Heidelberg, New York, Dordrecht, London 2014

30. Kroll S., *The Illiberality of Liberal International Law: Religion, Science, and the Peaceful Violence of Civilization* [in:] *Paradoxes of Peace in Nineteenth Century Europe*, T. Hippler, M. Vec (eds.), Oxford 2015
31. Kusaj M., *Narodziny amerykańskiego realizmu – Common Law Olivera Wendella Holmesa*, [in:] M. Sadowski (ed.), *Ze studiów nad prawem, administracją i ekonomią, Acta Erasmiana VI*, Wrocław 2014
32. Maciejewski M., *Odniesienia między prawem naturalnym i prawem stanowionym w wybranych doktrynach filozoficznych, politycznych i prawnych*, [in:] *Pozytywizm prawniczy i szkoła prawa natury – tradycje sporu i jego współczesne implikacje*, P. Kaczmarek, Ł. Machaj (eds.), Wrocław 2010
33. Maciejewski M., Scheffler T., *O doktrynologii: Rozważania dotyczące przedmiotu oraz metody doktryn politycznych i prawnych* [in:] *Myślenie o Polityce i Prawie, przedmiot, metoda, praktyka*
34. Maciejewski M., *Zarys dziejów kontraktualistycznych koncepcji genezy społeczeństwa i państwa,*[in:] *O źródłach państwa i władzy politycznej*, A. Wielomski, C. Kalita (eds.), Biała Podlaska 2011
35. Maus I., *Entwicklung und Funktionswandel der Theorie des bürgerlichen Rechtsstaats*, [in:] *Der bürgerliche Rechtsstaat*, M. Tohipidur (ed.), Frankfurt am Main 1978
36. Müller-Schmid P. P., *Adam Müller (1779–1829)*, [in:] *Politische Theorien des 19. Jahhunderts Konservatismus, Liberalismus, Sozialismus*, B. Heidenreich (ed.), Berlin 2002
37. Nasiłowski M., *Próba zdefiniowania społecznej gospodarki rynkowej*, [in:] E. Okoń-Horodyńska (ed.), *Społeczna Gospodarka Rynkowa, Materiały z ogólnopolskiej konferencji naukowej w Jaworze 27–29 Maja 1991*, Katowice 1991
38. Nordblom P., *Robert von Mohl*, [in:] *Gelehrte in der Revolution. Heidelberger Abgeordnete in der deutschen Nationalversammlung 1848/49*, F. Engehausen, A. Kohnle (eds.), Ubstadt-Weiher 1998
39. Nowacki J., *Państwo prawne w typologii państw Roberta von Mohla*, [in:] *Przybliżanie przeszłości. Księga pamiątkowa ofiarowana Profesorowi Czesławowi Głombikowi z okazji czterdziestolecia pracy nauczycielskiej*, J. Bańka (ed.), Katowice 1998
40. Pfordten D. v. d, *On the Foundations of the Rule of Law and the Principle of Legal State/Rechtsstaat*, [in:] *The Legal Doctrines of the Rule of Law and the Legal State (Rechtsstaat)*, J. R. Silkenat, J. E. Hickey Jr., P. D. Barenboim (eds.), Heidelberg, New York, Dordrecht, London 2014.

41. Pietrzyk-Reeves D., *Republikańska koncepcja umowy społecznej Jana Jakuba Rousseau*, [in:] *Umowa społeczna i jej krytycy*, Z. Rau, M. Chmieliński (eds.), Warszawa 2010

42. Piotrowski B., *O romantycznej wizji narodu niemieckiego uwag kilka*, [in:] *Pojęcia "Volk" i "Nation" w historii Niemiec*, A. Czubiński (ed.), Poznań 1980

43. Pulzer P., *Responsible Party Government in the German Political System*, [in:] *Party Government and Political Culture in Western Germany*, H. Döring, G. Smith (eds.), London and Basingstoke 1982

44. Rau Z., *Umowa społeczna w doktrynie Johna Locke'a*, [in:] *Umowa społeczna i jej krytycy*, Z. Rau, M. Chmieliński (eds.), Warszawa 2010

45. Reif M., *Public Sociology? Nicht mit uns!*, [in:] *2015: Routinen der Krise - Krise der Routinen. Verhandlungen des 37. Kongresses der Deutschen Gesellschaft für Soziologie in Trier 2014*, S. Lessenich (ed.)

46. Schulze H., *Preußen als konstituionelle Monarchie 1850–1867*, [in:] *Handbuch der Preussischen Geschichte*, O. Büsch (ed.), Berlin, New York 1992

47. Schüttemeyer S.S., *The Current State of Political Science in Germany*, [in:] *The State of Political Science in Europe*, H.-D. Klingemann (ed.), Opladen/Farmington Hills 2007

48. Sobkowiak L., *Obywatelskie nieposłuszeństwo*, [in:] *Encyklopedia politologii*, t.1, W. Sokół, M. Żmigrodzki (eds.), Kraków 1999.

49. Sokół W., *Partia polityczna*, [in:] *Encyklopedia politologii*, t.1, W. Sokół, M. Żmigrodzki (eds.), Kraków 1999.

50. Sokół W., *System partyjny* [in:] *Encyklopedia politologii*, t.1, W. Sokół, M. Żmigrodzki (eds.), Kraków 1999.

51. Sombart W., *Die Fehlurteile Robert von Mohls und Paul Barths über den Begriff der Soziologie*, [in:] *Hauptprobleme Der Soziologie Erinnerungsgabe Für Max Weber*, I Band, M. Palyi (eds.), München und Leipzig 1923

52. Strunz H., *Der Verwaltungsbegriff*, [in:] *Gestaltung öffentlicher Verwaltungen*, M. Hofmann, K. Zapotoczky, H. Strunz (eds.), Berlin-Heidelberg 1993

53. Szwarc W., *Zarys ewolucji pojęcia "policji" w monarchii pruskiej w XVIII i XIX w.*, [in:] *Wybrane problemy teorii i praktyki państwa i prawa*, H. Groszyk, L. Dubel (eds.), Lublin 1986

54. Thompson M. P., *Locke's contract in context*, [in:] *The social contract from Hobbes to Rawls*, London and New York 2005

55. Tokarczyk R. A., *Paradygmatyczne ujęcie koncepcyjnych i ustrojowych aspektów demokratycznego państwa prawa*, [in:] M. Aleksandrowicz, A. Jamróz, L. Jamróz (eds.), *Demokratyczne państwo prawa. Zagadnienia wybrane*, Białystok 2014
56. Vec M., *From Invisible Peace to the Legitimation of War: Paradoxes of a Concept in Nineteenth Century International Law Doctrine*, [in:] *Paradoxes of Peace in Nineteenth Century Europe*, T. Hippler, M. Vec (eds.), Oxford 2015
57. Vierhaus R., *Liberalismus, Beamtenstand und konstitutionelles System*, [in:] *Liberalismus in der Gesellschaft des deutschen Vormärz*, W. Schieder (ed.), Göttingen 1983
58. Zacher H. F., *Vierzig Jahre Sozialstaat - Schwerpunkte der rechtlichen Ordnung*, [in:] N. Blüm, H. F. Zacher (eds.), *40 Jahre Sozialstaat Bundesrepublik Deutschland*, Baden-Baden 1989
59. Zagóra-Jonszta U., *System gospodarczy ordoliberalizmu a ekonomia klasyczna i keynesizm. Próba porównania*, [in:] E. Okoń-Horodyńska (ed.), *Społeczna Gospodarka Rynkowa, Materiały z ogólnopolskiej konferencji naukowej w Jaworze 27–29 Maja 1991*, Katowice 1991
60. Zmierczak M., *Kształtowanie się koncepcji państwa prawnego (na przykładzie niemieckiej myśli polityczno-prawnej)*, [in:] *Demokratyczne państwo prawne*, H. Rot (ed.), "Acta Universitatis Wratislaviensis," No 1457
61. Żmigrodzki M., *Racja stanu* [in:] *Encyklopedia politologii*, t.1, W. Sokół, M. Żmigrodzki (eds.), Kraków 1999
62. Jann W., *Staatslehre- Regierungslehre - Verwaltungslehre,* [in:] Bandemer S. v., Wewer G. (eds.), *Regierungssystem und Regierungslehre*, Opladen 1989
63. Wunder B., *Bürokratie: Die Geschichte eines politischen Schlagwortes*, [in:] Windhoff-Héritier A. (ed.) *Verwaltung und ihre Umwelt. Festschrift für Thomas Ellwein*, Opladen 1987

Scientific articles

1. Avraham D., *The Social and Religious Meaning of Nationalism: The Case of Prussian Conservatism 1815–1871*, "European History Quarterly," Vol. 38 (4)
2. Bacławski J., *Wola powszechna i jej stabilność według koncepcji J.J. Rousseau*, "Przegląd filozoficzny - Nowa Seria," R. 21: 2012, Nr 4 (84)
3. Bhat G. N., *Recovering the Historical Rechtsstaat*, "Review of Central and East European Law," 32, 2007

4. Bosiacki A., *Polski klasyczny liberalizm. O recepcji liberalizmu w polskiej myśli politycznej pierwszej połowy XIX w.*, "Studia Iuridica Lublinensia," vol. XXV, 3, 2016
5. Budyn-Kulik M., Kulik M., *Społeczna szkodliwość czynu jako klauzula generalna w prawie karnym*, "Annales Universitatis Mariae Curie-Sklodowska" Sectio G "IUS," vol. LXIII 2, 2016
6. Buksiński T., *Trzy teologie polityczne Carla Schmitta*, "Filozofia Publiczna i Edukacja Demokratyczna," T. III, Nr. 1, 2014
7. Chmieliński M., *Dwa niemieckie indywidualizmy: Liberalny Humboldta i anarchistyczny Stirnera*, "Studia Prawno-Ekonomiczne," t. LX, 1991
8. Chmieliński M., *Wilhelma Humboldta idee ograniczenia państwa*, "Czasopismo prawno-historyczne," t. LIV 2002, z.1
9. Cohen M. R., *Justice Holmes and the Nature of Law*, "Columbia Law Review," vol. 31, no. 3 (Mar. 1931)
10. Dąbrowski K., *Ewolucja pojęcia policji w kontekście genezy żandarmerii w Niemczech*, "Annales Universitatis Mariae Curie-Sklodowska, Sectio G (IUS)," Vol. XXV, 3
11. Dubel L., *Idea "minimum państwa" w koncepcjach Frédérica Bastiata*, "Annales Universitatis Mariae Curie-Sklodowska, Sectio G (IUS)," Vol. LIX, 2
12. Dziadzio A., *Koncepcja państwa prawa w XIX wieku – idea i rzeczywistość*, "Czasopismo Prawno-Historyczne," t. LVII, 2005, Zeszyt 1
13. Eulau H. H. F., *Early Theories of Parliamentarism*, "The Canadian Journal of Economics and Political Science / Revue canadienne d'Economique et de Science politique," Vol. 8, No. 1 (Feb., 1942)
14. Fernandez-Villaverde J., *Magna Carta, the rule of law, and the limits on government*, 'International Review of Law and Economics,' 47 (2016) 22–28
15. Francis E. K., *The Nature of the ethnic group*, "Journal of American Sociology" 52, No 5 (March 1947)
16. Freyer H., *Gegenwartsaufgaben der Deutschen Soziologie*, "Zeitschrift für die gesamte Staatswissenschaft / Journal of Institutional and Theoretical Economics" Bd. 95, H.1 (1935)
17. Grygieńć J., *Jana Jakuba Rousseau koncepcja woli powszechnej. Czym jest, po co jest i dlaczego nie działa jak powinna?*, "Dialogi polityczne," 3–4/2004

18. Gugnin A., Pliszek T., *Instytucjonalny wymiar etyki w ujęciu Niccolo Machiavellego*, "Nierówności społeczne a wzrost gospodarczy," z. 15, 2009
19. Haselsberger B., *Decoding borders. Appreciating border impacts on space and people*, "Planning Theory & Practice," 2014, Vol. 15, No. 4
20. Hentschel V., *Die Staatswissenschaften an den deutschen Universitäten im 18. und frühen 19. Jahrhundert*, "Berichte zur Wissenschafts-Geschichte," 1 (1978)
21. Hilbert R. A., *Bureaucracy as Belief, Rationalization as Repair: Max Weber in a Post-Functionalist Age*, "Sociological Theory" 1987, Vol. 5(1)
22. Hoffmann R., *Beamtenstreik und Verfassungsverständnis vom Sozialstaat*, "Kritische Justiz," Vol. 4, No. 1 (1971)
23. Holmes O. W., *The Path of the Law*, "Harvard Law Review," Vol. X. March 25, 1897, no. 8
24. Hotel M., Rychlewska A., *Analogia jako metoda prawnicza*, "Kwartalnik Prawo-Społeczeństwo-Ekonomia," 2/2015
25. Huber E. R., *Die deutsche Staatswissenschaft*, "Zeitschrift für die gesamte Staatswissenschaft / Journal of Institutional and Theoretical Economics," Bd. 95, H. 1. (1935)
26. Hunter Taylor E., *H. L. A. Hart's Concept of Law in the Perspective of American Legal Realism*, "The Modern Law Review," vol. 35, No. 6 (Nov. 1972)
27. Hunter Taylor E., *H. L. A. Hart's Concept of Law in the Perspective of American Legal Realism*, "The Modern Law Review," vol. 35, No. 6 (Nov. 1972)
28. Isensee J., *Verfassung ohne Soziale Grundrechte: ein Wesenzug des Grundgesetzes*, "Der Staat," Vol. 19, No. 3 (1980)
29. Jarvard M., *Subsidiarity and Autonomy*, "History of European Ideas," Vol. 19, no. 4–6
30. Jaskólski M., *Szkice o Historii Doktryn Politycznych i Prawnych*, "Zeszyty Naukowe Uniwersytetu Jagiellońskiego DCCXII," "Prace z nauk politycznych," z. 23
31. Jaume L., *La théorie de l'autorité chez Benjamin Constant*, "Historical Reflections / Réflexions Historiques," Vol. 28, No. 3
32. Jońca K., *Ewolucja pojęcia "Państwa Prawnego" w Niemieckiej Doktrynie Prawnej*, "Acta Universitatis Wratislaviensis" No 307, Przegląd Prawa i Administracji VII, Wrocław 1976

33. Kaleta K. J., Koźmiński K., *Charakter władzy suwerennej w koncepcjach ładu konstytucyjnego Hansa Kelsena i Carla Schmitta*, "Filozofia Publiczna i Edukacja Demokratyczna," T.II, 2013, N. 2
34. Kaufmann F-X., *The idea of Social Policy in Western Societes: Origins and Diversity*, "International Journal of Social Quality" vol 3 number (2), Winter 2013
35. Kik M., *Leona Petrażyckiego Filozofia Prawa*, "Czasopismo Filozoficzne," nr 1, 2006
36. Kowalewski Z., *Historia nauki i naukoznawstwo. Zarys kierunków rozwoju i zmian organizacyjnych Zakładu Historii Nauki i Techniki*, "Kwartalnik Historii Nauki i Techniki" 15/3, 1970
37. Królak P., *"Dziewięćdziesiąt dziewięć cudzych pomysłów, i jeden autora." Porównanie myśli konstytucyjnej Wincentego Niemojowskiego i Benjamina Constanta*, "Czasopismo Prawno-Historyczne," T. LXIV, z.2, 2012
38. Kubiak M., Kubiak M., *Ordoliberalizm a koncepcja i praktyka społecznej gospodarki rynkowej*, "Studia Gdańskie" XXXI
39. Lesiński P., *«Rechtsstaat» and it's legal order according to Robert von Mohl*, "Zeszyty Naukowe Uniwersytetu Rzeszowskiego. Seria Prawnicza. Prawo." 31/2020
40. Leszczyński L., *Generalne klauzule odsyłające – ujęcie teoretycznoprawne*, Annales Universitatis Mariae Curie-Sklodowska" Sectio G "IUS," vol. LXIII 2, 2016
41. Leszczyński L., *Kategoria słuszności w wykładni prawa*, "Studia Iuridica Lublinensia," vol. XV, 1, 2011
42. Lichtblau K., *Die Stellung der Soziologie innerhalb der geistes- und sozialwissenschaftlichen Disziplinen*, "Soziologie" 2010, nr 39, z. 3
43. Liedke H. R., *The German Romanticists and Karl Ludwig von Haller's Doctrines of European Restoration*, "The Journal of English and Germanic Philology," Vol. 57, No. 3 (Jul., 1958)
44. Lötzsch R., *Was ist ein Volk und was eine Nation?*, "UTOPIE kreativ," H, 103/104 (Mai/Juni) 1999
45. Luban D., *The Rule of Law and Human Dignity: Re-examining Fuller's Canons*, "Hague Journal on the Rule of Law" 2, 2010
46. Łuszczyńska M., *Filozofia prawa: w poszukiwaniu tożsamości*, "Studia Iuridica Lublinensia" 16, 2011

47. Łuszczyńska M., *Prawo natury a prawo stanowione- dwa antagonistyczne ujęcia filozofii prawa*, "Annales UMCS Sectio G (Ius)," 2005–2006, vol LII/LIII
48. Łuszczyńska M., *Umowa społeczna jako fundament życia zbiorowego*, "Studia Iuridica Lublinensia" 21, 2014
49. Megay E. N., *Treitschke Reconsidered: The Hegelian Tradition of German Liberalism*, "Midwest Journal of Political Science," Vol. 2, No. 3 (Aug., 1958),
50 Meier E., *Robert von Mohl*, "Zeitschrift für die gesamte Staatswissenschaft," Nr 34, 1878
51. Murphy C., *Lon Fuller and the Moral Value of The Rule of Law*, "Law and Philosophy" 2005, 24
52. Nitschke P., *Von der Politeia zur Polizei: Ein Beitrag zur Entwicklungsgeschichte des Polizei-Begriffs und seiner herrschaftspolitischen Dimensionen von der Antike bis ins 19 Jahrhundert*, "Zeitschrift für Historische Forschung" Vol. 19, No. 1 (1992)
53. O'Malley M., *Currents in Nineteenth-Century German Law, and Subsidiarity's Emergence as a Social Principle in the Writings of Wilhelm Ketteler*, "Journal of Law, Philosophy and Culture," Vol. II, No. 1 (2008)
54. Opałek K., Wróblewski J., *Niemiecka szkoła historyczna w teorii prawa*, "Przegląd Nauk Historycznych i Społecznych," t. 5 1954
55. Orth J. v., *Exporting the Rule of Law*, "North Carolina Journal of International Law and Commercial Regulation," Vol. 24, N. 1
56. Papuziński A., *Filozoficzne dziedzictwo oświecenia a zrównoważony rozwój*, "Zeszyty naukowe Politechniki Śląskiej," seria: Organizacja i Zarządzanie z. 112, (2017),
57. Piloty R., *Das Parlamentarische System. Eine Untersuchung seines Wesens und Wertes*, "Archiv für Rechts- und Wirtschaftsphilosophie" Vol. 11, No. 1 (1917/1918)
58. Porębski Cz., *Umowa społeczna według Jana Jakuba Rousseau*, "Etyka" 22, 1966
59. Roberts D., *Jeremy Bentham and the Victorian Administrative State*, "Victorian Studies," Vol. 2, No. 3 (1959)
60. Rysiewicz M., *"Gdy prawo ustaje i wkracza siła…" Stan wyjątkowy w myśli prawno-państwowej Carla Schmitta*, "Dialogi Polityczne" 13/2010

61. Sauermann H., *Die gesamte Staatswissenschaft im Spiegel dieser Zeitschrift*, "Zietschrift für die gesamte Staatswissenschaft/ Journal of Institutional and Theoretical Economics," Bd. 134, H.1, März 1978
62. Scheuner U., *Der Rechtsstaat und die soziale Verantwortung des Staates: Das wissenschaftliche Lebenswerk von Robert von Mohl*, "Der Staat" Vol. 18, No.1 (1979)
63. Schwartz D., *Perfectionism and Subsidiarity: Comments on John Finnis' Human Rights and the Common Good*, "Jerusalem Review of Legal Studies," Vol. 8, No. 1 (2013)
64. Schwartz D., *Perfectionism and Subsidiarity: Comments on John Finnis' Human Rights and the Common Good*, "Jerusalem Review of Legal Studies," Vol. 8, No. 1 (2013)
65. Smyk G., *Początki ewolucji podstawowych pojęć i definicji w europejskiej nauce administracji*, "Studia z Dziejów Państwa i Prawa," 17, 2014
66. Sobolewski M., *Koncepcja państwa prawnego (Rechtsstaat) w doktrynie niemieckiego liberalizmu epoki klasycznej*, PIP 1980, z.2
67. Stoltenberg H. L., *Kurzer Abriß einer Geschichte der deutschen Soziologie*, "Weltwirtschaftliches Archiv" 1930, t. 32
68. Strzyczkowski K., *Zasada państwa sprawiedliwości społecznej jako zasada publicznego prawa gospodarczego*, "Ruch Prawniczy, Ekonomiczny i Socjologiczny," LXIX, z. 4, 2007
69. Sylwestrzak A., *Władza Trzecia "Neutralna,"* "Zeszyty Prawnicze UKSW," vol. 11, nr 4 (2011)
70. Tkacz S., *O "Pozytywności" i "Oficjalności" Prawa w Teorii Leona Petrażyckiego*, "Ruch Prawniczy, Ekonomiczny i Socjologiczny," ROK LXVII - zeszyt 1 - 2005
71. Tokarczyk R., *Relacje moralności i prawa w doktrynie Lona L. Fullera*, "Etyka" 15, 1977
72. Trzciński K., *Początki nowożytnego obywatelstwa w Europie - obywatel państwa i katalog jego praw w dokumentach Rewolucji Francuskiej*, "Studia Europejskie," 2/2005
73. Tulejski T., *Sir Robert Filmer. Sam przeciwko wszystkim! Część II*, "Studia Prawno-Ekonomiczne," t. CII
74. Tyrell H., *History and sociology - the First Century From Ranke to Weber*, "Inter Disciplines. Journal of History and Sociology," Vol. 1, No.1 (2010)
75. Vasciannie S., *Land-locked and geographically disadvantaged states*, "Commonwealth Law Bulletin," 2005, 31:1

76. Wahl R., *Rechtliche Wirkungen und Funktionen der Grundrechte im Deutschen Konstitutionalismus des 19. Jahrhunderts*, "Der Staat" Vol. 18, No. 3 (1979)
77. Wojtyszyn R., *Szkoła prawa natury od Hugona Grocjusza do Johna Locke'a*, "Studia Erasmiana Wratislaviensia Wrocławskie Studia Erazmiańskie, Zeszyt Naukowy Studentów, doktorantów i pracowników naukowych Uniwersytetu Wrocławskiego," 2007
78. Zacher H. F., *Der Sozialstaat als Prozeß*, "Zeitschrift für gesamte Staatswissenschaft / Journal of Institutional and Theoretical Economics," Bd. 134, H. 1. (1978)
79. Zahorski A., *Trzy syntezy Wielkiej Rewolucji Francuskiej: Albert Mathiez, Georges Lefebvre, Albert Soboul*, "Przegląd Historyczny," 55/1, 1964

Another sources

1. Banaszak B., *Konstytucja Rzeczypospolitej Polskiej. Komentarz*, Warszawa 2012
2. *Basic Law for the Federal Republic of Germany*, transl. Ch. Tomuschat, Berlin 2019.
3. Beyme K. v., *Einleitung*, [in:] R. v. Mohl, *Politische Schriften. Eine Auswahl*, K. v. Beyme (ed.), Köln und Opladen 1966
4. Białecki A., *Translator's note to the Reader*, [in:] R. v. Mohl, *Encyklopedia Umiejętności Politycznych*, t.1, Warszawa 2003
5. Biliński M., Żurawik A., *§ 15. Społeczna gospodarka rynkowa jako konstytucyjna zasada ustroju gospodarczego...*, thesis 5, [Legalis Legal Information System - access 02/08/2019]
6. Bosiacki A., *Wstęp*, [in:] R. v. Mohl, *Encyklopedia Umiejętności Politycznych*, Warszawa 2003
7. Chmaj M. (ed.), *Wolności i prawa człowieka w Konstytucji Rzeczypospolitej Polskiej*, Warszawa 2008
8. *Der europäische Rechtsstaat, 200 Zeugnisse seiner Geschichte*, J. Brand, H. Hattenhauer (eds.), Heidelberg 1994
9. *Doktryny polityczne XIX i XX wieku*, K. Chojnicka, W. Kozub-Ciembroniewicz (eds.), Kraków 2000
10. Domagała M., Podkowik J., Zubik M. (eds.), *Konstytucja RP w orzecznictwie Trybunału Konstytucyjnego oraz SN i NSA*, Warszawa 2018

11. Ehrle P. M., Schäfer V. (ed.), *Robert von Mohl (1799–1875) Austellung zu seinem 100. Todestag veranstaltet von der Universitätsbilbiothek und dem Universitätsarchiv Tübingen 4.–29. November 1975*, Tübingen 1975
12. Flügel F., *A practical dictionary of the English and German languages in two parts*, Part II, Hamburg, 1861
13. Muret-Sanders, *Encyclopaedic English-German and German-English Dictionary*, 2nd Part, H. Bauman (ed.), Berlin 1910, s. 911
14. *Niemiecko-Polsko Słownik Wyrazów Prawniczych i Administracyjnych*, Kraków 1874
15. Raberg F., *Biographisches Handbuch der württembergischen Landtagsabgeordneten 1815–1933. Im Auftrag der Kommission für geschichtliche Landeskunde in Baden-Württemberg*. Kohlhammer, Stuttgart 2001
16. Schulze H., *Robert von Mohl. Ein Erinnerungsblatt dargebracht zur fünfhundertjährigen Jubelfeier der Ruperto-Carola*, Heidelberg 1886
17. Skibicki W., *Słownik terminologii prawniczej i ekonomicznej, niemiecko-polski*, Warszawa 1993
18. Stelmach, Ł. Kurek, K. Eliasz (eds.), *Naturalizm prawniczy: stanowiska*, Warszawa 2015
19. *The Oxford-Duden German dictionary*, W. Scholze-Stubenrecht, J.B. Sykes (eds.), Oxford 1994
20. *Verfassung des Deutschen Reiches, gegeben Berlin den 16. April 1871*, L v. Roenne (ed.), Berlin und Leipzig 1882
21. Zaradkiewicz K., *Art. 20 [Społeczna gospodarka rynkowa jako podstawa ustroju gospodarczego]*, [in:] M. Safian, L. Bosek (eds.), *Konstytucja RP. Tom I. Komentarz do art. 1–86*, Warszawa 2016, thesis 24, [Legalis Legal Information System - access 02/08/2019]
22. Zaradkiewicz K., *Art. 20 [Społeczna gospodarka rynkowa jako podstawa ustroju gospodarczego]*. . ., thesis 62, [Legalis Legal Information System - access 02/08/2019]

Internet sources

1. http://www.documentarchiv.de/nzjh/verfbaden.html
2. http://www.servat.unibe.ch/dfr/bv021073.html#Rn014
3. http://www.servat.unibe.ch/dfr/bv059231.html
4. http://www.verfassungen.de/bw/wuerttemberg/verf1819-i.htm
5. http://www.verfassungen.de/de/by/bayern18-index.htm

6. https://opinioiuris.de/entscheidung/766
7. https://www.bavarikon.de/object/GDA-OBJ-00000BAV80000807 [accessed 20/02/2019]
8. https://www.sejm.gov.pl/prawo/konst/angielski/kon1.htm

This work has been reviewed by: Lech Dubel (Maria Curie-Skłodowska University)

Lech Dubel (born 1948) is a professor of legal sciences at Maria Curie-Skłodowska University in Lublin, Poland. Until his retirement, he was a head of the Chair of Political and Legal Doctrines at Faculty of Law and Administration, UMCS. He is an author and co-author of numerous works on political sciences and legal and political doctrines, including popular textbooks. His research covers a wide range of topics such as the thought of Karl Kautsky and Leon Trotsky, medieval philosophy (John of Salisbury, St. Thomas Aquinas, Marsilius of Padua), or the doctrines of Callimachus and Andrzej Frycz Modrzewski. Professor Dubel is also an active member of the international academic community. He was awarded with an IREX Scholarship for a scientific stay at University of Michigan (USA). He is also a member of Lublin Scientific Society, Polish Society of Political Thought, Commission of Legal Sciences (Polish Academy of Sciences Department in Lublin). He received the National Education Medal and the Gold Medal for Long Service. He was a supervisor of six doctoral theses.

Index

Studies in Politics, Security and Society

Edited by Stanisław Sulowski

Vol. 1 Robert Wiszniowski (ed.): Challenges to Representative Democracy. A European Perspective. 2015.

Vol. 2 Jarosław Szymanek: Theory of Political Representation. 2015.

Vol. 3 Alojzy Z. Nowak (ed.): Global Financial Turbulence in the Euro Area. Polish Perspective. 2015.

Vol. 4 Jolanta Itrich-Drabarek: The Civil Service in Poland. Theory and Experience. 2015.

Vol. 5 Agnieszka Rothert: Power of Imagination. Education, Innovations and Democracy. 2016.

Vol. 6 Zbysław Dobrowolski: Combating Corruption and Other Organizational Pathologies. 2017.

Vol. 7 Vito Breda: The Objectivity of Judicial Decisions. A Comparative Analysis of Nine Jurisdictions. 2017.

Vol. 8 Anna Sroka: Accountability and democracy in Poland and Spain. 2017.

Vol. 9 Anna Sroka / Fanny Castro-Rial Garrone / Rubén Darío Torres Kumbrián (eds.): Radicalism and Terrorism in the 21st Century. Implications for Security. 2017.

Vol. 10 Filip Pierzchalski: Political Leadership in Morphogenetic Perspective. 2017.

Vol. 11 Alina Petra Marinescu: The Discursive Dimension of Employee Engagement and Disengagement. Accounts of keeping and leaving jobs in present-day Bucharest organizations. 2017.

Vol. 12 Jacek Giedrojć: Competition, Coordination, Social Order. Responsible Business, Civil Society, and Government in an Open Society. 2017.

Vol. 13 Filip Ilkowski: Capitalist Imperialism in Contemporary Theoretical Frameworks. 2017.

Vol. 14 Leszek Leszczyński / Adam Szot (eds.): Discretionary Power of Public Administration. Its Scope and Control. 2017.

Vol. 15 Tadeusz Klementewicz: Understanding Politics. Theory, Procedures, Narratives. 2017.

Vol. 16 Tomasz Bichta: Political Systems of the Former Yugoslavia. 2018

Vol. 17 Miroslav Palárik / Alena Mikulášová / Martin Hetényi / Róbert Arpáš: The City and Region Against the Backdrop of Totalitarianism. 2018

Vol. 18 Jolanta Itrich-Drabarek / Stanisław Mazur / Justyna Wiśniewska-Grzelak (eds.): Understanding Politics. Theory, Procedures, Narratives. 2017.

Vol. 19 Jerzy Juchnowski / R. Jan Sielezin / Ewa Maj: The Image of "White" and "Red" Russia in the Polish Political Thought of the 19th and 20th Century. Analogies and Parallels. 2017.

Vol. 20 Roman Kuźniar: Europe in the International Order. 2018.

Vol. 21 Piotr Jaroszyński: Europe - the Clash of Civilisations. 2018.

Vol. 22 Stanisław Filipowicz: Truth and the Will to Illusion. 2018.

Vol. 23 Andrzej Szeptycki: Contemporary Relations between Poland and Ukraine. The "Strategic Partnership" and the Limits Thereof. 2019.

Vol. 24 Sylwester Gardocki / Rafał Ożarowski / Rafał Ulatowski (eds.): The Islamic World in International Relations. 2019.

Vol. 25 Jacek Zaleśny (ed.): Constitutional Courts in Post-Soviet States. Between the Model of a State of Law and Its Local Application. 2019.

Vol. 26 Andrzej Antoszewski / Przemysław Żukiewicz / Mateusz Zieliński / Katarzyna. Domagała: Formation of Government Coalition in Westminster Democracies. Towards a Network Approach. 2020.

Vol. 27 Joanna Osiejewicz: Global Governance of Oil and Gas Resources in the International Legal Perspective. 2020.

Vol. 28 Anita Oberda-Monkiewicz : Poland-Mexico towards a Strategic Partnership. 2020.

Vol. 29 Bartosz Czepil / Wojciech Opioła: Ethnic diversity and local governance quality. The case of Opole Province in Po-land. 2020.

Vol. 30 Adam Szymański / Jakub Wódka / Wojciech Ufel / Amanda Dziubińska: Between Fair and Rigged. Elections as a Key Determinant of the 'Borderline Political Regime' - Turkey in Comparative Perspective. 2020.

Vol. 31 Tomasz Grzegorz Grosse (ed.): Fuel for Dominance. On the Economic Bases of Geopolitical Supremacy. 2020.

Vol. 32 Dariusz Jarosz / Maria Pasztor: From Subjection to Independence. Post-World War II Polish-Italian Relations. 2020.

Vol. 33 Paweł Sekuła: Chernobyl Liquidators. The Unknown Story. With the Testimony of the President of Latvia. 2020.

Vol. 34 Kamil Glinka (ed.): Urban Policy System in Strategic Perspective: From V4 to Ukraine. 2020.

Vol. 35 Paweł Lesiński: At the Origins of German Liberalism: the State in the Thought of Robert von Mohl. 2020.

www.peterlang.com

www.ingramcontent.com/pod-product-compliance
Ingram Content Group UK Ltd.
Pitfield, Milton Keynes, MK11 3LW, UK
UKHW021831100926
8556IPUK00004B/269

9 783631 813058